THE WORLD IN THE TWENTIETH CENTURY

THE AGE OF GLOBAL WAR AND REVOLUTION

Daniel R. Brower
University of California, Davis

PRENTICE HALL, Englewood Cliffs, New Jersey 07632

Library of Congress Cataloging-in-Publication Data

BROWER, DANIEL R.
  The world in the twentieth century.

  Includes bibliographies and index.
    1. History, Modern—20th century. 2. Revolutions—
History—20th century. I. Title.
D421.B725 1987   909.82   87-14554
ISBN 0-13-965526-3

Editorial/production supervision and interior design: *Mary A. Bardoni*
Cover design: *Photo Plus Art*
Manufacturing buyer: *Ray Keating*

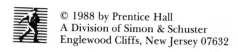

© 1988 by Prentice Hall
A Division of Simon & Schuster
Englewood Cliffs, New Jersey 07632

Printed in the United States of America

10 9 8 7 6 5 4 3 2 1

ISBN 0-13-965526-3 01

PRENTICE-HALL INTERNATIONAL (UK) LIMITED, *London*
PRENTICE-HALL OF AUSTRALIA PTY. LIMITED, *Sydney*
PRENTICE-HALL CANADA INC., *Toronto*
PRENTICE-HALL HISPANOAMERICANA, S.A., *Mexico*
PRENTICE-HALL OF INDIA PRIVATE LIMITED, *New Delhi*
PRENTICE-HALL OF JAPAN, INC., *Tokyo*
SIMON & SCHUSTER ASIA PTE. LTD., *Singapore*
EDITORA PRENTICE-HALL DO BRASIL, LTDA., *Rio de Janeiro*

CONTENTS

LIST OF MAPS

PREFACE

Priding ourselves on shaping history, we function day to day as slaves of the events that inexorably unroll themselves before our eyes, and fear possesses us and hatred follows in its train.

—Jawaharlal Nehru, 1949

Nehru, prime minister of India and one of the most respected Asian statesmen, confessed in the quotation above to a feeling of helplessness and bewilderment which many others have shared in the face of the unpredictable and destructive course of history in recent times. No era before the twentieth century has witnessed such dramatic, tumultuous, and often tragic changes in the lives of countless millions of people. We no longer share the easy optimism of Westerners before the First World War, who too readily assumed material and spiritual progress to be a logical and inevitable force, almost a natural law. Nehru had imagined a far happier time for his country than that which independence brought just two years before he made these comments. Those shattered dreams are as much a part of the story of the twentieth century as the achievements which countries such as India actually did experience. Knowledge of these events can help us to reach a balanced, sober understanding of human relations in our complex world.

The world-historical perspective adopted in this text rests on the premise that the single most important trend of the twentieth century has been the increasing interaction among states and peoples on a global scale. The principal questions I seek to answer follow directly from this, namely: What have been the significant characteristics of this interaction, how can we explain the emergence of these global patterns, and what have been their impact on the peoples in various parts of the world? This brief survey cannot possibly explore in detail all the dimensions of this interaction since the early century. It has of necessity to be very selective. Three topics have guided my selection of the major issues and events to be addressed. One is the international history of the major powers; the second is the role of ideology in political history; the third is the evolution of world economic relations.

All three direct attention to related, yet distinct, aspects of global interaction. International history examines the essential factors that have shaped the foreign policies of governments and the relations among states. These include, first, the political ideals and national interests of states; second, the relative power of states and of groups of states; and, third, the balance of power among countries. These three factors taken together explain in large measure the evolution of global conflict and cooperation in our century from the alliance system prior to the First World War to the domination of the superpowers following the Second World War.

The potent force of political ideology emerges from deeply felt convictions of right and wrong, justice and injustice, giving rise to powerful mass movements and guiding the policies of governments. The importance of these aspirations in our time is such that some scholars have suggested calling the twentieth century the age of ideology. Marxism, for one, has played a vital role in major countries and deserves particular attention. Nationalism, of Western origin like Marxism but without any single intellectual source or text, places the emergence of national identity and the formation of the nation-state at the center of human endeavor. It is debatably the single strongest political bond among peoples in the world today. In studying these ideologies we can appreciate better the motives of important political leaders and the manner in which social discontent has been articulated and expressed in political movements.

Finally, economic history stresses the significance of productive property, of new technology, and of ownership of these means of production. These factors have determined the global division of developed and developing nations, of wealth and poverty, and have shaped the economic conditions in which some countries became dependent on others for their very livelihood. The fact that the debate over international sanctions against the racist government of South Africa includes references to platinum, the bulk of whose world deposits are located there, is one example of the importance of global economic interests in international relations. All three topics—international, ideological, and economic history—help us to understand key changes in the interaction among peoples by suggesting where and how powerful new historical forces have emerged. In simplest terms, they illuminate the process by which human power in various forms has, for good and ill, reshaped the twentieth-century world.[1]

The power mobilized through collective action has had the greatest impact through wars, revolutions, and nation building. These themes are so important to our understanding of the evolution of global history in this century that they constitute the major subject of this text. The two great world wars represent key events in the disappearance of the Western-dominated world of pre-1914. It is therefore important to understand both how such catastrophic events occurred and what their consequences were. Other, smaller, wars since then have revealed to what extent hostility and rivalry have shaped the in-

---

[1]The usefulness of the theme of power in world history is discussed in a short essay by William H. McNeill, "'The World Is So Full of a Number of Things.'" in *The History Teacher*, vol. 18 (August 1985), pp. 507–10.

teraction among peoples and states; they provide clues to the antagonism which still deeply marks the relations among nations. It is important as well to study closely the origins and evolution of the rivalry between the Soviet Union and the United States, for this so-called "Cold War" dominated global international relations in the decades after the Second World War.

The terrible damage done by war has also created conditions for rapid political change. Actual revolutions, that is, sudden and violent transformations of political and social institutions, opened the way to new political movements to remake the lives of their people. The success of revolution in one country provided inspiration to parties in other lands to seek the same results. The Russian revolution of 1917 launched a process of political and social change, under the leadership of the Communist party, which later provided a model for leaders in other parts of the world. The political revolutions that accompanied the liberation of colonial countries gave expression to the hopes and the visions of nationalist leaders for their new nations.

Even where independence came without violence, there followed a complex and difficult period of formation of state institutions and of national leadership in the new nations. These developments, which we call nation building, have in many ways remade the lives of the peoples throughout the world. In the largest sense, destruction and creation represent inseparable parts to the history of this century. The bitterness and hostility generated by this struggle of ideals and interests make our world an uneasy, violent place. Perhaps the most appropriate—certainly the most optimistic—image of this process is provided by the Greek myth of the phoenix, the bird reborn from the ashes of its own destruction. To discern essential signs of the emerging new era represents the most challenging historical task of any survey of turbulent periods of change, particularly one so close to us.

The writing of this text has come through several years of teaching and innumerable discussions with colleagues who have proven generous with their time and indulgent of the author's endeavor. Students in the twentieth-century world history course at the University of California-Davis have lived through the several stages of conceptualization of this work. Particular sections have been read by specialists in the area, whose help was invaluable and to whom I would like to extend my deepest gratitude. In particular, I would like to thank the following scholars for their assistance: William Hagen, Donald Price, Kay Flavell, Karen Erickson, Ruth Rosen, Lovell Jarvis, Barbara Metcalf, and Arnold Bauer. They are absolved of all sins of omission and commission in the completed text, for which I bear full responsibility. This book is dedicated to my children, with the wish that they too may find the world a place to say "Fanfare for the Makers."

TWENTIETH-CENTURY WORLD HISTORY TIME CHART

	Global Events	Europe
1900	World population 1.5 billion	Anglo-French and Anglo-Russian entente (1904, 1907) Paris Exposition (1900) First Russian Revolution (1905)
1910	Outbreak of First World War (1914) U.S. entry into war (1917) Defeat of Central Powers (1918) Founding of Communist International (1919) Paris Peace Conference (1919)	Balkan Wars (1912–13) German military victories on Eastern Front (1915) Battle at Verdun (1916) Russian Revolution (1917) Russian civil war (1918–20) Bolshevik policy of war communism (1918–21) German Revolution (1918) Collapse of Austro-Hungarian Empire (1918)
1920	Founding of League of Nations (1920) Dawes plan (1924) Lindberg solo Atlantic flight (1927) Washington Conference (1920–21)	French Invasion of Ruhr (1923) Locarno Pact (1925) Fascist regime in Italy (1922) Soviet First Five-Year Plan (1928) Stalin Dictatorship (1929)
1930	World Depression (1930–35) End of war debts and reparations payments (1931) Second World War (1939)	Nazi rule in Germany (1933) Spanish Civil War (1936–39) German reoccupation of Rhineland (1936) Munich Agreement on Czechoslovakia (1938) Stalin's Great Terror (1936–38) Soviet-German Pact and partition of Poland (1939)
1940	U.S. entry in war (1941) Bretton Woods Agreement on international trade (1944) Teheran Conference (1943) Yalta Conference (1945) End of Second World War (1945) Start of Cold War (1947) United Nations (1945)	German invasion of Western Europe (1940) German-Soviet War (1941) Nazi extermination camps (1942–45) Stalingrad battle (1942–43) Normandy landing (1944) German Occupation Zones (1945) Marshall Plan and Truman Doctrine (1947) Berlin blockade (1948) Soviet-Yugoslav split (1948) North Atlantic Treaty (1949) British Labor government (1945–51) German Federal Republic (West Germany) (1949)
1950	Hydrogen bombs tested (U.S., 1952; USSR, 1955) Deployment of ballistic missiles (ICBM) (1958) Geneva meeting of U.S.–USSR (1955)	Death of Stalin (1953) Khrushchev new Soviet leader (1955) Soviet repression of Hungarian Revolution (1956) European Economic Community (Common Market) (1958) French Fifth Republic under de Gaulle (1958–) U.S. nuclear weapons in W. Europe (1953)

N. & S. America	Asia	Middle East & Africa
U.S. policy of intervention in Central America (1904)	Boxer Revolt in China (1900) Russo-Japanese War (1904–05)	Boer War (1899–1902) Discovery of Iranian oil (1901)
Opening of Panama Canal (1914) U.S. intervention in Mexican Revolution (1914, 1916)	End of Chinese Empire (1911) Gandhi leader of Indian National Congress, Amritsar massacre (1919)	Union of South Africa (1910)
	Provincial self-rule in India (1921) Chinese Nationalists control China (1928)	French and British mandates (1920) Greek-Turkish War (1920–22) Turkish Republic (1923) Agreement on "Red Line" (oil firms' partition of Middle Eastern oil fields) (1927) Egyptian independence (1924)
End of U.S. policy of intervention (1931) Batista in power in Cuba (1933)	Anti-salt tax movement in India (1931) Government of India Act (1935) Japanese invasion of Manchuria (1931) Sino-Japanese War (1937–)	Start of Arabian oil production (1939) Palestine Arab revolt (1936–38)
Mexico and other Latin countries in war (1942) Juan Perón Argentine president (1946–55) Vargas president of Second Brazilian Republic (1946)	Soviet war on Japan (1945) Hiroshima atomic bomb (1945) Chinese Communists in power (1949) U.S. occupation of Japan (1945–51) Indian independence and partition (1947) Indonesian independence (1945) Philippine independence (1946) French war in Indochina (1946–54)	Israeli independence (1948) First Arab-Israeli War (1948–49) Nationalist party in South Africa imposes apartheid (1948)
U.S. intervention in Guatemala (1954) Castro in power in Cuba (1959)	Beginning of Japanese "economic miracle" (1956) Mao's Great Leap Forward (1958–60) Indian Constitution (1951) Bandung Conference (1955)	Nasser in power (1952) Suez crisis (1956) Mossadeq in power in Iran (1951–53) Egyptian-Syrian Union (UAR) (1958–61) Ghana (Gold Coast) independence (1957) French war in Algeria (1955–63)

(*continued*)

TIME CHART (*cont.*)

	Global Events	Europe
1960	World Population est. 3 billion Organization of Petroleum Exporting Countries (OPEC) (1960) Cuban missile crisis (1962) First Communications Satellite (1965) Integrated-Circuit Computers Second Vatican Council (1962–65) Moon landing by American astronauts (1969) First terrorist plane hijacking (1969)	Berlin wall (1961) Brezhnev new Soviet leader (1964) Soviet repression of Czech reforms (1968) German Social Democrats in power (1968–)
1970	Nuclear arms treaty (SALT I) (1972) Second nuclear agreement (SALT II) (1979) OPEC price increases (1973, 1979) Nixon visit to China (1972) Manned U.S. Space Station (1973) First U.N. International Women's Year (1975)	Berlin Treaty (1972) British entry into Common Market (1971)
1980	World Population est. 5 billion (1987) Economic Recession (1980–83) Summit meeting: Reagan–Gorbachev (1985) First U.S. space shuttle (1981)	Solidarity movement in Poland (1980–82) Gorbachev Soviet leader (1985)

N. & S. America	Asia	Middle East & Africa
Soviet-Cuban cooperation (1960–) Cuban Bay of Pigs invasion (1961) Military dictatorship in Brazil (1964)	Sino-Indian War (1962) Death of Nehru (1964) End of Sukarno rule (1966) Chinese Cultural Revolution (1966–75) U.S. war in Vietnam (1965–73)	Belgian Congo (Zaire) independence (1960) Creation of Palestine Liberation Organization (1965) Israeli-Arab Six-Day War (1967) Biafra Civil War in Nigeria (1967–70) Independent Algeria (1963)
Military dictatorship in Chile (1973–) Sandinista regime in Nicaragua (1979)	Death of Mao (1975) "Market socialism" in China (1978–) Communist conquest of S. Vietnam (1975) Indo-Pakistan war and independence of Bangladesh (1973) 1971 Soviet invasion of Afghanistan (1979)	Cuban troops in Angola (1975) Soweto riots in South Africa (1976) Israeli-Arab War (1973) Egyptian-Israeli Treaty (1979) Iranian Revolution (1979)
Democratic government in Argentina (1985) U.S. aid to anti-Sandinistas in Nicaragua (1981–)	Philippine Revolution (1985) Assassination of Indian leader Indira Gandhi (1984)	South African protests at apartheid constitution (1984–) Israeli invasion of Lebanon (1982)

chapter 1

THE WESTERN WORLD, 1900–1914

No public spectacle so well typified the Western world before the First World War as the Paris Universal Exposition of 1900. To mark the first year of the new century, its organizers conceived the ambitious plan to celebrate human progress during the previous one hundred years. Exhibit halls, lining the Seine River in central Paris, attracted fifty million visitors. They, upon leaving the exposition, had no reason to doubt that Western civilization was the source of all progress. The great success of the 1900 Paris Exposition tells us how much that image pleased them. We can discover there important clues to the life of an era that, we know now, was rapidly approaching its end.

The exhibits revealed a firm confidence in the future of the West. They did so by presenting in a variety of ways the great power of Western states, the wealth and productivity of their economies, and the improvements which science, industry, and the arts were making available to Europeans. Electric lighting turned night into day at the exhibition. Overhead, the tallest structure in the world, the Eiffel Tower (built in 1889), demonstrated the ability of industry to create new buildings of iron and steel. Visitors looking through microscopes could see for themselves the lethal bacteria which doctors were for the first time able to identify and destroy in the war on infectious diseases. National exhibit halls arrayed along the Street of Nations rivaled each other in an effort to impress the public with the achievements of their nation-states. The German building resembled an enormous medieval town hall, the United States chose the design of a Roman temple, and the British hall looked like the comfortable house of a country squire. One French display contained a miniature naval battle of its forces destroying an (un-

Monumental Exhibit-Halls of the Western Nation-States: The "Street of Nations," Paris World Exposition, 1900. (The Paris Exhibition 1900 [*London, 1901*], *p. 110*)

named) enemy fleet. An entire series of exhibits revealed the curious customs and dress of the colonial peoples of Asia and Africa, the possession of Western empires. In these and many other ways, the exposition conveyed the impression that Western civilization was the greatest ever achieved in human history.

The exposition did not reveal every important aspect to Western life, however. Its industrial machinery was entirely given to peaceful use; the new weaponry of war was not displayed. It did not provide room for the socialist parties to present their picture of the cruel conditions the industrial economy inflicted on the labor force of farms and factories. No exhibit illustrated the enormous gap which separated the very wealthy from the very poor. The opponents of colonial empire had no place to portray the treatment of the conquered peoples by the imperialists. There was no room presenting visitors with the new, ugly features of racism and anti-Semitism. Behind the image of progress there existed economic inequality and exploitation, the source of social and political conflict in every Western state. The predominance of Western civilization, everywhere visible at the exposition, came at the expense of the weak; the might of the Western nation-states made the diplomatic rivalries among states an increasingly dangerous source of military conflict. Technology was creating instruments of destruction and death as well as marvelous tools for a better life. We now realize how misleading was that comfortable, peaceful picture of life presented at the exposition. At the time, most Westerners believed the image to be reality.

This history of the twentieth-century world begins with a brief survey of the West in those years. Although, later, Western empires vanished and European nation-states lost their international preeminence, global relations were permanently altered. Industrial technology remained the foundation of the international economy. Political ideals of freedom and equality for individuals and for nations, first championed by Europeans, were adapted by non-Western political movements in their own struggle for national independence and social justice. The forces leading to global war and revolutions had their roots in the West.

INDUSTRIALIZATION
AND THE INTERNATIONAL ECONOMY

A century of rapid economic growth and technological innovation in the West had laid the foundations of an international economy. The world's natural resources were available to Western companies possessing the wealth and the skills to extract and transform the coal, oil, iron ore, timber, cotton, and other raw materials into finished products to be sold in the West and increasingly in other countries as well. Food production

from distant lands fed the urban populations of Europe. Few tariff barriers impeded trade among states, while Western overseas empires allowed national goods and investment to go unobstructed wherever the flag of that nation flew.

These sales and investments generated profits for private corporations; banks earned an increasingly important share of their income from international finance. The West provided most of the manufactured goods for the world, for it possessed the technological skill and the financial means necessary for industrial growth. Its capitalist system of private ownership of the means of production assured that the increased wealth generated by the international economy remained largely in Western hands. Socialists bitterly protested the inequalities it caused, yet admired its technological advances; nationalists from colonial lands attacked Western exploitation of their resources and people and looked to the day when their countries would possess developed economies. In this sense, the West provided an enduring model of economic change.

The Industrial Economy

Two developments in the late nineteenth century accelerated the trend toward Western economic expansion. One was the result of technological innovation, the other of the reorganization of business firms. Communication and transportation, vital for the growth of an international economy, became increasingly rapid and inexpensive as a result of new inventions. The telegraph provided for the first time instant communication between distant lands. The British proudly announced, during their celebrations of Queen Victoria's Diamond Jubilee in 1897, that they had sent a message by telegraph completely around the world. Transportation by land and sea moved more rapidly as well with the introduction of new motors, of which the most important were the internal combustion engine and the diesel engine. The dream of flying became reality when the Wright brothers in 1908 successfully demonstrated their airplanes in flights in Europe and America. The most potent innovation in Western economic growth, however, came from the development of electric power. With the invention of efficient electrical motors factories were freed from their dependence on coal. Cities could provide public and private electrical lighting. Electric streetcar lines could move people at little cost within big cities. These and other inventions gave the West the mechanical tools on which its global economic ascendance rested.

New international corporations made great profits in finding the resources needed for the Western economy and in selling industrial products. International commerce had from the beginning of the Industrial Revolution been a source of investment funds and of raw materials for production. By the early twentieth century, the need for new resources drove the search for raw materials farther and farther outside Europe; at the same time, Western producers sought increasingly a mass market for their goods beyond the borders of the West. The rise of giant corporations indicated the path of Western capitalism in the century ahead. The most vivid example is provided by the petroleum industry. The rising demand for petroleum in the 1890s led to the exploitation of new oil fields in Asia. To compete with the major American oil company, Standard Oil, the Royal Dutch-Shell Company was formed in 1906, whose major reserves lay in the Dutch East Indies. Petroleum appeared by then so vital a resource for naval power that the British government decided

to purchase an oil company which had begun exploiting the rich Iranian oil deposits, creating in early 1914 the British Petroleum Company. Oil was becoming so widely used and so strategic a commodity that it was an affair of state and a driving force in Western exploitation of global natural resources.

The expansion of the oil industry represented only one instance of Western predominance in the international economy. Other companies sought out markets for their products. In America, the Singer Company was so successful in expanding its international sales and controlling the market that its name became synonymous with sewing machines. Western banks, enriched by decades of profits from investments in industry, lent a substantial share of their funds to companies operating in non-Western lands as well as to non-Western governments.

Great Britain possessed through its mercantile fleet, its commerce, and its financial operations the most extensive international economic network of any Western country. In the course of the nineteenth century it had laid down the basic rules by which trade and financial affairs were conducted. It had for a long time promoted free trade, based on the principle that everyone benefited when no tariffs impeded access to the inexpensive goods and on the practical consideration that the cheapest goods were often British. It established the practice of guaranteeing the value of its currency, the pound sterling, by establishing a fixed equivalent value in gold. Anyone with pounds could purchase gold and, when this gold standard was adopted by the other industrial countries, could transfer funds easily from one currency to another. When, in the 1890s, large gold deposits were discovered in South Africa, Australia, and the Yukon, the West expanded its money supply and increased

...tment. The Lon-... ter of financial af-... restment network. ...nal trade and fi-... economies depen-... markets and invest-... and nonindustrial ...Vest.

...hnology of the in-... in the late nine-... centuries to new ...eyond. Innovation ...restricted to the ...ties. The so-called ...the 1880s slowed ...ne emergence and ...rial areas. Both the ...what later Russia ...artly with the help ..., partly thanks to ...es, and partly with ...ve tariffs, imposed ...90s. The resources ...of the U.S. econo-...entieth century. It ...lustrial societies. It ...profit to European ...nds into the coun-...hey did into Russia. ...he other hand, was ...mpoverished peas-...r political conflict ...overnment and its ...stances, industrial-...a new source of

...nomy had to make ...on-Western country. ...loped, with remark-...dustry and interna-...prises. Its success ...echnology and cap-...the monopoly of the ...of the United States,

Russia, and Japan signaled the beginning of a momentous shift in economic power away from the old industrial states of Europe toward other regions of the globe.

Despite the struggle for markets that pitted capitalists of these states against one another, manufacturers, traders, and investors found their best customers in other industrial countries where there existed a large, relatively stable market. Until 1914, close trade ties existed between Great Britain and Germany in spite of worsening diplomatic rivalry. The British and French empires assured protected markets for the capitalists of those nations, yet these areas absorbed only a small part of their exports. Capitalist competition did not cause imperialism and war, but created the economic conditions within which both evolved. Economic growth had been rapid in first years of the twentieth century. World trade boomed, rising to a level by 1910 fifteen times that of the midnineteenth century. Yet serious social problems accompanied these "good times."

Urbanization and Social Protest

The most dramatic social consequence of the Industrial Revolution in the West was the population explosion and urbanization, not, as Karl Marx had argued, the appearance of the industrial proletariat. The extraordinary productivity of the new technology—applied in agriculture as well as industry—and the factory system provided food and shelter for twice as many Europeans in 1900 as in 1800 (400 million). Greatest hardship—and massive migration to the Western Hemisphere—occurred in Eastern and Southern Europe, where industrialization had just begun. Cities expanded everywhere, their inhabitants enjoying on an average better living conditions than ever before. They attracted migrants from the countryside seeking an escape from rural poverty. Disappointment awaited many new urban dwellers, but still they came. By the first years of the twentieth century, urbanization had led to the rise of major metropolises throughout the West. Later in the century the same forces led to massive urbanization in the non-Western world as well.

Within these cities family and class relations experienced dramatic changes. The older business classes were closely tied to industrial production and commerce. The fastest-growing middle-class positions at the turn of the century were in professions ranging from bank clerk to doctor and lawyer. New terms appeared, such as "white collar," to designate a large array of new occupations which required skills provided by secondary and advanced education. Access to these jobs was restricted by both custom and limited schooling. The poor laboring population had little hope to qualify, for social barriers and minimal elementary education stood in their way. A few unmarried women from the middle classes struggled to enter educational institutions to acquire advanced training, but most had no choice except less rewarding positions such as schoolteacher or nurse. Even then, custom dictated that upon marriage the wife immediately abandon outside work. To be a wife was in that social sphere synonymous with being a housewife. Discontent with this condition contributed to the rise of a new movement called "feminism," defined by one of its leaders as "the emancipation of woman as a personality." Although it later became a powerful, and controversial cause throughout the world, in the early century it was still the affair of a small group of activists. In that "Victorian" age, power and wealth lay in the hands of middle-class men.

The laboring classes of the Western countries were still deprived of both the benefits of the industrial economy and influential voice in government. Although fewer than ever before suffered constant privation, their adult years were spent in unrelieved labor in conditions which stunted their bodies and shortened their lives. Conditions were worst in the countryside, where the old paternalistic rule of landlords and the indifference of the state left peasant farmers and farm workers at the mercy of fate and local authorities. In the cities, work depended on economic demand and the needs of private businesses; depression meant unemployment and hunger. In the early twentieth century, governments did little or nothing to help those unable to work, still honoring the old precept that "God helps those who help themselves."

Economic exploitation and social repression gave workers of the industrial societies substantial reason to join in protest movements. Their principal means of organized opposition was the strike, increasingly led by labor unions. The principal demands centered on work conditions and pay, with the eight-hour day the single most potent objective among workers still forced to labor as much as twelve or fourteen hours, six days a week. The rise of organized labor represented as well a political challenge to rule by the middle classes. In those years of economic prosperity labor agitation showed signs of spreading and growing in strength. In Russia, for the first time in any country, a general strike in the fall of 1905 paralyzed for a short time economic life in all major cities. The strength of the Russian political revolution that year resulted largely from the working-class movement. In 1911 and 1912, English miners, railroad workers, and dockworkers, turning to direct action to demand the eight-hour workday and better wages, launched a wave of strikes almost as powerful as those earlier in Russia. When mobilized, the working class constituted a potent force for social protest and for political reform or revolution.

Profound social and cultural changes were already under way among the working classes in the West. Literacy was becoming widespread as a result of universal elementary education. Worker family life was beginning to adjust to new economic conditions. Improved health and food brought longer life expectancy and lower infant mortality. At the same time, birth-control methods became available, their use encouraged by socialist leaders who viewed emancipation of women as part of their larger struggle for the liberation of the working classes. For reasons which we still understand only poorly, birth rates were declining throughout the West in the early century as families chose to have fewer children than before. This trend, called the "demographic transition" (lower birth and death rates), signaled the end of Europe's population explosion of the previous century. The same demographic process, one of the most important for the balance of global resources and human needs, spread to other parts of the world later in the twentieth century.

THE WESTERN POLITICAL ORDER

The political stability of Western democracies depended partly on their ability to satisfy popular demands for new political and social reforms and partly on widespread agreement on the importance of liberalism and individualism, that is, of political liberty to protect the individual citizen. Individualism had become a pivotal feature of the Western intellectual tradition, and appeared to many Europeans the key to their superiority as a civilization. The image that best conveys the sense of confidence and su-

periority of Westerners in the nineteenth century was that of the rational individual. It gave meaning to political democracy, a benefit if controlled by representative government chosen by an enlightened electorate. It also sanctioned capitalist economic relations, governed by rational choices of material interests. It found justification in the conviction of scientists from Newton's time in the orderliness and harmony of the universe, whose basic laws reason could describe. It found expression in the artistic taste for harmonious music, for painting and sculpture portraying the real, tangible external world, and for public architecture which relied heavily still on the Classical style of Ancient Rome and Greece, models for Westerners of rational truth and beauty (and inspiration for the U.S. exhibit hall at the 1900 Paris Exposition).

This image of the rational individual extended into all areas of culture and politics and was deeply anchored in the Western mind to the end of the nineteenth century. It shaped the plans of imperialists who looked forward to a time when they would bring "civilization" to the colonial peoples. It helped to sustain the conviction among political leaders that liberal political values were a permanent achievement. Here and there the emergence of extremist political movements whose leaders glorified racism and nationalism suggested that this assumption was wrong, that the optimism was ill-founded. At the time, political liberty appeared triumphant in the West.

This confidence in liberalism was due to two factors. In the first place, government in most countries rested on democratic vote and majority rule, permitting new political parties to rise to power and encouraging existing parties to formulate new programs to win votes. Only Russia went through a period of political violence. Its revolution of

1905 ended the absolute power of the monarch, Nicholas II, who had to grant his people laws guaranteeing an elected legislature and civil and political liberties. Elsewhere these institutions already existed. The right to vote remained a male privilege except in a few states in the United States; universal manhood suffrage slowly was spreading through Europe. In most countries a majority vote in the legislature (called in England the Parliament) chose the executive, a cabinet of ministers. This parliamentary system, as opposed to the presidential system in the United States, left in place in many countries a monarch, stripped of power and symbol of stability and unity, and provided protection against the danger of dictatorial rule. These restrictions made rapid change difficult to achieve, but as long as most citizens accepted gradual reform, political stability was assured.

Liberalism, Socialism, and Nationalism

Reform represented an acceptable means to deal with political and social conflict for a second reason as well. Many citizens and political leaders shared a readiness to tolerate new political parties and to make certain concessions to new social and political programs to avoid violence. Government in the West down to 1914 remained in all countries in the hands of the middle and upper classes, yet liberal politics represented much more than class rule. Considerable political debate and controversy characterized political life everywhere; bitter quarrels divided political parties on issues such as property rights versus social welfare, protection of religious faith versus secular public education, the rights of nationalities versus state unity. In most cases, the issues were fought out in parliament and the press, not in the streets.

Liberal leadership was challenged principally by the socialist and labor movements. Inspired largely by the socialist theories of Karl Marx, intellectuals and leaders of socialist parties proposed a radically different view of human relations and of the future of the West. Intellectuals, eager to assist the working-class movement, had over the previous half-century studied the rise of capitalism and the hardships it caused and had sought to forecast the historical process by which inequality and economic exploitation would end, to be replaced by social equality and collective control of the means of production. "Socialism" is the general term by which we designate this ideology, a vision of a more just society and a program of action to reach that goal. The most influential socialist intellectual, Karl Marx, had anticipated that capitalism was a global historical process and therefore that proletarian revolution and socialism would ultimately constitute a common experience of all humanity. His Communist Manifesto of 1847 concluded by calling for the union of all "the workers of the world." His theories became the inspiration for new political parties, most calling themselves "social democratic," which appeared in many Western countries by the late nineteenth century. To strengthen their efforts to defend workers everywhere and to oppose capitalist and imperialist policies, they competed actively where possible in parliamentary struggles, and elsewhere operated within the revolutionary underground opposition. In addition, they strengthened their international ties by joining together in 1889 in the Second International (the first had existed briefly in the 1860's), meeting in international congresses to formulate common policies. The spread of these parties in Europe and later in many other countries throughout the world made Marxism a potent force in the transformation of states and societies in the twentieth century.

Marxist socialism was based on three important concepts: (1) the dominance of property in human relations; (2) the necessity of class conflict between those possessing productive property and those without, between the "exploiters" and the "exploited"; and (3) the inevitability of violent revolutions until property became the possession of everyone in a collective, "communist" society. To Marxists the basic issue in any society concerned ownership of property. It determined who were wealthy and poor, and who controlled the repressive powers of the state. The nature of productive property changed when technology altered the means of production. Nineteenth-century capitalists had taken full advantage of the inventions which gave rise to the industrial economy. This "bourgeoisie" had become the ruling class and dominated the states of Europe. Marxists all agreed that industrialism represented the most advanced form of production ever to exist and would ensure well-being for everyone, if only wealth were shared equally.

They also were convinced that the capitalist economy was locked in a deadly struggle among producers for markets, both within Western societies and in non-Western lands. Marxist writers linked the international economy and Western imperialism, which they attributed to European economic expansion in search of markets, pursued by capitalists throughout the world. The working masses, deprived of their rightful share of the value of production, could not buy the flood of products turned out by industry. In the early twentieth century some Marxists argued that imperial conquest was one product of this frantic economic competition. Even so, markets could not expand rapidly enough; some enterprises would grow at the expense of the weak in a "struggle for survival," but these firms were ultimately doomed by depressions and class conflict. Marxist intellectuals at the end of the century (with a few exceptions) looked ahead still to the final economic crisis which Marx had foretold would end the capitalist system.

The agents of this revolution would be the working class, the "proletariat." Their conditions of exploitation would cease only after they had participated in the overthrow of the capitalist system. Although some Marxists argued in the early twentieth century that universal suffrage permitted their parties to take power peacefully, most still held to the belief that only revolution could end capitalist domination. They viewed all history as a series of stages marked by the dominance of one class. The feudal system, controlled by the landed nobility, had fallen in a revolutionary struggle to the capitalists, the inevitable victors since they controlled the new, superior means of production. Capitalism itself created its own enemy in the industrial proletariat whose numbers would grow until they became the vast majority of the population. They would not be deflected from their struggle by "myths" such as religion, which Marx had dismissed as the "opiate of the masses," or nationalism.

A new stage in history would open when workers, led by their socialist parties, had triumphed. After an initial transition period of "dictatorship of the proletariat," the ultimate, communist stage would ensure that wealth be shared equally, that productive property would be the collective possession of the people, and that individuals would work in a manner best suited to their abilities ("from each according to his ability, to each according to his need"). Marxists anticipated that this process would spread throughout the world. All humanity would thus share in the benefits of this classless society. Like the organizers of the Paris Universal Exposition of 1900, Marxists extolled industry and thought in terms of power and progress. Their plans called, however, for proletarian power to end the rule of the bourgeoisie.

Their ultimate dream of progress for all humanity would then and only then come true.

The socialist parties had become by the early twentieth century a powerful political force in all democratic states in Europe. Nowhere had they won a majority of the vote, but their demands for social and economic reform had forced governments to begin to take action. Laws appeared restricting working hours, particularly for women and children. The practice of taxing the income of the well-to-do did spread. In a few states, notably Germany, the government undertook a major social program to assist the aged and the unemployed. No government conceived of introducing a program of nationalization, that is, state ownership of the means of production. Social welfare and nationalization, to become later in the century central features of socialist reforms in many Western and non-Western countries, remained at that time still socialist dreams.

The unity of the Western and certain Central European states depended as much on national loyalty as on allegiance to liberal political institutions. Although it was much written about, nationalism was not a coherent ideology like socialism, or even a well-defined set of political ideals like liberalism. It designated principally the ideal of a political community, the nation-state, whose people were bound by common language, history, and customs. When, as in the case of England and France, one nationality had for long constituted the majority of the population, it tended to reinforce the bonds among citizens.

When nationalism spread further east, it created the conditions for social conflict, revolution, and war. It had already remade the map of Central Europe through the unification in the 1860s of Italy and Germany. In both cases political leaders had turned to limited wars to achieve their goal of national unity. Further to the east in the Austro-Hun-

garian Empire of southeastern Europe and in the Russian Empire, many minority nationalities were denied political recognition. Poles were found within both states as well as in Germany. Many South Slavs (Yugoslavs) were citizens of Austro-Hungary, though a few lived in the small independent state of Serbia. Jews were scattered throughout the states of Central and Eastern Europe, a minority people often regarded with suspicion or even hatred by their Christian neighbors. In reaction to the rising anti-Semitism in that region, a Jewish nationalist movement, calling itself the Zionist Organization, appeared in 1897. Its leaders, using the rhetoric of European nationalism, argued that the Jewish people had to form their own nation-state by returning to the "homeland" in Palestine, in 1900 a province of the Ottoman Empire, from which they had been driven almost two thousand years before.

Nationalist political movements in Eastern Europe confronted bitter opposition from their rulers, rightly fearful that the creation of a Polish or a Yugoslav nation-state would destroy their multinational empires. To the nationalist leaders and their followers, national unity was an ideal worthy of great sacrifices. In its name a small organization of Serbian nationalists was prepared in 1914 to assassinate the heir to the Austrian throne. Nationalism in Eastern Europe, as later in other parts of the world, proved a potent revolutionary force.

The Great Powers of Europe

The political history of the West was dominated by the principal states of Europe: Great Britain, France, Germany, and Russia. We can more easily appreciate both the diversity of those states and their importance in the affairs of Europe and the world by a brief discussion of each in the first decade of the twentieth century. Three—Great Brit-

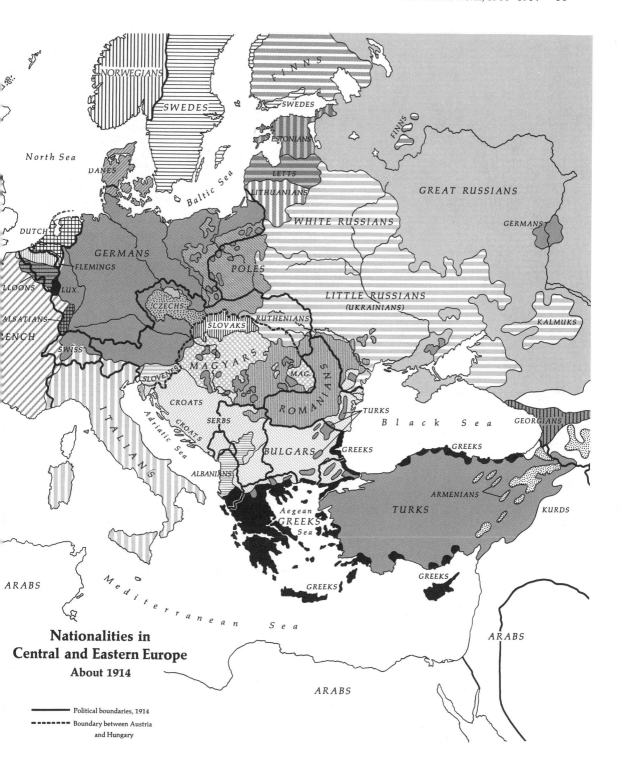

**Nationalities in
Central and Eastern Europe**
About 1914

——————— Political boundaries, 1914

- - - - - - - Boundary between Austria
and Hungary

Meeting of Two Emperors and Families: Nicholas II of Russia (center left) and Edward VII of Great Britain (center right), 1910 (*National Archives*)

ain, Germany, and Russia—were ruled by monarchs, close relatives by descent from Queen Victoria; when royal families paid visits to one another, the gathering (like that Nicholas II of Russia paid to Edward VII of Great Britain in 1910) resembled a friendly family reunion. All three held the title of emporer and ruled distant regions of the globe. They were to various degrees limited in their real powers (the Russian ruler only after 1905). The British king could represent his country, but did not govern it. Monarchy there symbolized political continuity.

Great Britain remained still the center of the Western world. Its fleet ruled the high seas; its global empire was the largest in size

and population. World trade was controlled by British shippers, and world finance passed primarily through London. Real political power in Great Britain lay in the hands of the British parliament and the cabinet that it chose. Elections in those years were contested by two principal parties, the Conservatives and Liberals. In 1905, the Liberals won and in the next years undertook a new program of reform. Confronted by a new party representing the working classes, the Labor party, the Liberals introduced for the first time a National Insurance Act to protect workers in case of illness or unemployment, to be paid for by a progressive income tax. The reforms at the time provoked bitter opposition from Conservatives; workers found the measures inadequate and launched in 1911 massive protest strikes. In other areas the Liberals did not achieve any reform. Plans to grant Ireland self-rule could not overcome the bitter opposition of the Protestant population living in the northern part of the island (Ulster) to rule by the majority Catholics. (After the Second World War the British would encounter similar intractable hostility between religious communities in India and Palestine.) A small but militant women's suffrage movement could not win Liberal backing to grant women the right to vote. Reform came slowly in Britain and in the midst of intense public debate and even violence.

Yet it moved more rapidly than in France. There the principal political issues involved not social welfare, but religion and national defense. The French Republic was governed by a multiparty coalition cabinet, for no one party could obtain a majority in the legislature. It possessed a strong state administration and army, with which it ruled the second largest colonial empire. Within France, cabinet politics of compromise avoided substantial new reforms and centered on issues of the rights of citizens, the unity of the nation, and the need for a standing army. In the first years of the century political leaders finally exonerated a Jewish army officer, Dreyfus, unjustly convicted of spying, after long years of public quarreling whether the army should be forced to admit it had committed an act of injustice to a French citizen. In the same years they adopted secular reforms limiting the role of the French Catholic church in education and stopping all state financial support to the clergy. Many Catholics were outraged and deeply opposed to the liberal parties in the cabinet. The government had separated church and state and vindicated the rights of citizens of all faiths, but at the price of divisive political conflict.

Still, over vehement opposition, it demanded obligatory military service of three years from all young Frenchmen, swelling the size of the army in anticipation of a new war with Germany. Socialists threatened to call the workers to strike rather than to accept participation in a conflict which they believed a struggle between capitalist states. France was a country divided by political and religious controversy, where worker protest was met with repression, not reform.

The newest of the large nation-states was the German Empire, which included most Germans of Central Europe. Its core was the old state of Prussia, whose armies had in the 1860s been victorious against the enemies of German unification. The last of these conflicts was against France, which as a result of its defeat lost the eastern provinces of Alsace and Lorraine. Forged in war, the German state remained deeply marked by militarism, that is, the glorification of the army and of military might. Emperor William II, ruler from 1888, believed firmly in Germany's destiny to become a world power and took a direct hand in making German foreign policy. Beginning in 1897 he encouraged his government to develop a strong German army and navy, to demand new colonial territories, and to extend German diplomatic influence into the Middle Eastern lands of the Ottoman Empire. His "world policy" *(Weltpolitik)* challenged the leading international role of the British. It encountered in Germany the opposition of the Marxist Social Democratic party, which by 1912 had become the largest mass party in Germany (though it did not control a majority in the parliament—the *Reichstag*) and strongest of all the Marxist parties in Europe. The German government had the most extensive program of social welfare for the workers of any state in Europe, yet these workers supported the opponents of the German government. In becoming a nation-state the

German Empire had made an enemy of France; in seeking to expand the international position of Germany, its nationalist leaders provoked serious internal conflict. Awareness of this political instability made them, however, not less but more prepared to risk foreign war.

This contradiction between an image of great power and the realities of social and political conflict was most apparent in the Russian Empire. In 1905, Nicholas II confronted a war with Japan which his army could not win and a revolution in his own country which defied his absolute powers. The war against the Japanese, a contest for East Asian territory begun in 1904, revealed the weakness of his army and navy and had to be settled by a compromise peace in mid-1905. The political revolution which had begun earlier that year was the result of the combined opposition to his rule of most of the peoples of his vast continental empire. Minority nationalities fought for self-rule. Peasant farmers, who constituted the majority of his subjects, began to seize by force the estates of noble landlords. Liberals joined the revolution to press their demands for representative government and political and civil liberties. The greatest threat to his rule came from the labor movement and socialist parties which emerged in a general strike that fall and formed revolutionary assemblies, called "soviets," which some revolutionaries thought could become the basis of a new worker state.

Confronting such massive opposition, Nicholas was forced to concede to his subjects some of the rights of democratic rule, including a parliament. But he was determined to hold the dominant hand in his demi-constitutional monarchy, ordering his army to repress the rebellious worker, peasant, and nationalist uprisings. The successful repression in 1906 of the revolution could not ensure the regime's political stability, however, and a new war threatened to erupt with Austria-Hungary. The country remained deeply divided. Nicholas II, still persuaded of his God-given right to absolute rule but incapable of governing effectively, turned for help to an unscrupulous religious zealot, Rasputin, whose political influence outraged the tsar's supporters. By 1914, even conservative Russians were predicting a new political revolution directed against the monarchy. In all the principal European countries, political and social conflicts lay near the surface, some in the years after 1900 partially resolved by reform, others threatening or actually causing revolutionary violence. In 1914, it was not clear which form of political change would prevail.

WESTERN IMPERIALISM

The imperialist expansion of the Western nations was driven by a spirit of conquest. Confidence in the power of their states and in the superiority of their civilization shaped the attitudes of most Westerners in their contacts with other peoples. At the end of the century, a handful of daring artists turned to the "primitive" art of Africa and Polynesia for inspiration to portray on canvas their deepest inner emotions. The French painter Paul Gauguin, who proudly called himself a "primitive," looked to his painting to express his sensual vision of life and nature. A rebel against French society and traditional art, Gauguin's search for inspiration and insight into these emotional forces took him to the French Polynesian colonies in the 1890s. His works from those years created an imaginary world of pagan idols, savage natives, and brilliant colors. Although his work scandalized art critics, his example was followed by Pablo Picasso and other creators of Cubist art. Their achievements helped to lay the foundations of the artistic revolution we call "modern art."

Yet their use of tribal art was not accompanied by an appreciation of the culture of those peoples. These artists dreamed of a future in which their art would shape a new life supported by modern machinery and urban comforts. Paul Gauguin condemned the French colonial policy of ruling Polynesia "for the sole glory of the conquering power." Yet he too believed it "noble" to colonize if the result was "to cultivate a country, to make an undeveloped area produce things which are useful to those who live there." He shared the belief of the English novelist Rudyard Kipling in the "white man's burden." A new manner of understanding human behavior and the quality of life was needed to appreciate the achievements of non-Western cultures. In those years the first anthropologists were discovering through their studies of these peoples a cultural richness and complexity which the terms "primitive" and "civilized" could not possibly comprehend. Only after barriers of racial prejudice and cultural stereotypes had fallen would Western and non-Western peoples be able better to communicate and to understand one another.

Missionaries, Merchants, and Soldiers

In the years around 1900, three groups of Westerners were most active in seeking to spread their ideas, skills, and power outside their countries: missionaries, merchants, and soldiers. Christian missionaries continued as in past centuries their preaching and ministering to win over the souls of the "heathens." By the late nineteenth century, this quest took some into the vast interior areas of China, where popular resentment at their proselytizing and special treatment contributed to the rise of an anti-Western movement called the Boxers. It took others into unexplored areas of Africa. One Scottish missionary, David Livingstone, gave his entire life to caring for the East African tribes among whom he lived. There he was "discovered" by a British journalist, Henry Stanley, in search of a sensational story for his mass-circulation newspaper, whose readers enjoyed accounts of valorous Westerners lost among the "savages."

Merchants sought to conquer markets and to discover raw materials, not to spread the Christian religion. The emergence of an international economy led adventurous and enterprising traders, miners, engineers, bankers, and industrialists to seek profit in far-off lands. Railroad builders brought their tracks and locomotives everywhere from the plains of India to the jungles of Central America, where one entrepreneur decided to plant banana trees to have something worth selling to transport on his railroad. Western investors rushed to Southern Africa to exploit the rich diamond and gold deposits of the Transvaal, despite the protest of the Boer (Dutch) farmers who had moved into the region before them. European settlers in the African Congo basin compelled local tribes, in conditions of forced labor, to extract the liquid from rubber trees to satisfy the demand for rubber in Europe. Traders with cheap cottons from Western textile mills sold their products so effectively that, in countries like India, the work of native hand weavers became worthless and an entire industry was virtually wiped out. The effects of Western capitalist activity were not everywhere as devastating as in the Congo or among Indian weavers, but Western merchants in general had little regard for the impact of their products and of their search for profit. The human and ecological consequences of the economic victories of the Western merchants were sweeping and profound, changing the face of the earth and the way of life of entire societies.

The soldiers of Western states found in the decades before 1914 adventure, honor, and heroism in their foreign conquests. The world to them appeared in the form of battles to win and land to seize, not of markets or souls to save. The military might of the major powers gave them the ability on land and sea to dominate small states; the nationalist pride of large numbers of their fellow countrymen and the ambition of political leaders sanctioned their wars. Vague ideas of the "survival of the fittest," called Social Darwinism, made military victory and colonial conquest appear a kind of law of nature. Seeking to "expand our territory, our legitimate moral, economic, and political influence," wrote one adviser to Tsar Nicholas II, was "in the order of things." Many other Westerners shared this view of peoples and land beyond their states.

Modern "imperialism" in the strict historical sense refers to the expansion in the nineteenth century of Western political domination to large areas beyond Europe. It was the work of political leaders and soldiers; occasionally it occurred to protect and encourage the merchants, but economic interests played generally a minor role in the initial steps toward conquest. Opposition to imperial expansion existed in all Western countries, the result largely of objections to the brutality of war and to the high cost of administering colonial lands, but also of a concern that expansion would defer necessary internal reforms. Still, nationalist ambition, the sense of superiority of many Westerners, and the power of the Western states and economies drove imperialism on. By the end of the century the empire builders had virtually completed their work.

What appeared at the time the triumph of the West proved, however, short-lived. The twentieth century turned out to be a period of decolonization. The reasons for this lay partly in the inability of the Western states to sustain the burden of empire, partly in the conflicts which their conquests provoked. Disputes among imperial states erupted in the struggle for the spoils of conquest. Resistance by colonial peoples revealed the depth of their hostility to imperial rule. Both factors gradually undermined Western domination. We can best understand the hidden weakness of Western imperialism by examining some of these conflicts in the early twentieth century.

The Empire of the United States

Even the United States, with its own continental empire to develop, joined in the expansionist drive by moving into Latin America and the Pacific. By 1898 the Spanish Empire had almost vanished from the New World, possessing territory only in the Caribbean Sea (notably Cuba) and the Philippines. The independent states in South and Central America were by comparison with the United States and Western Europe weak, most of their population poor, their economies dependent on the export of raw materials to, and the import of finished products from, the industrial countries. A small, very rich elite dominated their governments, controlled most of the mines and plantations, and collaborated with the foreign traders, bankers, and investors. In most countries governments proved very unstable as small factions of military and civilian leaders struggled for power. When this instability threatened foreign lives and investments, European states intervened in the conflicts. Intervention did not lead to actual conquest, in part because Great Britain, the dominant naval power, preferred to protect the independence of these states

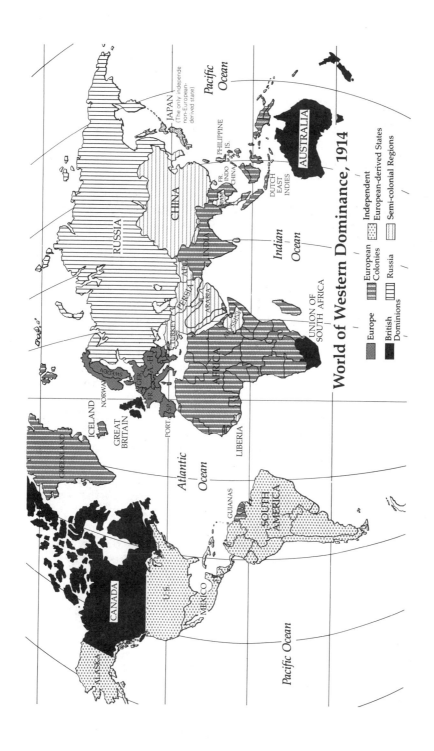

World of Western Dominance, 1914

Europe | European Colonies | Independent European-derived States
British Dominions | Russia | Semi-colonial Regions

JAPAN (The only independent non-European-derived state)

Pacific Ocean

CHINA

RUSSIA

PHILIPPINE IS.

FR. INDO-CHINA

DUTCH EAST INDIES

AUSTRALIA

Indian Ocean

INDIA

TURKEY

PERSIA

ARABIA

EGYPT

UNION OF SOUTH AFRICA

AFRICA

SWEDEN

NORWAY

ICELAND

GREAT BRITAIN

PORT. SP.

GERMANY

LIBERIA

GREENLAND

Atlantic Ocean

GUIANAS

SOUTH AMERICA

CANADA

U.S.

MEXICO

ALASKA

Pacific Ocean

and its freedom of trade there. The new spirit of military conquest did not reach Latin America until the United States in 1898 defeated Spain in a "glorious little war" and took over the remnants of the Spanish empire in the Caribbean Sea.

How did the United States become involved in imperial expansion? Democratic revolutionaries in Cuba, in revolt since 1895 against Spanish rule, had appealed for help to the United States. Some American leaders, notably Theodore Roosevelt, believed his "really great nation" had the responsibility to expand its naval and diplomatic power beyond its borders. The newspaper editor William Randolph Hearst found a large audience indignant at stories of "Spanish atrocities" and sympathetic to his call for a new American "destiny" to support democracy and fight tyranny in other lands. In this aggressive atmosphere, a simple incident caused by the explosion of the American battleship *Maine* in Havana harbor was sufficient pretext for a U.S. declaration of war on Spain. The war ended quickly after a major naval victory over Spanish naval forces in the Pacific and the rapid defeat of Spanish land forces in the Caribbean.

The consequences were long-lasting. The United States annexed Spanish territory in the Caribbean (Puerto Rico) and the entire Philippine archipelago as well. Nationalist leaders of the Philippines resisted, proclaiming the independence of their country and mobilizing their supporters to oppose U.S. annexation. As a result, the U.S. army had for several years to wage a war of occupation to defeat the Filipino rebels. While promising ultimate freedom, U.S. leaders argued that another European state would at that time seize the Philippines if they did not keep control. In fact, they treated the country as the fruits of their victory over Spain. Cuba itself received independence,

but only on the condition that it be a protectorate of the United States, granted the right to intervene "to protect life, liberty, and individual property." By annexation or by treaty, the United States had created its own small empire.

U.S. leaders shared with Europeans the same sense of their superiority in dealing with other peoples. The United States quickly became the dominant power in the Caribbean region. With the consent of Great Britain, President Roosevelt negotiated with Colombia for the construction of a canal across the Panamanian isthmus between the Caribbean and the Pacific Ocean. When the Colombians proved difficult, he helped Panamanian rebels create their own state and obtained their consent to the canal. In 1914 the Panama Canal opened to maritime transportation. The canal zone, controlled by the United States, was a base for American Navy and Marine forces. Having defeated Spain, Roosevelt made it clear to other European states that his state considered the area a U.S. "sphere of influence," that is, a region from which other major powers were excluded and where the U.S. government would use its influence to dictate policies to the small states when it judged necessary.

In the two succeeding decades, American leaders assumed that U.S. diplomatic and military interests justified direct intervention in the affairs of these states. Caribbean states had to pay their foreign debts or else U.S. advisers would take charge of their finances; they had to maintain internal order and protect foreign lives and property or else U.S. gunboats and Marines would do the job for them. When in 1911 civil war threatened Nicaragua, Marines moved in, remaining for another twenty years. To Roosevelt, this "gunboat diplomacy" was needed to protect U.S. power and was justified by the fact that his country was a "civilized nation" responsible to repress "chronic wrongdoing" among lesser peoples. Americans' faith in the superiority of their nation lay at the heart of U.S. imperial policy, but in the background, nationalist resistance to "Yankee imperialism" was already emerging.

Imperialism in East Asia

Imperial ambitions and conquest produced new conflicts in Asian lands as well. In some areas European empires were by the late nineteenth century firmly in place. The British Empire included the entire subcontinent of India, as well as Burma and Malaya; the Dutch controlled the East Indies; the French held Indochina. Serious international dispute erupted in the Chinese Empire, still nominally independent but in fact the prey to foreign intervention. Christian missionaries, protected by Western states, moved throughout the land to win converts. In doing so, they threatened the social customs and cultural values of the Chinese peasant masses. Western traders and railroad builders created hardship among those Chinese dependent on traditional labor and manufacturing. Antiforeign hostility had by the late 1890s spread widely among the Chinese population.

The humiliating treatment of the Chinese government by foreign powers heightened the anger of patriotic Chinese. Since the middle of the century the Western states had forced China to grant such sweeping political and economic concessions that Westerners could move about the country like conquerors. They obtained special trading rights to prevent the Chinese state from imposing high tariffs on their imported goods. They occupied in thirty-three cities special settlements with their own administration and police. Wherever they traveled they were protected by their own laws under the principle of "extraterritoriality." Western states even enjoyed the right to have their own naval vessels patrol the Chinese coast and rivers. They had taken from the Chinese Empire virtually everything except the appearance of independence.

The empire confronted a new threat from abroad when Japan joined in the 1890s the ranks of imperialist powers. This remarkable transformation of the formerly isolated island empire had begun in the 1860s, after Western diplomats backed by naval forces had obliged the old government to accept Western traders on the same unequal terms as those imposed in China. Faced with the likelihood that their state, like China, would be humbled by the Western imperial powers, in the 1860s a group of young Japanese reformers seized control of their government. This so-called Meiji Restoration (Meiji meaning "enlightened rule") mobilized the antiforeign sentiment of the Japanese in support of a daring effort to make their state and economy as powerful as those of the Western nations. Their motto was "rich country, strong military."

Claiming to have "restored" their emperor to power, the new leaders in fact ruled in his name, launching what amounted to a "revolution from above." Consciously borrowing Western technology and institutions, they succeeded in laying the foundations of an industrial economy, a well-equipped army and navy, and a constitutional monarchy. To obtain the cooperation of the population, they appealed to the people's patriotic loyalty to the emperor. By the end of the century, the reforms had proven so effective that the government could launch its own plan of imperial conquest. In 1894–95 it waged a quick, successful war against China to seize territory (notably Korea) and trade concessions. Japanese expansion took advantage of the weakness of the Chinese Empire and worsened the hatred of foreigners among the Chinese.

In reaction, a massive antiforeign rebellion broke out in China in 1900. Secret societies joined together to form a popular movement, called by Westerners the Boxers, whose objective was compressed into one slogan: "Support the Qing [the imperial dynasty]; destroy the foreigners." They received the secret backing of the Chinese government. Their revolt grew in scope and violence until by mid-1900 they were able to seize the capital itself, Beijing, and to lay siege to the foreign embassies. Western reaction was quick and brutal. A combined invasion force of British, Russian, American, and Japanese troops defeated the poorly equipped Boxer soldiers (in the process looting and destroying many buildings in Beijing). The victors demanded the execution of leaders of the rebellion, financial indemnity for damages, and even more humiliating concessions. The Chinese Empire survived for only another eleven years, unable to resist Western demands and increasingly incapable of governing the country. The imperialist powers had no need of annexing mainland China to reduce it to the level of a semicolonial land.

Imperialist rivalries in the Far East led to one last major conflict in those years. Tempted by the riches of the northern Chinese province of Manchuria, Russia and Japan each hoped to exploit its economic resources and to enlarge their sphere of influence at the expense of the powerless Chinese state. Fearing that Russia was on the brink of seizing the territory, the Japanese launched in early 1904 a surprise naval attack on the Russian Pacific fleet, followed by an offensive against the Russian forces in north China. By 1905 the Japanese had defeated the Russian navy and had forced the Russian army to retreat far into northern Manchuria. A peace treaty that year recognized the Japanese victory. Although Manchuria remained nominally a part of China, in fact the Japanese state established a sphere of influence in the southern area of the province and Japanese industrialists were able to exploit its mineral wealth. Russian plans for economic and political conquest were thwarted. Japan had become the leading state in East Asia, the equal to Western countries in self-confidence, international might, and expansionist ambitions. In the process, however, it had contributed to a rising wave of Chinese nationalism and had opened a conflict with Russia that would not end until after another brief war in 1945.

Imperialism in Africa

Of all the regions of the world where Western missionaries, merchants, and soldiers were active in the late nineteenth century, sub-Saharan Africa presented the greatest physical dangers and widest diversity of societies and cultures, and appealed most keenly to their spirit of adventure. Missionaries were challenged to learn new languages and to find new symbols of their Christian faith to win converts. Exploration of the unknown inner regions of the continent revealed great reserves of natural resources. Vast territories and exotic adventures awaited the small military expeditions sent by European states. In all respects Africa appeared a continent open to Westerners, to be molded and remade according to their plans.

The "scramble for Africa" had come to an end by 1900. The French and British governments had carved out the biggest shares of territory for themselves. Although rivals, they managed to settle peaceably their disputes. The most serious conflict occurred in 1898 when a French expedition contested the British claim to the upper Nile (Sudan). It withdrew when the French government decided not to risk war over that distant land. By then the British controlled a broad band of territory running "from the Cape [of Good Hope] to Cairo," interrupted only by German Tanganyika (Tanzania) and the small republics in southern Africa of the Boers (also known as Afrikaners).

These European colonists, descendants of Protestant settlers from the Low Countries, had in their search for independence from the British moved north from the Cape to the high plains where they established their farms and practiced their faith. They found in their creed religious justification to treat the Africans as inferiors and to expel the tribes from their land. But they could not remove so easily the Europeans who joined the gold rush when the precious metal was found in the late century in their territory. The Boers wanted to keep control of their "new Zion"; British imperialists like Cecil Rhodes had a very different vision of southern Africa, which they wanted incorporated in the British Empire and exploited by British capitalists. The two plans were irreconcilable.

As a result, Great Britain became involved in an imperialist war in sub-Saharan Africa. British administrators and officers in South Africa handled the dispute with the Boers with such arrogance and used their superior military force so provocatively that the Boers in 1899 resolved to fight. The military odds were hopelessly against the Boers, but they fought with the determination of religious zealots and the skill of guerrilla soldiers. The war did not end until 1902, by which time even the British government was aware of the destructive folly of that expansionist war. Soon after it had won the war, it set up the Union of South Africa, leaving the Boers free to run their own internal affairs in their territories and to participate in the leadership of the federal Union as well. The Africans themselves had no part in the conflict. They as well as their land had become the spoils and the objects of conquest. The Boers remained as determined as before to dominate their country. Their nationalism and racism became even stronger as a result of that bitter war.

The Ottoman Empire and the West

European imperialists could not so easily dispose of the territory or peoples of the Middle East, ruled by the Ottoman Empire. This vast state of the Ottoman Turks, in place since the fifteenth century, had declined in power in the nineteenth century. It lost wars and territory to the Russian Empire and went heavily into debt to European banks. To repay the debts, it had to give control of its taxes to European financiers. To Europeans it represented the "sick man of Europe," an area of exotic "Oriental" appeal but one incapable of governing itself effectively or of economic development. Still, it remained a potent political and diplomatic force in and around its vast territory, stretching from the Caucasus mountains to Arabia and from the Balkans to Egypt. It ruled over many peoples, some Christian, most Sunni Muslims for whom the Ottoman sultan was supreme religious authority (caliph) as well as political leader. One of its provinces was Palestine, which the Zionist Organization hoped to make once again homeland for the Jews. It was of strategic importance to Western states, for in its territory lay key waterways—the straits between the Black and Mediterranean seas and the new Suez Canal. An area where nationalist movements hoped to carve out new nation-states and where imperialist states competed for power, its very existence appeared threatened by the early twentieth century.

The most serious danger confronting the Ottoman ruler was the loss of control over his outlying provinces. Egypt, through whose territory ran the Suez Canal, ceased to be under his direct rule after the British government had in 1881 made that province a "protectorate." Theoretically still part of the Ottoman Empire and ruled by a Turkish *khedive,* Egypt came in fact under the control of the British consul-general and his aides. British officers commanded the small Egyptian army. British administrators supervised the construction of railroads, the building of dams, the expansion of irrigation, and the development of a public health program. Egypt for them constituted virtually another part of their empire, to be improved and molded as progress, civilization, and British interests dictated.

Other European states also had plans for the disposal of Ottoman lands. The Russian Empire to the north had for a century sought to extend its influence farther and farther toward the straits, as vital to its strategic and economic interests as the Suez Canal was to the British. Its armies and diplomats provided protection to nationalist movements among the Balkan peoples of southeastern Europe, in revolt in the late nineteenth century against their Ottoman rulers. While the Ottomans were powerless to stop the Russian advance, other European states did stand in the way. The Austro-Hungarian Empire was pushing its frontiers farther into the Balkan region. Its leaders feared that the Balkan nations, once victorious over their Ottoman rulers, might then begin to take apart the Austrian multinational empire. To them, the fate of the Ottoman Empire was bound to their own survival. The German Empire became involved as well when it decided to supply military aid to the Ottoman army and economic and engineering assistance for the construction of a strategic railroad through the Middle Eastern lands of the empire. Each European state in its own way was laying claim to a share of Ottoman land. All measured their own power in part by their ability to obtain the spoils of what they anticipated to be the coming partition of the Ottoman Empire.

The Ottoman collapse appeared under way in the early years of the twentieth century. The Austrian Empire took control in 1908 of the province of Bosnia, whose capital was Sarajevo and which was inhabited largely by Serbs. In 1912, the small state of Serbia, whose leaders hoped to gather together all South Slavs in one nation-state, joined with other Balkan states in a short war against the Ottoman forces to seize the remainder of the Balkan territory still under Ottoman rule. Their victory that year led to another brief war the next year when these little states fought over the territorial spoils taken from the empire. In the negotiations that followed that conflict, the Austrian government used its influence to ensure that Serbia remained weak. Serbian nationalists in Serbia and Bosnia vowed vengeance against the Austria-Hungarian Empire.

In that area, imperialist conquest was bringing military conflict closer and closer to Europe. Until then it had led only to small wars and to uprisings of conquered peoples quickly repressed. Vast regions of the world experienced more intensely or for the first time the impact of Western capitalism and imperialism. The expansion of the international economy and of Western empires accentuated the political and economic inequality of Western and non-Western peoples. We can see clearly now that these conditions of Western domination prepared the way for revolutionary opposition and for profound changes in the world order. The global might of the West was not destined to endure for long. In the early years of the twentieth century, conflicts in distant African and Asian lands did not disturb the peaceful, stable conditions in Europe. The crisis caused by the decline of the Ottoman Empire posed a new and far more serious problem. It brought the imperial ambitions of Russia and the nationalism of the Serbs in conflict with the interests of the Austrian and German states. It created the conditions for European war.

THE EUROPEAN BALANCE OF POWER

Industrial technology, science, and political institutions in Western countries had changed dramatically by the end of the nineteenth century, but not the diplomatic system of international relations or the battle plans which governed military operations in the event of war. The discoveries of scientists still had little direct impact on the weapons of war. The creative genius of Albert Einstein had, in theories worked out before 1914, proposed a fundamentally new view of time and space, and of matter and energy which he argued were bound one to the other (a bond expressed in the formula $E = mc^2$—energy is equal to matter multiplied by the square of the speed of light). At the same time, researchers were beginning to investigate the manifestations of the conversion of matter into energy through radioactivity. The physicists Marie and Pierre Curie isolated actual minerals which produced radiation and correctly identified the source to be a physical property of the atom, not a chemical reaction. For their work (as a result of which Pierre died of leukemia), they were awarded one of the first Nobel prizes for physics. The mysterious, unsuspected world of the atom was gradually revealing itself to these scientific explorers, who had no suspicion of the terrible potential for destruction to which their discoveries could be turned.

Industrial technology and mass production were already directly involved in the manufacture of new arms revolutionizing warfare. These included cannons of great power and accuracy, barbed wire as effective in stopping infantry charges as it was in keeping cattle from farmers' fields, and the machine gun, the most deadly of the new weapons. Infantry had in the past confronted volleys of rifle fire before reaching enemy trenches where the bayonet decided the battle. Each machine gun, firing hundreds of bullets a minute, covered a battlefield with devastating fire and turned an infantry charge into mass slaughter. With the appearance of these weapons, each major power spent great sums of money to equip its army as effectively as its rivals. By 1914 all had to some extent incorporated the new arms into their fighting forces. The advantage lay with the states whose industry could produce the best weapons in greatest number. By that measure Germany enjoyed military superiority.

European statesmen continued to rely on military might and diplomatic alliances to protect their countries and to achieve the political objectives they judged in the interest of their states. No international organization restrained their freedom of action; no effective international law set limits on warfare to resolve conflicts. Certain diplomatic conventions did seek to distinguish between combatants, who might kill and be killed, and civilians, theoretically protected from such mayhem on land and on sea. The sovereignty of each state meant that its leaders had the ultimate choice between war and peace. In those circumstances European diplomats had come to judge the relative strength or weakness of their countries in terms of the "balance of power," that is, the relative might of their state and allied states as opposed to that of rival countries. Depending upon their international ambitions, they might be satisfied with a balance sufficient to deter war, or might seek to swing the balance in their favor in order, by intimidation if not actual war, to achieve international gains. None considered war an end in itself, merely a means which their government or other states might employ to reach certain diplomatic objectives. Since the end of the Napoleonic wars in 1815, conflicts among states had followed this pattern. It appeared in the early years of the twentieth century that the system had worked fairly well. The Franco-Prussian war of 1870 had been the last serious European conflict, out of which had emerged the German Empire. It had left a deep scar on European diplomatic relations, however.

The Alliance System

In the years that followed, European alliances had altered to take into account the presence of this new major power in central Europe. The annexation by Germany of the former French provinces of Alsace and Lorraine had created a serious source of conflict between the two states. No French leader could, even if he himself was prepared to accept the permanent loss of that territory, raise the question publicly and hope to be reelected. French nationalist outrage was too strong. German leaders therefore signed in 1879 a defensive treaty with the Austro-Hungarian Empire, an ally in the event of a new war with France. In exchange, they promised protection to Austria in case of attack by its most likely enemy, Russia. The logical consequence of this agreement between the so-called Central Powers was the formation in the 1890s of an opposing alliance between Russia and France. Both trea-

ties were defensive, but each alliance anticipated war against the other side. The balance-of-power system rested ultimately on this "logic of force."

War plans took the next step in the preparations for conflict. On both sides they aimed at a quick military triumph. The French and Russian generals proposed, if war broke out with the Central Powers, to attack Germany simultaneously on its eastern and western frontiers. They expected the Russian army, drawn from a much larger territory and unable to move rapidly for lack of sufficient railroads, to begin its operations later than the French. Still, they hoped that the combined attack would split the German army and bring victory to their forces within a few months. The motto of the Russian army in 1914 was to be "in Berlin by Christmas."

The German plan required even greater speed to defeat the enemy. This Schlieffen Plan, named for the general who conceived it, sought to parry the threat of a two-front war by concentrating all available German forces first against the French, to be defeated within six weeks, then against the Russians. Success of this daring plan required rapid mobility of infantry, a dubious assumption in view of the new defensive armaments, and the passage of German forces through neutral Belgium to avoid French defenses and to encircle the French armies. Occupation of Belgium defied a century-old British demand for the neutrality of this small state, whose coast lay just a few miles from Britain. The German leaders expected their action would provoke war with Great Britain but looked forward to military triumph in Europe before British forces could take action. Of all the military plans, Germany's methods and objectives came closest to preparing an aggressive war of conquest.

German readiness to launch such a war reflected partly the German leaders' fear of encirclement. It embodied as well their expansionist ambitions. The "world policy" formulated in 1897 by Emperor William II sought the rapid rise of his country to the rank of world power. His principal rival was Great Britain, greatest naval and imperial state but still committed to its "splendid isolation" from alliances with continental states. The German leaders made plans to build a powerful navy and to use it to enlarge Germany's global empire. Their policy sought as well to enlarge their country's role in the international economy, yet the ambitious dreams of some German capitalists played a secondary role to the diplomatic goals of German statesmen. Power, not profit, represented their aim, justified in their eyes by their superior culture and their country's weakness relative to Great Britain. Their ambitions were not unique; the expansion of the English global empire had provided the first model of a world policy. Challenging Great Britain, German leaders looked forward to making their state the dominant state in Europe and the world.

The German world policy constituted the principal factor undermining European peace. Germany's alliance with Austria-Hungary had earlier assured it protection against the French and did not extend to support for Austrian expansion into Ottoman lands. On the continent the alliances did represent a fairly stable balance of power. By pursuing an expansionist world policy, the German leaders upset that balance. Their actions caused the British government to take two unprecedented steps. It withdrew naval forces from the Far East and from Latin America to strengthen its Atlantic fleet, choosing to rely on Japan and the United States to protect its interests in those areas. Second, it abandoned its policy of avoiding alliances in Europe. Negotiations in 1904 with France created an *entente* (that is, a diplomatic understanding) between the two states, ending their imperial disputes and

creating a defense agreement in case of war with Germany. Anglo-Russian negotiations in 1907 completed the process of associating Britain informally with the Franco-Russian alliance. German imperial ambitions, instead of forcing rival powers to acquiesce, had the opposite effect of cementing good relations among these states to resist more effectively. Neither Great Britain nor France planned a preventive war against Germany, but they did augment their armaments program and expanded their military forces. Most serious of all, the French leaders decided in 1914 that they would support Russia if it became involved in a war with Austria over control of Balkan territory. Peace in Europe thus came to depend upon peace in that one European area where imperialist ambitions, Slavic nationalism, and great power rivalry made war most likely to erupt.

Conflict in the Balkans

The immediate source of conflict opposed the Austro-Hungarian Empire and the small South Slav state of Serbia. The empire had survived internal revolutions and defeats in foreign wars in the nineteenth century by making political concessions when necessary and relying on its army to repress its enemies whenever possible. It had granted special powers to the Hungarian people in a peculiar "dual monarchy" which left the eastern half of the state, where most Slavic peoples lived, under the rule of Hungarians. When the Serbian state became the supporter of the Slavic nationalist movement in the Balkans, it threatened the power of the Hungarians and the very existence of the Austro-Hungarian Empire. Serbia was too weak to take any direct action against the empire; in fact its economy depended upon the Austrian market and its diplomatic actions were, willingly or unwillingly, controlled by the Austrians. Some of its leaders, however, supported a Serbian terrorist organization, many of whose members were Austrian subjects but whose nationalism made them bitter enemies of the Austrian empire. Like other terrorists, they became assassins not to avenge particular deeds, but to use murder to publicize their cause and to inspire less committed supporters to participate in their struggle. Terrorism represented a desperate, destructive gesture of the weak. It also created a grave risk of war when states blamed one another for terrorist action.

In 1914, some Serbian nationalists were prepared to provoke this conflict. Although we still do not know the full story, the head of the Serbian military intelligence appears secretly to have lent his support to a small terrorist organization, the Black Hand, to organize the assassination of the heir to the Austrian throne on a visit to Bosnia in June of that year. The terrorists conceived of their deed as a gesture in defense of Serbian nationalism; their Serbian patron may have welcomed the possibility that their terrorist act would provoke war. Serbia's protector was Russia, whose leaders had in 1914 made clear their determination to defend its independence from Austria, if necessary by war. On June 28, the Bosnian student Gavrilo Princip shot the Austrian grand duke, Francis-Ferdinand. One month later war spread over Europe.

This dramatic sequence of events did not follow any state's logical plan for war. Leaders struggled to resolve the dispute peaceably, but used the threat of war to make clear their determination to achieve their objectives. A point was reached when generals demanded the power to respond to those threats, taking out of the hands of diplomats the decision for war. In that sense, the outbreak of the war was an "accidental" event over which statesmen had lost control. It represented a cautionary tale for political leaders later in the century (including President Kennedy in the Cuban missile crisis of 1962) seeking to understand how they could avoid inadvertently causing war.

The first move was the decision by the Austrian government, backed by Germany, to end the independence of the Serbian state. The assassination provided Austria with the pretext in late July to declare war on Serbia. Both Austrian and German leaders expected Russia to protest, but not to risk war over Serbia. They were only partially correct, for to demonstrate its support for Serbia the Russian government ordered the mobilization of its army on the western (German and Austrian) frontier. The Russian action was the second step leading to European conflict. The German generals understood only the military implications of Russian mobilization, which threatened their own war plans for attack first against France. They convinced their emperor that war was inevitable. After Russia refused to end mobilization, William II on August 3 ordered the Schlieffen Plan in effect and declared war on France. When German troops marched into Belgium, Great Britain in its turn joined the conflict on the side of the French. The local Austrian-Serbian war had become a general European war.

Why had peace in Europe come to an end? The debate over the causes of the First World War began with the first shots and continues to this day. Two general theories have emerged out of the research and interpretations of historians. One places principal responsibility on the conditions that exacerbated international conflict in those years. It points to the aggressive imperialist conquests worsening relations among states, to the nationalist hostility dividing peoples of Europe, to the armaments race tempting the best armed state to prefer war to diplomatic compromise, and to the alliance system creating hostile groups of states. In this perspective no one state was to blame, for all contributed to the worsening of relations and to the preparations for war. The other theory isolates specifically the expansionist plans of the German state and the dangerous German-Austrian decision in 1914 to destroy Serbia. By picking out policies implemented by German and Austrian leaders, it attributes to these governments the key actions responsible for the chain of events leading to the outbreak of war. In the end, our judgment rests partially on how we read the evidence, partially on how much control we assume statesmen had over the system of international relations. Whatever answer we give, we must recognize that the outbreak of war constituted a terrible failure of European leaders to anticipate the true character of war and the full extent of the destruction that war would cause.

SUMMARY

The world was changing rapidly in the early years of the century, a time of widespread optimism in the West. A few intellectuals, such as the psychologist Sigmund Freud, were skeptical of the naive faith of Westerners in human progress. Others, notably the artists, demonstrated in their creativity a passionate joy in life and confidence in the future. When one French poet wrote in 1913 that "the world has changed less since Jesus Christ than it has in the last thirty years," he revealed his excitement at the emergence of that new world.

Intellectuals saw about them in the cities of the West the worrisome signs of social antagonism and inequality but also witnessed a greater activity in popular culture than ever before. Newspapers and popular novels reached out to a mass reading public. The new motion pictures, product of the combination of photographic film and electric light, enchanted viewers with escapist tales of romance, comedy, and adventure. Few then realized how these, and other means of mass communication, could be used to mobilize political movements and to exalt fanatical leaders seeking dictatorial power. These dark visions of the future held far less appeal than did the optimistic image of progress and prosperity presented by the Paris Exposition of 1900. The war destroyed that image. It marked the end of a period of prosperity for many and unprecedented intellectual and artistic creativity. It began an era of wars and revolutions, ending Western global domination and leading to the world we know today.

RECOMMENDED READING[1]

World History Studies

*William Keylor, *The Twentieth-Century World: An International History* (1984)

*William McNeill, *The Rise of the West: A History of the Human Community* (1963)

*L. S. Stavrianos, *Global Rift: The Third World Comes of Age* (1981)

Europe Before 1914

*Brian Bond, *War and Society in Europe, 1870–1970* (1984)

*Felix Gilbert, *The End of the European Era, 1890 to the Present* (third ed., 1984)

*H. Stuart Hughes, *Consciousness and Society: The Reorientation of European Social Thought, 1890–1930* (1958)

*Robert Hughes, *The Shock of the New: The Hundred-Year History of Modern Art* (1980)

A. J. H. Latham, *The International Economy and the Undeveloped World, 1865–1914* (1978)

Norman Stone, *Europe Transformed, 1878–1919* (1984)

A. J. P. Taylor, *The Struggle for Mastery in Europe* (1954)

---

[1]Books marked * are available in paperback.

Memoirs and Novels

*JOSEPH CONRAD, *The Heart of Darkness* (1902); also, *Almeyer's Folly* (1895)

*THOMAS MANN, *Buddenbrooks* (1900)

*GABRIEL GARCIA MARQUEZ, *One Hundred Years of Solitude* (1970)

chapter 2

THE FIRST WORLD WAR AND THE RUSSIAN REVOLUTION

The course of battle in the First World War determined the future of the European nation-states. Had the war plans of either side succeeded, peace would have come quickly after decisive encounters on a few battlefields. The European balance of power would have shifted, but victors and vanquished alike would have remained prosperous and powerful, dominating the world as before the war. The failure of all the battle plans condemned the nations of Europe to a war so long and destructive it undermined the very foundations on which their power and prosperity were built. The war of movement lasted only a few months in the West, replaced by prolonged, dreary trench warfare broken by bloody, inconclusive battles. The destruction caused by the deadly weapons of war shattered illusions of quick victory and turned bright-colored military uniforms to the drab browns and grays of the trenches where soldiers desperately sought shelter from artillery shells and machine-gun bullets. New war leaders condemned "defeatism" and demanded discipline and sacrifice of all the citizens of their nation. Their call was heeded in some countries, but not all.

That conflict became known as the "world" war not because major battles occurred in distant parts of the globe, but because for the first time the resources and peoples of distant, non-Western lands played an important part in the European fighting. The voracious demand of armies for men and materiel forced the Western leaders to mobilize their empires for war. Very early in the conflict, they had also to begin purchasing vast amounts of war supplies in the United States, whose entry in 1917 into the war on the side of the Allies marked the real beginning of the involvement of that state in global international affairs. The balance of power in the world was never the same again.

The course of the war changed dramatically as a result of the 1917 revolution in Russia. In that country the terrible pressures of war fatally weakened the monarchical regime of Nicholas II. The revolutionary transformation of Russia brought to power a Marxist party, the Bolsheviks, dedicated to the overthrow of Western capitalism and the emancipation of colonial peoples. Western states were unsuccessful in their effort to overthrow the new Russian government by aiding its enemies in a bloody civil war. The Bolshevik leaders looked forward to new wars and revolutions, a process which for them represented the necessary turmoil before the triumph of the Marxist dream of communism. They were prepared to extend aid to anti-imperialist movements, even if these parties were not Marxist, in the hope of weakening Western domination. The survival of Bolshevik Russia signaled the beginning of a new revolutionary age in world history.

THE EUROPEAN WAR, 1914–1917

Mobilization for war in August 1914 aroused in all fighting countries a wave of national solidarity and popular enthusiasm. For many Europeans this "August community" offered an escape from their petty lives to join in a glorious national crusade. The war appealed to their nationalist pride and to their patriotic loyalty to their country and its leadership. All socialist parties, save a few extremist revolutionary groups, supported their governments' declaration of war. Conscripts willingly abandoned civilian life to join in their army units; crowds in the streets cheered troops marching to the trains carrying them to battle. A young Austrian named Adolph Hitler volunteered for service in the German army and recalled later that he "sank down upon my knees and thanked Heaven" for the opportunity to "serve the German nation." For him as for many other young men, war "came as a deliverance." We may wonder at their blind enthusiasm, yet it was sincere, the mass expression perhaps of that spirit of adventure and conquest which had previously impelled overseas imperialism.

The Global War

The outcome of the great battles in 1914 on the eastern and western fronts represented a failure of all the war plans. The Austrians were unable to defeat Serbia; the French and Russian offensives stalled on the German frontiers. The German drive to destroy the French army reached in September as far as the Marne River near Paris before it was halted by a French counteroffensive. What had gone wrong? For one thing, the German and Austrian generals underestimated the might of the Russian armies, whose attacks against German East Prussia and Austrian Galicia forced them to divert troops to the east and to weaken their main operations. The Franco-Russian alliance proved that year its value to prevent the victory of the Central Powers. In the west, the arrival of the first British troops late that summer blocked a new encircling movement of German armies along the Belgian and French coasts. Most important, on all fronts were the new defensive weapons, stopping offensives with a terrible toll in human life. Mobile, rapid-firing cannon and machine guns proved the real victors of those battles.

The German armies were the first to discover the simple piece of equipment to protect their soldiers. Their trench spades permitted the infantry to resist the French and British attacks by throwing up walls of earth behind which they manned machine-gun

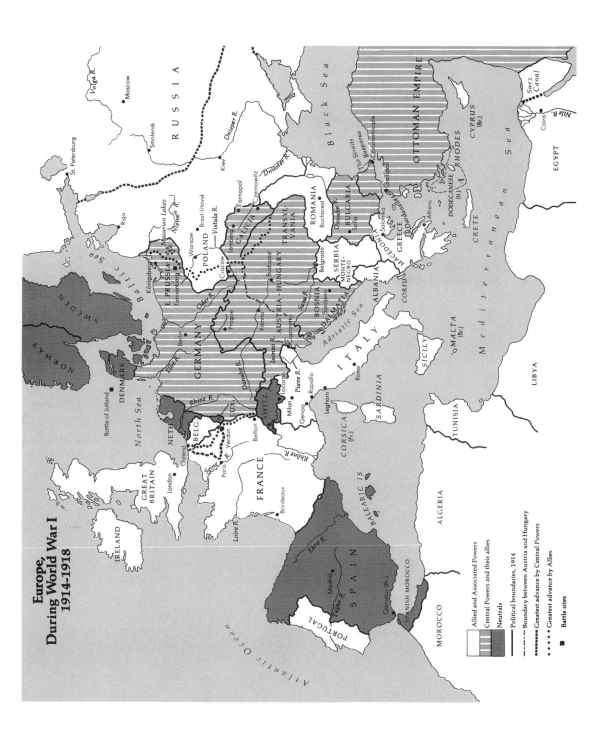

**Europe,
During World War I
1914-1918**

RUSSIA

Moscow

Volga R.

Smolensk

St. Petersburg

Riga

Dnieper R.

Kiev

Black Sea

OTTOMAN EMPIRE

Constantinople

Bosporus

The Straits

CYPRUS (Br.)

Suez Canal

Nile R.

Cairo

EGYPT

RHODES

DODECANESE (It.)

CRETE

Mediterranean Sea

Baltic Sea

Königsberg

E. PRUSSIA

Tannenberg

Masurian Lakes

Niemen R.

Brest-Litovsk

Vistula R.

Warsaw

POLAND

Cracow

Lemberg

GALICIA

Dniester R.

Tarnopol

Czernowitz

TRANSYL-
VANIA

ROMANIA

Bucharest

Danube R.

BULGARIA

Sofia

Solonika

GREECE

MACEDONIA

Athens

Dardanelles

Gallipoli

CORFU

ALBANIA

MONTE-
NEGRO

SERBIA

Belgrade

Sarajevo

BOSNIA

DALMATIA

Adriatic Sea

AUSTRIA-HUNGARY

Budapest

Vienna

Isonzo R.

Caporetto

Prague

GERMANY

Berlin

Oder R.

Elbe R.

Danube R.

Rhine R.

SWITZ.

LUX.

BELG.

Ostend

NETH.

Verdun

Belfort

Milan

Locarno

Genoa

Piave R.

Rapallo

Leghorn

Rome

ITALY

SICILY

SARDINIA

CORSICA (Fr.)

MALTA (Br.)

LIBYA

TUNISIA

ALGERIA

MOROCCO

BALEARIC IS.

SPAIN

Madrid

Ebro R.

Tagus R.

Gibraltar (Br.)

SPANISH MOROCCO

PORTUGAL

FRANCE

Paris

Seine R.

Loire R.

Rhône R.

Bordeaux

GREAT
BRITAIN

London

IRELAND

North Sea

Battle of Jutland

DENMARK

NORWAY

SWEDEN

Atlantic Ocean

SWEDEN

Legend:
- Allied and Associated Powers
- Central Powers and their allies
- Neutrals
- Political boundaries, 1914
- Boundary between Austria and Hungary
- Greatest advance by Central Powers
- Greatest advance by Allies
- Battle sites

and sniper posts. Their offensive had failed, but they remained in enemy territory. The front in the west became a band of territory, several miles wide, running through Belgium and northern France from the North Sea to Switzerland. In the east it extended from the Baltic south around Russian Poland into eastern Austria. The most accurate image of war by year's end was the deep trench, symbol of the "war of position" and the grave ultimately for many soldiers.

Despite the stalemate, generals and political leaders on both sides promised that they would soon achieve victory. German leaders were determined to retain territorial gains in the west to ensure German domination. France and Great Britain were committed to expelling German forces and, in addition, to ending German efforts at supremacy in Europe. Neither side anticipated the dire consequences of their decision to continue fighting. Defensive war fought from trenches along hundreds of miles of front line required of the belligerents millions of men in arms and immense quantities of war materiel. Although conditions varied from one country to another, the pattern of warfare determined everywhere a common set of policies. The alliances were enlarged until the European war extended into Asia and Africa; the resources of empires were called up; governments assumed semidictatorial powers; severe controls over production and consumption curtailed the free market economy; most serious of all, European nations poured their economic wealth and their most precious resource, human lives, into the inferno of battle. In the words of one embittered German officer, the First World War became "the grave of nations."

The global consequences of total war brought distant areas and states into the conflict. Battles were fought on sea as well as on land. The British navy quickly took control of the high seas, forcing the German fleet into the Baltic and declaring a naval blockade of Germany. German admirals turned to a new arm of naval warfare, the submarine, to be used to destroy both warships and merchant vessels carrying goods to the enemy. Both the British and the French mobilized the manpower and the resources of their empires for the war effort. Great Britain declared all colonies and Dominion lands, where the white settlers had received self-government, to be at war with the Central Powers. The Indian Army and troops from Canada, New Zealand, Australia, and South Africa participated in the battles on the Western Front and fought in Africa and the Middle East.

Food and industrial production from the empires proved vital in the war effort, and laborers from non-Western lands for the first time were needed in the Western economies to replace the men called to arms. Colonial regions ceased being simply areas for conquest and became a valuable part in the war effort. Labor conscription was imposed on conquered peoples, whose hostility toward their imperialist rulers led in these conditions at times to open resistance. From Russian Central Asia, where Turkic nomadic tribes fled to China rather than serve in the tsarist forces, to French West Africa, where a large-scale revolt among African tribes greeted French efforts to mobilize labor brigades, the war worsened the relations between conquerors and conquered. In this way it contributed to the emergence of nationalist opposition to imperialism.

Both the Allies and the Central Powers enlarged their military alliances. In the fall of 1914, Germany succeeded in bringing the Ottoman Empire into the war on its side. Ottoman leaders believed the Central Powers would soon win and looked forward to restoring their dominance of the Middle East. Their decision, a terrible blunder in the long run, had serious consequences for the Allies.

It shut off the shipment of military supplies through the straits to Russia, whose industry lacked sufficient capacity for total war. It opened as well a new front in the Middle East against Russia and Great Britain, threatening British control of the Suez Canal.

The Allies in turn were able in 1915 to obtain the support of Italy, whose leaders hoped to conquer territory from Austria-Hungary along the Adriatic Sea. That same year the Japanese government joined the Allies, declaring war on Germany. It immediately seized the small German concession in China, and at the same time forced the Chinese government to agree to special economic privileges in all north China. It found in wartime conditions new possibilities to expand Japanese power in East Asia. These new belligerents sought advantages for themselves; desperate for help, the Allies were prepared to grant major concessions. The war was thus preparing the way for a profound shift in the global balance of power.

The Consequences of Total War

The needs of total war placed demands on government which civilian leadership operating under constitutional limits could not meet. Everywhere governments assumed exceptional powers. The extreme case was Russia, where Nicholas II immediately reclaimed his autocratic powers and permitted the legislature (called the *Duma*) to meet solely to debate current affairs. Liberal leaders attempted without success to persuade him to appoint a war cabinet "responsive to the people." Instead, he relied on his wife, the Empress Alexandra, and on Rasputin for advice on policy and leadership. Too incompetent to create an effective wartime government, blamed by conservatives and liberals alike for military defeats and civilian hardships, the Russian tsarist regime proved the

least capable of mobilizing its people for total war. The Austrian state, though not as badly ruled as the Russian Empire, relied as well on traditional monarchical powers to lead the people in war, refusing any concession to nationalist movements in its lands. In Germany triumphs in battle in the first years of war increased the authority of the army generals, in particular Hindenburg and Ludendorf. Civilian leaders increasingly deferred to their leadership and to their demands for political authority to win military victory. Finally, in early 1917 these two generals assumed governmental powers, creating military rule and ensuring that Germany would end the war in triumph—or defeat.

In Great Britain and France the strengthening of political leadership came under civilian rule. "National union" coalitions of parties ended—temporarily—old political rivalries. No new elections were held for the war's duration. Parliaments authorized censorship to ensure that the press would not encourage "defeatism"—a new word to condemn opposition to the war—and permitted lengthy imprisonment without trial for suspected enemy agents and sympathizers. In 1917 real leadership in both countries passed into the hands of strong prowar politicians—George Clemenceau in France (called the "Tiger" by friends and enemies alike) and Lloyd George in England. Mobilization for military victory led everywhere to the decline of representative institutions and individual liberties, previously judged the core of progressive government. War constituted a dangerous education in authoritarian rule, sanctioned by military necessity.

Startling innovations altered wartime economies as well. Total war demanded the mobilization of all resources. Millions of able-bodied men left for the front, many never to return. The acute labor shortage overrode earlier prejudices against women in the economy. Women were encouraged (temporarily) to leave their homes to work on the "home front" (the language of war sanctioning this sudden abandonment of hallowed custom). For married women, work in factories could not make up for the loss of their husband's income and the burden of assuming added responsibilities at a time of worsening living conditions.

War powers introduced a sort of military discipline over the economy to fix prices, to allocate scarce resources to industry, and to distribute goods by rationing. Governments sacrificed the free market of the capitalist system to military necessity; they turned to corporate bureaucracy and capitalist management to provide the agents and institutions for the centralization and planning of economic activities. The need of armies for munitions, clothing, and food took precedence over all other requirements. Bureaucratic controls substituted for supply and demand. Industrialists implemented state orders for military supplies and collaborated in setting up guidelines to determine the most effective use of scarce resources. Much of the foreign investments of the British and French were sold to pay for imports of goods from neutral countries, yet these states still had to go deeply into debt to foreign manufacturers. Germany, without access to an overseas market, confronted the most serious shortages and introduced the most rigorous state economic controls. One German industrialist judged the wartime economic reforms so radical that he called the experience "an education in state socialism."

The results proved satisfactory for the armies, much less so for working classes. Even in Russia, armies were by 1916 adequately supplied in the necessities of war. Troops everywhere were receiving supplies of new weapons turned out by scientists, engineers, and industrialists. Poison gas made its appearance in 1915, followed quickly by masks to protect soldiers' throats and lungs from the lethal gas attacks. Fighter planes made airspace another arena of war. In 1915 the first British tanks appeared, too primitive yet to overwhelm the trenches and suspect to generals who still believed that human heroism, not an armored tractor, was the key to the war of movement.

Social conflicts, muted in the early months of the war, returned as the cost of living for the laboring population rose. The price for war production was the decline in the standard of living of the workers, especially in the cities. Wage increases lagged behind prices; farmers preferred to deal in the black market rather than to sell under government regulations. Those countries with the least developed industry, Austria-Hungary and Russia, experienced the most serious shortages and, as a consequence, the greatest social unrest among their working population. War leaders called for patriotism and self-sacrifice, but in those countries they enjoyed less and less support.

In the winter of 1916–17 a wave of strikes spread among factories in Russian cities, sparked partly by food shortages, partly by opposition to the tsarist regime. Women workers took an active part in the movement. Their hardship led some to join protest actions, participating in strikes and antiwar demonstrations. In February 1917, women employed in factories in Petrograd (formerly St. Petersburg) went on strike on Women's Day (a new socialist holiday) to demand more food. Their cries of "Give us bread!" quickly brought massive support from other workers, launching the movement that would within two weeks overthrow the Russian monarchy.

Governments undertook secret as well as public propaganda efforts to foment these conflicts in the enemy camp. Central and Eastern Europe provided the most promising area for "subversive" campaigns of political warfare. The German state offered secret financial backing to Russian antiwar revolutionary parties. Its most spectacular (and shortsighted) act came in 1917, when it permitted some of their leaders (including Lenin) to travel from Switzerland across Germany to participate in the Russian revolution. The Allies for their part aided independence parties among Austria-Hungary's minority nationalities. Both sides encouraged revolutionary movements to create disorder and to weaken their enemies.

The Ottoman Empire proved the area where political warfare contributed to the greatest violence and unrest. Armenian nationalists, backed by Russia, called on Armenians in the empire to fight the Turks for their own nation-state. In retaliation, Ottoman authorities forcibly evacuated 1.5 million Armenians from eastern Turkey. In the course of this violent operation and for reasons which are still not clear, Turks were responsible for the death of perhaps a half-million Armenians. These so-called "Armenian massacres" set a pattern, repeated many times later in the century, of mass persecution in wartime motivated by ethnic hatred.

The British government supported a national uprising among the Arabs of the empire, promising that their victory would lead to an Arab state in the Middle East. The most successful agent in this campaign was the British officer T. E. Lawrence. Working with and encouraging the revolt of the tribes in the Arabian peninsula under the leadership of the Hashim clan, headed by Hussein, his forces fought for two years against the Ottomans in support of regular British forces. He himself believed in the cause of Arab national revolution; his superiors in London had, on the contrary, plans for the partition among the Allies of Ottoman Arab lands. They also promised formally, in the 1917 Balfour Declaration, to support the Zionist demand for a Jewish homeland in the Palestine area of the Ottoman Empire. Encour-

aging Arab and Jewish dreams of lands of their own while still dealing with the Middle East in the imperialist spirit of conquest, the British sowed in those years the seeds of bitter conflict and war in the future. The atmosphere of total war encouraged European governments to employ any means to weaken the enemy's ability to fight. Their methods of political warfare, added to the economic hardship imposed everywhere by the war, increased the likelihood that war would lead to revolution.

German Victory in Eastern Europe

The confrontation of the Central Powers and the Allies in Europe remained the key to the outcome of the war. The military advantage shifted increasingly to Germany, whose forces played the key role on all major fronts. Germany provided the spearhead in the great 1915 offensive against Russian forces in Polish territory. Its victory there caused over 1 million Russian casualties and pushed the eastern front far into Russian territory. It also aided the Austrians in the conquest of Serbia and Rumania and bolstered the Ottoman army in the Middle East. In 1916, the German High Command launched its principal attack against the French armies around the fortress of Verdun. Its new strategy anticipated an all-out French defense, not a breakthrough, for it desired French casualties so severe the enemy would be unable to sustain the war effort. By year's end, French dead in the battle of Verdun numbered nearly 400,000, but German casualties were almost as great. A British offensive on the Somme River that summer led to nearly as many dead, with no substantial change in the front. Despite the awful bloodletting, the stalemate continued.

That terrible fighting was destroying the very foundations of economic productivity and political influence which war leaders imagined victory would enhance. The realization of the futility of the war began to spread among the belligerents, appearing in the "defeatism" increasingly apparent among the civilian population, and also in the cautious peace discussions among a few European political leaders. The United States, still neutral, undertook serious peace contacts late in 1916. President Wilson's ambition, made public in a speech in January 1917, encompassed not only a compromise "peace without victory," but also an end to the "struggle for a new balance of power" and "entangling alliances." In place of power politics he envisioned a "concert of power," that is, international collaboration in defense of peace. In effect, he sought to alter the very nature of relations among Western states.

But insurmountable obstacles stood in the way of any serious negotiations that winter. Both sides refused a return to prewar conditions, adopting intransigent positions justified partly by state interest, partly by the bitterness the war had engendered. The Allied governments set peace terms which included the withdrawal of German forces from all Russian and French territories and national rights for the peoples of the Austro-Hungarian Empire. In Germany, the war party was firmly in control of the government. The plans laid in 1914 for German expansion continued to lure generals and industrialists, and the military believed that they still had victory within their grasp. Submarines appeared to them the key. Possessing by then over two hundred "U-boats," they estimated that such a force would destroy all shipping around Great Britain. This supposedly impenetrable blockade would reduce Britain to economic chaos and thereby defeat the Allies. Destruction of neutral shipping and loss of lives created the serious danger of war against the United States, yet quick victory appeared to the German leaders worth the risk. In January 1917, Germany declared un-

restricted submarine warfare in effect in the waters of the British Isles. Peace negotiations collapsed; the war dragged on.

Germany did win a victory, but in the east, not the west. It came in the wake not of military triumph but of political revolution. The social unrest spreading among the Russian urban population swelled to become in late February (early March by the Western calendar) 1917, a full-scale uprising in the capital city of Petrograd. A wave of strikes led to political demonstrations under banners proclaiming "Down with the autocracy!" When Nicholas II called on his army to repress the uprising, the garrison troops mutinied and joined the demonstrators. His own generals chose to abandon him rather than to risk civil conflict to protect a monarch in whom they had lost confidence. Nicholas had to abdicate.

In place of the monarchy emerged in early March a new Provisional Government, supported by the army and the revolutionary crowds. It was made up of liberal political leaders and backed by most socialist parties (except Lenin's Bolshevik party). Its most forceful members (including a young lawyer named Alexander Kerensky) believed that their first duty lay in pursuing the war, for they could not conceive of abandoning the Western Allies and hoped that a victory would strengthen their country, and their own regime. This decision proved a fatal mistake. They hoped to introduce democracy in the midst of war, but the two objectives proved incompatible.

Within a few months, the Provisional Government had lost the allegiance of the revolutionary masses. The soldiers and workers were by then sickened of the war and eager for peace and a new revolutionary social order in their country. They associated "democracy" with popular rule and proletarian revolution and viewed with increasing suspicion the government's efforts to maintain order by supporting army officers, industrialists, and "bourgeois" property owners. The split between revolutionary forces and the liberal-socialist leadership was worsened by food shortages and unemployment in the cities, the consequences of the war and social unrest. When Russian generals attempted to launch a major offensive that summer, the front-line troops mutinied. That fall, both soldiers and workers turned to the one group promising to end the war and to defend the "proletarian revolution," the Bolshevik party of Vladimir Lenin.

In the growing revolutionary chaos of late 1917, the Bolsheviks had the great advantage of defending a radical program of "peace, bread, and land" for the Russian people. This set of demands brought them the support of armed soldiers and workers, the real force behind the revolution. They carried their program of peace and social reform to the revolutionary assemblies, called "soviets," whose representatives were chosen by soldiers and factory workers in all Russian cities. There they won the backing of the delegates that fall, taking leadership of the soviets and organizing them for armed insurrection against the Provisional Government. In October (November on the Western calendar), they seized power virtually without violence, for the government had lost the support even of its own army officers. The Bolsheviks formed a one-party dictatorship and, in their first important action, declared an armistice on the eastern front.

Peace negotiations began with the Central Powers. The German military leaders demanded of the new Russian regime a peace of capitulation, that is, the occupation by their armies of all the eastern territory they had conquered and the creation in southern Russia (the Ukraine) of a new state under their protection. Lenin had, in March 1918, to accept these terms, for by then the Russian army had ceased to exist as a fighting force.

The Peace of Brest-Litovsk reduced the size of the Communist state to the old northern lands of Muscovite Russia and made Germany the dominant power in Eastern Europe, giving the Central Powers their greatest military triumph in the war. The Bolshevik leaders claimed their revolution to be a victory for humanity. Western governments, left without the Russian front, condemned the Bolsheviks for abandoning the alliance. Both sides chose to ignore the fact that the forces of war had played a greater part than human choice in the immediate origins and outcome of the Russian revolution.

THE FIRST WORLD WAR AND THE UNITED STATES

The German leaders were convinced in early 1918 that they would soon win on the western front as well. Signs of the decline of Allied power encouraged them in this hope. The Italian army had virtually collapsed in late 1917 at the battle of Caporetto, though it did manage after weeks of retreat to form a new front line to stop the Austrian forces. The French army appeared in even worse condition after several front-line divisions had mutinied in the summer of that year, refusing to participate in more bloody and futile offensives. Its troops were not "defeatist," for they remained in their trenches to resist German attack. Without strong reinforcements, however, they would cease to be capable of more major offensives. In these conditions, the German generals believed their armies prepared in 1918 to break the stalemate. Despite serious food shortages in Germany, the population remained patriotic and the troops disciplined, some (like a young corporal named Adolph Hitler) still enthusiastic for battle. They moved their best troops from the east to participate in the spring of 1918 in a series of attacks that brought the front to within fifty miles of Paris. There the offensive stopped, however, halted by Allied resistance. The balance of military power began to shift at last to the Allies

U.S. Neutrality and the Allies

The key factor explaining this turn of events was the participation in the war of the United States. Without massive American military supplies followed by hundreds of thousands of fresh troops, Imperial Germany would almost certainly have won the struggle for mastery in Europe. With them, the tide of battle changed and so too did the diplomatic objectives of the Allies. For the first time in its history the United States became an important actor in deciding the outcome of world war and the shape of the peace to follow. The First World War transformed the United States into a great power.

What are the reasons for U.S. entry into the war? The answer lies partly in economic ties linking America to the Allies, partly in the political objectives pursued by the U.S. president, Woodrow Wilson. In the first decade of the twentieth century, American political life was dominated by "progressivism," a reform movement that identified progress with the strengthening of democratic government and protecting free enterprise from Big Business. In the previous half-century the American economy had grown rapidly as western lands were settled and put in cultivation, and as industry boomed. Prosperity brought with it serious abuses of political power and social inequalities between farmer and banker, worker and industrialist. Progressivism promised to correct these injustices. Wilson, nominated by the Democratic party on a progressive platform in 1912, vowed to restore "national life to its pristine strength and freedom" and ensure that "fair competition" and "industrial freedom" would permit "any man who has the brains to get into the game" of business. His program drew on visions of a Golden Past in American life and won him the presidency that year.

Nationalist ambitions and economic expansion were pulling the United States into international relations, yet most Americans still paid little attention to the world beyond U.S. borders. The United States had already established a sphere of influence in the Caribbean and Central America (see Chapter 1) and had become actively involved in East Asian affairs, where it insisted on free trade with China (the "open door" policy). A new factor which strongly influenced U.S. policy toward foreign lands was a product of progressivism itself. Its emphasis on the superiority of democratic government gave its followers the conviction that the United States could and ought to help other peoples introduce democracy in their political life. Wilson believed deeply in this cause. Mexico, beginning its great revolution, was in the throes of civil war when he became president. Arguing that it was the United States' "duty" to support "constitutional government and the rights of the people," he sent troops into Mexico briefly in 1914 to try to impose "ordered self-government." His policy, bitterly resisted by Mexicans opposed to Yankee imperialism, remained a regional matter. The U.S. government still followed a century-long tradition of nonintervention in European international rivalries, which appeared to one Wilson adviser "militarism run stark mad." The outbreak of the First World War, however, thrust these rivalries into the center of U.S. political life.

Wilson's first reaction was to proclaim U.S. neutrality in the conflict. He urged Americans to be "neutral in fact as well as in name, impartial in thought as well as in action." Noninvolvement was difficult to enforce, for nationalist as well as ideological reasons. Strong ties still bound many immigrants to their home countries, involved on one side or the other of the war; in addition, many Americans, including Wilson, admired the British system of government and disapproved of the strong militaristic cast to German rule. Some realized as well that the presence of the powerful British Atlantic fleet helped to assure the protection of U.S. shores. A "special partnership" existed between the two states. What would happen if Germany won? Wilson feared that his country would "be forced to take such measures of defense which would be fatal to our form of Government and American ideals." Yet for three years he managed to keep the United States out of the conflict.

Wilson's strong backing for neutrality rested on both political and personal grounds. Large numbers of Americans judged their country's affairs far more important than international conflicts, an attitude termed "isolationism." When Wilson ran for reelection in 1916, his most popular slogan was "He kept us out of war." He himself adhered to a strict Christian belief in right and justice, with which he associated liberty, peace, and progress. Even though by 1912 the United States possessed the mightiest industrial economy in the world, he did not seek to use that wealth in making the United States a world power. As the war dragged on, he attempted to mediate between the belligerents for the sake of a compromise settlement which would end the fighting and avoid U.S. involvement. As already noted, his peace initiative in late 1916 failed, principally because of German hopes for victory. Despite his ultimate failure to keep the United States out of the war, he retained his vision of a new international order to follow the conflict. His progressive ideology and his

belief in his own leadership together explain his later promise to help build a just peace which would "make the world safe for democracy."

Despite his efforts to maintain U.S. neutrality, Wilson found that the Allies' need for American goods quickly made his country an indirect collaborator in the war against the Central Powers. From the perspective of the warring states, access to the U.S. market represented an important factor in their plans for war. Denial of U.S. goods to one side might contribute to the military victory of the other. Whatever policy the U.S. government adopted toward trade with the belligerents, it would have a decisive impact on the outcome of the war.

The American economy quickly became a major source of war supplies for the Allies. The United States had to accept the blockade set up by Great Britain. The British fleet dominated the Atlantic and used its naval vessels to stop and search freighters bound even for neutral countries to prevent goods from reaching Germany. Within a year it had effectively halted U.S. commerce with the Central Powers. At the same time, France and Great Britain took full advantage of the U.S. market to place enormous orders for food, clothing, and munitions. By 1915 they had virtually exhausted their reserves of gold and capital investments with which to pay for these purchases and turned to U.S. banks for large loans.

Was this action in the spirit of neutrality? Some of Wilson's advisers said "no," but he finally agreed to allow these bank credits to continue U.S. sales to the Allies. He knew that not to support trade with France and Britain in the long run would weaken the Allies, and in the short term would lose political support from business, agricultural, and labor groups in the United States. The war had disrupted international commerce at the very time American industry and agriculture was beginning to recover from a serious recession, and all these groups looked to trade to sustain economic recovery. By 1916 U.S. trade to these countries increased four times, the American economy boomed, and American supplies became an important part of the Allied war effort. In commercial relations real U.S. neutrality proved impossible to achieve.

The German submarine blockade of the British Isles, begun in February 1917, pushed the United States into the European war. That spring one of every four freighters headed for British ports was sunk by German torpedoes, and among them were U.S. ships manned by U.S. citizens. Wilson had only two options. He could refuse to let American lives and property become involved by banning all U.S. shipping in the war zone, or he could propose war against the Central Powers. The first choice would greatly increase the chances of German victory, particularly since revolution had just begun in Russia. The second would force America to mobilize for war and would, Wilson feared, "overturn the world we have known."

Why did he decide on war? In the first place, he believed strongly in nineteenth-century international law, by whose standards the German destruction of U.S. shipping constituted an act of war. In the second place, he and his advisers had decided German military domination represented a threat to U.S. security. One clumsy German proposal that winter to bring Mexico into a military alliance against its Yankee neighbor, uncovered by British intelligence, revealed how near German international ambitions had come to U.S. borders. In April 1917, he asked Congress to declare war on the Central Powers, condemning German "warfare against mankind," pledging that the United States was not fighting for "conquest or domination" but rather for "the ultimate peace of the world and for the liberation of its peoples. The world must be made safe for democracy." He looked forward to a new era to follow the terrible conflict. Behind his rhetoric lay a vision of political progress and international peace.

U.S. Leadership in War

Before he could attempt to implement his peace plan the Allies had to defeat the Central Powers. The immediate demands on the United States were for military supplies and troops. The U.S. government mobilized the country for war and in doing so, as in other belligerent countries, instituted economic centralization and planning. It created a Council of National Defense to organize the civilian war effort and set up a War Industries Board to allocate scarce resources to ensure that production met military needs. It assumed control of the railroads to speed the shipment of war material. It made its own funds available to extend war loans for expanded Allied purchases, a boon to all sectors of the American economy.

U.S. military might grew more slowly. The first priority consisted in fighting the German "U-boat" blockade of the British Isles. In collaboration with the British navy, U.S. naval commanders set up a system of "convoys" of large numbers of merchant ships, protected by warships, during their crossing of the Atlantic. By late 1917 this technique cut shipping losses in half; when the time came to send U.S. troops to Europe, it ensured that not one troop ship was sunk. An entire year elapsed, however, before the army was prepared to fight in France. Finally in the summer of 1918, hundreds of thousands of U.S. infantry began arriving on the continent every month, forming a separate armed force of one million troops by that fall. Their presence destroyed the last German hopes of victory on the western front.

The military collapse of the Central Powers came that summer and fall. The Allied armies in the west launched a combined offensive in July (using for the first time hundreds of tanks). Outnumbered and increasingly demoralized, German troops began a steady, uninterrupted retreat across France and Belgium. Small Allied armies in northern Italy and Greece began late that summer their own offensives toward Austria-Hungary and in October broke through Austrian defenses. At the same time British and Arab forces in the Middle East advanced to the city of Damascus. By late October, the Central Powers ceased to exist as a military alliance. The Austrian armies broke up into units of the various nationalities of the empire (Czechs, Hungarians, etc.), each prepared to protect only its own territory and nation. These groups formed the core of the new nation-states of southeastern Europe which emerged in the ruins of the Austro-Hungarian Empire.

In Germany, defeatism was turning to revolutionary uprisings, directed both against the war and against the imperial government. Sailors of the Baltic fleet mutinied, followed by army units in other parts of the country. Joined by workers, they formed revolutionary assemblies resembling the Russian soviets which had provided the mass organization of the Bolshevik Revolution the previous year. Close to victory that spring, in the fall of 1918 the Central Powers were headed toward defeat and revolutionary chaos. In October, the German government asked for an armistice.

The terms of armistice and the plans for peace came principally from the United States. Although France and Great Britain had borne the principal burden of war on the western front, their leaders could no longer dictate peace conditions. They had fought for mastery in Europe and, in secret, had laid extensive plans for territorial annexation. Interests of state defined their goals: security and territorial expansion. These traditional war aims offered no promise of a new era of peace and supposed that the people would continue to defer to their political leaders. But too many sacrifices had been inflicted on that population and too many claims made of a "just" war. The nature of the war itself led the Allied peoples to expect that their hardships would find reward in a new peace. Their rejection of power politics was heightened by the campaign of the new Communist (Bolshevik) government in Russia to discredit what it called the "imperialist" war and the war leaders. Even before it signed the peace treaty with Germany, it made public the secret, annexationist treaties between Russia and the Western Allies, to prove that the war had been imposed on the people in all countries by greedy capitalists. Their action damned in the eyes of many Europeans the old war aims.

The United States had the only plans for peace with which to answer the Communist accusations. President Wilson's humanitarian vision, apparent first in his proposal for compromise peace and then in his call as war leader for a "peace without victory," appealed to an enormous audience in Europe. In addition, the economic and military power of the United States forced even those European politicians who were skeptical of his vision of future world relations to heed his pronouncements. Wilson's principal statement of war aims came in the Fourteen Points, presented in January 1918. Supplemented by later additions, they constituted a rebuttal of Lenin's condemnation of the war and offered a democratic alternative to the Communist call for proletarian revolution.

Three points were central to Wilson's plan: national self-determination for all European peoples, democratic governments, and the creation of an international association of states to protect the peace. In concrete terms, his plan foresaw the withdrawal of German troops from all the land seized in Eastern Europe by the Treaty of Brest-Litovsk, the formation of nation-states throughout Central Europe, and the elimination from the German state of its militaristic leadership. Wilson placed the prestige and the power of the United States behind democratic and national revolutions. The British and French war leaders, Lloyd George and Clemenceau, accepted Wilson's peace principles. The importance of the United States within the alliance gave them no choice.

Victory on Wilson's terms came in early November. Although no Allied forces had yet reached German soil, the German High Command concluded German troops would not continue fighting. Heeding the warning, the German government accepted the armistice, which went into effect on November 11. At last, in the words of a famous German antiwar novel, all appeared permanently "quiet on the western front." Demonstrators in Allied capitals celebrated both the victory of their side and the end of the fighting.

The Ottoman and Austro-Hungarian

Armistice Day Celebration, Paris, November 11, 1918. (*National Archives*)

empires had already ceased fighting. Even before the final shots were fired, political revolutions were under way among the Central Powers. Nationalist leaders of the Slavic peoples of Austria-Hungary proclaimed in late October the formation of the nation-states of Poland, Czechoslovakia, and Yugoslavia. The German emperor abdicated, discredited by defeat and condemned in the West for his militarism, and was followed shortly by the Austrian emperor. Their disappearance immediately brought rival claims for political succession in those lands. The Russian precedent was on the minds of many people, some fearing the Communist path, others welcoming it. In the revolutionary turmoil erupting throughout Central and Eastern Europe, Lenin's vision of a new international and political order and Wilson's plan for democratic self-determination both had many supporters.

After four years of bitter, bloody fighting, the shape of the postwar world depended only partly on the decisions of statesmen. Political events took a course of their own as nationalist movements grew in strength and as workers and other urban groups looked to social revolution to end their sufferings. The very ability of the victorious states to impose their settlement was weakened as a result of the terrible price they had paid for victory. Allied statesmen used whatever force their armies and diplomats could exert to protect the power and interests of their states in remaking the European order. Their armies had lost the will to pursue new wars, however, and their countries were weak.

The casualties of battle, numbering everywhere in the millions, were concentrated among draft-age men. The war caused over 10 million deaths and another 20 million wounded. France lost 1.5 million, the highest proportion of dead to the population in any country. In all European lands the hardships of war weakened the population and opened the way to epidemics at war's end, the worst of which was the Spanish influenza. The fighting had made a mockery of the images of power and progress of prewar years. Although Allied political leaders held fast to their conviction of European domination, events to the east proved that their power had dwindled.

COMMUNIST REVOLUTION IN RUSSIA

The formal end of the First World War did not stop fighting throughout Europe. Revolutions brought in their wake civil strife. Civil wars raged in some countries, while foreign states intervened elsewhere in support of particular political leaders and parties. Everywhere large numbers of people, many former soldiers, joined political movements whose goals were shaped by an ideological vision of the future and whose means to this end included agitation, demonstrations, and even violence. Having mobilized for total war, European societies upon war's end returned only slowly to peacetime conditions, and some by then had changed dramatically. Nowhere was the conflict over political ideals more acute and the revolution more extreme than in Russia.

The Communist insurrection of October 1917 marked a new stage in the revolutionary transformation of Russia. It ended the hopes of liberals that the country would evolve toward a democratic state and capitalist economy. The Communist regime defied Russian patriots and Western Allies alike by signing the peace with Germany. These forces united in 1918 to oppose the new state in a bloody civil war. This ideological conflict acquired much greater amplitude and force as a result of the social revolution pitting classes and nationalities against one another. Peasants took up arms to seize the property of landlords, workers expelled industrialists from their factories and prosperous urban families from their homes, Ukrainians fought Russians, Jews were attacked and murdered by Christians.

In this extraordinary violence it is remarkable that any state managed to survive. Lenin's Communist party (the name was changed from Bolshevik party in 1918) demonstrated extraordinary ability in holding power in Russia. The Communist victory imposed a new ideological blueprint on Russia, and later served as an inspiration to revolutionary movements in other countries. It provided in concrete form the image of a socialist future and the model of how a small "vanguard" of political militants could change the course of history. We need therefore to examine closely the origins and leadership of the Communist revolutionary movement.

Lenin and the Bolshevik Party

Lenin and his followers were unique in 1917 among European Marxist parties in two respects. First, they adhered firmly to the belief that their party constituted the organization capable of mobilizing and heading a proletarian revolution. Second, they were convinced that the war had brought the entire Western capitalist society to the verge of social revolution. The two principles together justified in their eyes proletarian revolution in Russia.

The party was in large measure the creation of a young Marxist radical, Vladimir Lenin. A brilliant student, he had chosen in the 1890s to devote his entire life to the destruction of the Russian autocratic regime and of capitalist society. Many other radicals shared his vision of a society of freedom and equality, but few matched his fanatical dedication and organizational ability. After having worked for a few years to build a working-class movement in Russia, he came to the conviction that workers by themselves would abandon the cause of revolution for the sake of better wages and living conditions—what he termed "Gomperism" (from the name of the head of the American Federation of Labor, Samuel Gompers).

Lenin defended his new theory of Marxist revolutionary action in a short book, *What's to Be Done?*, one of the most influential political works of the twentieth century. The key concept he proposed was embodied in the term "vanguard." Other Marxists continued to talk of a working-class mass movement aided and organized by a revolutionary party, led by radical militants. Lenin, on the contrary, considered the latter to be the "vanguard fighters" whose understanding of "revolutionary theory" and total commitment to the movement elevated them above ordinary workers in the struggle against the state and against capitalism. These "professional revolutionaries" constituted the elite force without whom the workers would be led astray—hence the term "vanguard." While Marxism taught Lenin that proletarian revolution was inevitable, his theory explained how important was the role of men like himself. Leninism was based on one simple proposition: "Give us an organization of revolutionaries, and we shall overturn Russia!"

He created his own Marxist party to carry out this program. Although he encountered considerable opposition from other Marxists in the Russian Social Democratic party, he gradually pulled together supporters he chose to call the "majority" (in Russian, *bol'shevik* means a member of the majority). Finally, in 1912 he organized his own Bolshevik party. A Central Committee, of which he was the leading member, decided revolutionary policy and tactics, to be carried out by followers organized in secret cells. He and his followers had not played an influential role in the Revolution of 1905. By 1914, though, the Bolsheviks had attracted considerable support among militant workers. When the Revolution of 1917 began, his party possessed a strong organization and a small but dedicated group of followers (among whom was a former seminary student of Georgian nationality, Joseph Stalin). Most important of all, he returned that April from exile prepared to organize the proletarian revolution in his country.

No other Marxist movement in Europe had at the time such a daring plan. Some parties believed that the class conflict between workers and capitalists had not progressed far enough; others had in fact abandoned revolutionary tactics to seek political reform through democratic institutions. All judged that support for their countries during the war came before other political issues. Lenin reversed these priorities. He did so in the belief that the war marked the ultimate crisis of the capitalist order. Studying the war while in exile, he concluded that capitalism had evolved into a last phase of "monopoly capitalism." Large companies and banks had forced their states to compete for colonies. The result was, in his opinion, an "intensification of antagonisms among imperialist nations for a division of the world," the last desperate outburst of "moribund capitalism." He called on soldiers in all nations not to join in the unjust war, but rather to turn their rifles on their own officers and political leaders to transform the "imperialist war into a civil war."

His was a voice in the wilderness until Tsar Nicholas II was overthrown in February 1917. He had argued that Russia, though backward, still constituted one key part of the capitalist world. It was "the weakest link in the capitalist chain" which would break completely if proletarian revo-lution succeeded in Russia. He viewed his party in 1917 as the revolutionary spearhead, not just in his country, but in Europe as well. Sharing his impatience for proletarian revolution in Russia was another Marxist radical, Leon Trotsky, who joined the Bolsheviks that summer. Lenin's vision, which proved quite mistaken ultimately, gave him and his followers the conviction that on their actions that year depended the fate of humanity.

The Bolshevik Revolution and Civil War

In a country the size of a continent with a population of over 200 million, the chances that the Bolsheviks could seize and retain power appeared very slim. The mutiny of the Russian army, numbering 6 million men, had by the fall of 1917 destroyed military discipline both in garrisons and on the front lines. Many soldiers turned to the Bolsheviks, but solely to end the war and to free them from the trenches. The rapid decline of industrial production worsened conditions among the country's small working class—about 2.5 million—inciting some to back the Bolsheviks, others to return to the villages from which they had migrated. Throughout the enormous Russian countryside peasant farmers banded together, often with the help of soldiers returning from the front, to seize the estates and to divide up the possessions of noble landlords. Freed from serfdom in the middle of the nineteenth century, they farmed small plots of land, relying on household labor and consuming much of what they produced. As inflation destroyed the value of money that year, they sold less and less agricultural produce, worsening the food shortages in the cities.

This social revolution created its own images of friends and adversaries which, when identified with the Bolsheviks and their opponents, provided Lenin with vital support from the revolutionary masses. The Bolshevik ideology had simple answers to resolve the complex problems confronting the country in 1917. Its language of class conflict drew a picture of evil caused by capitalism and imperialism and proposed a new vision of a just society of the working population. A young American reporter in Russia that fall overheard one soldier justify his support for the Bolsheviks by explaining that "there are just two classes, you see, the bourgeoisie and the proletariat, and if you aren't for one, you're for the other." Under banners reading "Bread, Land, and Peace," demonstrators paraded through the streets of Petrograd defying the Provisional Government and risking their lives for Bolshevism. In the popular mind, Lenin's program

linked the Bolshevik party with the immediate aims of the social revolution.

Thus what armed force remained in the country by the fall of 1917 was largely sympathetic to Bolshevik leadership. Infantry garrisons were more likely to heed Bolshevik appeals to support the "revolution" than to repress worker demonstrations in the cities. Armed worker militias, the Red Guards, obeyed the orders of the popularly elected assemblies called *soviets,* where Bolshevik leaders were in command. The new chairman that fall of the Petrograd Soviet was Leon Trotsky, Lenin's close aide in organizing the insurrection. When the Central Committee agreed that October to take power from the Provisional Government, Trotsky and the other Bolshevik leaders of soviets in the cities provided the key forces to seize the reigns of power. The Bolshevik

Revolution in the Streets: Petrograd Street Demonstration under Fire, July, 1917. (*National Archives*)

slogan "All Power to the Soviets" symbolized Lenin's claim to act in the name of the working masses organized in the soviets. Power in the October Revolution passed in fact into the hands of the Communist party (Bolshevik), ruling a state Lenin called the "Russian Soviet Socialist Republic."

Bolshevik dreams and Russian reality came into immediate conflict. Appeals to "German brothers in arms" to turn against their officers failed miserably, as did appeals to other armies to mutiny. The Communists stood alone, first of all against the German and Austrian armies. Over bitter opposition from some party leaders who preferred "revolutionary death" to compromise with German reactionary imperialists, Lenin obtained in early 1918 his party's support for the treaty of Brest-Litovsk. His argument was simple: "the fate of the socialist revolution" is not worth a "reckless gamble" on revolution in Germany.

Critical political and economic problems confronted the new regime. Peasants stopped marketing their food at low state prices, preferring the black market. Workers had to be fed, however, to keep factories operating. At first the new state issued decrees authorizing peasant seizure of all large estates, putting the regime on the side of the rural revolution and petty peasant farming. The hunger sweeping the cities, however, soon incited the Communist authorities to use force to obtain the produce the peasants would not willingly sell. In the spring of 1918, they set up armed worker brigades in a "food army" to move through the villages seizing food from the peasant population. The Communist government was assuming dictatorial powers over the Russian population more extreme than any exercised by the war cabinets of the other European states.

The Bolsheviks justified these decisions in the name of their ideological vision of progress. For the sake of the communist society, the highest stage of historical development, they were prepared to demand of themselves and of all Russians terrible sacrifices. In their minds, the future governed the present. Shortly after they had seized power, local officials throughout the country had organized the long-deferred elections to choose delegates for the constituent assembly, a plan of the Provisional Government which the Communist regime had not dared to annul. As expected, the Communist candidates did not win the majority—though they did gain 25 percent of the vote, second largest among all the parties competing. The assembly met only once, immediately disbanded by force by the police. Lenin had no intention of permitting "bourgeois parliamentarism" (i.e., rule by a majority) to stand in the way of "the workers' and peasants' revolution." In other words, his state would not permit majority rule to block Communist government.

These political and social policies caused in the summer of 1918 a crisis so severe it almost destroyed the Communist regime. Opposition had been swelling for several months. Many workers, once strong supporters of the Bolshevik Revolution, went on strike and organized demonstrations to demand that the Communists obtain food to keep them alive and permit other socialist parties to participate in a real "Soviet democracy." To put down the strikes and demonstrations, the regime called out its new military police force, organized under the name of "Special Commission for the Struggle Against Counterrevolution" (the Russian acronym was *Cheka*), the embryo of a new internal secret police. The leadership of the largest democratic opposition party, the Socialist Revolutionary party, decided that summer that armed insurrection offered the only hope of ending the Communist dictatorship. Although their uprising failed, Lenin himself was wounded in an assassination attempt. In retaliation, the Communist state authorized mass arrest and execution of suspected enemies by the secret police. The Red Terror had begun.

Opposition came as well from Russia's former allies. These states quickly discovered how completely the Bolshevik Revolution had broken the ties that bound Russia to the West. Lenin's regime abandoned the alliance to make peace with Germany. It canceled the entire Russian foreign debt, totaling several billion dollars, owed largely to the Western states and investors. Its acts of defiance gave real substance to the appeal from Communist leaders for "international socialist revolution." Its very existence challenged the international order which the Allies sought to create following victory over Germany.

Western leaders decided in the summer of 1918 to deal with the Communists by measures they had employed against rebellious political movements in other parts of the world—military intervention. They provided supplies and military advisers for the anti-Communist opposition in Russia, declared an economic blockade of Soviet territory, and sent troops to key port areas along the Russian coast (where large amounts of Allied munitions for Russia had been stored). Even the Japanese government participated, sending troops to eastern Siberia (though it was less interested in opposing Communist revolution than in creating another Japanese puppet state on the Russian Pacific coast). The Allies and the Communists were at war.

By mid-1918 Russia was in the grips of a bitter civil war. Large parts of the country escaped the control of the Soviet government, seized by anti-Communist forces intent on overthrowing the Communist regime. A small force of forty thousand Czech soldiers, originally moving along the Trans-Siberian railroad toward the Pacific, became the spearhead of the first important military threat to the Communists. Supported by the Allies and collaborating with the Russian Socialist Revolutionary leadership, its disciplined forces quickly seized the entire railroad across Siberia and soon threatened Moscow itself. Unprepared for war and beset by foreign and domestic enemies from all sides, the young Communist state could only rely on its own meager forces.

The response of Lenin and the other Communist leaders to the civil war was to forge the weapons of a revolutionary warfare state. They abandoned their Marxist idealism to mobilize all their country's resources for war and to destroy the "counterrevolution." Theirs was the language of war, which identified all opponents with hostile classes in league with Western imperialism. Lenin described his state as a "fortress besieged by world capital" and demanded that it become "a single military camp." It employed the instruments of political repression and economic mobilization. The government, called the Council of People's Commissars, became the center of a bureaucratic state, supporting a new army and running a nationalized economy.

Lenin authorized Leon Trotsky to constitute a regular army and gave him complete power to take whatever measures were needed to defeat the enemy forces. By the end of the war, the Red Army had grown to five million men, a conscript army led by former tsarist officers under the control of Communist commissars. The Cheka expanded in size and power, imprisoning and executing on its own authority all suspected counterrevolutionaries and enemy agents. To provide the necessary supplies for the army, a policy later called War Communism went into effect. It included nationalization

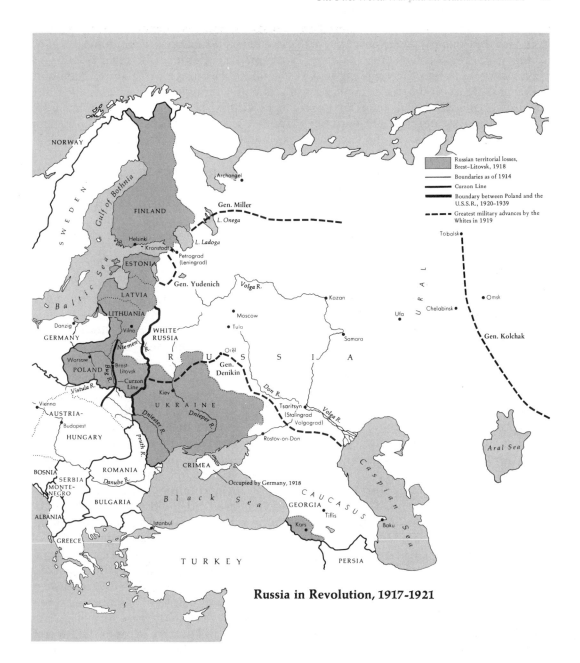

Russian territorial losses, Brest–Litovsk, 1918

Boundaries as of 1914

Curzon Line

Boundary between Poland and the U.S.S.R., 1920–1939

Greatest military advances by the Whites in 1919

NORWAY

SWEDEN

Archangel

Gen. Miller

FINLAND

Gulf of Bothnia

L. Onega

Helsinki

Kronstadt

L. Ladoga

ESTONIA

Petrograd (Leningrad)

Gen. Yudenich

Volga R.

Kazan

Tobolsk

Omsk

LATVIA

Moscow

Ufa

Chelabinsk

U R A L

LITHUANIA

Tula

Danzig

Vilna

WHITE RUSSIA

Samara

Gen. Kolchak

GERMANY

Niemen R.

R   U   S   S   I   A

Warsaw

Brest-Litovsk

Bug R.

Orël

POLAND

Curzon Line

Gen. Denikin

Vistula R.

Kiev

Don R.

Vienna

UKRAINE

Volga R.

AUSTRIA-

Dniester R.

Dnieper R.

Tsaritsyn (Stalingrad Volgograd)

Budapest

HUNGARY

Prath R.

Rostov-on-Don

Aral Sea

BOSNIA

ROMANIA

CRIMEA

SERBIA

MONTE-NEGRO

Danube

Occupied by Germany, 1918

C A U C A S U S

Caspian Sea

ALBANIA

BULGARIA

Black   Sea

GEORGIA

Tiflis

GREECE

Istanbul

Kars

Baku

T U R K E Y

PERSIA

Russia in Revolution, 1917-1921

(i.e., state ownership) of all industry and commerce and requisitioning of all needed produce from peasant farmers.

The struggle to win the civil war had a permanent impact on the new regime, for it put in place the basic institutions of Communist dictatorship and trained Communist militants in the ruthless methods of class war. The party, which grew to 500,000 in those years, changed from an underground revolutionary movement to the sole political force in the country, recruiting many of its new members from soldiers scarcely educated in Marxism and proven fighters for the new state. It remained under the control of the central leadership in a new committee, the Politburo. There Lenin, Trotsky, Stalin, and a handful of other leaders made the decisions that determined the survival of the regime. Their remarkable leadership ability combined with the fanatical commitment of party members to the victory of the socialist revolution constituted the key factors in the defeat of the anti-Communist forces in the civil war. The power of that ideological vision and of Lenin's concept of the vanguard party was confirmed in the bloody triumph of the "Reds" over the "Whites."

The Communist regime confronted military crisis after crisis in the years of civil strife. The struggle against the Czech Legion in the summer and fall of 1918 ended in Communist occupation of most of eastern Russia, but not Siberia. Its forces had to turn instead to the Ukraine and western Russia, for in the winter of 1918–19 German and Austrian troops withdrew from that enormous territory in fulfillment of the conditions of the November 1918 armistice. The end of the European war gave the Communists new hope that revolution was about to sweep over Europe. They welcomed the few foreign supporters able to reach their country, including the American journalist John Reed, and organized them in a new international revolutionary organization, the Communist (Third) International, to encourage proletarian revolution. Lenin still thought inconceivable the "ultimate victory" of his Soviet state "if it were to remain alone." But no revolution in Europe brought to power supporters of his dictatorial socialist ideology.

Instead, Allied military aid helped anti-Communist generals in Russia to organize major offensives in 1919, one from Siberia under Admiral Kolchak in the spring, another in the summer and fall under General Denikin from the Ukraine. These military dictators had taken the place of democratic parties at the head of the "White," that is, anti-Communist movement. Both started with large armies and considerable popular support. Their forces were, however, uncoordinated, poorly led, and as brutal in their own way as was the Communist dictatorship. The Red Army stopped first Kolchak's offensive, then that of Denikin, and gradually reoccupied the southern and eastern regions of the country. The Allied intervention had failed. Western troops, some of whom mutinied rather than participate in yet another war, did not take any important part in the civil war. Allied arms and financial aid could not compensate for the incompetence and disorganization of the White generals. The peasant population of Russia, victimized by both sides in the fighting, chose to support only their own guerrilla bands (known as the "Greens") to protect their land and their food. Numbering several hundred thousand, these armed groups operated at will in large areas of the Russian countryside. At the end of the White campaigns, the Communist regime had survived, but it controlled only the cities.

Before it could deal with internal disorder, it confronted one final military conflict. The Polish War of 1920 settled the boundaries of the new state and sealed the fate of Communist revolution in Europe. The leaders of the new Polish nation-state, formed in 1919 and aided by France, dreamed of a country whose boundaries would extend far into Eastern Europe, an area of mixed population where centuries before the Polish monarchy had ruled. Their troops attacked the Soviet Republic in the summer of 1920, but quickly were forced to retreat by the far larger forces of the Red Army. Lenin, for his part, imagined that the time had come at last to let his army carry revolution into Central Europe in support of the Polish and German workers. The Red Army entered Poland, but the Polish workers proved loyal to their nation, not Russian communism, and the Polish army in turn stopped the Russian offensive. The war ended in a stalemate, leaving the Polish frontier far inside former Russian land. The Communist regime had to proceed with its socialist revolution alone in the world, surrounded by hostile capitalist states and in the midst of a rebellious peasant population.

The NEP Compromise

The end of the Russian civil war left the country in a state of economic collapse, its population living in impoverished conditions, epidemic disease affecting millions with little medical care, and large cities partially depopulated after townspeople fled to the countryside. No one knows how many died in the fighting or as a result of disease and famine. Industrial production had fallen to one-fourth prewar levels, and most factories no longer operated. Many of those remaining workers were at war's end unwilling to continue living in such terrible conditions, but the Communists made no concessions. As a result serious strikes broke out even in Petrograd, where police and soldiers shot demonstrating workers and arrested strik-

ers. These events represented a cruel rebuttal to Communist claims of forming a "proletarian state." Angry sailors at the nearby naval fortress of Kronstadt, formerly ardent Communists, mutinied in March 1921, demanding a return to "Soviet democracy" and restrictions on the repressive powers of the Cheka. But Red Army troops crushed the uprising, termed a "counterrevolutionary plot" by Lenin. The single-party dictatorship remained the foundation of Communist rule.

Economic ruin and social unrest required new policies, however. Deprived of any incentive to grow food beyond their own needs, peasant farmers had curtailed production so drastically that they themselves suffered when crops failed in 1921. Hunger in the eastern and southern regions became so acute, in fact, that the Communist regime reluctantly had to request famine relief from the American Relief Administration (a private organization formed by Herbert Hoover to provide aid to war-torn Europe), an action that revealed to the outside world how impoverished the population really was. Before relief arrived, the famine killed untold millions of people. If Russia was to recover, it needed once again to raise sufficient food. The revolution of 1917 had permitted the peasant farmers to seize all the land, farmed largely still in small strips scattered about great fields. No large estates remained; the Communists had been able to set aside only a few "state farms" to demonstrate their plans for cooperative farming. Their vision of socialism in the countryside represented a pipedream as long as real control over agricultural production rested in the hands of 25 million peasant households.

To obtain the collaboration of those "petty capitalists" constituted the first priority for economic recovery from the war. Recognizing that Russia remained a "small peasant country," Lenin reluctantly decided in 1921 to allow free trade in food produce. This New Economic Policy (NEP) excluded requisitioning of peasant production and was soon expanded to permit traders in towns and villages to sell manufactured goods, a concrete incentive to peasants to market their surplus. The state introduced a new currency to replace the old money which inflation had made worthless. All these measures strengthened the role of the market and of petty capitalism. One Communist leader enthusiastically urged the peasants to "Get rich!" In the mid-1920s, agricultural production did grow rapidly and hunger no longer threatened Russian society.

By then party leadership had passed into the hands of Lenin's colleagues. The revolutionary leader, though only "one among equals" in the central party committees, had enjoyed such authority among party members that his word usually set party and state policy. In 1922, however, he suffered a debilitating stroke, forcing him to leave the daily affairs of state in the hands of the other members of the Politburo. He made one effort to designate an heir, asking Leon Trotsky to become his assistant as chairman of the Council of Commissars. Trotsky refused, for reasons which still remain unclear. At the same time, Lenin concluded that Stalin did not possess the qualities of a party leader and asked the Politburo to remove him from office. Shortly afterward, in early 1923 a second stroke deprived him of any active political role. A complete invalid, he watched helplessly as the other Politburo members disregarded his recommendation to deprive Stalin of political power.

Instead, Lenin's heirs preferred to govern as a "collective leadership" and to decide among themselves the succession. Fearing Trotsky, whom they imagined a new Napoleon, and believing Stalin's claims of loyalty to the party, they reversed their for-

mer leader's plan by joining with Stalin to expel Trotsky from the party. Lenin's most serious defeat thus came at the hands of his own colleagues, who later themselves paid with their lives for having rejected his advice. In early 1924, Lenin died, honored by his party and by revolutionaries all over the world, his body embalmed and preserved in a mausoleum to be gazed upon in religious awe by the Russian people. The spirit of the new faith was captured by one Soviet poet, who proclaimed: "Lenin lived, Lenin lives, Lenin will live!"

The economic policies he put in place remained in effect, but their success created new economic problems. Industry continued to be run by the state, dependent on state subsidies for reconstruction and expansion. Communist hopes to build a socialist society (the stage before communism) depended above all on industry and technology. Lenin was fascinated by the power of electricity, the key to "communist economic development," and by the "up-to-date achievements of capitalism" (including the American engineer Taylor's system for labor efficiency). The Soviet government formed in 1924 a State Planning Commission to provide the "scientific guidance" for state economic policy. But how was wealth to be channeled toward industrial growth, the real material base for socialism, if peasant farmers held in their hands the largest share of the productive property of the Russian economy? Communists debated these questions at length, searching for the guidelines by which to plan their country's economic development. They knew that no help was available from outside and that they, as one of their leaders stated, had to "build socialism in one country."

Implicit in NEP was the hope that encouragement of peasant production and farm cooperatives would win peasant support for socialism and increase taxes to pay for slow industrialization. It did not satisfy many Communists, who rejected the thought of building socialism at a "snail's pace" and resented deeply the reappearance of petty capitalists and prosperous farmers (called *kulaks*). Lenin himself had warned of the dangers of the "revival of the petty bourgeoisie and of capitalism," which undermined social equality and took control over economic affairs partially out of the hands of the party. The Soviet government's retreat to a "mixed economy," combining private and nationalized productive property and a free market, was in his eyes a temporary concession to peasant "backwardness." Some leaders called for patience and education to close the gap between workers and peasants, between Communist ideology and peasant "greed." Others preferred to use force, as the civil war years had taught them. Lenin's authority in the early 1920s had imposed the NEP methods of compromise, to be continued temporarily while his heirs debated the future course for Soviet socialism.

Revolutionary dreams were put into action more quickly in other areas. Learning represented to the Communists a necessary tool to bring their message to the masses, and they organized volunteers to wipe out illiteracy among the poor. Secondary and higher education was opened to the lower classes through special "worker colleges" to provide rapid remedial training. The socialist vision of a new era of human achievement following the end of capitalism included the end of the unequal treatment of women. Communist leaders protested that they were not feminists—true liberation for women could result only from proletarian revolution, according to Marxism—but their new laws incorporated many ideas from the feminist movement. Marriage became a simple legal procedure and divorce could be obtained on demand. Abortions were legalized. Communist writers extolled the "new Soviet woman," equal in her rights to men and free in her decisions on marriage and the family. In reality, women's place in Russian society changed slowly, particularly among the peasant population. In the cities and among party members, women were able to assert their new rights. Stalin's young wife, Nadezhda Allilueva, was an emancipated woman with both children and a career in party work. A scandal among many Westerners, the Soviet feminist reforms became later a model for other socialist countries.

Soviet art in the 1920s displayed in abstract and surrealistic form the revolutionary visions of painters and sculptors. The newest art form, the motion picture, became the center of experimental work in form and content. Sergei Eisenstein created a new revolutionary plot for his movies, in which the masses were the heroes and the drama emerged in the conflict between characters and groups embodying the class struggle from which the proletarian revolution had emerged. In the 1920s the Communist leaders tolerated artistic creativity and intellectual experimentation, even when they did not approve of the results.

The Struggle Against Imperialism

Their attention was directed in those years as much to international as to internal affairs. Their ideological view of global relations blurred the lines between the two, for socialist revolution recognized no boundaries. They confronted a world in their opinion dominated by the imperialist Western powers, from whom they expected another interventionist war as inevitable as the class war they foresaw in the industrial societies. The Communist International grew in size as more and more revolutionary Marxists joined, accepting the leadership of Moscow and reshaping their parties on the Leninist model. It promised new proletarian revolutions some time in the future. In the meantime, the Soviet state had to deal directly with the Western states.

The Communist leaders sought new policies by which to protect their state and to encourage revolutions in the colonial areas. The end of the civil war brought the withdrawal of foreign troops from Russian territory (though the Japanese did not leave Siberia until 1922) and the cessation of the Allied economic blockade. It also permitted the Soviet state to take advantage of the divisions within the "imperialist camp," namely, the presence of a defeated, isolated Germany. Both the German and Soviet governments had need of the assistance of the other for diplomatic backing, economic trade, and even armaments. In 1921, their military leaders began secret military collaboration for the development and testing of new weapons (forbidden the Germans and beyond the means of the Communists). In 1922, the two states formally opened diplomatic relations. Soviet-German cooperation marked the entry of the Soviet state into the realm of power politics, forced there by its isolation among the capitalist states.

Complicating the new Soviet policies were the nationalist movements which had altered drastically the map of Europe and which were creating unrest in non-Western, colonial lands. Surrounding the Russian population of the Soviet Republic were non-Russians, some with their own nationalist movements. In the course of the civil war nationalists in some of these areas had created their own independent states, usually under the protection of the Western powers. The Ukraine and Finland had been protected by Germany until 1919; the Baltic Republics and the small states in the Caucasus received the aid of Great Britain. Caught between Russia and the Western states, their

leaders preferred Western help to the risk of social revolution and Communist intervention.

After the withdrawal of Western forces, the Soviet government did in fact seize those areas where there was no risk of war with the West. Defeat of the Whites in 1919 in the Ukraine left the Ukrainian Communist party in command. In 1920–21 the Red Army brought Soviet power on the point of its bayonets to the Caucasus and occupied Central Asian territories, north of Iran and Afghanistan, which tsarist forces had conquered a half-century earlier. In the south and the east, the frontiers of the Soviet state resembled those of the Russian Empire. The nationalities there received in theory special rights in a new federal constitution, adopted in 1923, creating the Union of Soviet Socialist Republics (USSR). In fact, the entire area was ruled from Moscow.

In colonial lands beyond the Soviet borders, on the other hand, the Communist leaders gave strong encouragement and support to the new nationalist movements which emerged in the years after the First World War. In their global view of the conflict with the Western states, this growing resistance to Western imperialism represented a new stage leading toward the inevitable collapse of world capitalism. They sponsored in 1920 a Conference of Oppressed Peoples, held in Baku, a Soviet city on the Caspian Sea between Europe and Asia. It was the first time Asian and African opponents gathered in one place, and the spirit of the meetings was revolutionary. The delegates urged the peoples of colonial lands to rise up against their imperialist rulers. This appeal presented a radical new conception of future global relations and Western imperial rule and placed the Communist regime clearly on the side of nationalist revolutions in non-Western lands.

Twice in the 1920s the Communists intervened in conflicts occurring along Soviet borders to aid nationalist parties opposed to Western domination. In 1922 the Chinese Nationalist party *(Kuomintang)* requested Soviet aid in its campaign to conquer China and to forge a new Chinese nation-state (see Chapter 5). The Russian Communists agreed, providing military aid and training and economic assistance, and ordering the Chinese Communist party to collaborate in that "bourgeois-nationalist" revolution. The interests of the Soviet state benefited as well as the cause of Asian nationalism, for the Chinese had to accept a Soviet sphere of influence along their northern border (in Manchuria and Mongolia).

The importance of power politics in the new Soviet foreign policy appeared even more clearly in its aid to the revolutionary nationalist regime in Turkey. The Western Allies had agreed to partition the Ottoman Empire but encountered militant opposition from Turkish nationalist officers under the leadership of Kemal Ataturk (see Chapter 3). In 1920 war had broken out between Greece, supported by the Allies, and the Turkish forces. Although Ataturk was openly anticommunist, he needed aid. The Russian Communists were prepared to help his cause with their limited means, since in their eyes any conflict weakening the West represented a step toward socialism and reduced the danger of a new imperialist war on Soviet Russia. As in the civil war in Russia, the Western forces in Turkey were unable to impose their peace settlement. In 1922, the Turkish war ended, leaving intact the new Turkish nation-state. It was in fact the last act in the fighting begun in 1914.

SUMMARY

In Russia, war had led to successful Communist revolution despite the intervention of the Western states. The Turkish war repeated in its own way the same experience. How could the victors over Germany have been unable to control the outcome of the Russian civil war? The explanation lies partly in the nature and outcome of the world war. It so drained the human and material resources of all the belligerents that victors and vanquished alike were severely weakened. It is no wonder that Allied troops were at war's end hostile to the prospect of participating in distant conflicts at the orders of leaders they no longer trusted. One measure of the decline of the military might of France was the mutiny of troops it had sent to Russia in 1918. Like many other Europeans, these French soldiers were sickened of war.

Another reason for the failure of Allied intervention was the new direction given the war effort by the United States. Its entry into the war ensured the defeat of Germany, whose withdrawal from Eastern Europe left open the door to revolution. The strongest world power by war's end, its leaders spoke out against the methods of international power politics in favor of new principles of self-determination and collaboration among nations. They did join the intervention in the Russian civil war, but did so halfheartedly and refused to follow the British example of supporting the White counterrevolution.

Finally, the Russian Communists possessed an extraordinary ability to forge and to defend their revolutionary regime. Once before in the 1790s, French revolutionaries had created in their country the structure of a new state and a new culture and had mobilized the people to defeat foreign enemies. The Bolsheviks in some ways repeated the same experience. They too believed fervently in the justice of their revolutionary cause and obtained the help of other Russians ready to overlook questions of ideology to defend the independence of their country from foreign enemies. Lenin's Communist ideology did mold the new regime, but so too did the pressures of war and a growing identification between communism and Russian national interests. Out of this mixture emerged slowly a new communist political culture, shaping the policies of the new leadership. Defense of Soviet Russia was their first priority; the second was to assist in the birth of a new revolutionary world order. The First World War, like the next global conflict to come twenty years later, prepared the ground on which revolutions flourished.

RECOMMENDED READING

The First World War

Ross Gregory, *The Origins of American Intervention in the First World War* (1971)

Basil Liddell Hart, *History of the First World War* (1970)

*Alstair Horne, *The Price of Glory: Verdun, 1916* (1979)

N. Gordon Levin, *Woodrow Wilson and World Politics* (1968)

Norman Stone, *The Eastern Front, 1914–1917* (1975)

Edmond Taylor, *The Fall of the Dynasties: The Collapse of the Old Order, 1905–1922* (1963)

John Toland, *No Man's Land: 1918* (1980)

*Barbara Tuchman, *The Guns of August* (1962)

The Russian Revolution and the Communist Regime

*William Chamberlin, *The Russian Revolution* (2 vols., 1935)

*Robert Daniels, *Red October: The Bolshevik Revolution of 1917* (1967)

Sheila Fitzpatrick, *The Russian Revolution, 1917–1932* (1984)

*Adam Ulam, *The Bolsheviks* (1968)

Memoirs and Novels

Robert Graves, *Goodbye to All That: An Autobiography* (1980)

*Erik Maria Remarque, *All Quiet on the Western Front* (1929)

*Boris Pasternak, *Doctor Zhivago* (1958)

John Reed, *Ten Days that Shook the World* (1919)

chapter 3

THE RECOVERY FROM WORLD WAR, 1918–1928

The work of peacemaking lasted for a longer time than had the war itself. It presented the monumental tasks, on the one hand, of reconstructing civilian life and, on the other, of rebuilding stable international relations on the ruins of the fallen eastern empires and in the face of European revolutions and anti-imperialist movements in the Middle East and Asia. Political leaders all over Europe confronted internal political turmoil and economic hardship. The new nation-states in Central Europe struggled with their neighbors over frontiers while fashioning their own political institutions. The specter of Communist revolution frightened liberals and conservatives everywhere and intruded into the peace negotiations in Paris, even though the Soviet leaders were not invited to participate. One panicked American negotiator, concluding that "the whole world is in revolt," consoled himself with the idea that

"all we care about is that it be a thoughtful revolt and a gradual one."

In reality, the new economic and political order which emerged in the mid-1920s resembled strongly that of prewar years. A number of new nation-states had appeared in Central Europe, while, to replace the Ottoman Empire, the Middle East was divided into new "mandated" states in theory under League of Nations supervision. These boundaries placed new barriers between and within cultural and economic communities, suddenly reorganizing human relations as well as political leadership in a manner to be repeated many times after the Second World War. But the appearance of these new states in the 1920s did not mark a complete political transformation. In the Middle East, the new Arab states were closely controlled by the Western powers, who treated them much like new territories in their empires. The leaders of the Central European states looked west to France and Great Britain for models of state building and for diplomatic alliances, not east to Soviet Russia.

Among Western states, the political preeminence of the United States quickly faded after the war. Great war debts reminded the European states of the new economic wealth of the United States, without whose aid (in the form of loans) international trade and investment could not recover from the dislocation of war. Diplomatic leadership returned to Western Europe, however, when the U.S. government reverted in the 1920s to its old isolationist policies. The great promises Wilson had made of a new era had strongly shaped the peace treaties of 1919, but these had to be supplemented in the mid-1920s by a new European security treaty, minus the United States. The League of Nations met regularly, but it lacked the peacekeeping powers to be an effective guarantor of peace. Pacifism and disarmament campaigns were popular political movements, but in the background lurked potential conflicts over territory in Eastern Europe and a new militaristic movement called fascism, first triumphant in Italy but with followers in other lands. The plans for permanent peace lacked solid foundations in the political conditions of postwar Europe.

In the lands beyond Europe, Western empires appeared still to dominate global relations, but beneath the surface new forces were at work. Nationalist movements in colonial areas had gathered strength during the war; in the postwar years, resistance to Western rule was stronger than ever. Investment and trade in these lands remained largely in the hands of Western companies, but they now confronted serious competition from Asian businessmen, among whom the Japanese proved the most active. Japan had emerged from the war an influential and powerful Asian state, whose leaders were for

the first time accepted as equals by Western statesmen in discussing East Asian and League affairs. Slowly and painfully, a new pattern of global political and economic relations was beginning to emerge.

EUROPEAN PEACEMAKING, 1919–1925

Two conceptions of peacemaking dominated the Paris negotiations in 1919. The idea of a peace of victors assumed that the defeated states would have to sacrifice territory and wealth to ensure the permanence of the settlement, honoring the old adage that "to the victors belong the spoils." In the course of the war, Allied states had signed treaties promising annexation of enemy territory when they achieved victory. Great Britain and France had from the start agreed that Alsace-Lorraine, seized by Germany in 1870, should return to France. They also looked forward to dividing between themselves the oil-rich Middle Eastern lands of the Ottoman Empire and Germany's African colonies. Japan had seized the German concession in China. Italy claimed the former Austrian land along the eastern Adriatic coast. In addition, the French government of Clemenceau proposed to force on Germany severe limits on its military might as a guarantee that it would never be able to launch a new attack on their country. Issues of national rights and justice had a secondary place in this view of a new European order.

Contrary in spirit and content was Wilson's principle of a "peace without victors or vanquished." His vision of the settlement called for self-determination for all important nationalities. In his Fourteen Points, he had recognized the right of the Polish people to a new nation-state and had acknowledged as well the claims to self-rule of the Slavic nationalities of the Austro-Hungarian Empire. His hope for a just settlement rested on the assumption that peoples, granted national and democratic rights, would never again support militaristic leaders. A peace of territorial annexation was contrary to the spirit of reconciliation among peoples. With the assistance of an international organization which would coordinate the collective resistance to aggression, states would trade freely among themselves and prosper without fear of war. Wilson looked to an end to power politics to ensure real progress for humanity. The bitter debates among Western statesmen reflected in large part the profound difference dividing them on the very nature of peace.

Before the treaties were even completed, certain features of the new Europe were already in place. The old imperial states of Germany, Austria-Hungary, and Russia had vanished; the armies of the Central Powers had surrendered and occupation Allied forces had moved into key areas. National governments of Poland, Yugoslavia, and Czechoslovakia had come into existence and had hastily put together small armies made up of war veterans. Before and during negotiations, revolutionaries in Central Europe made sporadic efforts to create Communist regimes but lacked the support of their laboring populations. The real fight over Bolshevism was restricted to Russian lands. Thus the treaties had to take into account both the conflicting conceptions of peace and the political realities of postwar Europe. They could not possibly satisfy all the demands of the participants in the Paris conference.

The Paris Peace Treaties

The peace negotiations were dominated, but not controlled, by the American delegation. Wilson went to Paris determined to "fight for what is right." His influence there was great, for he was at the peak of his popularity in Europe and the economic aid of the United States was essential for the first steps of postwar recovery. The American Relief Administration (ARA) brought public and private assistance to the war-ravaged economies of Central Europe, providing food to millions and technical assistance to reopen coal mines and railroads. The head of the ARA, Herbert Hoover, ran the operation with a combination of practical engineering efficiency, charitable concern for social hardship, and faith in the ultimate triumph of free enterprise. He argued that his aim was "to prevent Europe from going Bolshevik," but his larger vision looked forward to a prosperous European market for U.S. agricultural and manufacturing goods, both in oversupply after the end of the war. The prominence of the ARA testified to the importance to Europe of U.S. help in the recovery from war.

In peace negotiations, however, Wilson's powers were limited. The major decisions were made in the Supreme Council, where Great Britain, France, and the United States all played key roles in treaty making. When the Italian negotiators demanded the Adriatic lands promised in a secret treaty, Wilson refused in the name of the national rights of the Yugoslavs inhabiting the area. The Italians walked out of the conference. But the French could not be so easily thwarted. Clemenceau challenged Wilson's claim that an international association provided a better means to keep the peace than the old balance of power. He demanded that the new Polish state be granted German lands to make it a strong French ally in the east. At one point Wilson himself threatened to abandon the negotiations in the face of French resistance, but in the end, he had to accept part of the French program. The treaties, chief among which was the Versailles Treaty for Germany, constituted a compromise among the Allied powers. The defeated states had no voice in negotiations. The treaties were in this sense a peace of victors.

Yet in concrete terms the peace provisions were more conciliatory than punitive. They reflected the complexity of the territorial questions and incorporated the conflicting objectives of national self-determination, security against Germany, and collective peacekeeping. Five main provisions of the treaties embodied the major features of the compromise reached after months of negotiations. These were (1) a weakened but still united German nation-state, (2) a large Polish state, (3) a new state of Slavic peoples in Central Europe called Czechoslovakia, (4) German reparations for war damages, and (5) the formation of the League of Nations.

The fate of Germany dominated all other issues. The Alsace-Lorraine provinces were returned to France. Wilson and the British leader, Lloyd George, refused the French demand for the separation of the western German region of the Rhineland from the rest of the country, judging the proposal a violation of the principle of national self-determination. They did accept the incorporation of a strip of northeastern Germany into the Polish state despite the fact that it remained the home of 1 million Germans. The new Germany emerged nonetheless almost as large as the prewar German Empire. The German industrial and agricultural economy was still potentially the most productive in Europe, and the population remained the largest of any European country, save Soviet Russia. French agreement to these provisions came only after the negotiators accepted to limit the size of the German army to 100,000 men and to "demilitarize" the Rhineland, that is, to forbid the German army from occupying the area. Wilson also promised that the United States would participate in a defense treaty with France and

Great Britain to guarantee these restrictions on German might. Wilson made this defense commitment to protect the new balance of power in return for French participation in the League of Nations, in his eyes the real promise of future peace.

Two new states in Eastern Europe received special consideration at the conference. Both Poland and Czechoslovakia bordered on Germany; both claimed territory inhabited by Germans to ensure their independence and protection against their powerful western neighbor. The Allies satisfied their demands, but the price was abiding German opposition to these eastern settlements. Poland received a "corridor" of territory extending from Polish land to the Baltic coast, where the German port city of Danzig, outlet to the sea, became an "international city." Twenty years later, Nazi Germany began another war to take back these lands. French military advisers helped create a new Polish army. The new Polish state re-emerged in 1918 only because the eastern empires had all collapsed, the troops of Germany and Russia both withdrawn from the region. Its survival required Western military support, assured in the 1920s by France. The prewar alliance with Russia, which had saved France in 1914, was gone; Poland provided the French a meager substitute.

Out of northern provinces of the Austro-Hungarian Empire emerged the state of Czechoslovakia. It grouped in one nation-state separate Slavic peoples (Czechs and Slovaks) granted the right to govern themselves in lands with large minorities of Germans and Hungarians. The Germans lived primarily in a mountainous area in the west, the Sudetenland, the only defensible frontier in the event of war with Germany. Czechoslovakia's borders, like those of Poland, represented a compromise between the principles of national self-determination and security. It too had to depend on the West-

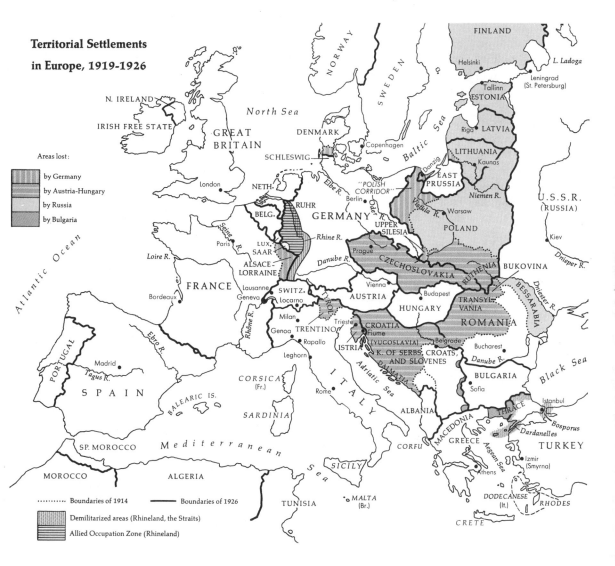

Territorial Settlements in Europe, 1919-1926

Areas lost:

- by Germany
- by Austria-Hungary
- by Russia
- by Bulgaria

·········· Boundaries of 1914 ——— Boundaries of 1926

Demilitarized areas (Rhineland, the Straits)

Allied Occupation Zone (Rhineland)

ern states if a new war broke out with Germany.

Of all the issues which aroused public debate, reparations for war damages provoked the most controversy in the immediate postwar years. The war had placed a heavy financial burden on all the belligerents; among the Western allies, France had suffered the greatest physical destruction. The Allied states all agreed to seek reparations from Germany, a practice centuries old in which the losers in war had to make financial payment to the victors. In 1919, Western political leaders promised their people that Germany would pay for human as well as material damages, though in private they themselves realized European economic recovery and heavy German reparations were incompatible. They sought U.S. financial aid in rebuilding their countries' devastated areas. Their first request was that the American government reduce the size of their war debts, which totaled over $15 billion.

Wilson's refusal to consider granting this "gift" forced the Allies to use reparations for reconstruction in place of U.S. aid. From this decision began a long and bitter controversy with Germany. The treaty recognized German "responsibility" (not "war guilt," as German nationalists later claimed) to make reparations to the Allies, but left the actual amount to be set later. The reparations requirement and the loss of territory in the east appeared to many Germans the proof that the Versailles Treaty constituted an unjust, punitive peace. In 1919, German leaders could do nothing to alter the peace settlement, for their country was occupied by Allied troops and was still under naval blockade, their people suffering serious shortages of food. Despite bitter opposition, they had to sign the treaty.

Wilson's plan for an international peace-keeping organization took the form of the League of Nations. He believed the project to be the key to peace. He thought that collaboration among states committed to peaceful relations could replace the balance-of-power system of alliances and armaments. He and other farsighted leaders saw in the League a means by which the practice of imperialist conquest could give way slowly to the principle of self-rule by all non-European, colonial peoples. The Covenant, or binding agreement among League members, included a new "mandate" system for granting the former German colonies and Arab territories of the Ottoman Empire to Western states until such time as the peoples there were judged ready to rule themselves. The new policy toward empire implied that all colonial lands would ultimately emerge

from European imperial domination. In fact, its effects remained so limited at the time that leaders of nationalist movements in Asia and elsewhere considered it a failure. The United States excluded from League surveillance its right to intervene in the internal affairs of Latin American countries. The European states governed their mandated areas in a manner similar to their other colonies. Real liberation from imperial rule came after the Second World War and as a result of the struggle of nationalist movements for self-determination.

The heart of Wilson's plan to end militarism and war was contained in Article Ten of the League Covenant. It declared that each signatory to the document would "respect and preserve against external aggression the territorial integrity and political independence of all members of the League." Governments were to act together to stop any war of aggression, if necessary by waging war themselves on the aggressor. This key provision required that states decide the question of war not solely from the perspective of their own national interests but also in the interests of other states. It also tied the League to the defense of the provisions of the treaties drawn up that year, including the new frontiers and the restrictions on German military power.

Nowhere was Wilson's internationalist idealism more clearly revealed. Article Ten introduced a radical new concept into international relations—the idea of a community of states bound together by a moral commitment to peace and to collective action, regardless of their immediate interests, to protect all independent states against aggression. Wilson recognized that among sovereign states some were more powerful and had greater influence in international affairs than others. The Covenant, therefore, provided for the creation of an executive council, whose permanent members were the United States, Great Britain, France, Italy, and Japan (plus four other states chosen by the assembly). These countries bore principal responsibility for the decision to resist aggression. This vision of a new international order represented to Wilson "the hope of the world." He returned to the United States convinced that the participation of his country was vital. Isolationism must not return, for in his view the United States was "the only nation which has sufficient moral force with the rest of the world to guarantee the substitution of discussion for war."

His idealism blinded him to the new political realities of postwar America. Wartime internationalism gave way to peacetime isolationism. Confronted by a large minority in the U.S. Senate hostile to his concept of international peacekeeping, he turned to the American people for support. While on his national campaign, however, he suffered a stroke so severe he could no longer participate in public affairs. His unwillingness to compromise on the League Covenant led the senate to reject the entire Versailles Treaty.

That action represented only one step in the resurgence of isolationism in the United States. Among political leaders domestic issues became their most important concern. Business came first to the Republicans, triumphant in the 1920 elections. The U.S. government relied upon and supported American financial and corporate leaders in their efforts to restore world trade and finance, essential to U.S. prosperity and to corporate profits. International debts had to be paid, even if the debts were incurred in a war that the United States had made its own. International commerce provided a means to promote the sales abroad of American goods. To appease domestic producers, the government enacted in 1922 a protective tariff law to keep out foreign imports, though the restraint on trade made more difficult

the repayment by European states of their war debts. In those years antiforeign pressure among Americans led the government to enact the first restrictive immigration act in American history, curtailing so severely the entry of migrants that it effectively shut the door to any further large-scale foreign settlement of American land. The United States applied to international relations the shortsighted precept that private American interests assured the public good.

Foreign alliances had no place in these isolationist policies, a return to the old pattern of noninvolvement in the European balance of power. The U.S. government never ratified the Versailles Treaty, never joined the League of Nations, and never became a member of a defensive alliance with Great Britain and France to protect them in the event of another war with Germany. With hindsight we can see that the withdrawal of the United States from European affairs seriously crippled the attempt to rebuild a stable system of state relations. As damaging was the decision of the government to treat war debts and trade relations solely from the perspective of U.S. short-term interests. The United States, having altered profoundly the outcome of the war, left the preservation of the peace to the European states.

Wilson had sought to make the United States a party to major world events, believing that it had the obligation and the moral responsibility to do so. Whether or not his new international system based on the League of Nations proved successful, diplomatic and economic decisions taken in the United States would have a vital impact on the rest of the world. Wilson understood this. American isolationism in the 1920s and 1930s rested on the illusion that the United States could live apart from the other industrial and military centers of power. By pretending that world affairs did not require

U.S. involvement, it contributed by default to the outbreak of a new world war twenty years after the first had ended.

The Versailles settlement without the United States could not succeed. Its weaknesses appeared in the very compromises which it contained. In the first place, it depended for implementation on the dominance of the Western Allies. That power was seriously diminished by the withdrawal of the United States. In addition, the British government refused to back the intransigent demands of the French, for it had affirmed once again its control of the High Seas and preferred collaboration with Germany on the continent. Even in France, the bellicose spirit of war of some conservatives hid serious economic weakness and a revulsion for warlike policies on the part of many citizens. They, like other Europeans, desperately hoped the First World War had been the "war to end all wars" and, hoping it was so, came to believe it. From this mood developed a strong pacifist movement in the West, particularly in Great Britain.

In the second place, the treaty had established the right of the Allies to demand reparations from Germany without fixing the total amount. This unresolved issue opened the way to one last act of war against Germany and ultimately a new financial agreement. Finally, the settlement required that the German government renounce any ambition to become a great power, limiting the size of its army and forbidding military occupation of the Rhineland. Yet Germany retained the potential for such a recovery. In all these respects the treaty created conditions not for peace, but for further conflict. The crises it produced in the following years ended only when a revised peace settlement, put together in bits and pieces, emerged in the mid-1920s. The new agreements represented a fragile peace, the best that European statesmen could achieve after the terrible years of war and without the direct backing of the United States.

The Revised Peace Settlement

The reparations issue proved the source of greatest dispute in the years after 1919. It lay at the heart of the difficulties confronting the West in establishing a new international financial system. The methods before the war by which governments had borrowed funds and borrowers had found foreign creditors had relied on the free flow of money from one country to another. All trading nations had committed themselves to the free exchange of currency, and most states had permitted relatively free international commerce by holding down tariffs. After the war, however, commerce was in turmoil, for the end of military production meant the end of war jobs and war markets. After a brief spurt of production, a recession set in. European manufacturers needed to find foreign buyers. They had to compete for markets where traders and manufacturers from the United States, Japan, and other Asian countries had during the war taken their places. Their sales to the American market were hindered by the high U.S. tariff of 1922. Yet the war debts placed particular pressure on the Allied countries to sell abroad to make regular payments. The U.S. government stipulated in 1922 that the funds had to be repaid in 25 years at a 4.5 percent rate of interest. In turn, the Allied countries insisted on a high level of German reparations. Until 1921, no precise total was agreed upon. Finally that year the International Reparations Commission fixed the sum at $35 billion.

The German government refused to accept this decision. It had already paid billions to cover the cost of the Allied army of occupation stationed in Germany. Its political power was limited, for it relied on a coalition of parties for support. Many Germans considered any reparations to be unjustified and punitive, claiming that Germany was not "guilty" of starting the war and thus bore no special responsibility for the damages. This opposition and the weakness of the ruling political coalition led the government to avoid the painful economic policies necessary to make reparations. Historians now conclude that this lack of cooperation, not the supposed burden of reparations themselves, produced the crisis of 1922–23. German leaders fell behind in their payments and even then relied on deficit spending, that is, spending more than the state took in taxes, to meet these payments. The problem worsened in 1922; repeated failure to pay led to warnings from France that it would use force if necessary to obtain German compliance with the treaty. In effect, the French and German leaders treated each other as enemies still, a conflict in which France had the advantage of a victorious army occupying German territory.

Tempted to return to the methods of war, the conservative French government ordered its troops in January 1923 to occupy the industrial region of the Ruhr to seize the coal it claimed due for reparations. German leaders responded by the only means of opposition available, passive resistance. They called on German workers in the Ruhr to strike, promising to pay their wages from government funds. German army veterans and civilians initiated acts of industrial sabotage and attacks on French army units. The French responded with more force. Ultimately they deported over 100,000 Germans from the occupied territory. In the violence that erupted, 20 Allied troops and 70 Germans were killed. The French found that though they held military control, they could not force the Germans to bow to their will. The German government, for its part, could not force the French to withdraw. In addi-

tion, it had by its massive payments to the striking workers in the Ruhr worsened the incredible inflation sweeping Germany. So serious was the crisis that it threatened the whole peace settlement and global economic recovery.

Neither state could win that new undeclared war. In late 1923 the German government called a halt to passive resistance. A new liberal French government ended the policy to impose reparations payments, concluding it could not afford the cost of the Ruhr conflict and preferring conciliation in the hope of achieving a stable peace. Although its troops stayed in the Ruhr until 1925, it was ready to settle the question by international negotiations. Never again did the French government use its army to enforce its terms of peace with Germany.

The conflict over reparations involved all European governments, intent on avoiding another war. It hurt investors and banking interests of Europe and the United States, whose plans for economic expansion and profitable financial investments were disrupted by the political crisis and the uncertainty caused by the Ruhr invasion. The Republican administration in Washington realized that its war debts would be paid only when German reparations payments flowed regularly to the Allied states. It therefore encouraged U.S. bankers to take part in the formulation of a workable reparations plan. The entire settlement depended in fact on the participation of the American financial community, called upon to join in a sort of "dollar diplomacy" in Europe.

Charles Dawes, an American banker, agreed to head a commission to prepare the plan. Presented to a conference in London in 1924, this Dawes plan set up a regular schedule of yearly German payments, starting at $250 million—far lower than that originally demanded by France. At the same time it arranged for a massive loan of private funds, mostly from U.S. banks, to assist the German government in making its first payments. In effect, the Dawes plan put in place a cumbersome system for international financial exchange. German reparations flowed primarily to France and to Great Britain. These countries applied the funds to regular payments on their war debts to the United States. American investors continued their profitable short-term loans to Germany, where the dollars proceeded back once again in reparations.

Dollars sustained the system, which in turn reassured international financial interests. Although German nationalists complained bitterly of the terrible imposition reparations placed on their country, in fact the payments came from U.S. loans, attracted until 1928 by high interest rates. The total paid by Germany before it abandoned payments in 1931 was about $2 billion; the total U.S. investments over that period was slightly over $2 billion. When these loans dwindled after U.S. investors in 1928 discovered Wall Street stock speculation more rewarding, the exchange began to fall apart. While it worked, governments avoided conflict, and U.S. dollars fueled the growth of the Western economy and indirectly of the entire international economy.

Agreement on reparations constituted one important element in the new international order put together in the mid-1920s. The second part of the system consisted of a security treaty among all the major European states. The new French cabinet abandoned the policy of imposing the Versailles peace settlement on Germany. Following the initiative of the British government, it turned to a new policy of collaboration with Germany. German cooperation was assured by the leadership of Gustav Stresemann, the outstanding German statesman of the 1920s, who anticipated that by working with Germany's former enemies he could gradually revise the peace settlement.

Thus the German, British, and French governments found new grounds on which to reach an agreement for their collective security. In 1925, their leaders met in Locarno, Switzerland, to negotiate a comprehensive diplomatic settlement. The Locarno Treaty had two major provisions; (1) the participating European states recognized the permanence of the western frontiers of Germany, a guarantee which constituted a regional security agreement, and (2) Germany accepted the permanent demilitarization of the Rhineland, leaving that region bordering on France and Belgium free of its troops. In return for agreeing to these limits on its sovereign powers, Germany obtained from the Allies the promise to withdraw part of their occupation troops (completely withdrawn in 1930). It also was granted admission to the League of Nations, an act which symbolized Germany's restored status as a major power in Europe.

The League of Nations in those years did hold out still the hope that, as Wilson had promised, it embodied a new collective force to protect peace. In the absence of the United States, Great Britain and France became the most important participants. Their leaders collaborated in debates of the executive council, where proposals emerged to settle peacefully conflicts among smaller states. As long as no great power was involved, the League appeared capable of preventing war. The World Court, made up of jurists elected by the League, offered its assistance to settle international disputes when the states involved accepted outside mediation. A third important component to the new system was the International Labor Organization, whose purpose was to improve conditions of labor. "Social justice," proclaimed the charter of the organization, was the only sound basis for "the establishment of universal peace." What was social justice? The League, dominated by Western states and minus the membership of the Soviet Union, looked to equality of opportunity, not collective property ownership and shared wealth, for the answer.

All three organizations operated on the principle that war was avoidable, that the causes for disputes among states were subject to discussion and compromise, and that statesmen would agree as reasonable people to international cooperation to protect the interests of their nations. The activities of the League represented a new direction in international affairs, but in reality it could not lead the way. The consensus among delegates rested on its narrow membership, excluding all colonial peoples and the Soviet Union. Its promises to resist aggression sounded hollow in the absence of the most powerful Western state, the United States. The ideal of the peaceful resolution of international disputes had become a European affair.

The chances for permanent peace in the 1920s were weakened also by political and economic shortcomings in the peace settlements themselves. In the first place, the European security system fashioned at Locarno had not provided any guarantee of the eastern borders of Germany. German conservatives such as Stresemann and military leaders refused to accept the permanence of Polish annexation of German lands. Some even dreamed of reestablishing German domination in the east, where for a few months in 1918 Germany had reigned supreme. Czechoslovakia held western territory inhabited largely by Germans, many of whom looked to Germany to replace their former Austrian rulers. France had signed alliances with Poland and Czechoslovakia, but Locarno revealed how heavily the French relied on Great Britain, itself not committed to protect those frontiers.

In the second place, international financial cooperation based on the Dawes plan depended not on the wisdom of statesmen but on the decision of private U.S. investors to use their wealth wisely. Uncontrolled, reckless investments on a large scale risked undermining the stability of this system. Stock speculation on Wall Street constituted a danger to the entire Western economy. In the third place, nationalist resistance to European empires was growing in Asian countries. Encouraging these anti-imperialist movements was the Soviet Union, whose Communist leaders were prepared to provide assistance to revolutionary nationalism. The link between anti-imperialist nationalism and war first became clear in East Asia. The success in the late 1920s of the nationalist movement in China, aided by Russia, challenged Japanese interests in north China. In response, the Japanese invaded Manchuria in 1931, the first act in what soon became Asian war. Neither the League nor the Western empires could contain the forces which within a decade destroyed the settlement of the 1920s.

THE YEARS OF PROSPERITY

Called by exuberant Americans the Roaring Twenties, the ten years following the end of the war gave Westerners good reason to believe that peace and prosperity had returned. Intellectuals created new forms of art and scientists explored uncharted areas of the natural world; inventors added basic discoveries to the technological marvels of the industrial economy; democratic government managed, with some exceptions, to permit citizens a voice in politics and provided many nationalities the opportunity to choose their own political leadership.

The cultural world of those years bound together intellectuals from all the countries of the West. Paris provided a home for American writers, among them Ernest Hemingway and Gertrude Stein, who found there the excitement and encouragement they lacked in their own country. Composers such as the Russians Sergei Prokofiev and Igor Stravinsky created new forms of classical music while jazz musicians from America introduced Europeans to a new popular music. The "International" school of modern architecture, under Walter Gropius, grew and flourished in Germany and found disciples in France and the United States. The discoveries of Albert Einstein set the direction for new developments in the scientific community, where atomic physicists came closer than ever to understanding the forces of matter and energy. The Freudian school of psychoanalysis spread across the West from the United States to the Soviet Union and provided inspiration for artists and writers exploring new dimension of human behavior. All these trends, emerging before the war, became major intellectual features of the cultural life of the 1920s.

In that age of exciting discoveries, pessimistic voices warned of darker human forces of destruction. Some writers extolled the glories of violent struggle and national supremacy, carrying into the years of peace the rhetorical violence which had characterized the wartime. The Expressionist artists of Germany exposed on canvas the ugliness and hatred which they sensed continued to divide classes and nations. The German philosopher Oswald Spengler singled out the postwar "revolutions of stupidity and vulgarity" to prove that Western civilization had, like Roman civilization millenia earlier, entered its inevitable final stage of decline. His major work, *The Decline of the West,* had particular success among fellow Germans, who found comfort in projecting their pessimism at the future of their country onto a larger Western stage.

Economic Recovery

While these debates and discoveries reverberated within the world of intellectuals, technological developments produced startling changes in everyday life. The automobile emerged as a vehicle for individual transportation, cheap enough in the United States to be accessible to the middle classes. Architects raised to greater and greater heights the building which epitomized the new metropolis, the skyscraper. Electricity spread through cities and into homes in rural and urban areas. With it came the radio, a new form of communication bringing global events almost instantaneously within reach of individuals. The plane, used extensively first as an instrument of war, became in years of peace a means of rapid transportation across continents and even oceans. Of all the public events of the 1920s, Charles Lindberg's solo crossing of the Atlantic in 1927 aroused the greatest enthusiasm and captured best the popular vision of the future. Acclaimed throughout Europe and America, he appeared the new civilian hero who used the power of technology for the conquest of space, not territory, and whose exploit dissolved national frontiers. In this respect, as in others, the "old" continent looked to the "new" for inspiration.

Postwar social trends carried forward some of the changes which war had introduced. The demand for "white-collar" positions, from clerical to professional, grew particularly rapidly. Filling these jobs were an increasing number of women, for whom the end of the fighting had brought a decline in war-related work. Their opportunities remained restricted both by social prejudice and by continued difficulty to obtain advanced education. Their work was more likely to be clerical than professional; some low-level positions, such as operators of the new telephone exchanges, became exclusively feminine work.

Still, the gradual trend in the West toward women's emancipation was continuing. Women's right to vote became law among northern countries from the United States to Great Britain and Scandinavia. These reforms came slowly, for they encountered strong opposition from conservatives to whom the proper woman's role remained, in the German saying, "children, kitchen, church." A new Western image of the liberated woman was the "flapper" (a term drawn from the new popular dances, applied generally to women who enjoyed partying and a free life), a scandal to many people, but to others the symbol of a woman asserting her right to her own private life.

Economic prosperity was the foundation on which rested postwar recovery from the material and psychological damage of war. The first five years after the war were a period of economic instability and reconstruction. The most dramatic sign of the continued shortages and of popular pessimism toward the future was inflation, which disrupted economic life in many countries. The worst price increases occurred in the defeated states. In Germany money virtually ceased in 1922–23 to function as a medium of exchange; by late 1923, boxes had replaced wallets and handbags to carry the depreciated currency, which just before its replacement had one-trillioneth its prewar value. France too suffered from rapid price increases in 1924. In both countries, the means to end runaway inflation came when the governments replaced the old currency, taken out of circulation in exchange for new bills. The confidence that had once characterized those who saved was undermined. Before the inflation ended many debtors had repaid their creditors with devalued

money. Savings became worthless; the resulting insecurity of the middle classes weakened their loyalty to moderate political leadership and prepared them, when a new economic crisis appeared in the 1930s, to support conservative, even antidemocratic movements.

Global trade and finance remained concentrated in Western hands, but no longer did Great Britain coordinate and stabilize investments and encourage free trade. World trade expanded in the 1920s, with Japan and the United States enjoying the highest rate of growth in exports. New York, not London, became the financial capital of the West; the United States, once a debtor nation to European investors, became the major creditor, lending over $6 billion to foreign countries between 1924 and 1929. Great Britain, by contrast, lent half that amount, another indication of its declining financial role in the world economy.

The governments of the European states had in these conditions to assume greater responsibility than before for economic growth. One important new policy was major investments to assist in the reconstruction of devastated areas and to help industry to adapt to peacetime conditions. Some industries never recovered. British coal production, encountering new competition from foreign coal and losing markets to diesel motors, could not maintain its wartime levels. Hundreds of thousands of British miners remained permanently unemployed.

A second innovation in economic policy among European states was their effort to promote foreign trade. They took steps to stimulate commercial exports, disrupted by the needs of war, and to protect their own producers from foreign competition. Some devised new means to open up foreign markets. The French government undervalued its new 1924 franc, thereby lowering the foreign price of its goods and encouraging exports. Great Britain, on the other hand, continued to defend free trade and returned the pound sterling to its prewar value on the gold standard. The British leaders' attempt to resist the statist tide was not successful, for they discovered that they had made British goods less competitive overseas while facilitating foreign sales in Great Britain. The smaller states in Eastern and Southern Europe, which suffered from the decline of international food prices after 1925, raised tariff barriers on imports. Thus state intervention in economic affairs, though not as intensive as during the war, remained far greater than in prewar times. Increasingly, trade and financial policies tended to reflect national interests, a move toward economic "autarchy," that is, isolation, which accelerated in the 1930s.

New economic and social trends were appearing in non-Western countries, colonial and independent, in those same years. With the advantage of hindsight, we can identify two key developments which would continue into the postimperial era. First, these lands were becoming the source of vital minerals and of agricultural produce in the international economy, providing raw materials for industry and the urban populations located principally in the West. Second, the gradual diffusion of medical care and the improved food supplies launched in the 1920s a global population explosion. For the first time the rate of population growth in Asia and Africa rose above that of Europe. Terrible famines and epidemics, previously the principal natural limits on growth, declined in severity. By 1930 the estimated world population had reached 2 billion, up from 1.5 billion in 1900. The short life expectancy of the bulk of the population in these regions remained far below that of the Western peoples, and the living conditions for most were barely sufficient for survival. The basic improvements suggested by the growing population were at best imperceptible, yet they heralded a gradual change in attitudes of the poor masses from resignation to the hope of better conditions for themselves and their offspring. This profound "revolution of rising expectations," just beginning to appear in those years, was to become one of the central features of public activity and private life in the decades following the Second World War.

The price paid for these improvements was the increased dependency of the economies of these non-Western lands on the international economy. Gradually more small farmers were beginning to raise cash crops for sale, entering for the first time a national or foreign market. In Africa, crops such as cotton and cocoa spread, under the encouragement of good prices in the 1920s and of merchants linked with European companies such as Unilever. At the same time, Western mining corporations were expanding their exploitation of the rich mineral deposits of certain African regions, providing employment for African labor. The companies paid miserable wages to these African miners, who migrated from great distances to work in the copper mines of Katanga in the Belgian Congo, in the tin mines of Niger, or in the gold mines of South Africa where employers forced out the white workers to hire cheap black miners. Gradually an African working class was beginning to appear around these European-owned enterprises.

In Asian lands the expansion of the production of food and of raw materials was accompanied by the development here and there of industry, some of which was owned by Asians. The principal food crop grown for the international market was rice, which became a vital part of the economy of countries such as Burma. The increased demand in the West for tires led to a boom as well in rubber production, extracted from rubber trees in South Asia as well as in Central Africa and in South America. As long as Europe and North America prospered, so to a far lesser extent did the farmers and growers of such commodities and so, in a very meager way, did the laborers working on the plantations. Only in a few locations did an industrial economy in Asia develop in those years, principally in Japan, and to a lesser extent in India. In both lands, textile manufacturing had expanded rapidly during the war, and continued to grow in the 1920s. The dominant characteristic–and their greatest weakness—of the Asian and even more the African economies, however, was their role in providing raw materials to the international economy. Their markets lay elsewhere, and the prices received for their goods depended on global forces of supply and demand over which they had no control.

Until the mid-1920s, prices on these commodities tended to rise. Those good years came to an end in the mid-1920s, when world prices on these commodities began a long, steady fall. By the end of the decade rubber had lost two-thirds of its value; areas in Latin America and Asia dependent on rubber sales experienced a severe depression. Similar difficulties, though not so acute, affected the rice-growing areas, for production of rice, along with wheat, was increasing far more rapidly than demand. Farmers and laborers, dependent on the sale of a single commodity, were the first to suffer. The economic decline of these regions hurt in turn international industrial exports and, even before the 1929 financial crisis, pointed to the coming global depression.

International economic expansion developed particularly in new industries, such as petroleum. The principal international oil corporations—Standard Oil of New Jersey, Royal Dutch-Shell, British Petroleum—moved into the Middle East where vast petroleum deposits were being discovered. With the backing of their governments, they set up an informal agreement to dominate the area near the Per-

sian Gulf with greatest known reserves (a territory marked on their map by a Red Line, the name by which their agreement was known). They also fixed international crude oil prices to protect the profits of American producers competing in Europe with cheaper Middle Eastern oil, whose sale price in Europe was kept at the level of American petroleum prices (the "Gulf-plus system"). The control these companies possessed over the extraction and price of petroleum made them international political as well as economic powers. Oil from the Middle Eastern wells found new markets as petroleum demand rose in the industrial West. The oil companies enjoyed excellent profits, only a small fraction of which went in the form of royalties to the governments on whose territory the oil was extracted. The low price of crude oil (below $2.00 a barrel) provided a new source of cheap energy for transportation and industry in the Western economies. In this manner new inventions such as the internal combustion engine sparked new industries in the West, and led to a demand for raw materials such as oil and rubber provided by distant lands where Western corporations controlled sales and prices. The international economy of 1900 was gradually evolving into an interdependent global economy, divided between a prosperous "North" and dependent "South."

The economic recovery of Europe brought national incomes to prewar levels by 1925. Industrial growth continued at a steady, though slow pace for three more years in Europe and North America. The benefits appeared in rising standards of living for many Europeans and in employment for most workers. The recovery remained incomplete—the unemployed miners of England were one reminder of that fact. Farm incomes could not keep up with manufacturing, preventing the rural population from enjoying the benefits of the new consumer society. The United States played a key role in the economic prosperity of those years. It provided the bulk of the investment funds for public and private lenders and constituted the single most important foreign market for European and Japanese manufactured goods.

The U.S. political and financial leaders relied on the impersonal operations of the capitalist system to ensure that economic growth continued, ignoring the reckless speculation on the stock market and intervening in economic affairs only to raise tariffs to protect U.S. farmers and manufacturers. Protective tariffs and benign neglect of stock speculation both appeared in the short-term profitable to the American economy. Economists would later conclude that these two aspects of U.S. domestic policy damaged seriously world economic relations. The United States failed in this area to provide the constructive leadership which Great Britain had once given the global capitalist system. The prosperity of the Roaring Twenties was not built on solid foundations.

European Democracies

The new postwar settlement depended on political stability as well as on economic growth. Diplomatic collaboration among Western states relied upon a shared political faith in democratic government and human rights. With the exception of Italy, the major powers in those years all returned to a political system that recognized majority rule, minority rights, and the obligation to serve in one manner or another the needs of the people. Great Britain and France resumed politics as usual through the workings of their parliamentary systems. Elections brought shifts in parliamentary majorities and new cabinets, but they did not change the fundamental institutions or challenge the democratic and capitalist consensus on which political stability rested. No outstanding leaders emerged in those years. No new reforms were introduced to resolve continuing

problems of social inequality and the impoverishment of part of the population. Communist parties called for proletarian revolution but attracted only a small following. For the first time the British Labor party won in 1923 sufficient parliamentary seats to lead a coalition cabinet, but it lasted less than a year and lacked the political support to implement Labor's socialist program. Political stability came at the price of reform; power remained in the hands of prewar leaders lacking a new political vision and preoccupied with healing the wounds of war. To most British and French citizens, adherence to the old ways represented a reassuring sign of security.

Many other European states adopted the parliamentary system in the years after the war. Political revolutions produced new leadership and new political institutions throughout Central Europe. The common characteristics of most were democratic constitutions and parliamentary government. New states in Poland, Czechoslovakia, and Yugoslavia respected at least the form, often the substance, of liberalism. The attraction of the liberal political system remained strong in Europe.

Germany's experience in democratic government constituted the key to the success of postwar peacemaking. Moderate political leadership there depended upon the cooperation of socialists, liberals, and conservatives. When coalition politics later failed, so did democratic government, opening the way to fanatical nationalists to lead the country toward dictatorship and new war. The constitutional monarchy of the German Empire had placed great powers in the emperor and his chancellor; the militaristic wartime regime concentrated leadership in even fewer hands. Those institutions and leaders vanished in the November 1918 revolution. Political leadership of the new regime passed to the largest democratic movement, the Social-Democratic party, whose leader became chancellor on November 9. Supported by crowds of demonstrators in the streets of Berlin, he proclaimed the founding of the German Republic.

What shape would the new German state assume? The outcome of the revolution depended partly upon the new political leaders, partly upon the violent conflicts among demobilized officers and soldiers, workers and revolutionaries, which swept the country in the winter of 1918–19. Revolutionary socialists planned to introduce, if necessary by armed insurrection, a workers' state similar to that the Russian Communists had formed one year before. They did not receive the backing of the German workers' councils, formed in many cities that winter. Representatives from the councils agreed in December to support a democratic constitutional regime and to disband their organization. The

German workers preferred orderly democratic reform to proletarian revolution and radical dictatorship.

In the struggle over Germany's political future, socialist leaders relied on this working-class support. But they depended also on the backing of the officers of the German army, with whom they were prepared to collaborate against their radical enemies. To preserve public order they kept in place the officer corps, a bastion of Prussian militarism and doubtful ally of German democracy. An uprising did occur in Berlin in January 1919, organized by the revolutionary Spartacist movement seeking to overthrow German capitalism. It was quickly and ruthlessly repressed by military units. The spirit of war reigned in the streets of Berlin and other cities, where groups of self-proclaimed "patriotic" officers and soldiers attacked "Bol-

Visions of the German Revolution (1): Poster Entitled "Elect Spartacus," 1919. (*Poster Collection/Hoover Institution Archives*)

Visions of the German Revolution (2): Poster entitled "Spartacus at Work" by the Union of Struggle against Bolshevism, approx. 1919. (*Poster Collection/Hoover Institution Archives*)

sheviks," by which they designated any radical socialist movement. The new state had made a dangerous decision to leave in place the military elite, along with the administration and judiciary, of the old imperial state.

In 1919, the institutions of the democratic republic took shape. Its constitution, prepared in the city of Weimar, was a model of political equity. It created a cabinet system of government, chosen by a majority in the parliament (*Reichstag*). An elected president had few powers save in time of emergency when he could rule by decree. When the first elec-

tions were held, German voters had the choice among many parties, no one of which won a majority in parliament. The Social Democratic party was still the largest parliamentary group, but it had to share power in a coalition with liberal parties supporting free enterprise and opposed to major social reforms. This new leadership was obliged to sign the Versailles Treaty when called to France by the Allies in mid-1919. Required to carry out the provisions of the treaty and limited in its powers by coalition politics, the new democratic regime began under difficult conditions.

Its task was made even harder by the militaristic illusions of many German conservatives and war veterans. Very quickly nationalists obliterated the historical truth of military defeat by inventing the myth of a mighty Germany "stabbed in the back" at war's end by defeatist Jewish and socialist traitors whom they blamed for the armistice. They preserved the memory of a "greater Germany" victorious in Eastern Europe and damned the Versailles Treaty for its supposed—and nonexistent— "war guilt" clause. We cannot easily explain such widespread mystification, except by pointing to the social and political turmoil of postwar Germany and to the extraordinary nationalist fervor of many Germans. One important group prepared to believe these myths was made up of war veterans who clung to their identity of national warriors and refused the transition to civilian life. One eloquent veteran (and future Nazi Stormtrooper) dismissed "those people who told us the war was over," arguing that "we ourselves are the war. It fascinates us with the enticing urge to destroy." In their fight against "traitors" and "Bolsheviks," he and his comrades in arms "marched onto the battlefields of the postwar world just as we had gone into battle on the western front."

These fanatical nationalists kept German politics in a state of siege for several years. They were responsible for hundreds of assassinations. Some veterans formed special military units, called Free Corps, to carry the war into public life. In March 1920, an armed insurrection of Free Corps units in Berlin seized control of the state for a few days until a general strike by workers and state administrators forced them to surrender. Others joined new political parties. One, calling itself the German National Socialist Workers' party, promised to overthrow the Versailles Treaty and to build a powerful new German nation-state purged of aliens, especially the Jews. Its leader was a war veteran named Adolph Hitler.

The year 1923 provided these groups another opportunity to overthrow the democratic state. The French occupation of the Ruhr and the ruinous inflation stirred up widespread opposition to the Weimar government. The National Socialists began an armed insurrection in Munich which they hoped would produce a "march on Berlin" by Weimar's enemies and the creation of a new nationalist regime. (They took hope from the example of the Italian Fascist party, which had one year before succeeded in this manner in seizing power.) The uprising failed, largely because most of the regular army stood by its agreement to defend the Weimar Republic.

Under these conditions the very survival of German democracy was noteworthy. It was protected by labor unions on the one hand, by the regular army on the other. A majority of voters indicated throughout the 1920s that they preferred parties committed to democratic rule. Conservative politicians like Gustav Stresemann, originally hostile to the Weimar regime, came to accept its existence. Enthusiasm for freedom appeared less noticeable than satisfaction at improved economic conditions of the post-1923 years. It may well be, as one German historian claimed at the time, that "a secret Germany" longed for "its emperors and heroes." If so,

the yearning did not disrupt the political stability of those years.

The peak of Weimar democracy came in the period following the diplomatic and financial settlements of 1924–25. Workers benefited from social welfare and public housing reforms, the work primarily of the Social Democratic party. U.S. investors, attracted by high interest rates, poured billions of dollars into Germany. Industry revived and resumed its international operations. The giant chemical firm I. G. Farben signed an agreement in 1926 with Standard Oil of New Jersey to share patents and research developments in petroleum products, some of which proved of vital military importance. A U.S. official observed that the arrangement proved these international corporations considered "war a transitory phenomenon and business a kind of permanent thing." U.S.-German economic ties were strong. Profits and technological innovation constituted the common bonds. Less fortunate were the German farmers, caught in the global agricultural depression, and small businesses and savers for whom the inflation had been ruinous. Their bitter voices were not heard, however, in those years.

The Weimar cabinets provided adquate leadership for a country so recently in the throes of war and revolution. Coalition governments brought together representatives of the various competing moderate political parties. Extremist parties such as the National Socialists lost votes, appearing a lunatic fringe grouping a handful of fanatics. The new German foreign policy, the work of Foreign Minister Gustav Stresemann, incorporated Germany in the European security system and earned the state a place in the League of Nations. The government obtained the backing of parliament for this policy, a convincing sign Germany had accepted the Versailles Treaty. Stresemann's plans for the recovery of German land in the east and the secret buildup of German military did not disturb the public image of international tranquility.

In 1925 the first popular election of the president of the Republic took place. Candidates from all major parties competed, and so too did the war hero, Marshal von Hindenburg. A majority of Germans, drawn more by memories of past imperial glories than by hopes for a restoration of the old regime, chose Hindenburg. Although he once had embodied the militarism of the empire, he swore a presidential oath to uphold the democratic constitution and kept his word during his early years in office. He was old, however; as the years passed he proved increasingly dependent on trusted aides, nationalist conservatives more prone than he to use power to undermine the Weimar regime. In the prosperous years of the late 1920s, political and social hostility was muted and the parliamentary government assured political stability. Germany appeared a part of the new European system.

Italian Fascism

Only Italy among the principal states of Western Europe abandoned democratic rule. The political transformation there constituted a revolution, producing a regime whose very title came to designate a new ideology and method of government. Until the 1920s, Italian political evolution had followed the general pattern of other European countries. After national unification in the 1860s, the country was governed by a cabinet chosen by a parliament, under the authority of a constitutional monarch. Actual power lay in the hands of a small political elite, altered only slightly by periodic elections. Coalition cabinets protected property interests, largely by limiting social reforms. The poverty of southern laborers and northern workers was not their concern. Their bitterest opponent was the Catholic church,

whose powers had been severely curtailed by the new nation-state. These hidden weaknesses became serious after war and economic mobilization created new opponents and revealed the shortcomings of the parliamentary regime.

In 1915, Italian nationalist leaders brought Italy into the First World War on the side of the Allies. They did so primarily in the hope of substantial territorial rewards, promised in a secret treaty. Although Italy emerged from the fighting on the side of the victors, the experience of total war proved a defeat for the Italian state and people. Its armies won no great victories until the very end and suffered a major defeat at Caporetto in 1917. Soldiers blamed the "civilians" and most particularly political leaders for lack of support, corruption, and incompetence. Nationalists were outraged by the refusal of the Allies in 1919 to cede to Italy land along the eastern Adriatic—the Dalmatian coast south of Trieste—and made the government the scapegoat for their disillusionment.

Demobilized soldiers returned to their homes to face unemployment, and many turned to political movements promising radical reform. Some joined workers in the new Communist movement; others became members of the Fascist party founded by the army veteran and nationalist Benito Mussolini. Fear of "Bolshevism" spread in Italy when workers seized factories and farm laborers claimed estate land for themselves. Political leaders preferred to let the conflicts slowly subside rather than to call out troops and risk bloody rioting. In fact socialist revolution never threatened Italy. Nonetheless, some industrialists and large landowners saw radicals everywhere and organized for their own protection private armed guards. In those conditions, politicians lost authority, and voices, in and out of parliament, were raised calling for a new nationalist order to impose discipline and unity and to restore

Italian honor. These postwar social and political conflicts existed in other countries. The peculiarity of Italy consisted in the weakness of its political leadership, on the one hand, and on the other the extraordinary skill of a political demagogue, Benito Mussolini, and the unrestrained violence of his Fascist movement.

The leader of the Fascists was a former antiwar socialist who had become a fanatical nationalist in the war. The image of the warrior fighting for Italy suited his personality better than the proletarian hero of socialism. Mussolini served in the Italian army, an experience that marked his personality and his political philosophy. Demobilized after being wounded, he launched a political movement intended to carry the spirit of the front-line soldier into civilian life. Prone to violence himself, the war gave him a new vocabulary for the glorification of struggle, both the end and means of his nationalist cause. He brought to the Fascist movement his talents, in the words of one biographer, as "an actor, a dissimulator, an exhibitionist,"[1] who gloried in violence and the pursuit of power. The war provided him, as it did Hitler, schooling for political combat on the national stage.

Backed by other disillusioned war veterans, he preached a message of militaristic rejuvenation of the Italian nation. He called for the expulsion of the "corrupt" politicians from government, the end of labor strikes and agitation, and the defeat of the "subversive, internationalist" Communists and socialists. He scorned ideals such as "liberty," preferring "discipline" for the Italian nation. In place of a parliamentary regime he proposed a strong state purged of all democratic parties under a real leader—himself. Fascism in its original Italian version was more a

set of nationalist slogans and images of masculine valor and violence than a precise doctrine. It constituted a vague political ideology for nationalist revolution and dictatorship, turning the spirit of war into a revolutionary creed.

To achieve his goal of overthrowing parliamentary government, Mussolini organized a new type of combat party, the *Fasci di combattimento* (Groups of Combat). From this term came the name of his party. The elite of the movement were the "fighters," a paramilitary group dressed in black shirts with heavy belt buckles useful in street fighting against Communists, labor leaders, and other groups they accused of undermining the strength of the nation. Mussolini glorified war and combat as the true test of a man and of a nation. He turned his party into an instrument for the violent seizure of power, bringing war into politics. His supporters came in large numbers from war veterans, his money from nationalists and Italian businessmen frightened by the rise of revolutionary social protest.

Between 1920 and 1922, he gradually made a place for his party in Italian political life by defying public order and democratic ideals. The fact that the Fascists never won over 15 percent of the vote in free elections meant nothing to Mussolini, since he believed that he and his followers proved their fitness to lead the nation not by popularity but by determination and struggle. He used his armed bands to attack elected socialist city governments—even expelling the municipal leaders in the major city of Milan—to close socialist newspapers, and to attack rival political groups. His movement had no concrete political program, replaced by emotional appeals to national unity, by warnings of Communist subversion, and by attacks on parliamentary incompetence and corruption.

Although beatings and even murder were

---

[1] Denis Mack Smith, *Mussolini* (New York, 1982), p. 111.

an integral part of his tactics, he still received support from Italy's political and business elite. Businessmen contributed funds to a movement promising to destroy socialism. Army officers despised Italian politics and sympathized with Mussolini's call for new national leadership. Powerful political leaders were prepared to collaborate with him to end what they considered the growing disorder of parliamentary rule. Even the Italian king was reluctant to order the use of force against these "good patriots." Mussolini turned these internal weaknesses to his advantage in his plan to seize power. In October 1922, he ordered his fighting squads to "march on Rome" to overthrow the democratically elected government. His action was largely bluff, for troops and police forces could easily have dispersed his squads. He counted mainly on the reluctance of the authorities to use force, and he was right. Before his squads even reached the capital, the king had invited him to become prime minister of the Italian cabinet. Mussolini began his rule as the legal head of government.

Within three years Italian democracy ceased to exist. Political opponents were intimidated by threats of violence, others were attacked, and some were murdered. Elections were held for the last time in 1924 but were so manipulated that the Fascist party was assured absolute control of parliament. Most political leaders quietly dropped out of politics, preferring their own safety to the physical danger of resistance or placing a higher value on order and "discipline" than on democratic liberties. Soon political parties were banned and the free press closed. Labor unions were placed under the direct control of the state and strikes outlawed. Property owners felt secure in their possessions.

A policy of "corporatism" created a large state bureaucracy to oversee industry and agriculture but left real control and profits in the hands of owners. The Fascist state made peace with the Catholic church by granting it control over marriage and the family and making payment for property seized by the state in 1870. No social or economic revolution occurred. On the contrary, this "revolution" defended traditional values and protected the wealthy. It was "radical" only in its destruction of democratic government.

Italy became a single-party dictatorship, controlled by the Fascist party and headed by Mussolini. He encouraged the cult of his leadership, extolled by his followers as "divine Caesar" and "sublime redeemer in the Roman heavens." In a divided country such as Italy, he proved that a small but violent political movement could use democratic liberties to destroy democracy. The conditions which gave birth to the Fascist movement in Italy were created by the war—the social unrest produced by the economic hardships and demobilization, the disillusionment of veterans trained to kill and persuaded they had special rights to lead the nation, the arousal of nationalist passions which no postwar settlement could satisfy, and finally the weakness and corruption of a parliamentary regime more concerned with its own interests than with popular discontent. Fascism provided Europe and the world with a new political ideology and a model of a new type of dictatorship. In place of the Communist message of class conflict and proletarian dictatorship, it proposed national unity and conservative dictatorship. In the 1920s it appeared a peculiar Italian product. When hard times returned in the 1930s, fascism emerged as a powerful political movement in other European countries. In the political turmoil of nation building in non-Western countries that followed the Second World War, elements of fascism appeared in the programs of some nationalist leaders in those lands as well.

POSTWAR IMPERIAL DIPLOMACY AND NEW PROBLEMS OF IMPERIALISM

Allied peacemaking reached out beyond Europe to distant parts of the globe. Everywhere, the Allies confronted as a result of the war political problems which had not existed before. They redrew the map of large parts of the Middle East where the Ottoman Empire had once ruled, creating new political boundaries to form Syria, Iraq, and other small states. Within these artificial boundaries, they established new Arab leaders. Great Britain could not so easily dominate Egypt, where nationalist opposition to their protectorate forced the British to grant formal independence. The Turkish officers, intent on saving their homeland, were able to call on the support of their own people to defeat Allied plans for partition. In Africa, the colonies of Germany passed under Allied "trusteeship," joining their other colonies. Only in the Far East did the imperial states adopt a new formula for international collaboration, based on an American proposal to renounce spheres of influence in Chinese and Russian lands and to reduce naval armaments. Here as elsewhere, the key decisions regarding peace and political power were made in Allied capitals.

Islam in the Middle East

The Middle East presented Western statesmen with complex problems of postwar rule. They had agreed among themselves to divide up the lands of the Ottoman Empire, but they faced opposition both from the Arabs, whose armed uprising they had backed, and from the Turks, the ruling elite of the defeated empire. The lands of the Middle East, the cradle of civilization five thousand years before, had suffered over the millenia from interminable wars and the decay of agriculture. The population, partly nomadic, partly peasant, partly urban, was deeply divided as well by religion, language, and tribal bonds.

Most of the peoples of the empire were Muslim, of the Sunni branch which honored the succession of Muslim political and religious authorities from Mohammed's time through the medieval Arab empires down to the Ottoman Empire. All Muslims, in total numbers the second largest religion in the world, looked to the Koran for the word of God and obeyed the key rites and practices of Islam. They prostrated themselves daily in prayer to show their submission and homage to their God and to his prophet—"there is no god but Allah and Mohammed is His prophet." They obeyed the law of the Koran, the sacred book of Islam. Religious rules dictated important elements in their daily lives, including daily prayer, fasting in the month called Ramadan, and pilgrimage to the Arabian city of Mecca, most sacred of Muslim holy places.

The strength of Islam in the early twentieth century was great by comparison with Christianity, many of whose followers had by then come to place more importance on secular values such as material success and to identify most closely with members of their nation. The Muslim religion remained still the most important force in the lives of most of the faithful throughout the Ottoman lands and elsewhere. Yet it too suffered from bitter internal divisions, the most important of which was the split between Sunnis and the Shia, concentrated in Iran, who honored their own line of descendants from Mohammed and rejected the leadership of the caliph. The impact of secularism, that is, the acceptance of rational ethical guidelines in the place of the Koran, was making itself felt among some Muslims, including many of the

Turkish military elite of the Ottoman Empire.

The Turkish National Revolution

The Ottoman Empire had provided for centuries political stability under despotic rule. Having joined the coalition of Central Powers, it shared in their defeat. The sultan was supreme ruler of his lands and religious leader, or caliph, of the Sunni Muslims. His powers had been challenged once already before the war by reformist officers attempting to strengthen the army and the state against Western imperialism. These "Young Turks" had failed in their effort then, and the war kept them loyal to their ruler. Their army could not, however, defeat the combined forces of the Allies, which included British, Arab, and later Greek troops. That war and the threatened partition of Turkish lands revived the plans of these officers to undertake radical political changes. As in Eastern Europe, the harsh lessons of war led there to political revolution.

After the Ottoman Empire surrendered to the Allies in November 1918, much of its territory was occupied by Allied military forces. British troops and their Arab allies controlled the Fertile Crescent, the area from the Tigris and Euphrates Rivers to Palestine. Greek troops took control of the islands of the Aegean Sea and the Anatolian coast around the port of Smyrna, where half a million Greeks lived. The straits, including Constantinople, were under Allied military and naval occupation. The wartime plans for the partition of the empire became the central feature of the peace treaty drawn up in 1919. Presented to the sultan for his approval, it left only central Turkey in a dwarfed Ottoman Empire.

The fate of the empire and their sultan mattered less to the Turkish officers than that of the Turkish people. If implemented, the treaty would have left many Turks under foreign (and Christian) rule, some incorporated in the Greek state. Refusing to bow to Allied terms or the sultan's orders, they gathered about a military commander, Mustafa Kemal (later to take the name of Kemal Ataturk), to organize in 1920 a nationalist revolutionary movement. Their aim was to create a Turkish state and to form a Turkish army to defend their new nation-state from partition. Opposed by the sultan, they at first ignored him. Later, in 1923, they abolished the empire and the positions of sultan and caliph. In doing so they made clear the importance they attached to the secular (nonreligious) as well as the national goal of their movement. Their army was a national force, recruited solely from the Turkish population, and united under Kemal's leadership to gather into one Western-type state the area inhabited by Turks. Combating foreign invaders to create their own nation-state, the Turkish population supported the movement with the zeal of Muslim warriors in a Holy War.

The task of military conquest was made easier by the weakness of the surrounding states and the unwillingness of the Allies to intervene in yet another war. In the East, the Turkish army encountered little resistance in Armenia, where few Armenians were left after the wartime tragedy of evacuation and massacre. In the Northeast were Red Army forces, but both Soviet and Turkish leaders preferred cooperation to war. Turkey agreed to leave to the Soviet state a small part of eastern Armenia; in exchange, the Communist regime provided military aid to the Turkish nationalists. Good relations with Turkey fitted the Soviet policy of supporting enemies of the Western states and gave the Turks, surrounded by enemies, one ally. The Turkish nationalists did not support Marxist revolution. In fact, at the time they had arrested and executed the leaders of the

Turkish Communist party. Sharing common enemies, however, the two young states overlooked political differences. In that temporary alliance appeared the pattern of nationalist and socialist collaboration, apparent elsewhere in later years, which played a major role in the decline of Western imperial ascendance.

Having come to terms with the Soviet state, the Turkish army turned west to attack Greek forces. In 1920, Greek leaders had ordered their troops to invade central Anatolia. They, like other nationalists in Eastern Europe whose dreams far exceeded the means at their disposal, imagined a Greater Greece that would control all the lands around the Aegean Sea, in ancient times dominated by Greek city-states. They realized that the new Turkish nation-state stood in the way of their goal. Their decision to seek territory by conquest proved a political blunder and a tragedy for many of their people. In the Greek-Turkish war of 1920–22, the Turkish army succeeded in expelling Greek forces from all Asia Minor. The distrust which had long divided Greeks and Turks turned in the war to violent hatred. Of the Greeks living in Anatolia (1.3 million in all), many died in the course of the fighting. Others abandoned their homes when the Greek army retreated, seeking refuge in the Greek mainland; the remainder followed after the war. At the same time, half a million Turks left their homes in Greek territory to live in Turkey.

For the first time, nation building was accompanied by mass death and the flight of millions of refugees to escape rule by another people. Nationalism was a two-faced ideology, presenting on one side an image of strong bonds of trust and solidarity among the people of one nation and on the other the ugly mask of hatred toward other nations. The Turkish nationalist revolution had succeeded. The Western powers prepared a

new peace treaty in 1923, leaving most of Asia Minor, including the straits, within Turkish borders. The Turkish nationalist leaders introduced sweeping internal reforms, creating a new constitutional order, including a parliament and elected president, and replacing Koranic law by civil law. The events in Turkey represented in their broad outline the prototype of nationalist revolutions of later decades. The extraordinary influence of Kemal Ataturk resembled that of other nationalist leaders later who, at a time of social and political turmoil, won popular devotion and loyalty to both their policies and to themselves. This power, peculiar to times of crisis, is called "charisma." Second, the Turkish leaders were able to create a mass movement in support of national unity. Finally, they relied particularly on an elite organization—in this case, the army—from which the cadres of the new state came. Out of the ruins of the Ottoman Empire had emerged a new Turkish nation-state.

In achieving this goal, the Turks had distanced themselves from the rest of the Middle East. Having once ruled as conquerors, they pulled back into their own land and created new borders which were national and cultural frontiers as well. The single strongest bond among peoples of that region had been Islam. Ataturk set out to exclude Muslim law and the Muslim religious leaders from his new nation-state and to replace customary social practice, sanctioned by Islam, with Western models. The emancipation of women became a major symbol of his crusade to modernize his country. The new laws of Turkey ended the legal subordination of women to the head of the family, made schooling and jobs available to them, and forbade women to wear the veil, symbol of their seclusion from public life. In defying religious custom, Ataturk was seeking to rid his country of the dead weight of the past to

create a new Turkey. Even though he ultimately failed in his most ambitious plans, he
launched his country on a nationalist revolution.

Imperialism in the Middle East

Among the Arab peoples of the Middle East
there emerged after the war other nationalist
movements, but nowhere so powerful as Turkish nationalism. The war had destroyed the old
order and mobilized Arab forces, but it had
also strengthened the influence of Great Britain and France in the area. During the war
Arab tribesmen under the Hashim clan (headed by Sheik Hussein) had organized with the
assistance of the British a large-scale revolt
against Ottoman rule. They had extended
their conquest as far north as the city of
Damascus, capital of the Syrian province
whose borders extended from the eastern
shores of the Mediterranean to the province of
Iraq.

Hussein and his followers dreamed of creating a large Arab state in the Middle East, a
vision which Arab nationalists drew from the
Arab empires of the Middle Ages. But in the
twentieth century the Arab-speaking peoples
were deeply divided. Even in Arabia, Hussein's
leadership was opposed by the clan of Ibn
Saud, who in the mid-1920s led his own forces
in a successful revolt to form the state of Saudi
Arabia. In Syrian lands the population was divided into many religious and clan groups.
Muslims were split into five separate sects (of
which the Sunni were the most important) and
Christians into ten different sects. These divisions prevented the emergence of a powerful
nationalist movement and permitted the Allied
states to divide and rule separate parts of the
area.

During the Allied peace negotiations, the
British and French leaders laid claim to Middle Eastern land. They had agreed in a secret
treaty to this partition of Ottoman territory.
Standing in the way of the agreement in
1919 were the new peace objectives of
Wilson, who defended the right of colonial
peoples to ultimate self-rule. The negotiators reached a compromise between these
contradictory objectives by creating the mandate system, applied to all non-Western areas
taken over by the Allies. In the Middle East,
Great Britain and France assumed responsibility in "mandated" territories to provide
"advice and assistance" until the peoples
there could rule themselves. In effect,
French and British troops and colonial administrators took in one form or another
control of government. French troops
moved into the northern part of the former
Ottoman province of Syria, expelling Hussein's forces from Damascus and setting up
the states of Syria and, in the coastal area
where most Christians lived, Lebanon. The
British allowed two sons of Hussein to rule as
kings in most of their mandated lands—the
states of Iraq and Transjordan (the area between Iraq and the Jordan River).

In all these territories Arabs enjoyed some
degree of political autonomy, but real independence remained a distant promise, and
Arab political protest was immediately repressed. Why did the Western states hold
firmly to this area? Petroleum was a major
reason, for both Syria and Iraq possessed
abundant oil reserves, increasingly profitable to oil corporations and of great strategic
importance to Western Europe. Freed from
Ottoman rule, these small states enjoyed only
the appearance of national independence.
No Arab leader had appeared to unify the
people and to resist the partition of this region by the Western powers. Rivalries among
Arab leaders and Western domination had
led to the emergence of rival small states, the
permanent inheritance of postwar peacemaking.

In the territory of Palestine, the peace settlement also brought serious conflict among the population, divided between Arabs and a growing Jewish community. The 1917 Balfour Declaration promising a "national home for the Jewish people" bound the British government to allow them to migrate to that coastal region where twenty centuries earlier the Jewish tribes had lived. The number of Jewish settlers, most from Eastern Europe, rose slowly to 180,000 at the end of the 1920s, when Arabs (Christians and Muslims) totaled 750,000. Although British leaders promised limits on Jewish settlement and protection of Arab political and economic rights, the Arabs in the region rejected Jewish settlers and refused any cooperation in a mandated state as long as Britain supported this policy.

What explains their adamant opposition? Religious intolerance had not been a part of Arab or Ottoman rule, but segregation and restrictions on Jews and Christians had existed. More important was the fact that no established Arab leadership existed in Palestine in the 1920s, leaving power in the hands of rival clans. These groups responded with great hostility to the alien presence of Jewish migrants of European culture, educated, economically enterprising, and individualistic. The Jews bought Arab property to set up businesses and to establish their communal farms *(kibbutzim)*. The Muslims of the area, many of whom had themselves settled there in recent decades, remained closely bound to their communal customs, many following a largely pastoral way of life and unable to compete economically with the Jews. Religious disputes over access to the holy places of Jerusalem brought to a head conflicts whose roots lay in the deep differences separating the two communities. Anti-Jewish riots erupted first in 1921 and were repeated on a much larger scale in 1929. The Zionist Organization formed its own armed security forces. Palestine was becoming a land of communal hatred and sporadic civil conflict.

Under these conditions the British themselves had to rule the Palestine mandate. No Arab leaders would collaborate, and the British could not encourage the Jewish minority to assist in rule without provoking Arab violence. Instead, a British high commissioner governed with the assistance of imperial military forces. His task became increasingly difficult as Jewish migration accelerated in the early 1930s. The persecution of Jews in Europe forced increasing numbers to abandon their homes, and the United States accepted only a relative handful following passage in the 1920s of the restrictive immigration law. Palestine was the Jews' last haven as well as their religious homeland. This influx of settlers set off in 1936 a large-scale Arab revolt, not finally repressed until 1938 with the loss of several thousand lives (Arabs and Jews). By then, British leaders were seriously considering the partition of Palestine into separate Jewish and Arab regions. The proposal was unacceptable to Arab leaders there and elsewhere. They rejected the right of Jews to Palestinian land and continued to call for the formation of a unified Middle Eastern Arab state. By then the conditions already existed for civil war.

Arab nationalism was strongest in the one state in the area unaffected by the peace settlement. At the outbreak of war, Great Britain had severed Egypt's ties to the Ottoman Empire, formally declaring the state a British protectorate. Imperial troops protected the Suez Canal and British economic interests. British administrators supervised the government, nominally under the authority of the Egyptian king. The war spared Egypt itself but brought economic hardship to Egyptian peasants, conscripted into a civilian labor force and obliged to pay much higher food prices. Popular resistance to British rule encouraged political leaders to appeal to the Allied peacemakers in 1919 to support Egyptian independence. When the British refused even to allow the Egyptian delegation to leave the country, violent protest broke out in several cities. The nationalists formed their own party, called Wafd (meaning "delegation") and organized a mass campaign against the British in support of Egyptian national independence.

Confronted with this opposition, the British in 1923 proposed independence on the condition that the Wafd party allow their military forces to remain for the protection of the Suez Canal. The Wafd leaders agreed to the compromise and became the governing party in the new parliamentary regime. The reform was peaceful. It left in place the Turkish monarch, whose powers were restricted by a constitution, and the wealthy landowning elite. The economy of the country depended on agriculture, nourished by the waters of the Nile, producing new cash crops (principally cotton) for foreign markets and staple food crops for an impoverished and rapidly growing peasant population. Western influences were penetrating Egyptian society from many directions, attractive to some Egyptians drawn to Western models of progress, a threat to others for whom the West represented foreign domination and the loss of Egyptian identity. One young nationalist student of the 1930s, Gamal Abdul Nasser, recalled later that "our spirits were still in the thirteenth century" but everywhere "the symptoms of the nineteenth and twentieth centuries infiltrated" Egyptian society.

These Western pressures led in Egypt, first of any Arab land, to an organized effort to protect social customs and the Islamic faith, a response we call "Muslim fundamentalism." Religious conservatives formed in 1928 an organization, the Muslim Brotherhood, to defend religious authority and Koranic law. Their principal enemies were fellow Egyptians, the political leaders of the Wafd party who, like Ataturk in Turkey, supported social and cultural reforms including state education, civil marriage, and women's rights. The Brotherhood's methods of resistance included the promotion of religious practice and education, but also mass street demonstrations to protest reforms and even assassination of their political enemies. The Brotherhood soon appeared in other Arab lands where Western secular (i.e., nonreligious) practices and values threatened Islamic ways. Although Egypt was freed after 1923 from direct British control and became the leading independent Arab state in the Middle East, it could not escape the cultural and social tensions created by the Western international economy and secularization.

Imperialism in Africa

The Allied peace settlements reached beyond the Middle East into sub-Saharan Africa. The European colonies there had become involved in the war, partly as a result of the acute need of the Western states for African raw materials and manpower, partly because fighting broke out there too between German and Allied forces. The Western industrial demand then and after the war for minerals stimulated the expansion of mining, the most important center of which was South Africa. The recruitment of African workers from tribal areas to work in the mines and in other industries created a new social and political problem, especially in South Africa where white rule was strongly influenced by the racism of the Afrikaners (Boers). To control these migrants, South Africa expanded its segregation policies to include a "pass" system which required South African blacks to carry internal passports, severely restricting their right to residence in towns. In that country, more than anywhere else in Africa, economic and social development was leading to increasingly oppressive measures of White domination.

The war was also responsible for the conscription of Africans, especially in French West Africa, into military service. Revolts among the tribes there forced the French to curtail their policy, but nonetheless large numbers of Africans found themselves mobilized in a war whose origins and objectives meant little to them. Gradually more and more Africans were willingly or unwillingly becoming familiar with Western ways. They ultimately formed the vanguard of nationalist movements in these lands.

Western political domination of Africa altered little in the years following the war. The Allies took control of all German colonies. The League's mandate system distributed the areas in both East and West Africa to the British and French empires, and to South Africa (granted Southwest Africa, now called Namibia), to be "trustees" of the peoples there until they should be judged fit for self-rule. In effect, these areas were integrated into the system of colonial rule established by the Western powers before the war. A handful of Western administrators governed vast territories, relying largely on African "tribal" leaders to carry out their orders. In fact, the Europeans understood little of tribal power relations, and in their search for "chiefs" they frequently had to appoint "native authorities" of their own choosing. Both the French and the British did permit some Africans, able to obtain Western education, to work in their colonial administration. This small, educated elite constituted a second important feature of colonial rule, gradually introducing new groups into the political life of Africa.

The bulk of the African population, however, experienced western economic and cultural forces more directly than political pressures. The spread of cash crops altered their daily lives and made them more dependent than before on the market for their livelihood. Western medicine spread slowly beyond the cities into rural areas. Medical help, like that provided by the clinic set up by Dr. Albert Schweitzer in West Africa, provided assistance against the endemic tropical diseases afflicting the population in those lands. Later testimony from Africans revealed to what extent some resented the alien forces brought by the Westerners. "They have given us a road we did not need," recalled one African tribal chief in the Congo, bringing "foreigners and enemies into our midst, . . . making our women unclean, forcing us to a way of life that is not ours, planting crops we do not want, doing slave's work. . . . He sends us missions to destroy our belief."[2] The Western imperial states forced upon Africans painful and often destructive changes in their lives. Some of these new influences did improve living conditions and create possibilities for a better life. But few Westerners were concerned about the damaging effects of the clash of cultures caused by their reforms, which to most appeared to replace "primitive" customs with their "civilized" ways.

The social and psychological stress of imperial rule opened the way to large-scale religious conversion to Christianity and to Islam. Christian missions received usually the backing of Western administrators and offered to the Africans who came to their centers social services and schooling in addition to teaching in their faith. Many factors explain the mass conversions to Christianity among Africans in the years after the First World War. Partly, imperial conquest undermined the credibility of the old gods and

---

[2]Oral testimony recorded by Colin Turnbull, *The Lonely African* (London, 1963), pp. 81–83.

made Christianity the way of the conqueror. Partly, Christianity provided a sort of "cultural baggage" for those Africans eager to learn and to profit from new economic and political conditions. Alongside Christianity, Islam appeared very distinct from Western ways, but it also offered a coherent religious view and a strong religious community. The Muslim faith spread rapidly in the postwar years in both East and West Africa, until in the latter region over half the population was Muslim. Under the pressure of Western imperialism, the old bonds of tribal unity were gradually dissolving, but new unifying institutions and ideologies were slow to emerge. The drama and tragedy of postimperial Africa had their roots in the disruptive impact of the West.

Great Powers in East Asia

Imperialist claims on new territory and great power rivalries in East Asia led to a new diplomatic settlement, as important in its own way as the Paris treaties were for Europe and the Middle East. The end of the war left the Japanese state in a stronger position than ever before. Its navy was the largest fleet in the Far East, and its army far stronger than either the Chinese or the new Soviet Red Army. At the beginning of the war it had joined the Allies, though its forces had taken no direct role in the European conflict.

Those war years were a time of further Japanese expansion onto the Asian mainland. Japanese troops had occupied the territory in north China (the Shantung peninsula) which had been Imperial Germany's "concession." Following the Allied decision in 1918 to intervene in the Russian civil war, they had moved north to take control of the Pacific Coast regions. Japanese leaders forced the Chinese government during the war to accept a Japanese economic sphere of influence in north China and Manchuria, subjecting its great neighbor to the same humiliating treatment as the Western states earlier. What pushed Japan on this expansionist path? The initiative lay primarily with the Japanese military, where the old feudal militarist traditions glorified conquest and power. It lay as well in the economic ambitions of industrialists who looked to the Asian mainland for markets and mineral resources.

The war in Europe had opened the way to the expansionist party, but peace presented new difficulties to Japan. The Chinese protested Japanese economic privileges and in retaliation declared a trade boycott of Japanese goods. The military intervention in Siberia proved costly and gave Japan no direct benefits. Most serious of all was the opposition of the U.S. government to Japanese expansion. The United States had become an important customer for Japanese goods and a vital source of raw materials, especially petroleum and iron ore. It was Japan's only serious naval rival in the Pacific, and had expanded its Pacific fleet as part of the U.S. policy to oppose Japanese domination in East Asia. The economic importance and naval might of the United States led the Japanese government to end its expansionist policies. It reasserted control over the Japanese military, ending (temporarily) the "autonomy of command" of its generals and blocking their plans of Asian conquest. In 1921 it accepted the offer of the U.S. government to join an international conference in Washington to discuss Far Eastern affairs.

The Washington Conference introduced into Asian international relations a model of collective peacekeeping similar to that the U.S. negotiators had taken to Paris in 1919. Wilson was no longer president, but the Republican administration came to the 1921 conference as eager as Wilson once had been to end "spheres of influence" and power politics. The principle of national self-determination strengthened the long-standing policy of the United States to protect China from foreign intervention and to keep its market open to American goods. The hope to reduce the danger of war through international collaboration was reinforced by U.S. opposition to a Japanese sphere of influence in the Far East and by the costly naval armaments race with Japan. The other major powers were prepared to accept the U.S. proposals for an end to the "diplomacy of imperialism" in the Far East. Great Britain and France collaborated because they were weakened by the war. Japan joined because its civilian leaders hoped that cooperation with the United States would bring Japan economic prosperity.

When its work was finally completed in 1922, the conference produced a remarkable set of agreements. The most important was the treaty to restrict the number of the warships. It fixed a ratio among the participating states of the relative number of capital ships they were permitted, leaving Great Britain and the United States with the largest navies, followed by Japan, then France and Italy. Great Britain, the United States, and Japan all scrapped a large number of vessels—thirty-two for the United States. The British and the Americans promised not to establish any new military bases in the Pacific or to strengthen fortifications in their existing bases at Singapore and at Corregidor in the Philippines; in exchange, the Japanese withdrew their troops from Soviet territory. For a few years the treaties effectively halted power politics in the Far East and ended the naval armaments race. Additional treaties set up a procedure for peaceful settlement of conflicts among the major powers in the Far East and guaranteed the independence and territorial boundaries of China. Like the Locarno Treaty in Europe, the Washington treaties held out the hope of a new peaceful era in Asian international relations.

Their success depended on cooperation between Japan and the United States. Misunderstanding over their terms came easily, for these agreements represented very different approaches in Japan and the United States to political realities. The political culture which formed the outlook of American leaders placed all states on a common level, but instilled a sense of superiority toward "Oriental" peoples. It assigned universal value of the concepts of peace and progress. Japanese culture, on the contrary, presented its people with images and symbols of their uniqueness and of the primacy of the interests of their own state. The role played by Japanese negotiators at the Washington Conference (and their delegates to the League of Nations) confirmed in their eyes the importance of their country as a world power. Civilian leaders adopted wholeheartedly the American program of international cooperation, but had to justify its results to the military and industrial elite by direct benefits to Japan. The unstated Japanese condition in signing the treaties was the expansion of U.S.-Japanese trade and the continuation of economic growth. When prosperity ended, so too did Japanese compliance with the treaties; imperialism vanished from the Far East only briefly.

SUMMARY

We now look back at the 1920s as a time of transition toward a new and even more terrible war. The "normalcy" acclaimed by one U.S. president of the 1920s had only a short time to survive. The new order put together by European statesmen represented a timid effort to find new solutions to the problems of international conflict and economic growth. We may judge these men short-sighted, but should recognize that their powers were limited, their peoples exhausted by the war and fearful of "Bolshevism" as much as of another war.

A return to old ways was reassuring. To pretend the Soviet Union was inconsequential, as the U.S. government did by refusing to recognize the new state in those years, avoided fundamental questions about social justice and revolution. The persistence of German militarism revealed how tenacious were the illusions of national grandeur even in a defeated country. Italian fascism, though it occasionally spoke of revolution, looked to the Italian past for its images of national grandeur.

The weakness of the new order lay as well in grave defects in the system itself. International economic relations did not duplicate prewar conditions, a hope impossible to achieve since the United States refused to assume the leading role in trade and finance. The relations among major powers suffered from the naive assumption of U.S. leaders that the complex set of international financial and diplomatic arrangements—the League of Nations, the Locarno agreement, the Dawes plan, the Washington treaties—would function by themselves, leaving the United States at peace behind its ocean frontiers. The events of the 1930s ended these illusions.

RECOMMENDED READING

International History of the 1920s

DEREK ALDCROFT, *From Versailles to Wall Street: 1918–1929* (1977)

FRANK COSTIGLIOLA, *Awkward Dominion: American Political, Economic, and Cultural Relations with Europe 1919–33* (1984)

SALLY MARKS, *The Illusion of Security: Europe's International Relations 1918–1933* (1976)

DAN SILVERMAN, *Reconstructing Europe After the Great War* (1982)

European States

ERICH EYCK, *A History of the Weimar Republic* (1963)

PETER GAY, *Weimar Culture: The Outsider as Insider* (1968)

DENIS MACK SMITH, *Mussolini* (1982)

A. J. P. TAYLOR, *English History, 1914–1939* (1965)

Imperial Diplomacy and Non-Western Lands

BILL FREUND, *The Making of Contemporary Africa: The Development of African Society Since 1800* (1984)

AKIRA IRIYE, *After Imperialism: The Search for Order in the Far East 1921–31* (1965)

A. J. H. LATHAM, *The Depression and the Developing World, 1914–1939* (1981)

Memoirs and Novels

*ERICH MARIA REMARQUE, *The Road Back* (1931)

CHINUA ACHEBE, *Things Fall Apart* (1969)

chapter 4

DEPRESSION AND DICTATORS IN EUROPE: 1929–1939

The visions in the West of peace and progress of the 1920s faded in the next decade. Economic prosperity gave way to a depression more pervasive and severe than ever before. Cycles of economic growth and decline had marked the industrial world for a century, yet the collapse of economic production of the 1930s was worse both in scope and intensity. It constituted truly a global depression, vivid proof of the growing economic interdependence among industrial countries and between the developed and developing lands.

In its wake came bitter political conflicts and violence. The increased role of government in economic life, and the spreading belief in the responsibility of the state for the social welfare of the population, both aroused among the population greater demands than in the past for political action to deal with the crisis. Prophets of a "new way" attacked the old leaders and promised new solutions. Fascism won many new converts, ready to place their faith in militant nationalist leaders and in dictatorship to provide security in those troubling times. The triumph of the Nazi party in Germany represented the most spectacular victory of European fascism. At the same time, Communist parties increased their following among those who despaired of capitalism and imagined that Soviet Russia had created a better, "socialist" society. Between these two extremes, the democratic countries experimented also with new economic and social policies, but their innovations were far less spectacular and their public image less impressive than those of the Nazi and Soviet states. In these terms, the 1930s was the great era of the dictators.

The depression turned the attention of peoples of the democratic states inward,

89

away from the problems of war and security, and in so doing undermined the peace settlement of the 1920s. Conflicts among states in the years before 1914 had grown out of rivalries and ambitions shared to a greater or lesser extent by all the major powers. The threat to peace in the 1930s arose from the policies of two aggressive states, Nazi Germany in Europe and the Japanese Empire in East Asia. The measures for peacekeeping put in place in the 1920s relied on collective action to prevent war. That consensus no longer existed in the following decade, victim of the depression and of isolationist illusions of security. Joseph Stalin, perhaps the most cynical of the political leaders in those years, considered global politics a "jungle" in which only the ruthless could survive. Although he himself contributed to that situation, the foreign policies of other states confirmed his judgment. The world was headed for a new war.

GLOBAL DEPRESSION

The economic decline that began at the end of the 1920s damaged all the industrial economies of the world as well as the areas supplying food and raw materials to the West. It had the characteristics of earlier recessions, including a severe decline in production and trade, a rapid rise in unemployment, and a drastic fall in the standard of living of the population. Businesses declared bankruptcy; banks were unable to make loans and some even to pay their debts to depositors; food prices fell so low that farmers let fields lie fallow though the urban poor went hungry. The recession began in 1929 in the United States, and gradually spread throughout the Western world and into East Asia. By the early 1930s a global economic depression existed. It represented a human tragedy of monumental proportions, creating hardship and suffering, destroying confidence in governments, undermining hope in the future. It led in many countries to a serious political crisis.

The United States and the Global Depression

The American economy led the way in recession after having launched the prosperity of the 1920s. By early 1929 U.S. industrial production had begun to decline, led by the new automobile industry. Unemployment among workers had started to climb the year before, reaching two million by the end of 1928. Farm prices had been falling for several years, cutting back on farm incomes and reducing the standard of living of rural families. Declining demand for industrial goods represented an important factor in triggering recession. Added to this condition, however, were other grave problems of American finance and trade that complicated and prolonged the international and national effects of the recession.

Many middle- and upper-class Americans pursued the illusion of easy money by speculating on the stock market. They borrowed heavily from banks, also eager for quick gain even if risks were high. Stock values on Wall Street doubled between 1927 and the fall of 1929. Prices reflected speculative dreams, not economic reality, a fact that led some major investors to abandon Wall Street in late 1929 for less risky ventures. Their decision, coupled with financial problems in London, burst the speculative bubble and started massive selling. By the winter of 1929, stock prices had declined by one-third, and many speculators who had borrowed heavily were ruined. When they failed to repay their loans and banks raised their interest rates, investment funds for industry dwindled by almost one-half. Factories cut back production even more. The decline in sales of U.S. goods and rising unemployment produced political pressure to keep out foreign goods. In response, in 1930 the U.S. Congress enacted the Smoot-Hawley tariff, setting tariff barriers 50 percent higher on imports and spreading the harmful effects of declining demand to industrial producers in Europe and Japan.

The impact of the American recession on other economies was crucial. In the first place, the United States ceased making abundant investments in foreign countries. The financial crisis caused by the Wall Street crash of 1929 penetrated deeply into the world economy. U.S. foreign investments fell two-thirds by 1932. The decline in the flow of dollars to Germany forced the German government to abandon in 1931 its reparations payments. European manufacturers, in turn, curtailed factory investments. At the beginning of the depression, financial orthodoxy in ruling circles still dictated balanced budgets and high interest rates to attract foreign money, both techniques severely criticized later for hindering recovery. The United States, center of world financial dealings since the war, could not provide those funds, and the entire system of foreign investments in Europe fell apart as creditors called in their loans.

The long-term effect of the U.S. financial collapse produced a major banking and financial crisis in Europe in 1931. Banks in Germany and Austria defaulted on their own loans; Germany forbade withdrawal of funds to other countries. In Great Britain, the flight of money abroad forced the British government late that year to end its guaranteed exchange of pounds for gold at a fixed value, the key to its efforts to protect stable international finances. In 1931 Great Britain and France stopped repayment of their war debt to the United States; in retaliation, the U.S. Congress prohibited purchase of British and French government securities by U.S. investors. No other country besides the United States had the economic resources to restore world financial stability. However, U.S. investors had recklessly gambled away their funds and the U.S. government sought primarily to protect U.S. banks and investments.

The second area in which the U.S. recession contributed directly to the global economic decline lay in trade. Instead of opening its market to foreign products falling in price, the U.S. government undertook to exclude imports. Recovery in earlier recessions had come in part as producers lowered prices on goods to attract buyers. The United States did not permit that process to occur, for its 1930 tariff helped reduce U.S. imports almost by one-half. Country after country retaliated by raising their tariffs; even Britain abandoned free trade in 1931. In the next two years world trade declined by one-third. Most countries exporting food and raw materials lost over half their foreign sales by the early 1930s. Japan, dependent on exports to pay for imports of vital raw materials, saw its American market suddenly contract and its total exports decline by 50 percent. The standard of living of its workers fell by one-third. Japan's vulnerability to the Western depression encouraged its political leaders to consider East Asia their special market and strengthened the plans by Japanese generals to conquer Asian territory. Economic crisis and war were closely linked.

By 1932 industrial production had declined by one-fourth worldwide and by one-third in Europe. In concrete terms, only three-fourths of the quantity of the manufactured goods once available were still produced. The wealth of the industrial world was shrinking. The economic crisis was particularly acute in the most industrialized countries. Production fell in Germany by 40 percent. As a result, one out of every four German workers was unemployed, and many others were surviving on lower pay. Small business confronted bankruptcy. The German government, to which employers and workers looked for help, appeared at a loss to devise new remedies to the crisis.

The economic depression undermined the international financial and commercial network of the capitalist economies. States increasingly relied on their own internal markets for recovery. A major international conference gathered in London in 1933 to attempt to put the international trade and finance system back together. European leaders turned to the U.S. government to guarantee a stable dollar, to serve as a source of new investment funds, and to open the United States to increased imports. However, the new U.S. president, Franklin Roosevelt, refused to cooperate, fearing that an international program to promote economic growth would worsen the depression in his own country. International cooperation gave way to shortsighted national interests, and the lack of American leadership proved crucial to the financial and trade impasse hindering the recovery.

The capitalist system's promise to provide people with work and to satisfy their needs had failed miserably. Gradually economic production did begin to rise after 1932, but in many countries, it remained for years below the level of prosperity of the late 1920s. Where did the basic problem lie? The inequalities of wealth within the industrial countries and between industrial and nonindustrial lands weakened demand, but this factor appears less important than two others. First, global economic growth required effective means for the free movement of investment funds and goods. The 1920s system had disappeared, replaced by "autarky," a nationalist system of self-reliance and rivalry with competing economies. "Beggar thy neighbor" was the motto of the day. Second,

the complex domestic forces of the industrial economy could no longer function satisfactorily without state intervention. The free market left idle economic resources and labor. Conservative fiscal policies did not offer an adequate solution to the crisis.

Critics condemned state inaction and classical economic theory that relied on the "laws" of supply and demand to ensure prosperity. Franklin Roosevelt, Democratic candidate for the U.S. presidency in 1932, stated this new view of economic relations when he argued that "economic laws are not made by nature. They are made by human beings." His conclusion was that, since "men and women are starving," the state had to take action. He, like other political leaders in the early 1930s, had little regard for the advice of professional economists, for the crisis in the United States, in his opinion, called above all for political leadership.

A long-term solution to the depression called for a fundamental revision of economic thought. The most promising ideas came from a British economist, John Maynard Keynes, who proposed a radical new theory to deal with the crisis. He argued that the free market might never produce complete recovery and full employment. By itself, the demand for producer and consumer goods would never, in his opinion, rise sufficiently to meet these objectives. Instead, he proposed that governments use their own financial means to invest, spending if necessary more than they earned in hard times to compensate for the inadequacy of private consumption and investment. His call for government intervention encountered vehement opposition among conservatives, for it violated deeply cherished beliefs in the limits to government powers and in the benefits of the free enterprise system.

Nonetheless, Keynes's theories did provide suggestions for state action to politicians like Roosevelt, who later in the decade applied Keynesian policies. Even earlier, measures partially in conformity with Keynes's views were introduced, in Great Britain and Germany and did stimulate recovery from depression. His proposals did not address, however, the problem of the global dimensions of the depression. The old system of international trade and finance had collapsed, and its absence constituted an abiding obstacle to the return of prosperity in an age of global economic interdependence. Only at the end of the Second World War did a new system take its place.

The Western Democracies in the Depression Years

The crisis created by the depression in the Western countries brought out the differences in the political cultures of the United States, Great Britain, and France. New leaders followed differing policies in each state, yet similarities did appear. All three held firmly to democratic methods of rule, turning aside demogogic politicians and authoritarian movements seeking power. In all three cases, domestic needs came before international economic problems, though the European states did make one effort in 1933 to involve the United States in the formation of a new system of trade and finance. Finally, each government became more active than ever before in helping to alleviate the economic hardship caused by the depression. Under strong pressure from their citizens, they expanded the meager aid previously granted the unemployed, the aged, and the sick, and granted new rights to labor unions to protect the interests of the workers. We call these state efforts to assist the needy social welfare policies. Once considered socialistic by liberals and conservatives alike, they became important not only to protect the welfare of the poor but also to ensure the democratic consensus on which the political stability of these countries depended.

In the United States, Franklin Roosevelt's victory in the 1932 presidential elections began a period of sweeping social and economic reforms. He came to office having been active in New York politics and having served as secretary of the navy in Woodrow Wilson's cabinet. Although he was from a very wealthy family, he had little knowledge of economic affairs. But compensating for this was an extraordinary sensitivity to the needs of Americans in those hard times. Perhaps this concern stemmed from the long years of suffering he endured after contracting polio in the early 1920s. He remained for the rest of his life paralyzed in both legs. On becoming president in early 1933, his program for recovery called for immediate government action to save the banking system, in a state of collapse at the time, and to revive the economy. His first period of reforms emphasized the protection of productive property and included efforts to save the farmers from foreclosure and businessmen from bankruptcy. Regulatory federal agencies were set up to prevent the abusive action of speculators, judged responsible among other things for the stock market crash of 1929. The only major effort to assist the poor at that time was a massive public works campaign, offering the unemployed state-funded jobs in construction, manufacturing, and other public projects.

These measures to help the needy proved inadequate, and the economic recovery was disappointing. Popular demands for welfare measures grew, pushing Roosevelt in 1935 and 1936 to begin a second important period of reforms. The emphasis this time lay in aid to those groups in America in need of protection—and with the political influence to make Roosevelt heed their wishes (the Southern blacks, excluded from political life by racist segregation measures, received no help). The Social Security system went into effect to provide minimum pensions for retired people, and was paid for by obligatory contributions from employers and employees. Labor unions obtained the legal right of collective bargaining, and in the following years organized industrial labor and struggled with management in the most intensive period of union activity in U.S. history. Conservatives called Roosevelt a "socialist" for using federal powers to regulate and limit the powers of business, but Roosevelt answered that he was trying to save the capitalist system from collapse. The voters in 1936 proved that they supported his measures, giving him an overwhelming victory in the elections that year.

Still, Roosevelt's reforms had only limited success. Full recovery from the depression did not come, and millions remained unemployed. Even the introduction of government spending measures in 1937, inspired by Keynes's theories, were not sufficient. Only the beginning of intensive armament production in 1940 restored full employment and prosperity. Domestic measures for economic growth, even in a country as large as the United States, were no longer sufficient. A new system of global economic expansion was needed, but Roosevelt and his government had no plan for such measures. Political leadership and the majority of the population were as isolationist as ever in those years. While the threat of war spread across Europe and East Asia, the United States tended to its own business. Events soon proved that U.S. security, as well as economic recovery, was a global affair.

The governments of Great Britain and France followed very different paths in guiding their countries through the crisis. In Britain, the Conservative party dominated political life, though for several years it collaborated in a national government with Liberal and Labor leaders. The coalition relied on compromise and moderate reform to maintain political stability and to cope with the depression. It introduced a large-scale public housing program, the first in British history, to improve lodging for Britain's poor. These state investments, combined with low interest rates, brought the British economy back to its predepression level of production by the middle of the decade. The British cabinet searched as well that decade for new policies to govern its greatest colony, India, where a powerful nationalist movement, led by Mahatma Gandhi's National Congress, demanded freedom for the subcontinent. In the 1935 Government of India Act, the British government agreed to grant the Indian people self-rule, with the promise of ultimate independence.

The principal concern of the British leaders was to preserve peace in Europe. They realized Great Britain was far weaker than in 1914, its navy shrunk in size and quality, its air force just beginning to develop new fighter planes and bombers. The depression further strengthened their readiness to accept the gradual revision of the peace settlements at the demand of Nazi Germany. To them this policy of "appeasement" represented a conciliatory and reasonable means toward the noble aim of a peaceful world. By conceding Hitler's demands for German expansion, they found, however, that they were destroying the fragile European balance of power, their only real protection from new war.

In France the economic depression swung French voters in the middle of the decade toward new political leadership. Challenging conservative rule in 1936 was a coalition of reform parties, led by the Socialist party but including as well the Communists. These former outcasts of French political life had recently joined the democratic parties as part of a shift in the policies of the Communist International in Moscow, where Stalin sought of foreign Communists above all their help in fighting the enemies of the Soviet Union. They received orders to join popular-front coalitions wherever allies could be found to combat fascism. After years of opposing "bourgeois democracy," the French party adopted the new policy and was welcomed by socialist and liberal parties in a political reform movement to bring to French people substantial measures for social welfare and economic recovery. The victory of the Popular Front in 1936 made Communists the partners in a ruling coalition for the first time in French history.

For the next two years, the new cabinet, headed at first by the Socialist Léon Blum, implemented an extensive social reform program, including for workers the forty-hour work-week and two-week paid vacations every year. Expensive benefits of this sort needed government policies to stimulate economic growth by increasing demand for producer and consumer goods, but in this respect the government failed. Economic production stagnated, and bitter political quarrels divided the country. The Popular Front soon had to make international issues of war and peace, not domestic reforms, its first priority. Its leaders, sickened of war and dependent upon the diplomatic and military alliance with Great Britain, joined in the policy of appeasement of Nazi Germany. Democratic government in Britain and France in those years found leaders who, like most of the population, desired nothing so much as peace. The greatest tragedy of that time was that the world was no longer, as Wilson had so optimistically promised in 1917, "safe for democracy."

The Collapse of German Democracy

Germans lacked the strong democratic traditions of the British and French people. As a result, when the depression set in, over half of the German electorate voted for parties whose solutions to the crisis included an end in one form or another to parliamentary democracy. Some voters opted for the Communist party; many more chose the National Socialist party of Adolph Hitler. Economic hardship did not cause Nazism and the triumph of the Nazi regime. It did, however, produce a social crisis in which many Germans lost confidence in the leadership provided by their party system and cabinet rule.

The depression was responsible as well for a political conflict in 1930, the solution to which began the move away from democratic rule. The coalition cabinet which governed the country at the beginning of the recession saw its tax revenues decline and its social welfare payments, particularly unemployment relief, rise dramatically. This budgetary dilemma tore the coalition apart; socialists urged raising taxes to sustain financial help for the needy, while conservatives demanded fiscal austerity to balance the budget. Neither side knew how to stop the recession. In March 1930, the political stalemate ended when President Hindenburg appointed a conservative chancellor, Bruening. When new elections failed to win a parliamentary majority for the chancellor's policies, the aged president invoked his emergency powers, which permitted Bruening to remain chancellor without a majority in the legislature and to rule by special presidential decree. The decline of German democratic government began then.

Although Chancellor Bruening won the budget battle, the real victors were the Nazis. This fanatical nationalist movement, whose propaganda blamed Germany's ills on traitors, Jews, and Bolsheviks, attracted millions of German voters, many of whom had previously supported the moderate parliamentary parties. The legislative elections in the fall of 1930 increased the National Socialist vote to six million, almost eight times as many as in 1928. By 1932, the party received the backing of one-third of all German voters. The only other movement which gained substantially was the Communist party, though it never exceeded 17 percent of the vote. Together the two extremist parties attracted over 50 percent of German voters. This extraordinary electoral shift revealed a mood of protest among Germans, not only against the ineffectiveness of government policies but also against the democratic system so recently adopted. Their collective rejection of parliamentary politics constituted the second step toward Nazi dictatorship.

By the laws of parliamentary rule, the National Socialist party had earned in 1932 the right to head the German cabinet. It had one-third of representatives in the legislature and was the largest party in the country. Yet it was an avowed enemy of democracy, and Hitler had stipulated that his party would agree to support a cabinet only if he himself became chancellor. President Hindenburg looked with scorn on that lowly "corporal" and political demagogue. He was old, however, and depended on the advice of his close advisers, including army generals and conservative aristocrats. In that political vacuum, a handful of men made the fateful decision to accept Hitler's conditions. They believed the solution to the political crisis had to be the appointment of a new coalition government headed by the Nazis.

Unable to understand Hitler's ruthless ambition and fanaticism, they thought that they could control Hitler as easily as they dominated Hindenburg. Like Italian political leaders in 1922, they ignored the brutality and violence of the Nazi party, seeing in it a mass movement which they could use in support of nationalism and conservatism. They shared Hitler's hatred of the Versailles system and thought his nationalist program of German expansion the right course for their country. In January 1933, the president yielded to their arguments and appointed Hitler chancellor of the German Republic. Germany had taken a long step toward Nazism.

THE NAZI REVOLUTION AND THE DESTRUCTION OF THE VERSAILLES PEACE

What was this National Socialist party? In outward appearance it was modeled on the Italian Fascist party, which had spawned imitations in many Western countries since seizing power in 1922. Among these parties were the Phalange in Spain, to play an important role later in the civil war, and the Arrow Cross in Hungary. The term "fascism" is often used to describe all these movements, which glorified national unity and militarism, vilified democracy and socialism, promised to care for the masses, and demanded rule by a political elite to protect conservative values and property. Fascism was in the 1930s an international movement, a symptom of a deep crisis in European civilization. It was diagnosed by one observer as a collective "escape from freedom" by Europeans, who sought the security of simple truths and elementary loyalties fixed upon reassuring national symbols and a charismatic leader.

Nazism

Nazism was in important respects unique among fascist parties. It embodied the peculiar ideological vision of its leader, Adolph Hitler. On the one hand, he focused the hatred of his followers on the Jewish community of Europe, buttressing the image of the Jew as national enemy with a myth of racial inferiority. This anti-Semitism marked the movement deeply and led ultimately to the greatest human tragedy in Western history. Second, he expanded the militaristic impulse of fascism to encompass a dream of German conquest of a continental and ultimately a world empire. None of his ideas and prejudices was original to him; the combination however made of Nazism a ominous new political force in the Western world.

Hitler's own personality and ambitions were transformed by war. His early life in Austria was a failure. As a child he had few friends and found little affection in his family. After failing to complete his secondary schooling he made a shabby living as a commercial artist in Vienna and then Munich, where he was living when the 1914 war began. In the enthusiasm of the first weeks he volunteered for the German army. The warrior brotherhood of the front lines provided, he wrote later, "a deliverance from the distress that had weighed upon me during the days of my youth." It was "the greatest of all experiences" and produced a profound change in his character.

Although he identified himself with "the great heroic struggle of our people," the "people" became synonymous with his own ego, whose appetite for power was insatiable. He proved himself a courageous soldier and made the "manly virtues" of the warrior his measure of individual worth. He emerged from the war a political activist and orator of talent in the cause of German nationalism and militarism. In 1920 he became the leader of the National Socialist German Workers' party. He had found his calling.

The basic elements in his program for a new Germany appeared in his writings of the 1920s. His principal work, *Mein Kampf* (My Struggle), described in a disorganized man-

ner his political beliefs, intermingled with flattering references to his own life. Like Mussolini, he glorified triumph through combat as the way "the strong raise themselves about the weak." In this struggle, the elite led the masses, to him passive creatures "like a woman" waiting to submit to a forceful ruler to end the confusion which "liberalistic freedom" created. He echoed the fascists also in conjuring up a "Bolshevist" threat to the nation. He added however a second enemy, the Jew. Identifying German nationalism with "racial" purity, he turned the Jewish people into the image of the implacable adversary, corrupting "German blood," seizing German wealth, dividing the German nation, seeking "the complete destruction of Germany." He demanded that they be deprived of citizenship and political office, ultimately to be removed entirely from German territory. Nazism placed anti-Semitism at the very core of its distorted view of the world and its plans for Germany's future.

In his writings of the 1920s Hitler also made clear his determination to expand German power and territory. He referred most frequently to the destruction of the Versailles Treaty and the unification of all Germans in one large nation-state. He wrote as well of a new "world policy" more ambitious than that pursued by German statesmen of the prewar empire. He envisioned the rise of Germany first to the rank of continental power dominating all Europe, including Russia, whose Communist regime he vowed to destroy and much of whose territory he sought to annex. Germany would rank among the great powers of the world alongside Great Britain, the United States, and the Japanese Empire. The second stage, which he imagined at that time would come after his death, entailed a global "battle of the continents" pitting the German Empire against the United States in a struggle for "world domination."[1] This dream appeared pure fantasy in Germany of the 1920s. It possessed Hitler's mind so firmly that it led his country ultimately into global war.

The concept of the leader crystallized the role of Hitler as dictator. The image of the party became fused with that of the leader (*fuehrer*), to be glorified and obeyed as much as the *duce* in Italy. The identification extended to the German nation itself; later one of his disciples proclaimed at a party meeting that "Hitler is the People; the People is Hitler!" In concrete terms, the party program became whatever Hitler judged best. Some in the party believed that National Socialism included the struggle against the German elites in business, finance, and the military. Hitler accepted their collaboration as long as they did not challenge his leadership. He understood "socialist," however, to mean someone "who knows no higher ideal than the welfare of the nation." The Nazi program offered no real promise of social reform, for, similar in this to Italian fascism, it clung to conservative, middle-class values and institutions, all subordinated to the party and to the leader. Nazism consisted of a mixture of German nationalism, militarism, anti-Semitism, and obedience to the leader. The message appealed to the discontented, of whom there were great numbers in the early 1930s. It promised national strength and unity, a potent appeal to nationalists who rejected the 1918 defeat and to conservatives who feared revolution.

During the 1920s the movement acquired its special organization and structure. First, Hitler formed within the party a special paramilitary group, the Stormtroopers (*Sturmabteilung*, or SA), composed largely of war veterans dressed in a special uniform and

prepared for street battle to defend the party against its enemies. Later he added an elite bodyguard dressed in black uniforms called the *Schutzstaffel* (SS). He demanded of the SS a loyalty greater than that of any soldier in the German army. The SS members had to present documents proving racial purity and to take a personal oath of loyalty to Hitler promising absolute obedience—"the word of Hitler has the force of law."

Gradually the party spread its sections throughout the country and built up its membership. At the end of the 1920s it still had only 100,000 members and fewer than 1 million voters, but the depression made it a mass political movement. The great increase in Nazi votes was paralleled by the influx of members into the party, growing by 1932 to 800,000, and into the SA, numbering .5 million men by then. Nazi members came from the middle and lower-middle classes of Germany, and from the working class as well. Many were war veterans or people who had found in the national community of wartime a sense of purpose in moments of crisis. They became the warriors in the struggle against Weimar democracy.

We may wonder still why so little opposition emerged to Nazi domination of the German state. Nazism embodied everything the liberals and socialists had opposed in 1919. Yet power virtually fell into Nazi hands. Although German democratic leaders realized that the Nazi party constituted a threat to the very existence of democracy, they were divided among themselves and paralyzed by their strict adherence to parliamentary action. The labor unions, once firm supporters of the republic, had suffered in the depression and no longer were prepared to undertake a massive strike movement for the sake of the discredited Weimar leadership. The military, sworn to the Republic, believed their loyalties lay with the president. When

---

[1]Andreas Hillgruber, *Germany and the Two World Wars*, trans. William Kirby (Cambridge, Mass., 1981), p. 50.

Hindenburg, respecting all the legal formalities, gave the position of chancellor to Hitler, no serious protests were made.

The Nazi Dictatorship

In the early months of 1932, Germany remained legally a constitutional democracy. Hitler governed with the powers of chancellor in a coalition government responsible to parliament. Taking the law in its own hands, however, the Nazi party moved during that winter and spring into more and more positions of power. The SA and SS operated freely in the country, able to intimidate or terrorize Nazi opponents at will. Their members filled the ranks of the police force of Prussia, the largest state within the Republic, where Hitler's close aide Goering was chief of police.

Using his powers as chancellor, Hitler dissolved the Reichstag and called for new elections in March. He employed all the means at his party's disposal to obtain a majority. The building in Berlin housing the parliament burned in late February (possibly an action engineered by Nazis). Hitler blamed the Communists and persuaded the president to grant him extraordinary powers "for the protection of the people and the state." He suspended individual liberties, including press and assembly. Although the elections gave the Nazis only 44 percent of the vote, Hitler obtained by intimidation and bluster parliamentary approval of the Enabling Act, granting the cabinet (that is, Hitler) the power to rule without parliamentary restraints. Only the Social Democrats voted against the bill. With the passage of the Enabling Act, he was virtual dictator.

During the next several years, the Nazis extended their control over the entire state and population. Local governments came under Nazi rule; the German state lost its federal structure. Nazis replaced the labor unions with their own German Labor Front. Political parties disappeared one by one. The Communist party vanished shortly after the Nazi rise to power, its underground organization destroyed and many of its members thrown into the first concentration camps. The Social Democratic party was banned next as an "enemy of the people and state." In July 1933, the cabinet proclaimed that the Nazi party "constitutes the only political party in Germany."

The country had become a one-party dictatorship. Hitler's cabinet became in theory the instrument of his will. Nazi organizations reached out to all elements of the population, including youth, labor, and professional associations. Even the churches came under state control or made their peace with the Nazis. Whenever individual religious leaders dared to protest Nazi injustices, they risked jail or concentration camp. By 1934 the voices publicly opposing Nazism had fallen silent.

The German army still remained beyond Nazi control. Its officer corps retained the traditional solidarity of the old German army; its generals could rely on the political support of President Hindenburg. The Nazi movement came to power with its own military forces. The head of the Stormtroopers, Ernst Roehm, believed in the promises of "national revolution" against the old elite, among whom he included the officer corps. He sought to become head of a new "people's army," made up of his Stormtroopers. By the end of 1933 they numbered between two and three million men, many of them war veterans who hated the rigid discipline and arrogance of the officers. Roehm called for a purge of the army; with control of the SA, he represented one of the party's most powerful leaders.

Hitler chose to side with the army against

the SA. He knew Hindenburg was close to death and sought army backing to become the new head of state. He promised the generals an expanded army and immunity from political attack. In doing so he became Roehm's enemy. To end the SA threat, he resolved in June 1934 to remove by force the SA leadership. SS squads seized and executed during the "night of the long knives" over seventy political leaders whom Hitler wished eliminated, including Roehm and other SA officials, as well as several non-Nazis. Hitler justified the executions by claiming that he made the law, for he was "responsible for the fate of the German people." The army leaders condoned by their silence this blood purge, satisfied to see the radical SA leaders disappear. That September, Hitler obtained from them his reward. Following Hindenburg's death, he proclaimed himself head of state and commander-in-chief of the Armed Forces. In a special oath, each soldier and officer in the army swore "unconditional obedience to the Leader of the German State and People, Adolph Hitler," and vowed "as a brave soldier, to stake my life at any time for this oath." Police terror and absolute loyalty constituted two central features of the Nazi state.

In fact there existed two states. On the one hand, the regular state administration functioned much as it had in the past. Most bureaucrats accepted their new leaders, many joining the Nazi party to ensure the security of their job. The judicial and educational officials adjusted their methods to the new political conditions, though new courts enforced political repression. New masters set the rules; the regular state apparatus remained virtually unchanged. The other state ruled behind the scenes. It did not abide by ordinary laws nor were its personnel at all like those of the state administration.

This was the "SS state," a system of power dedicated to absolute, unquestioning service to the leader. The Nazi party symbolized the new leadership, its giant party rallies in the medieval city of Nuremberg orchestrated to display Nazi might. It provided the recruits to the two key groups in the "SS state"—the SS, expanded in numbers and power after June 1934 to supplant the SA, and the secret police, the Gestapo, soon incorporated into the SS organization. The powers of the SS extended to the jails for political prisoners and concentration camps for the "reeducation" of undesirables. Probably around ten thousand individuals, mostly political opponents of the Nazis, were confined to these camps in the 1930s, but the number who passed through the camps was much higher. This "SS state" enjoyed unrestricted power to arrest and to punish; its only law was the simple command: "The will of the Leader has the force of law." Hitler's dream of a new German nation took the form of a warfare state, led by warriors and supported by the efforts of the entire population. Hitler devoted vast resources to build great architectural monuments worthy of the new, Third Reich (Empire), which would, he proclaimed, last for a thousand years.

There was no place in this new empire for its Jewish population. Nazi hatred of the Jews became the inspiration for a policy of racial segregation and persecution. First in 1933 came the expulsion of Jews from any position in the German administration. Then came sweeping measures of discrimination contained in the Nuremberg Laws of 1935. All Germans with at least two Jewish grandparents lost their German citizenship. Marriages between Germans and Jews became illegal. The result of these laws was the expulsion of Jews from German society, into which they had assimilated generations before. In the wake of these laws municipalities issued edicts forbidding Jews entry into their cities, posting signs proclaiming themselves "Free of Jews [*Judenrein*]." By 1938 over

Nazism on Display: Hitler Addressing Party Rally, approx. 1935.
(*National Archives*)

100,000 Jews had emigrated, usually surrendering everything they owned to obtain their permit to leave. Among them were outstanding intellectuals such as Albert Einstein. Even more fled after the violent attack in November 1938 on Jews and Jewish property (the so-called "Crystal Night"), during which all Jewish synagogues were burned. In a country Westerners believed an advanced, civilized society, blind racism had become law. The foundations for the policy of genocide were in place.

To Germans supporting the new regime, those years before 1939 were good times.

They were expected to demonstrate public approval of Nazi policies and to serve the interests of the nation in the spirit of Nazism. In return Hitler promised to put Germans back to work. In its social and economic policies, the Nazi regime proved, as the Italian Fascists earlier, a conservative force. Hitler needed a strong German economy for his plans of rearmament. He knew no economic theory; he did believe that people had to be put to work, even if the state lacked sufficient tax revenues. His financial advisers were shocked by his deficit spending, used for public work projects, public housing, and other major building projects. The unemployed were required to enroll in the German Labor Service, which enforced the slogan (also applied to concentration camp inmates) that "Work makes one free."

Nazi deficit spending, public works projects, and the rearmament program spurred economic recovery. Public works had already begun under the Weimar regime, and improved international trade gave a boost to German exports. Still, the Nazis claimed the credit for better times, and it appears that Hitler's use of deficit spending to pay for his projects did accelerate economic growth. A Four-Year Economic Plan introduced in 1936 sought to make Germany economically self-sufficient (and hence better able to wage war). Nazi planners collaborated with and guaranteed profits to capitalists; their economic methods had nothing in common with planning in Russia in the same years. By the middle of the decade, unemployment had disappeared, and the standard of living of the population returned to 1920s levels. Germans had work and security, and most did not choose to ask for more.

The Nazi state extended its controls over social and cultural activities as well. Propaganda movies such as the documentary film *The Triumph of the Will*, which skillfully portrayed the 1934 Nazi party rally, were shown throughout the country. Censorship ensured that the press and books conformed to the Nazi ideology. "Corrupt" modern art was banned and replaced by monumental paintings and statues of heroic German men and women. The regime encouraged collective recreational activities in the "Strength Through Joy" organization. It even considered producing a German rival to the model A Ford, to be called the "strength through joy" car (much later appearing as the "people's car"—*Volkswagen*).

These social policies emphasized a way of life of earlier generations which had appeared threatened in the free atmosphere of the 1920s. Women's place in German society was summed up in the slogan "children, kitchen, church." Thus while the Nazi revolution swept aside old political institutions and leadership, it preserved under new political controls the social order and economic structure of Germany. The reason for this conservatism was in part Hitler's disdain for economic issues and his narrow view of proper German values and institutions. More important was his determination to turn the energies of Germany to foreign conquest.

The Nazi State and Foreign Expansion

Both expansionist and militarist, Nazism was an avowed enemy of the Weimar policy of collaboration with the Western states in the Locarno Treaty and of acceptance of Versailles Treaty limits on German military might. Hitler's fanatical hatred of Bolshevism ended as well Weimar's policy of good relations with the Soviet Union. He stated in 1937 that "German's problem can only be solved by force and this always entails risk." He had no plan of conquest; he had learned in his political career how to take advantage of circumstances and did the same in the pursuit of his goal to make Germany the "continental power" of Europe.

In the three years that followed the Nazi seizure of power, the German government destroyed the peace settlement of the 1920s. In late 1933 Germany abandoned the League of Nations, an action that symbolized Hitler's renunciation of the principles of collective security and peaceful relations which Wilson and the other framers of the League Covenant believed would guarantee a better world. In those same months, Hitler secretly terminated the military collaboration with the Soviet Union. The act revealed his deep hatred of "Bolshevism"; in the following years he rejected all Soviet offers of peaceful relations, calling publicly for the destruction of the "Bolshevistic international world oppressors" who championed a "destructive Asiatic world conception." Nazi expansionist aims in Central Europe were not aided by these statements and actions, which forced the Soviet Union to consider (temporarily) an alliance with the Western democracies. Hitler was possessed by a larger and more ambitious goal than simple interest of state.

The Nazi regime had first to end the Versailles limits on its military power. It secretly began to shift some industrial production to armaments; the Nazi Youth and the Labor Front became military training organizations. By early 1935 secrecy was no longer possible. In March, Hitler denounced the limitations imposed on the size of the German army included in the 1919 treaty. Immediately Germany adopted conscription and set out to increase the army to one-half million men. Hitler justified his action by demanding "equality of rights" for his country. The British government, desperately seeking to maintain peace by treating Germany "fairly," accepted the act. Once again Hitler had gambled and won.

The last act ending the peacekeeping agreements of the 1920s was German destruction in 1936 of the Locarno settlement. The most important security guarantee to the Western powers in that treaty was German acceptance of the demilitarized "buffer zone" in the Rhineland. The frontier area along the northeastern French and the Belgian borders had been kept free of German troops. In the 1930s, however, no Allied occupation forces remained to ensure compliance. The only assurance that Germany would honor this restriction on its sovereignty was the Locarno Treaty; should it violate that treaty, the other participants had the right to send their forces back into the Rhineland, and if necessary to declare war.

Hitler chose to take that risk, though his army remained small and his generals warned that German troops would have to retreat immediately if France chose war. He later admitted that "if the French had marched into the Rhineland we would have had to withdraw with our tail between our legs." He dismissed the fears of his generals, however, for he was persuaded that the British had lost faith in the Versailles settlement and that no Allied power had the determination to enforce its provisions. He was right. He possessed an extraordinary talent to pick out the weakness in his adversaries. German military reoccupation of the Rhineland in March 1936 took place peaceably, to the cheers of the Rhineland population.

A new European balance of power was beginning to take shape. The move into the Rhineland made Germany a major power. Yet all it had done was to eliminate the restrictions of 1919. What would take the place of the old system? The British relied on conciliation and negotiation with Germany, judging Hitler a statesman of reasonable goals defending German national security. The French government, concerned primarily with retaining its alliance with Great Britain, supported the British policy. The ambitions which drove Hitler remained to them mysterious and unimaginable. By 1936 it was clear that while they clung to peaceful compromise to resolve disputes, Germany relied increasingly on force and intimidation.

The Spanish civil war revealed the profound differences in international behavior that separated the Western democracies from the European dictators. In July 1936, a military uprising led by General Franco sought to overthrow the Spanish Republic, whose Popular Front government supported radical land reform and national autonomy for the non-Spanish peoples of the country. In the social turmoil of that year, the reformist leaders were powerless to prevent some of their followers from attacking property of the Spanish Catholic church, a supporter of conservatism. Franco's goal was a strong centralized state protecting property, the church, and the unity of Spain. He was not a fascist, though he accepted help from a fascist movement, the Phalange. The Republic, on the other hand, obtained its support from liberals and Marxists, from workers and peasants. Many Europeans judged the conflict in Spain to be between popular democracy and fascist dictatorship. The civil war became an international cause; volunteers from the Western democracies—socialists, communists, ardent democrats (including some Americans such as the writer Ernest Hemingway)—joined the Republic's forces.

The Spanish conflict had a second international dimension as well. It became an opportunity for fascist leaders in Europe to demonstrate their commitment to "destroy Bolshevism" and to expand their international power. The Italian Fascist state, eager to create an Italian sphere of influence in the Mediterranean, immediately sent troops and military equipment to Franco. The previous year, Italy had invaded Ethiopia in its first effort to create an "Italian Empire" that Mussolini dreamed would ultimately rival that of classical Rome. Only Nazi Germany backed his war of conquest. The Spanish civil war provided a second opportunity for collaboration, for Germany also supplied military aid to Franco's rebels. Included in this help were German fighter bombers and pilots, responsible for the brutal bombing of the Basque city of Guernica (the subject of the most famous antiwar painting of the century by the Spanish artist Pablo Picasso). In 1937 the two dictators agreed to collaborate in an alliance which they called the Axis.

Opposing their intervention was the Soviet Union. Once German and Italian support for Franco began, the Soviets sent military aid and helped to organize international fighting units, the International Brigades, to assist the Republic. Joseph Stalin, the Soviet leader, probably anticipated that Great Britain and France would also intervene on the side of the Republic, thus ending the period of Western appeasement and bringing both countries into conflict against Germany. Instead, the two countries, as well as the United States, chose a policy of nonintervention, which in practice meant they denied aid to the Republic (though France did later secretly supply arms). Their objective was to avoid the risk of international conflict for the sake of the Spanish Republic. Appeasement remained their highest priority. In early 1939 the civil war ended with the triumph of Franco's forces. The Spanish state, like many other European countries in those crisis years, became a dictatorship.

Strengthened by its rearmament and by the destruction of the Locarno Treaty, the Nazi regime set out on the more dangerous path of territorial expansion in the south and east. This region of small states, the successors of the Austro-Hungarian Empire, represented a "power vacuum" easily dominated by large states. The protection extended to these countries by the Versailles Treaty system and by the Western powers existed only on paper and dissolved when challenged by Nazi Germany. In early 1938, Hitler proclaimed that the Austrian people had to join his Greater Germany. When the Austrian government refused, he sent German troops to occupy without firing a shot the entire country. Austria became a province of the Third Reich; its eight million people now served the Nazi state. Most important, German domination of Eastern Europe moved ahead.

The second step came when Germany demanded the annexation of the area in western Czechoslovakia known as the Sudetenland. The proclaimed purpose was the protection of "oppressed" Germans living there; the real objective was the destruction of Czechoslovakia, a major obstacle in the path of German eastward expansion. Czechoslovakia possessed a strong army and had signed a defensive alliance with France and the Soviet Union. It represented a substantial military force on Germany's eastern borders. Hitler was ready for war that year, but may also have anticipated that the West would once again prefer conciliation, even if it entailed the sacrifice of an allied state and another key element in the Paris peace treaties.

When he threatened in September to invade the Czech lands unless his demands were met, Italy proposed a four-power meeting in Munich of Germany, Italy, France, and Great Britain. The Western states grabbed the olive branch, though both the Soviet Union and Czechoslovakia were excluded from the negotiations. The Munich Treaty which resulted from the conference gave Hitler all he wanted. Great Britain and France forced the Czechs to give up the Sudeten territory to Germany, fatally weakening Czechoslovakia. Their desperate effort to preserve peace in Europe came to symbolize capitulation to aggression.

In fact, neither government was prepared militarily and psychologically for war in defense, as the British leader Neville Chamberlain said, of a "far-off place inhabited by people of whom we know little." The treaty itself resulted from years of Western wishful thinking regarding Nazi objectives, an illusion to which Western statesmen and citizens clung in the fervent hope that European war would never return. A tragedy for Czechoslovakia, the agreement proved a diplomatic disaster for the Western states.

In 1939, the Nazi leaders took the third step toward becoming a "continental power." That spring, they removed the state of Czechoslovakia from the map of Europe by annexing the western half of the country and creating a puppet government over the eastern half (Slovakia). To the northeast lay Poland, situated between Germany and Soviet Russia and including territory taken from both states. The recovery of the "Polish corridor" and of the city of Danzig had constituted an objective of German policy even under the Weimar Republic.

Hitler publicly demanded no more but, as in the case of Czechoslovakia, his larger goal was domination of the region. His means remained as in the past force and intimidation. In March 1939, an appeal from President Roosevelt for a peaceful compromise evoked from him only ridicule of the distant Americans. Boasting that he, "who twenty-one years ago was an unknown worker and soldier of my people," had "reestablished the historical unity of German living space," he mocked Roosevelt's concern for "the fate of the world." He could easily afford to do so, since isolationism prevented the United States from exercising any real influence in European affairs.

The Soviet Union presented a more serious problem. Hitler had for years treated the Communist state as Germany's enemy, yet it possessed the largest army in Eastern Europe. That spring, the British government finally abandoned its policy of appeasement and refused any further revision of the Versailles Treaty. Instead, it pledged military aid to Poland in the event of war with Germany and began, with the French, to negotiate a military alliance with Soviet Russia. If Stalin decided to join with the Western democracies to protect Poland, he would force Germany into another two-front war. Reluctantly Hitler chose to negotiate with Communist Russia. Offering to divide Polish territory with the Soviet Union, he presented Stalin with an offer of spoils of war, that is, Polish territory, in exchange for Soviet collaboration in the destruction of Poland. Stalin accepted, and in August, 1939, the two states secretly agreed to partition Poland. The German-Soviet nonaggression pact opened the way to German war on Poland. Hitler urged his military commanders to "close your eyes to pity" and to "act brutally." In September 1939, his army invaded Poland. Two days later, in a desperate effort to contain German expansion and to save the Versailles settlement, Britain and France declared war on Germany. A new European war had begun.

Unlike the First World War, in whose origins responsibility had to be shared by the great powers, the immediate cause of the new war was obvious. Nazi militarism and expansionism drove Europe into the conflict. For all their defects, the Versailles settlement and Locarno treaties together had dealt in a fairly equitable manner with the problems of security and national self-determination. From the perspective of 1939, in fact, they were too fair, leaving Germany with the territory, population, and resources sufficient under Nazi leadership to mobilize for war. No one in 1919 had conceived of a German state so fanatical and brutal as that the Nazis had instituted after 1933.

STALIN'S RUSSIA

In the decade prior to the outbreak of that new war, the Soviet Union became a powerful, industrialized country under the control of a brutal, centralized dictatorship. Historians have termed the events of those years the "Stalin revolution," for in 1929 Stalin had become Lenin's heir and undisputed ruler of the Soviet Union. The most important changes occuring under his leadership consisted of (1) the rapid development of the Soviet industrial economy, (2) the forcible collectivization of all farmland brought together in collective farms, and (3) the expan-

sion of the repressive powers of the party and the secret police to perpetuate a system of terror, that is, of arbitrary arrest and punishment unhindered by legal restraints.

The Bolshevik Revolution of 1917 had put in place a Communist dictatorship governing a country predominantly agricultural whose land was held and worked by peasant farmers. Stalin created a one-man dictatorship and ended private farming, extending the powers of the state into all areas of the economy and society and developing Soviet industry at an extraordinary pace. He claimed that the social and economic transformation of his country raised Soviet society to the historical stage of "socialism." Critics called him a tyrant. How had he managed to become dictator and to transform so radically the Soviet Union?

Stalin and the End of NEP

The critical problems of Communist rule in the late 1920s and his own political ambition represent the key factors in his rise to power. In those years collective leadership rested in the hands of the members of the Politburo, the governing party committee which set state policies. Stalin was only one of the participants, possessing in addition the special responsibility of general secretary in charge of party membership and appointments. The Communist "vanguard" constituted a small ruling elite controlling a vast country and fearful of hostile Western states. The leaders believed that they confronted the "real and actual threat" of a new imperialist war.

Their country was weak and internally divided between a small working class, sympathetic to Communist aims, and peasant farmers determined to keep possession of their land. The New Economic Policy, introduced in 1921, had succeeded in raising farm production but did not provide adequate means to finance rapid industrial growth, necessary both to build a strong modern army and to create the socialist society of abundance of which the Communists dreamed. Thus two reasons, one practical and the other utopian, impelled the party leadership to propose in 1927 a campaign for rapid industrialization. Expensive investments required that agriculture, that is, the peasantry, be made to sacrifice income through taxes and low prices for farm produce. The peasants' refusal to cooperate on these terms, apparent in 1928, threw the country into its most serious crisis since the civil war and opened the way for Stalin's leadership.

The crisis took the form of a serious shortage of food for the urban population and for export. The state, which purchased almost all farm production, had lowered the price it paid for major commodities, and many peasant farmers refused to sell their crops. The decline in sales was so severe that food rationing appeared in 1928 in the cities, and Soviet agricultural exports, essential to pay for the import of industrial machinery, nearly collapsed. What caused the shortages? To Westerners accustomed to free enterprise, the problem lay in the market. The peasants demanded incentives—good prices, consumer products at cheap prices—which the Communists refused to grant them.

Many Communist leaders understood the crisis very differently. Suspicious of peasant "petty capitalism" and imbued with the ideological and civil war spirit of class war, they blamed wealthy peasants, the *kulaks,* for seeking to weaken the proletarian state. Stalin was their spokesman. He put in words their fears of peasant opposition and of imperialist attack, warning in the spring of 1928 that "we confront enemies outside the Soviet union [and] we confront enemies within the Soviet Union." He provided as well a simple solution to the crisis. That year

he ordered police and party officials to seize by force, as in the civil war, the surplus produce of the peasants. Moderate Communist leaders were appalled at his ruthless action. One even accused him of being a new Mongol "Genghis Khan," introducing Asiatic despotism in place of proletarian dictatorship.

That year marked the first time Stalin took political leadership in his hands. Why had he done so? He claimed to be defending the revolution in the spirit of Leninism. The consequences of his action, however, were to launch a new revolution and to replace Leninism with Stalinism. Most Western historians believe his personal ambition was fixed upon the goal of taking Lenin's place and that he turned the crisis of 1928 to his own advantage. We know little of his inner thoughts and motives, for he was a secretive man. His life had been one of struggle from poverty and of political combat in the name of proletarian revolution, which he appears to have associated with his own personal glory. He learned of class conflict and oppression, of the inevitable fall of capitalism, and of the future joys of communism, through his study of Marxism. We need not question his faith in these basic ideological precepts, for they gave him the essential conviction in the rightness of his cause and the necessity for conflict. His understanding of Marxism, in other words, fit his combative personality. Lenin was his teacher and leader in that period of learning and fighting. He remained loyal to Lenin through the years of underground agitation and then of war and revolution. All he achieved he owed to Lenin, including his position as general secretary.

Like the rebellious son, however, in the early 1920s he came to think himself worthy to take Lenin's place. His political methods were harsh, a fact Lenin discovered too late. After Lenin's stroke and then death in 1924, Stalin used his key party responsibilities gradually to build up a following among the party cadres, who played the key role in choosing new leaders and carrying out policy. They were sympathetic to his new policies in 1928, and supported his moves that year and the next to remove from leadership positions all his rivals in the Politburo. By 1929 he dominated that body and through it the Soviet Union. On his fiftieth birthday late that year his backers proclaimed that "Stalin is the Lenin of today!"

The Stalin Revolution

That year he began what he himself boasted was a "revolution from above." Previously the very term "revolution" was synonymous with popular uprising; in the new Stalinist vocabulary, it referred to the transformation of the economy and society at the command of the Communist party. It took shape through two separate policy decisions. One consisted in the adoption of a Five-Year Plan for industrial production, which was to triple by the early 1930s. The other was the party decision taken late in 1929 to force the 100 million peasants off their farms and into "collective farms" (referred to usually by the abbreviated Russian term *kolkhoz*), that is, producer cooperatives.

In theory "collectivization" of farms strengthened socialist cooperation; in reality it gave to the state direct access to agricultural production, since state officials would control administration of the farms. These measures marked the end of NEP and of conciliation of the peasantry. Their implementation required that the Communist dictatorship expand its repressive powers, in the hands of the secret police. Ultimately Stalin's ambition and the vast increase in arbitrary police power came together to turn the Soviet regime into a police dictatorship.

Industrialization in the first Five-Year Plan combined revolutionary dreams and the need to expand the state's military might. The production goals of the plan supposedly followed the guidelines of the plan elaborated by the State Planning Commission (*Gosplan*). In a burst of optimism, Stalin ordered the attainment of the plan's objectives by the end of 1932; the slogan was "The Five-Year Plan in four years!" The spirit of Soviet industrialization was warlike; workers had to "storm" ahead and "conquer fortresses" to build socialism. Economists in Gosplan objected that such extraordinary economic growth would lead to chaos; they were dismissed or arrested. Under this system of command planning, officials and managers in the state enterprises had to meet production targets or risk being fired or even arrested for "wrecking."

These brutal policies responded to the need to equip a modern army as well as to lay the material foundations for a socialist society. To Stalin the former objective was more important. The "tempo" of industrial growth "must not be reduced," he told a meeting of factory managers in 1931. The reason was simple: an advanced "socialist system of economy" would make Russia strong, ending its "backwardness." Stalin warned his audience that the world was still ruled by the "jungle law of capitalism," which he understood to be the simple rule of "beat the weak but be wary of the strong." Speaking more like a Russian ruler than like a Communist, he recited the long list of foreign enemies who had defeated the Russian state in past centuries, from the Mongol Khans in the thirteenth century to the Japanese in the twentieth (omitting the Germans for diplomatic reasons). Either the "Socialist homeland" would catch up to the capitalist countries in ten years "or they will crush us." Without realizing where the real danger would come from, he anticipated the terrible war which lay ahead.

The actual campaign of industrialization

proved as chaotic as the skeptics in 1929 had predicted. Russia needed to import foreign machinery and technicians to set up new industries. Among the imports was an entire tractor and truck factory build by the Ford Motor Company. German machinery for steel mills went to the new industrial city of Magnitogorsk in the Ural mountains. The worldwide depression lowered the price of agricultural commodities and raw materials, major source of Russia's foreign exchange with which to pay for these imports. The government chose to export more food, though part of the population starved in 1932–33. Within the country there were not enough railroads, not enough skilled workers, not enough housing, not enough steel and cement for all the new factories. The Five-Year Plan served primarily propaganda needs, used to cajole and threaten workers and managers. A priority system similar to wartime decided where the most pressing needs lay and where scarce resources should go.

The most spectacular accomplishments of the industrial plan consisted of giant industrial projects. Accompanied by great publicity, a 1,000-mile railroad, the Turksib, linked Turkestan in Central Asia with central Siberia; a mammoth dam (its size fixed by Stalin to be greater than the largest Western dam, the Hoover Dam in the United States) on the lower Dnepr river in the southern Ukraine generated hydroelectric power for industry. The mountainous region around Kuznetsk, north of China, became one of the country's major sources of coal. To the west, on the parched eastern slopes of the Ural Mountains emerged a giant iron and steel complex, Magnitogorsk, to exploit the rich iron ore deposits of the area (also on Stalin's orders to become the largest steel mill in the world). To these building sites went the precious machinery, foreign ex-

Machinery for the Collectivized Countryside: Soviet Factory Producing Locomobiles for Rural Power Houses, approx. 1939. (*Patty Ratliff Collection/Hoover Institution Archives*)

perts, and raw material necessary for rapid construction. Key party leaders personally supervised the work to ensure that the "tempo" never slackened.

The burden fell on great numbers of workers brought voluntarily or by force to these construction sites. Young Communists considered the projects a crusade; Communist workers abandoned their homes to join in the campaign. One Soviet writer observing them at work asked why they worked so hard in such primitive conditions. Their answer was simple: "We're building communism. The entire world is looking at us." Alongside them, however, were peasants fleeing the brutal collectivization campaign and misery in the countryside; they worked simply to avoid hunger. There too were hundreds of thousands of forced laborers, mostly peasants arrested for resisting collectivization. They lived in tent camps under police guard. The total size of the industrial labor force doubled by the end of the first Five-Year Plan. Their living conditions were miserable. Housing was inadequate, and food supplies were so short that rationing remained in effect during the entire period. Like it or not, they had to accept great sacrifices in Stalin's industrialization drive.

To supervise the work, the Soviet state needed an army of specialists. It inherited from tsarist Russia a small core of well-trained engineers, but their "bourgeois" origins made them suspect in Stalin's Russia. To force them to work for the new regime, the police arrested "traitorous" engineers accused of sabotage in the pay of capitalist enemies. In 1930 two "show trials" in Moscow put on display prominent engineers accused of "counterrevolutionary" activities. All the defendants confessed, to be shot or sent as prison labor to work in the industrial projects. "Justice" had become another tool to manipulate key segments of the population.

The atmosphere in the country resembled that of a besieged fortress, filled with enthusiasm for battle and with fear and suspicion of saboteurs and spies. Part of that battle consisted of the rapid training of "Red specialists," Communists from worker background given technical training on the job. By the end of the first Five-Year Plan, over one-half million people had received promotions to managerial and technical positions through this "affirmative action" plan. Among them were Nikita Khrushchev and Leonid Brezhnev, future leaders of the Soviet Union. These people owed their careers to the party and to Stalin; they became the new "Stalinist elite" of Soviet Russia.

By the end of 1932, industrial production had soared. New industrial plants in Siberia were beginning to turn out great amounts of iron and steel, whose total output doubled between 1928 and 1932. Oil production too doubled, while electricity increased three times. The standard of living of the urban population, on the other hand, declined by one-third to one-half; it had a low priority in Stalin's revolution. Stalin proclaimed that his country had "cast off the aspect of backwardness and medievalism." The price paid by the population, however, was terribly high.

The peasant farmers suffered worst of all. In November 1929, the party leaders ordered "mass collectivization" of private farms to begin. Stalin refused any compromise with the "capitalist way" of private farming; the "socialist way" of collective farms had to triumph. The party expected resistance and authorized the use of "administrative measures," that is, of repressive police action to punish those who resisted. The prime target was the so-called *kulak* group of well-to-do farmers, which the party decided in January 1930 to "liquidate," that is, to deprive of all their property. Police officials received secret instructions to exile, imprison, or shoot specific proportions of peasants in their regions.

The orders indicated that in the entire country, 1.2 million households (approximately 6 million individuals) would experience one form or other of repression. These peasants, the best private farmers in Russia, were excluded from the new collective farms. This "planned" class war represented a monstrous act of retribution against peasants condemned for lack of support for the Communist regime. By early 1932, collectivization was complete in the principal farming areas of the country. At the Seventeenth Party Congress in early 1934, Stalin proudly announced that 200,000 producer farm cooperatives existed. The regime had "eliminated capitalism" in the countryside, destroying the last bastion of privately owned productive wealth standing the way of socialism.

The result in the countryside was hardship and hunger. The state used its power over agriculture to extract the greatest amount of produce at the lowest possible price. It removed incentives from farming, at precisely the moment when Communist administrators on the collective farms were struggling to set up "cooperation" in farm work. Peasants had slaughtered nearly half their livestock rather than let it go to the collective farms. As a result, draft animals were in short supply, and the state had precious few tractors to replace them. Peasants on the new farms worked half-heartedly. All these factors led by 1932 to a fall in farm production. In late 1932, it was clear that collectivized agriculture was not producing enough to satisfy the state and to feed the rural population. Stalin chose to continue state procurements, ordering severe punishments for any officials who failed to deliver the produce.

Although never admitted by the state, hunger spread through the countryside, leading to famine, epidemics, and the death of untold millions of Russians. Word of the tragedy reached the cities, where even Communists were horrified at the betrayal of their hopes for a better life for all the people. Stalin's young wife, Nadezhda Allilueva, shared the dream and suffered the disillusionment at the new revolution. That fall, in the midst of the celebrations of the fifteenth anniversary of the Bolshevik Revolution, she had a bitter quarrel with her husband. Afterward, she shot herself in their Kremlin apartment. Her suicide made her another casualty of the Stalin Revolution.

Even Stalin's colleagues in the Politburo concluded that his leadership had led to serious abuses of power. In the spring of 1933 these moderates, including one of his close aides, Sergei Kirov, forced Stalin to end mass terror, to regularize the conditions of the collective farms, and to accept reasonable goals of industrial growth in the second Five-Year Plan. They hoped to revive the practice of "collective leadership" of the pre-1929 years and to curtail Stalin's own authority. The man they supported to lead this effort, perhaps even to replace Stalin, was Kirov. Suddenly, in December 1934 Kirov was assassinated. This event freed Stalin from the party restraints put on his rule. It led to bloody retribution against all Stalin's rivals, real and imagined, and produced a system of police terror that remained in place until his death.

The Terrorist Dictatorship

What permitted Stalin to set up his new dictatorial regime? Historians are still searching to understand the secret process by which terror installed itself in Soviet life. It is clear that the growing power of the secret police facilitated Stalin's task. Soviet leaders hinted after Stalin's death that the dictator himself, with the aid of agents in the secret police, was responsible for the Kirov murder. They also pointed to the Stalin "cult," the public adulation of the dictator, to explain the ease with which Stalin unleashed police terror. They omitted a third reason, namely, the backing he received from large numbers of Communists whose careers were linked to his. This "Stalin generation" of Communists were collaborators in terror.

The Stalin terror was based on unlimited repressive powers, exercised by the secret police controlled by Stalin himself. At his personal orders the secret police received immediately after Kirov's death the power to arrest, judge, and shoot or imprison anyone guilty of "counterrevolutionary activity." Since the police alone were the judge of the existence of this activity, they obtained arbitrary authority to punish at will those whom they considered enemies. To Stalin's suspicious mind, all Soviet officials, party members, or plain citizens who talked or acted in a manner to question his leadership and his policies were traitors. The Kirov assassination was followed by a wave of arrests of anyone remotely connected with opposition to his rule.

Stalin justified his recourse to terror by alleging the existence of a vast network of class enemies and foreign agents operating within Soviet Russia. He argued that "the further we advance toward socialism" the greater will be the "fury of the broken, exploiting classes" who used the "most desperate means of struggle" to undermine the Soviet state. Pitiless vigilance and repression alone could deal with these enemies, whom he perceived everywhere. So great was his suspiciousness that historians have since suggested he was mentally deranged. Yet his ruthless action revealed the careful, calculating mind of a tyrant. He turned the secret police into his chosen agents of rule. In

doing so he added a second key element to Stalinism. The first was revolution from above. The second was police terror.

The former leaders of the country vanished in the mass repression. The unrestricted power enjoyed by the secret police (known then by the initials of the People's Commissariat of Internal Affairs, *NKVD*) permitted Stalin to decimate the ranks of the party cadres, responsible for Communist dictatorship throughout the land, of the state bureaucracy (including even the officer and diplomatic corps), of the engineers and managers of nationalized industry, and of the intellectuals. His most dramatic acts comprised the arrest, trial, and execution of almost all the "Old Bolsheviks," Lenin's collaborators and leaders of the party since the revolution. Beginning in 1936, they went on trial in three major "show trials," the last of which was held in early 1938. All confessed after months of interrogation and torture to supposed (and completely fictitious) "crimes against the state"; all were convicted and shot, their names removed from party histories, their faces removed from group pictures of party officials. Leon Trotsky, whom Stalin had expelled from the Soviet Union in 1929, was tracked down in Mexico by NKVD agents and assassinated. No party leader was left to criticize Stalin or to remind him of his own inadequacies.

In an action that undermined the efforts to strengthen Russia's military might, the so-called Great Terror extended even to the Red Army. After having supported his generals in their effort to turn the army into a professional, highly trained military organization equipped for tank warfare, Stalin appears to have become afraid of their potential political power. No real evidence ever appeared to substantiate the accusation that these officers had plotted against Stalin or had become agents of foreign powers. Evidence was irrelevant. Even confessions proved unnecessary to convict, for Stalin and the police had judged the officer corps guilty in advance. The terror in the army began with the secret trial in 1937 of five outstanding generals, including the army commander-in-chief, Tukhachevsky. They were convicted and shot as spies for foreign powers. All officers then fell under suspicion, and half of the entire officer corps within a year was arrested, many executed or dying in prison camps. At a time of growing foreign danger, Stalin gambled his country's security for the sake of his brutal dictatorship.

Out of the terror emerged a enormous secret police empire. It consisted of prisons and a vast network of prison camps extending across the country, especially in the northern and eastern regions of Siberia. Millions of prisoners worked there, a large number dying in inhuman living conditions. In their brutality and hardship, the camps appeared to inmates an extreme form of the police rule which dominated the entire country. One prisoner from later years, Alexander Solzhenitsyn, conveyed this message in his story of camp life, *A Day in the Life of Ivan Denisovich.* The camps constituted a world unto themselves, though, where prison officials reigned as petty despots.

The secret police became in the Great Terror the most powerful political institution in the country. Stalin, probably aware of the potential threat it posed to his dictatorship, had its chief, Ezhov, and his followers arrested in 1938, to be shot in their turn as "counterrevolutionaries." The new chief, Lavrenty Beria, stayed at the head of the secret police until Stalin's death. The terror declined in intensity after 1938, but the system remained in place as long as Stalin lived.

The dictatorship extended into all areas of Soviet cultural life. The encouragement for experimentation and the toleration for artistic diversity which existed in the 1920s vanished. State-controlled organizations of writers, artists, musicians, and educators controlled the publication and diffusion of cultural work. Their censorship left little room for individual creativity. Instead, official canons dictated the form and substance of cultural activity. The model of "socialist realism," that is, of art reflecting the idealized "reality" of the socialist society, was imposed in literature, painting, and cinema. The only new theme was the glorification of Russian nationalism and old Russian military and political leaders (such as Tsar Ivan the Terrible, with whom apparently Stalin increasingly identified). Education became dogmatic, stressing simple truths among which the most important was the Marxist-Leninist-Stalinist ideology. Teachers became the absolute authority in the classroom, where pupils once again (as in tsarist times) dressed in uniforms. Culture was in the service of the Stalinist state.

What had the Stalin Revolution achieved? Some historians would answer that it raised Soviet Russia to the rank of second greatest industrial power in the world. The economic statistics prove this fact correct, though they cannot convey the true measure of human hardship endured in that effort. Others emphasize the social revolution achieved by the elimination of private farming, pointing to state ownership of the means of production in all areas of the economy as evidence that a new social system had appeared. Communists called it the first "socialist society" in the world; critics called it state capitalism ruled by a "new class" of party bureaucrats.

Finally, another historical view stresses the police dictatorship in which Stalin and his supporters controlled the party, the state, and the entire population. It in some respects resembled Nazi Germany; this fact led political scientists to describe both as "totalitarian," emphasizing the supposed "total control" of the state and its leaders over the population. We know now that Stalinism, like Nazism, could not so dominate society. George Orwell's novel *1984,* based largely on the author's observations of the Soviet regime in the 1940s, provides a nightmarish and exaggerated image of the brutal world of Stalinism.

Stalin's Foreign Policy in Asia and Europe

The new Soviet leadership demanded obedience not only from its own population but also from all Communist parties around the world. Stalin had a low opinion of foreign Communists. He valued the Communist International primarily for its service in defending the Soviet Union. He demanded of its sections help in repelling the new enemies of the Soviet Union. He sought to turn French Communist participation in the Popular Front into a means to encourage French opposition to Germany in the mid-1930s, when the Soviet leadership hoped to contain German power with a French alliance. He required Chinese Communist resistance to Japanese forces in northern China to turn the Japanese military away from Soviet territory. These instructions to foreign Communists were intended primarily not to promote revolution but to assist the "socialist homeland," the Soviet Union. The supremacy of the interests of the Soviet Union in the world revolutionary movement constituted the third major tenet of Stalinism.

Stalin followed a simple set of rules to fix Soviet foreign policy in the dangerous world of the 1930s. Judging Western ideals of collective peacekeeping and conciliation a sham, he adopted for his state what he believed to be real Western practice, power politics. He repeated again in 1934 his conviction, first voiced in 1931, that "in our times it is not the custom to respect the weak—only the strong are respected." What did states do with their power? He revealed in 1939, referring again to the practice of other states, that he believed they created around their territory "spheres of influence" in which they dominated smaller states for their own protection and profit.

The "jungle law of capitalism" which he had identified in 1931 dictated that "might made right" and greater territorial domination was the reward for success. By that elementary rule the Soviet Union had for its own sake to "respect" other strong states by accepting their own spheres. The real threat of war would arise when they disagreed on the borders of those spheres. This simplistic, brutal picture of world relations guided Stalin's conduct of Soviet foreign policy for the rest of his life.

In the 1930s his country was threatened by the Japanese state in the east and Nazi Germany in the west. In each case he had to prepare for possible war but welcomed agreements which would avoid conflict and protect Soviet security interests. In 1931, Japan had invaded Manchuria, and later in the decade, its troops launched several attacks on Red Army forces both in the Soviet Union and in Mongolia, part of the Soviet Asian sphere. The Red Army repelled each Japanese attack, inflicting heavy losses on the enemy forces. After the outbreak of war in 1937 between Japan and China, the Soviet government began to provide military assistance to China.

The real escape from Asian war came when in 1941 the Japanese government decided that its most important military objectives were in the Pacific and Southeast Asia, not in Northeast Asia. That spring, the Japanese foreign minister offered the Soviet government a neutrality treaty. Stalin accepted immediately. He cared not at all where Japanese forces might attack in other areas; he asked only that his country be spared.

Nazi Germany proved in the end the greater danger. Hitler's hatred of the Communist system filled his speeches. Stalin, on the contrary, stated publicly in early 1934 that he did not consider ideological differences between fascism and communism to be a serious obstacle in dealing with the new German regime. "It is not a question of fascism here," he argued. "If the interests of the U.S.S.R. demand good relations with one country or another which is not interested in disturbing the peace [i.e., not attacking the Soviet Union], we will adopt this course without hesitation." But Hitler refused the invitation. Stalin had good reason to believe that Nazi Germany would move east again, as in the First World War, this time with the dual goals of seizing territory and destroying his regime.

How could the Soviet Union protect itself from another war with Germany? The precedent of the pre-1914 Franco-Russian pact suggested reviving this alliance. Stalin did agree in 1935 to a defense treaty with France, but it never became the foundation for a Soviet collective security policy. At best it offered the possibility that Germany might have to fight first in the west. Soviet aid to the Spanish Republic in 1936 sought to encourage Western resistance to "fascism," that is, to Germany. The French government clung to its appeasement policy until 1939, however.

By then Stalin had returned to his earlier objective of reaching an agreement with Nazi Germany. He seems to have believed that he understood the expansionist policies of Hitler, judging him another follower, though in an extreme form, of the "jungle law of capitalism." Since the two states dominated Eastern Europe, by his reasoning they

could avoid war (temporarily) by dividing the region into respective spheres of influence. He therefore accepted Hitler's offer in the summer of 1939 of a nonaggression pact, which contained the secret provisions for the partition of Poland, and in addition recognized a Soviet sphere of influence over the small eastern Baltic states. The agreement used a language Stalin understood. A German war against France and Great Britain did not concern him; again all he sought was territorial control and peace, if only for a few years, with the other major power of Europe, Germany.

SUMMARY

The Western world had undergone dramatic political changes in the ten years since the depression began. Two powerful dictatorships had emerged in Germany and Russia. Their collaboration in the war on Poland signaled a remarkable shift in the European balance of power. These two states, whose ideologies presented diametrically opposing visions of humanity's future, bore strong resemblance in their structure and operations. Both concentrated political power in one party dominated by a dictatorial leader; both gave broad authority to a secret police; both demanded absolute obedience of the population. Were common forces at work shaping these two regimes? Perhaps war provides one link, for both Stalinism and Nazism carried into their political revolutions a warrior mentality, directed in the first case to class conflict, in the latter to national conquest. Both Stalin and Hitler used a mass movement to satisfy their own hunger for power. Finally, both turned the institutions and methods of a bureaucratic state and modern technology into instruments to dominate an entire society. Although both talked of freedom, the word as they used it really meant obedience. Deadly rivals for international power, their regimes each in their own way represented the antithesis of democratic government.

The peace settlements laboriously put together by the Western statesmen had vanished as well by 1939. The Western states had chosen not to enforce these agreements, partly out of reluctance to risk a new war, partly because they were weakened by the depression. The war which began that year would not be ended by their efforts. Instead, that new world war led to the victory of states whose power extended across continents. The Western empires could not survive the conflict. The Asian war was as important to the new balance of power as the European war.

RECOMMENDED READING

The Depression and the Western Democracies

JAMES BURNS, *Roosevelt: The Lion and the Fox* (1956)

M. COWLING, *The Impact of Hitler: British Politics and British Policy* (1975)

JOHN GARRATY, *The Great Depression* (1986)

CHARLES KINDELBERGER, *The World in Depression, 1929–1939* (1973)

The Nazi Dictatorship

*WILLIAM S. ALLEN *The Nazi Seizure of Power: The Experience of a Single German Town* (second ed., 1984)

*HANNAH ARENDT, *The Origins of Totalitarianism* (1973)

*ALAN BULLOCK, *Hitler: A Study in Tyranny* (1965)

*DAVID SCHOENBAUM, *Hitler's Social Revolution: Class and Status in Nazi Germany* (1980)

*A. J. P. TAYLOR, *The Origins of the Second World War* (1962)

HENRY TURNER, *German Big Business and the Rise of Hitler* (1985)

*EUGEN WEBER, *Varieties of Fascism* (1964)

The Stalin Dictatorship

ROBERT CONQUEST, *The Great Terror* (1968)

*ISAAC DEUTSCHER, *Stalin: A Political Biography* (second ed., 1955)

*SHEILA FITZPATRICK (ed.), *Cultural Revolution in Russia, 1928–1931* (1978)

*ROBERT TUCKER, *Stalin as Revolutionary, 1879–1929* (1973)

Memoirs and Novels

*ARTHUR KOESTLER, *Darkness at Noon* (1940)

NADEZHDA MANDELSTAM, *Hope Against Hope* (1976)

*JOHN SCOTT, *Behind the Urals: An American Worker in Russia* (1942)

chapter 5

THE ASIAN CHALLENGE TO EUROPEAN IMPERIALISM, 1918–1941

Nationalism in Asia developed in the decades after the First World War into a powerful political force. The war itself marked the beginning of a new era in the relations between the imperial powers and Asian peoples. No fighting occurred in India or in East Asia, and the peace settlements scarcely altered the prewar colonial divisions of the area. Indirectly, however, the war's impact extended throughout the area. Political leaders spoke out from Communist Russia proclaiming the end of the imperialist era. Wilson's war aims suggested in milder language that peoples everywhere could aspire to national self-determination. Even the British government indicated its readiness to concede some measure of self-rule to its greatest colony, India.

Giving greater force to this new climate of opinion was the fact that the Allies had had to accept Asian collaboration in the war effort. The independent state of Japan became a welcome ally in the war. Indian industrial production expanded and the Indian army participated in the fighting. A new Chinese government sought to protect its fragile powers by joining the Allied side. When the peace settlement recognized Japanese concessions in China, Chinese opposition to the Japanese presence was so strong it produced the first nationalist mass movement in the country's history. There, as in other lands, nationalism took the form first of all of popular opposition to foreign domination. National identity emerged in resistance to the "outsider," against whom political and social unity was needed. In this manner imperialism in the non-Western world led directly to nationalism.

The new political forces at work in Asia took different forms depending on the history of the colonial lands, and also on the colonial regimes. The Dutch, French, and British, dominant Western imperialists, ruled their territories each in a manner peculiar to their own political traditions and colonial practice. The Indian experience under the British combined centralization of political power with limited autonomy granted princely states, some very large, scattered throughout the area. India occupies a central place in the study of Asian nationalism, for it produced one of the most effective reformist independence movements of the twentieth century.

Chinese nationalism emerged in conditions of civil war, which began shortly after the collapse of the Chinese Empire in 1911. The last emperor disappeared without a struggle, deprived of his "mandate of heaven" in the eyes of many Chinese by his inability to reform his state and to resist Western imperialism. The real conflict began afterward, when military leaders and political parties fought one another for power and leadership of that vast country. As a result, China endured nearly a half-century of sporadic, but bloody civil war. In the 1920s the victor appeared to be the Nationalist party. But internal and foreign opposition stood in the way of its plans to be heir to the empire and creator of the Chinese nation-state.

The most serious enemy of the Chinese Republic proved to be Japan. The political and economic reforms of that island empire, begun after the Meiji Restoration of the 1860s, proved revolutionary in their scope though they occurred without violence. Japan had become before the First World War a nation-state in which popular patriotism had fused with loyalty to the emperor and democratic institutions and parties had supplanted the traditional leadership of feudal lords and nobles (*samurai*). The new army did provide a home for the former warrior caste, whose solidarity and code of honor (somewhat like the Prussian officer caste)

made them a political force within the new Japanese state. Militarism coexisted alongside democracy in the Japanese state.

BRITISH INDIA AND INDIAN NATIONALISM

To understand Indian nationalism after the First World War, we need first to survey Indian society in the early twentieth century. One of the oldest civilizations in the world, it was composed of a vast and diverse array of peoples, customs, and religious practices, Many different languages were spoken among the 300 million people of the Indian subcontinent, with Hindi and related languages like Bengali dominant in the north and a very different family of languages (such as Tamil) in the south. The British had left in place hundreds of principalities, each with its own ruler and political traditions. Along the coast merchants and manufacturers produced and traded as capably as Western entrepreneurs, while elsewhere peasants eked out a miserable existence.

In this diversity religion emerged in the colonial period as the principal social and cultural bond. Hinduism had deeply marked Indian society both by its spiritual values and by the caste system. The Islamic religion had become a vital force among a large number of Indians. The development of India during the two centuries of British rule turned these two religious groups into separate and often antagonistic communities.

Hinduism and Islam in India

Hinduism provided the common culture of most inhabitants of the subcontinent. It was an extremely complex religion, with no single sacred book or organization of spiritual leaders. It consisted of a set of beliefs drawn from many sources and of a large number of deities, no one of whom stood out as the principal god. A central theme was an understanding of a single Being beyond time and space present in all creation. Hinduism emphasized perpetual change, as the wheel of life transported souls through incarnation from one body to the next, as birth was followed by death. Through this cycle of life, souls carried with them the moral consequences of the acts of the individuals previously inhabited by these souls. No merit went unrewarded in the end, no sin unpunished. As a result, the individual, in principle, accepted his or her lot in life. The Western belief in historical progress through political reform was not present in Indian culture.

A second important aspect of Hinduism was the caste system. It divided the population into hereditary groups according to status and social responsibilities. It translated the moral duty of each Hindu into a specific social obligation. The structure included hundreds of separate castes (only some of which might be present in one community), all of which belonged to one of the four major orders of Hindu society. The orders, once actual occupations—priests, warriors, merchants, farmers—had long since become merely social ranks, of which the Brahmins were the highest. The Hindu social hierarchy included one other group, the untouchables, the "unclean," segregated from all recognized castes and condemned eternally to perform the most degrading, menial tasks. They represented a sizable group—perhaps 15 percent of the population. Taboos governed behavior, including eating, among castes; beef was forbidden to most groups since the cow was sacred. Marriage had to remain within the caste. The customs and taboos governing the caste system had existed for many centuries and were closely bound with the spiritual values of Hinduism. Hindu society had evolved a strong integrative set of social customs and prescriptions.

Before the arrival of Western imperialism, the most recent powerful foreign influence had been a religion, Islam. Carried by merchants and warriors from the Middle East, the Muslim religion had spread through the subcontinent. It embodied a radically different set of spiritual values and social practices. Worship demanded submission by the faithful to one God, Allah; His word was contained in one sacred book, the Koran. The Muslim religion forbade the segregation of the faithful into castes and the worship of other deities. Pork, not beef, was forbidden food. In a multitude of practices and habits of daily life, Islam and Hinduism differed.

Yet their populations lived side by side throughout the subcontinent. The greatest concentration of Muslims lay in the Indus River valley to the west and, in the east, in Bengal. Between the two communities existed barriers of religious doctrine and social custom. Beginning in the colonial period, "communal violence," that is, attacks by members of one religious community upon members of the other, had become increasingly common. Until the mid-twentieth century, no one imagined that the Muslims, a minority among Hindus, might form a separate nation-state to protect their faith and to defend their community.

Out of the contact between the two religions emerged one other important religious group. In northern India a sect calling itself *Sikh* joined Hindu philosophy with the Muslim worship of one God. Sikh men had during the years of British rule served in the Indian army, adopting a warrior code exalting military valor. They were concentrated around their holy city of Amritsar, located in the northern province of Punjab, surrounded by large Muslim and Hindu populations. When Pakistan became a reality, they judged it a deadly threat to their community, siding with the Hindus in the bloody civil war which followed independence.

British Imperial Rule in India

Ruling over this vast population were the British. India was their prize colony. It provided them with economic benefits, manpower for their imperial armies, and, as important as all these material advantages, with the glory of domination. The British monarch was its emperor, and it was, in the words of one British statesman, the "jewel in the crown" of the monarchy. This empire extended over the entire subcontinent, from Afghanistan in the west to Burma in the east. Political authority was in the hands of the viceroy, appointed by the British monarch (on advice from the cabinet). His powers in the early twentieth century were vast, for no parliament or constitution limited his authority. He declared war and set taxes, approved laws and mobilized troops.

In practice, important restrictions tempered the viceroy's absolute authority. In the first place, large areas remained under the domination of Indian princes. These rulers had proven their loyalty to Great Britain by supporting the empire; they were rewarded by being assured internal control over their territories as long as Britain governed India. They ruled in great splendor, but all had to accept British "advisers" at their courts. In the second place, the British sought to avoid disorders among the population by leaving in place most of the local laws and customs. Authoritarian rule came in times of internal unrest; it appeared often in the turbulent years of nationalist conflict after the First World War.

British rule created a structure of Western institutions which left a permanent mark on Indian public life. For one thing, the British organized an Indian Army, staffing it with regular British officers and joining one regular British brigade with two Indian brigades to form integrated regiments. They trained the soldiers in Western military techniques and promoted some to noncommissioned officers. The army proved its value in both world wars; by the 1940s Indians had become full officers. Ultimately, officers and soldiers from this army formed the core of the armies of the free nation-states of India and Pakistan; they proved a vital force in maintaining the unity of these new states.

Another essential institution of British rule was the Indian civil service. It slowly expanded in size as the British took on new responsibilities for public works and state railroads. Indians had for long regarded government service as a position of high status. They took advantage of the opportunities for advancement in the civil service. By 1914 one-fifth of the high civil servants were Indians. A few had even become high court judges, responsible in the English tradition for the observance of the rule of law; one of these men was a Brahmin named Motilal Nehru, father of the future prime minister of independent India. Gradually the colony acquired a political elite trained in Western methods of administration, ready to move into positions of political responsibility when India won its independence.

A third important legacy of British rule consisted in an extensive program of public works. The British constructed a network of roads and railroads, which became by the First World War the largest and best internal transportation system of any Asian country. The railroads, at first a military necessity for the movement of troops, facilitated extensive commercial and industrial growth; they served British economic interests, but increasingly were used by Indian traders and workers. Irrigation constituted another key element in British plans for the development of India. The imperial administrators sought crops such as cotton of benefit to British industry and food sufficient to alleviate famine in India and to export to Europe. An extensive network of canals opened for cultivation large areas in northern India, bringing water from the complex river system flowing out of the Himalayas to the parched plains of the Punjab province and elsewhere. By 1940 irrigation was essential for cultivation on one-fifth of India's arable land.

In these and other ways, measures undertaken by imperial administrators to strengthen their own rule opened the country to national economic development. Britain found a vast market for its industrial goods; gradually Indian entrepreneurs emerged to take advantage where possible of industrial technology and the capitalist system. The wartime demand in Britain for iron and steel led to the development of the largest metallurgical enterprise in Asia, owned by an Indian family. One small part of Indian society adapted Western capitalist practices; another larger segment became an urban labor force. India gradually began the transition toward an industrial economy.

The British *raj* (the Indian term for rule) had an equally profound impact on Indian political life, provoking growing opposition while at the same time training Indians in English administrative, legal, and political practices. At a distance, the example of the British state exercised a powerful attraction for Indians, both opponents and collaborators in imperial rule. By 1914 the dream of the return to a golden age following the expulsion of Westerners and of Western ways had been rejected by India's political leaders. If they were to defeat the British, they had to do so by learning British skills, acquiring Western knowledge. Upper-caste

Indians such as Motilal Nehru, who adopted a Western style of life and who made a place for themselves in the new Indian administration, won public esteem. Nehru had not abandoned the goal of Indian independence; on the contrary, he was for years one of the most influential leaders in the nationalist movement. For him, as for his son, liberation came through the acquisition of Western learning and the adaptation of British democratic values and practices to Indian society.

The educational efforts of the British rulers in India had a strong influence on the Indian social elite. By the First World War, few educated Indians denied that Western industrial and scientific achievements had the capacity to transform and improve the life of the people. Only Gandhi and his close disciples questioned the spiritual price paid for Western materialism. The network of English secondary and higher schools provided trained personnel to staff the civil service, courts, railroad administration, wherever Indian employees were needed. Grants were available to a few to study in England; families also helped their sons make the trip. Young Mohandas Gandhi traveled to London to study law in the 1890s with the aid of his family (though under the threat of ostracism from an outraged uncle). These Indians had to learn the English language, to master the necessary literary skills, and to acquire a grounding in modern mathematics and science.

Westernized Indians experienced the difficult adaptation to foreign ways, to which they often joined respect for traditional customs and rituals of their own society. Most found employment in the service of their imperial rulers, keeping their resentment of British rule to themselves or working quietly and peacefully for self-government. A few chose to use their knowledge and authority to become leaders of the political struggle to achieve full independence and to create a unified Indian nation-state.

Indian Nationalism

The center for Indian nationalist resistance to Great Britain became a party called the Indian National Congress. Formed in 1886, it gradually evolved into a political movement seeking a free, democratic India. In effect, the Congress borrowed from England the structure and practices of a political party to achieve recognition for Indian nationalism. At first it emphasized collaboration with the British administration to bring self-rule in India; after 1918, it pursued its goal in opposition to the British. It was not the only anti-imperialist movement; others stressed the needs of particular groups or regions, while a few promoted violent means of struggle, including political assassination.

Congress was the most influential, however, and it adhered firmly to nonviolent political agitation. Although its conflicts with the imperial authorities occurred with increasing frequency, the Congress retained its admiration for English rule of law, moderation, and democracy, accepting time and again dialogue and collaboration in reforms for regional and then national self-government. The British, for their part, resisted at times adamantly Congress demands for political reform leading to independence, yet slowly came to accept greater Indian self-rule and democratic liberties. As Congress pressure for reform mounted, the British repeatedly made compromise proposals leading to greater responsibilities for elected Indian leaders. Both the British and Congress, on the surface bitter enemies, in fact grudgingly continued to collaborate in the gradual move toward Indian independence. Out of that

collaboration emerged the Indian democratic nation-state.

The agitation for self-rule led also to the emergence of a Muslim political movement. In the early years of the twentieth century, a group of Muslims, supporters of Indian nationalism, created an organization to protect the political rights and cultural values of their minority religious community. Representatives of the Muslim League took their place alongside other Indians in the National Congress. With hindsight we can see that the formation of the League was the first step toward the political crisis among Indians which ultimately tore the country apart. Yet it had still deeper roots, in the profound differences separating the two religious communities. Those Muslims supporting the League (many more remained members solely of Congress) anticipated that the two great religious groups would coexist, not blend together, in a future independent India. They feared, with some reason, that a Hindu majority in a democratic state might become the persecutors of the Muslims. When in the 1920s the British extended self-rule to its Indian territories, Hindu-Muslim rioting only worsened. The solution proposed in those years by the leaders of the League was a separate voice in Indian public life for Muslims, to be guaranteed separate political representation. The creation of a unified Indian nation-state confronted serious obstacles arising from the religious and social diversity of its people.

The participation of India in the First World War proved the key event in the emergence of the National Congress as a mass political party. India, like the rest of the British Empire, joined the war against the Central Powers. Its economy grew rapidly to help the British war effort; the Indian Army fought in Europe, Africa, and the Middle East. The war caused economic hardship among Indians as goods became scarce and food prices rose; social discontent focused on the British. In addition, the leaders of the National Congress found encouragement for their dream of independence in the policy statements and events of the war. They read President Wilson's Fourteen-Point program for peace, which called for recognition of the "interests of the populations" in colonies and for national self-determination. They watched the Bolshevik Revolution in Russia and read Lenin's appeals for the united struggle of proletarian and colonial movements. War and revolution in Europe were shaking the foundations of Western imperial power. Within India, extremist nationalists began a terrorist campaign against British rule. Congress leaders responded to the new postwar conditions and the increased strength of their party by demanding democratic home rule for India.

The British government had itself recognized that Indian mobilization for war required concessions for self-rule. Yet the institutions and habits of imperial domination remained in place. In 1917 the cabinet issued an official declaration promising "the gradual development of self-governing institutions, with a view to the progressive realization of responsible government in India as an integral part of the Empire." Following war's end, laws were prepared to permit cabinet government in the Indian provinces (that is, ministries chosen by provincial legislatures) and to expand the Indian electorate.

To end the wave of terrorism, however, the British administration introduced new repressive laws. These measures permitted the temporary suspension of civil liberties and ended legal protection for "subversives." In April 1919, imperial troops fired upon an outlawed meeting of ten thousand Indians in the city of Amritsar; hundreds of unarmed Indians were killed and over a thousand wounded. The National Congress organized a national campaign of protest. It had a new leader to carry the movement to the people—Mohandas Gandhi.

In his early adult years, Gandhi belonged to India's new Westernized class. After legal studies in England, he practiced law in South Africa, where many Indians had emigrated in search of work. There he encountered racial prejudice and segregation and discovered his true vocation, political protest in defense of all oppressed Indians. He himself, caught between Indian and Western culture, had already set out on a spiritual quest to reconcile Indian religious values

The Apostle of Non-Violence: Mohandas Gandhi. (*Embassy of India, Washington, D.C.*)

and Western individualism. He sympathized deeply with Western socialist demands to improve the lives of the poor and oppressed. At the same time he remained faithful to the Indian belief in spiritual rejuvenation through meditation and to the principle of nonviolence to others. He read the writings of the Russian novelist Leo Tolstoi, who preached a new doctrine of spiritual renewal based on the principle that "the kingdom of God is within you." Gandhi attached great significance to Christ's message in the Sermon on the Mount that violence be met with love by "turning the other cheek." He studied as well Henry David Thoreau's theory of civil disobedience to resist unjust laws. In this long search he looked for the common humanitarian message that transcended creed and ideology.

Out of these readings and his own compassion for the sufferings of his fellow Indians, he put together a new political movement. In mobilizing Indians in South Africa to resist the racist laws there, he formulated his ethical theory of what he called "truth force," that is, the personal courage to resist injustice nonviolently through civil disobedience. He demanded of his followers that they accept willingly and peacefully imprisonment from their oppressors rather than obey unjust laws. He condemned all violence as evil, relying on an innate sense of justice and the "law of love" among all people to achieve the reforms he demanded. His political crusade in South Africa succeeded in ending (temporarily) the discriminatory legislation imposed by the white government. He returned to India in 1915 a famous champion of Indian rights.

There he quickly became an outstanding member of the National Congress. His mixture of political activism and spiritual purity appealed to lower-class Indians, to whom the political reform program of Congress appeared vague and remote from their needs.

Gandhi spoke to them in a language they could understand. The simplicity of his life—a vegetarian, he practiced frequent fasts and retreats for spiritual meditation—earned him their deep respect; his vow of sexual abstinence placed him in their eyes in the ranks of India's holy men.

The Westernized leaders of the Congress found him a peculiar mixture of political commitment and naive idealism. Jawaharlal Nehru shared his hope for "an India in which all communities shall live in perfect harmony" and admitted the justice of his call to end the callous segregation inflicted on the untouchables, whom Gandhi called the "children of God." Nehru refused the other side to Gandhi's moral crusade to reform India, namely, that the "salvation" of India lay in traditional peasant life, stripped of "railways, telegraphs, hospitals, lawyers, doctors." To emphasize his conviction that simple Indian ways were better, Gandhi began to wear homespun peasant garments, which he learned to spin himself. His teachings and way of life aroused feelings of love mingled with dismay within the National Congress. Among Indians, he quickly achieved the stature of spiritual as well as political leader, their *Mahatma,* or "great soul."

The crisis that resulted from the Amritsar massacre of 1919 revealed that the National Congress had become a potent nationalist movement. It already possessed an extensive political organization, to which was added Gandhi's inspired leadership and a mass following throughout India. In protest against the massacre and the imperial rule responsible for that outrage, Gandhi organized in 1920 his first movement of noncooperation. He proclaimed that "cooperation in any shape or form with this satanic government is sinful." Under his leadership Congress called for the resignation of Indians from government office, the boycott of all English schools and colleges, the refusal to participate in local elections. If successful, the campaign would have thrown British rule in turmoil.

It failed, however, to disrupt seriously public life. When one group of Congress demonstrators attacked a police station, burning it and the police inside, Gandhi called off the campaign. He would not tolerate violence. His protest movement was also weakened by internal dissension within Congress. Many leaders welcomed the British offer to participate in provincial self-rule. The Montford Reforms of 1921 carried out the promises of 1917 for provincial cabinet government. The British viceroy proclaimed that "the principle of autocracy [i.e., absolute rule by the British state through its viceroy] has been abandoned." Congress politicians accepted the offer to present candidates for the elections. Gandhi had to adjust his campaign to the electoral interests of the party.

Nehru and Indian Self-Rule

Experience in government reinforced the commitment of the National Congress to Indian independence. The conflict between the British and Congress did not vanish as a result of provincial self-rule. The unfulfilled longing to be rid of the British *raj* moved Congress leaders to new action. In 1928 the Congress voted formally for a motion stating "the goal of the Indian people to be complete national independence."

This new policy was the work of a talented young party leader, Jawaharlal Nehru. He had joined the National Congress following an upbringing deeply influenced by British culture. His eminent father provided him with tutors, then with the best English education. Having earned his law degree in London, he returned to India in 1912 prepared to take up a law career modeled on that of his

The "Semi-Naked Sons of India": Field Workers Winnowing Rice, South India. (*Indian National Congress Collection/Hoover Institution Archives*)

father. An aristocrat by birth and education, he believed deeply in the cause of Indian independence and joined the National Congress. Working for Gandhi gave him for the first time an awareness of the social exploitation of "this vast multitude of semi-naked sons and daughters of India."

In the 1920s he began a search for a solution to social injustice, looking first to British socialism, then to Marxism-Leninism and the Soviet Union. He traveled to Russia in 1927, coming away with the conviction that the struggle against imperialism had to be joined to that against capitalism. He never abandoned Gandhi's tactics of nonviolence or the goal of a democratic India, and rejected both the Leninist tactics of armed insurrection and the Soviet practice of single-party dictatorship. He began in the late 1920s a militant campaign for liberation of his country, which he envisioned both democratic and socialist. Western socialism encouraged him to become a nationalist revolutionary.

In 1930 Nehru obtained Congress's backing for a "declaration of independence" condemning Britain for "depriving the Indian people of their freedom" and for "exploitation of the masses." It called for civil disobedience and the nonpayment of taxes to disrupt imperial administration and to force British withdrawal. Gandhi remained the man capable of organizing this new mass movement. In 1931 he launched a campaign, the most effective and dramatic of his career, for the nonpayment of the salt tax. Touching directly the poor and symbolizing British domination, the tax provided the ideal target against which to mobilize well-to-do Congress supporters and Indian peasants. By the summer of that year, the movement had spread throughout the country. Gandhi himself walked halfway across the land to the Indian Ocean to publicize his readiness to use salt taken from the sea in defiance of the law. Jails filled with Indians convicted of il-

legally manufacturing salt or demonstrating against the tax. Over sixty thousand were imprisoned, most for short terms, and the numbers remained as great throughout that year.

Once again, the British replied first with repressive measures, and ultimately with political compromise. The Indian army and police arrested demonstrators, including Nehru and Gandhi. The campaign lasted another three years before dying away. Yet during that time negotiations between the National Congress and the British government took place as well. In 1931 Gandhi traveled to London, along with other Indian leaders, to negotiate Dominion status for his country. The British government had that year created an association of independent former colonies, the Commonwealth, whose members (Dominions) governed themselves yet accepted a common tariff among all associated states, pursued a common foreign policy, and recognized the British monarchy. Only those lands under white rule (Canada, Australia, New Zealand, South Africa) immediately became members. Congress demanded equal treatment for India, but the British refused. Yet the process leading toward self-rule. once begun, did not stop. Congress kept up its agitation, and the British government found in those years of depression and rising fear of new war in Europe ample reason to accelerate the process leading to self-rule for its largest colony.

After several years of hesitation, it issued in 1935 new laws for Indian self-government, the Government of India Act. This statute created the legal structure of Indian political life until independence. It gave India the institutions of a self-governing state, restricted still by special powers for the viceroy in the event of war or internal emergencies. That part of India under the direct rule of the British, eleven provinces in all, received a federal structure somewhat resembling the Canadian state. An Indian central government had its own cabinet, responsible to a federal legislature. The viceroy, representative of the throne, provided the direct link between Great Britain and the Indian government. In each province, local cabinets and legislatures were responsible for regional affairs. The six hundred princes had the choice of joining the federation or retaining their separate existence; all chose then to preserve their powers.

Elections in 1937 posed a new dilemma to Congress leaders: continued struggle against vestiges of British rule or collaboration in the implementation of the India Act. Among those Congress members who argued against compromise were some admirers of the fascist regimes in Europe, and others who found in Stalinist Russia inspiration for Indian revolution. Between these two extremes Nehru spoke for moderation. After some hesitation, he chose electoral collaboration, declaring "we have no choice but to contest the elections." His moderate policy won the support of Congress. Nehru proved in that electoral campaign to be Congress's outstanding political leader, speaking throughout India "to make the masses realize that we not only stand for them but that we are of them and seek to cooperate with them in removing their social and economic burdens." Congress won a resounding victory in the 1937 elections, gaining control of eight of the eleven provinces.

That victory proved a defeat for the cause of united India. The Muslim League had presented its own electoral candidates on a program of cooperation with Congress. When the provincial cabinets were formed, Congress leaders refused to appoint Muslim League members to their ministries. They followed Gandhi's principle that India must not allow separate religious representation to weaken the national community. The leader of the League, Muhammed Ali Jin-

nah, proclaimed that Islam was in danger, warning that a unified democratic India represented a menace to the Muslim faith and to the very existence of the Muslim community. In place of one India he proposed two states, one of which would be Pakistan. Perhaps at the time he conceived the plan to be a useful menace by which to force the National Congress to negotiate. If so, he was playing a dangerous game.

The idea of a Muslim nation-state had first been conceived in 1930. Fearing Hindu domination and determined to protect their religious practices and community from Western, secular influence, a growing number of Muslims were drawn to the nationalist creed of spiritual and political rejuvenation in a separate state. Their search for cultural unity fused with the Muslim League's struggle to defend its separate existence alongside and equal to the National Congress. Even among Muslims, however, the perspective of partition aroused bitter controversy. No real territorial limits separated the two communities, and many Muslims collaborated with the British in the Indian army and civil service. Others were loyal to the National Congress, a few holding powerful positions in the party.

Why did the Muslim League become the defender of a Muslim nation-state in India? It turned in this radically new direction only when independence appeared imminent. That circumstance forced Congress and the League to confront a future without British rule and revealed how far each side had gone in refusing to heed the program of the other. Gandhi would not compromise on the principle of national unity, a conviction which blinded him to the fears of Muslims that majority rule meant oppression for them.

Less moralistic, more ambitious leaders on both sides exploited religious differences to promote their own careers. Mohammed Ali Jinnah himself was a thoroughly

Westernized Indian lawyer who spoke exclusively English. He did not practice the Muslim religion, and did not even speak fluent Urdu, the language of most of his Muslim followers. The importance he attached to the Muslim League in defending Muslim interests, not a religious quarrel, explains his support for the cause of Pakistan. Yet political manipulation and nationalist idealism are not a sufficient explanation. Indian society was itself increasingly split by the communal hostility which political reform appeared only to worsen. Conditions were worst in urban areas such as Calcutta where poverty exacerbated religious and social antagonism. The growth of violence between the Muslim and Hindu communities made real national unity increasingly an illusory goal. Perhaps there still was time to avoid the tragedy of partition through wise leadership and compromise. But war intervened, and the time never came.

That war began for India, as for Great Britain, in 1939. The Indian viceroy proclaimed India at war with Germany. Congress, while it backed the English cause, refused to be the agents of the British government in a war imposed on India. All Congress cabinets resigned. The Muslim League took their place. Jinnah proclaimed a Day of Thanksgiving for all Indian Muslims at their deliverance from Hindu rule. Muslim deputies became ministers throughout India. The League's power grew. As the time of independence drew nearer, so too did the likelihood of conflict between India's great religious communities.

THE "NEW CHINA" AND THE NATIONALIST PARTY

The Chinese path to national independence began with the overthrow of the Chinese Empire in 1911 and ended with the Communist revolution in 1949. Once an integrated empire and social system, China underwent a prolonged period of disorder and struggle until a new order emerged. Foreign and civil war wrought terrible destruction and hardship, adding to the perennial sufferings of the population. Supporters of the Chinese Nationalist party looked to the example of Western states for their reforms, while the Communists conceived of China's future on the model of Soviet socialism. Deeply divided by political ideology, they both rejected the traditional Confucian order and opposed imperialist domination. Although bitter enemies, both looked forward to the appearance of a new Chinese nation-state.

The Chinese Empire had survived for thousands of years before disintegrating in the early twentieth century. The unity of the empire and the might of the emperor had rested partly on Chinese armies, even more on a unique political culture. A class of officials, the gentry, ensured public order and the implementation of imperial policies. They had earned their privileged position not by birth, but by passing an examination in the Classics of Confucian learning. The philosopher Confucius had written of a world order in which the state was the guarantor of harmony and order. His political philosophy became the ideology of the imperial system. It preached obligations, not freedom. It extolled the Three Bonds of subordination—subject to ruler, son to father, and wife to husband—stressing family ties along with political obedience. The extraordinary endurance of imperial power in the "central country" testified to the strength of this unique political culture.

The Rise of the Nationalist Party

Its fall was due, on the one hand, to Western imperialism, unchallenged since the repression of the Boxer Rebellion in 1900 (see Chapter 1) and, on the other, to internal

Students edu-
revolutionary
ew, "progres-
ils trained in
ere prepared
cal conquest.
eneral in 1911
Chinese Re-
lent, the em-
Its collapse
istory.
ted two prin-
power. One
s from the old
i ruled large
f Manchuria.
i their armies
ects to govern
iad a reform
able to create
ought among
with little ef-
of the civilian
the 1911 rev-
ublic in name
titutions and
e imperialist
id spheres of
th these petty
warlords had
ostacle to na-

g for power
ies. Their or-
icated in the
ad. The most
s the veteran
le had aban-
ng to Chris-
iedical career
onary move-
up in a set of
sm, by which
alist domina-
him repre-

sented Western constitutional government; and (3) socialism, which he understood as industry and equality of land holdings for the Chinese peasant farmers. He called his movement the Nationalist People's party (in Chinese, *Kuomintang* or *KMT*). For him as for other radicals, revolution constituted China's sole path to progress and independence.

The end of the First World War accelerated the revolutionary conflict in China. Japan's seizure of the German concessions and demands for special economic privileges in China provoked in the postwar years the first widespread nationalist movement in Chinese history. It was centered largely in the coastal cities, where new social groups were beginning to take the place of the old gentry leaders of society. Textile manufacturers and bankers in cities such as Shanghai proved themselves capable capitalists, eager to protect their own economy from foreigners and hostile to Japanese domination. Students and scholars in the new Western schools, defying the Confucian scholars, set out to create a "new culture."

When the Paris peace conference approved Japan's "special interests" in China, these groups united on May 4, 1919, in a national protest movement. Led and organized by students, it was directed against the warlords, some of whom collaborated with the Japanese, and against Japan itself. The May Fourth Movement summed up its objectives in the slogan: "China's territory may be conquered, but it cannot be given away! The Chinese people may be massacred, they will not surrender!" A national boycott of Japanese goods began. Ultimately Japan agreed to renounce its special rights at the Washington Conference in 1922. As important, the Nationalist party of Sun Yat-sen absorbed the May Fourth Movement into its organization. The anti-Japanese nationalist protest created a mass base for Sun's party.

The Nationalists soon found a valuable foreign ally. Their opposition to Japanese expansion and to Western imperialism was shared by the new Soviet regime in Russia. The Communist leaders considered nationalist revolutionary movements in colonial lands to be an important part of their global struggle against Western capitalism. Thus the two sides had common enemies. Some Chinese radicals found in the revolutionary experiment under way in Russia a model for their own country. They constituted the membership of the Chinese Communist party, created in 1921. Sun Yat-sen did not share their faith in the dictatorship of the proletariat and the inevitable triumph of communism. He did however recognize the practical benefits of an alliance with Soviet Russia. For one thing, the Nationalist party needed a centralized organization like the Russian Communist party if it was to organize a constitutional republic in China. For another, he realized that his movement required military aid if it were to defeat the warlords. The Russian Communists had set up an effective army in their fight for survival during their civil war. They could thus furnish the needed military training which would prepare Nationalist armies to conquer China.

In 1923, the Soviet state and the Communist International agreed to provide political and military assistance to the Chinese Nationalist party. Russian advisers helped to organize a Chinese "party army" and Chinese officers, including Sun's aide Chiang Kai-shek, went to Russia to learn the skills of modern war from Red Army officers. Russian assistance proved very effective, widening the base of support for the Nationalists and strengthening its leadership and its army. Russians reorganized the KMT to open it to mass participation. Sun Yat-sen had in return to pay a price, agreeing to Soviet control of the railroad crossing northern

Manchuria and Soviet domination of Outer Mongolia (soon to become the Mongolian People's Republic). Power politics was never absent, then or later, in the uneasy relations between China and the Soviet Union.

Sun's ideal of democracy did not extend to the Nationalist party, however, where his authority (and later that of his successor, Chiang Kai-shek) remained supreme. The Chinese Communist party collaborated with the Nationalists, helping in the KMT's reorganization. Communists, both foreign and Chinese, assisted in forming a mass movement of support for the nationalist revolution among the peasantry (where a young Communist named Mao Zedong was active) and among the workers in the industrial cities. This United Front coalition hid, but could not end, the political and ideological rivalry between the Communists and their supporters and moderates and business interests backing the KMT. The Communist party exploited its new political activities for its own benefit, secretly expanding its organization and building support among workers and peasants. KMT leaders were deeply hostile to peasant and worker revolution and saw in the Communist party a dangerous political challenger. The alliance between the Communists and the Nationalists could not endure.

In 1926 the Nationalist leadership launched its military offensive to defeat the warlords in northern China. From its base in the south its troops, commanded by Chiang Kai-shek, moved up the coast, their objective the city of Beijing (Peking). The success of this Northern Expedition, ending in 1928 in the capture of Beijing and the submission of the remaining warlords, proved of great benefit to Chiang Kai-shek. He had become leader of the KMT following Sun's death in 1925. His power depended largely on his control of the army, as much a political as a military weapon. For the rest of his life he relied primarily on the army. Chiang resembled in this respect the warlords, but he did retain Sun's political organization and the political program of nationalist reform. His military victory conferred on him the mantle of Sun's legitimate heir, for he could claim to have achieved Sun's dream of a new China unified under the National People's party.

In those years he set out to eliminate his principal political rival, the Chinese Communist party. In 1927 combined Nationalist military and police operations suddenly struck all major Communist organizations, with arrests and executions following quickly. Many of the fifty thousand party members vanished, either in the first KMT attack or after the Comintern late that year ordered the Chinese comrades to organize armed resistance against the Nationalists. These uprisings were immediately crushed. Urban worker support for the Communists declined as a result of repression and of disillusionment at the failure of proletarian revolution. The failure that year of Comintern policies in China gave some of the Communist survivors a bitter lesson in Moscow's inability to understand the Chinese revolutionary struggle.

Mao Zedong and Chinese Communism

Mao Zedong proved the most adept at finding new foundations on which to rebuild the Chinese Communist movement. He had joined the party after years of search for a political blueprint to reform the Chinese state and society. A student at the time of the 1911 revolution, he joined in the struggle against the old order. He rejected his father's wish that he return to help run the family farm, preferring the life of an activist scholar. He wrote in those years that the "four evil demons of the empire" were "religion, capitalism, autocracy, and the three bonds."

Moving to Beijing in 1918, he discovered there the cause to which he devoted his entire life. Some Chinese intellectuals that year were praising the Communist revolution in Russia as the "victory of the spirit of all humanity." He joined a Marxist study circle, becoming familiar there with Lenin's theory of the revolutionary vanguard. He uncovered a new vision of his country's path to progress within the global struggle against imperialism and capitalism. By the time the Chinese Communist party was founded in 1921, he was a dedicated Marxist-Leninist.

The years of collaboration with the Nationalists gave Mao invaluable experience in revolutionary organization. He paid particular attention to mobilizing Chinese peasants for political action in the campaign against the warlords. He discovered during those years the potential strength of the peasant protest movement. Despite their ignorance and superstition, the Chinese peasants did respond to calls for rebellion against their oppressors. Most were tenant farmers, subject to exploitation by landlords, by tax collectors, and by soldiers. Their only recourse in past centuries had been banditry and mass rebellion. Mao helped to form peasant unions in central China, where the membership grew to over one million.

In the course of this experience, Mao reached the conclusion that in China the success of the proletarian revolution depended on a parallel peasant revolution. He alone among Communist leaders grasped the fact that China's poor peasants could be mobilized to take up arms against their landlords and against foreign enemies. Marx had never considered the peasantry an important force in the proletarian movement; Lenin had based his revolutionary movement on the backing of the Russian workers. Mao was in effect proposing a fundamental revision in Communist revolutionary theory and practice.

The suppression of the urban Communist movement in 1927–28 forced Mao to turn to his own peasant forces. By 1929 he had carved out and defended a small area in the south China province of Jiangxi (old spelling—Kiangsi) where he and his peasant guerrilla army were able to construct a Red Base. Isolated from the central party and from Moscow, he organized and expanded his territory in spite of repeated "extermination" offensives by Nationalist troops. To survive, he needed above all an army, consisting of his peasants in arms. By 1931 his "liberated area" had expanded to include a population of 3 million under the control of a Red Army of 100,000. That year he formally proclaimed it a Chinese Soviet Republic.

In those years he formulated the theories to justify his new policies. He continued to believe that class struggle provided the sole path to the inevitable triumph of communism. He never doubted that the liberation of China constituted part of the world revolutionary movement of which Marx, Lenin, and Stalin were the great prophets. Still, he considered his "semicolonial" country to be a society in which the "peasant struggle" would "accelerate the revolutionary upsurge." He even suggested that the Chinese peasantry might prove "more powerful than the workers" in the revolutionary movement. Orthodox Chinese Communists condemned him as a maverick violating fundamental Marxist-Leninist ideological tenets in favor of "peasant guerrilla-ism." In purely intellectual terms they were correct to condemn his actions as heretical. Mao, however, judged revolutionary truth as much by results as by Marxist dogma. His arguments reveal that, though his views on world revolution and his respect for Stalin's policies remained unchanged, he had elaborated a new theory of revolution in China. He was con-

vinced that the most powerful revolutionary forces of his country were in the countryside, and he was right.

The success of his movement depended on the support of the Chinese peasantry and the organization of military forces capable of sustaining long and arduous guerrilla warfare. Mao implemented a policy of agrarian reform granting the poor peasants what they most desired—their own land. Landlords and rich peasants lost most of their property and the confiscated land was redistributed according to need. The land and its harvest belonged to individual peasants, who depended upon their new Communist rulers to retain their farms. They had substantial reasons to support their Communist rulers; many became the recruits in the Red Army on whom the survival of the Soviet Republic depended.

The army was the military arm of Mao's Communist movement. He and his followers considered it a revolutionary political organization as well as an instrument of war. They sought to convince the soldiers that their real enemy was "feudalism," a term which in the Chinese Communist vocabulary symbolized the cruel, harsh, and antiquated past, and that their goal was progressive revolution, not just their own land. The poor armaments of the Red Army forced it to fight in a manner much like peasant rebels so long a part of Chinese history. Mao devised over the years a unique strategy of guerrilla combat, summed up in a simple formula which every soldier learned: "The enemy advances, we retreat; the enemy camps, we harass; the enemy tires, we attack; the enemy retreats, we pursue." Mao had no real assurance of ultimate revolutionary triumph save his own unshakable faith in the world proletarian movement, and no protection from his Chinese enemies besides the rifles of his peasant soldiers. In those years of repression and weakness of the Chinese urban Communist forces, the very survival of Mao's Soviet Republic represented a victory.

Nationalist China versus the Chinese Communists

In the late 1920s, the Nationalist party consolidated its leadership of China. For a few years the country enjoyed relatively peaceful times. The Western powers made their peace with Chiang, for they were unprepared to maintain strong military forces to protect their concessions and knew that the Nationalists did not threaten their basic interests. The Chinese Republic took over control of tariffs, taxes, and postal services, previously run by Westerners. Many foreign concessions became once again a part of China; Chinese law extended throughout the country. The Nationalist leaders could fairly claim to be Sun Yat-sen's true heirs in working to end Western imperialist domination.

In other respects, however, they abandoned Sun's ideals. They never introduced a land reform to alleviate the poverty of the Chinese peasantry. No restrictions were placed on the accumulation of vast wealth in the hands of bankers and industrialists. Chiang himself was allied by marriage with the greatest of the banking "clans," the Soong family. Foreign and Chinese investors managed well, even in the years of depression.

We know little of the living conditions of the rural population, though its numbers did increase in those years. What is clear is that, on the one hand, the old cycle of poverty, flood, and famine remained a major threat to many millions and, on the other, that hopes of improvement, spread by reformer and radicals, were weakening the "Bonds" on which the old order rested. The Na-

tionalists promised an end to old abuses. They banned the cruel practice of footbinding, mark of the submission of women to the Chinese patriarchal order. Yet their regime was too weak to end the practice. As a result of its unwillingness or inability to institute important social reforms, the Nationalist government deprived itself of widespread support in the country.

Despite Sun's promise of constitutional democracy, the Chinese Republic under the Nationalists was an authoritarian state. The KMT army was the dominant political force in the country, under the command of Chiang. He held semidictatorial powers, justifying his rule by the need he saw for "guided democracy" in the young Chinese Republic. He took inspiration from the example of "supreme leaders" such as Mussolini in fascist Italy and Kemal Ataturk in Turkey. His claim to be the head of a unified China was, however, illusory. The Nationalist leadership was never able to govern effectively their country, whose vast population numbered by then over 400 million. Many areas escaped their control; Manchuria remained in the hands of its warlord, only nominally "allied" with the Nationalists. In Korea and on the southern Manchurian coasts were Japanese military forces, increasingly eager to extend their power in China. Manchuria was their most tempting target.

In 1931, the Japanese army invaded Manchuria north of its coastal zone. Army officers claimed (falsely) that Chinese terrorists had attacked Japanese property and military; in fact, they had resolved to seize the province before the Chinese Nationalists could do so. By early 1932 they had conquered the entire area and soon turned it into the "puppet" (i.e., satellite) state of Manchukuo under the fictitious rule of the last Chinese emperor, collaborating with them

Etat fantoche

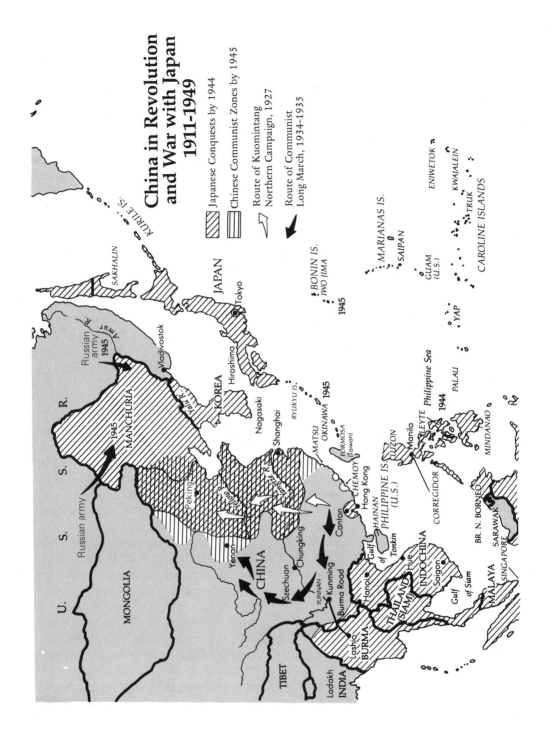

China in Revolution
and War with Japan
1911-1949

Japanese Conquests by 1944

Chinese Communist Zones by 1945

Route of Kuomintang
Northern Campaign, 1927

Route of Communist
Long March, 1934–1935

KURILE IS.

SAKHALIN

JAPAN
Tokyo

BONIN IS.
IWO JIMA
1945

MARIANAS IS.
SAIPAN

GUAM
(U.S.)

CAROLINE ISLANDS

ENIWETOK

KWAJALEIN

TRUK

YAP

PALAU

Philippine Sea
1944

LEYTE

MINDANAO

Russian army
1945

Amur R.

Vladivostok

KOREA
Hiroshima
Nagasaki
Yalu R.

Shanghai

RYUKYU IS.

MATSU
OKINAWA 1945

FORMOSA
(Taiwan)

Peking

Hwang R.

Yangtze R.

CHEMOY
Hong Kong
Canton
HAINAN

MANCHURIA
1945

Russian army

Yenan

Szechuan

Chungking

CHINA

YUNNAN
Kunming
Burma Road

MONGOLIA

U. S. S. R.

U.
S.

TIBET

Ladakh

INDIA

BURMA
Lashio

THAILAND
(SIAM)

Gulf
of Siam

INDOCHINA
Hanoi
Hue
Saigon
Tonkin
Gulf of
Tonkin

MALAYA
SINGAPORE

BR. N. BORNEO
SARAWAK

LUZON
Manila
CORREGIDOR

PHILIPPINE IS.
(U.S.)

134

against the Nationalists. Chiang made only token gestures of opposition. The Japanese campaign touched a peripheral area, destroying the power of another warlord. Rather than pursue actively a war with Japan which his forces could not win, he agreed to an armistice. He preferred instead to turn his own troops against an internal enemy.

His target was the Soviet Republic ruled by Mao's Communist forces. It was the stronghold for his most hated rivals for power in China. Its revolutionary program of land reform aroused bitter opposition from Chinese middle classes and landlords, on whose support Chiang heavily depended. In the early 1930s he launched four separate military offensives against the Communists. He turned for help to German military advisers, who taught his troops the methods of encirclement operations. By 1934 his siege had created a noose which was slowly strangling the Soviet area. The Communists' only hope of survival lay in abandoning the Jiangxi Soviet Republic.

The Long March of the Communist forces has become a legend in Chinese history. As such, Communist accounts of the yearlong trek mingle fact and fancy. It started out, in Mao's own words, as a "headlong flight" of about 120,000 soldiers, abandoning their families and possessions and setting out without any clear destination. They were pursued by Nationalist troops seeking their annihilation, through areas inhabited by people hostile to any Chinese. Taking charge after several months of dissension and debate within the party, Mao proved his remarkable leadership ability in saving his soldiers from death or imprisonment and his movement from destruction.

In that period he emerged in the eyes of Chinese Communists as their heroic "helmsman" and courageous warrior carrying forward the revolutionary flame. Mao selected the destination, which was the northwest

province of Shaanxi (old spelling—Shensi), center of another small "liberated area." The distance to be covered was enormous, almost six thousand miles, over mountainous terrain where few supplies could be found. Hunger and disease accompanied the marchers all the way. Those who survived required great moral and physical strength. The legend affirms that only eight thousand arrived in late 1935 in Yanan (old spelling—Yenan), a city in Shaanxi; whatever the actual number of casualties, the Long March proved the revolutionary commitment of Mao and his followers and forged the leadership which led the party to victory fifteen years later. Mao had saved the core of his movement and found a secure base to continue his struggle.

Recognition of his remarkable achievement came from Moscow. After years of opposition, the Comintern acknowledged Mao's position at the head of the Chinese Communist party. It had a particular objective for Mao's rural movement. The Soviet Union needed the foreign Communist parties to mobilize opposition to its enemies, Germany and Japan. The Chinese party was in 1935 ordered to organize an anti-Japanese, "united front" of Chinese forces, most important of which were Chiang's troops. Mao appears to have supported the new tactics wholeheartedly. He was himself a Chinese patriot, deeply committed to the defeat of all China's imperialist enemies. In the following years his party became the most fervent proponent of all-out war against the Japanese, gaining the sympathy of many Chinese attracted by its nationalist zeal as much as by its Leninist revolutionary program.

The Communist base of operations became north China, in the poor highland region of Shaanxi. Its military forces, numbering in 1936 about thirty thousand, were strong enough to defeat a new Nationalist encirclement campaign. Almost completely cut off from the outside world (the American Edgar Snow was one of the first foreigners to visit the area, describing it in a flattering book called *Red Star over China*), it had to rely solely on the resources of the region.

The Soviet Union provided no assistance, for Stalin distrusted what he later called Mao's "peasant bandits" and preferred dealing with the Nationalist regime. When in 1937 the Soviet government began sending military supplies to China, it directed them to Chiang's forces. Mao organized a new Chinese Soviet Republic, employing the same strategy of peasant reform and guerrilla war which he had applied in Jiangxi. He explained to his followers in 1936 that their "revolutionary war" carried forward the struggle to destroy imperialism and feudalism in China and to end the "counter-revolutionary" regime of the Nationalists. Chiang's forces were very strong, however, and they were "weak and small." The Communists' first task therefore consisted in the defeat of the Japanese imperialists; revolution came later.

War Against Japan

The alliance with Chiang finally began in 1937. The Nationalist leader until then had refused all offers from the Communists for an anti-Japanese "United Front." He was forced to consider joint action after one of his own generals had late in 1936 taken him prisoner in one of the most bizarre and humiliating episodes in his political career. Mao stepped into the dispute to free Chiang. In exchange, he obtained Chiang's agreement to Communist participation in the Nationalist state and collaboration in military operations. We will never know what his real feelings toward Chiang were; other Communists wanted their arch-enemy shot. Moscow needed a strong Nationalist regime under

Chiang to resist the Japanese, and Mao agreed to this policy.

Very reluctantly, Chiang became a partner in the United Front coalition, ending (temporarily) his attacks on the Communists. His most substantial benefit came in the form of abundant military aid from the Soviet Union (more than the United States gave his state in the period before 1941). The Chinese Communists renamed their Soviet Republic the "special regime of the Republic of China" and the Red Army became the "Eighth Route Army." Both sides secretly distrusted each other. Only the distance separating their core territories and the conflict with Japan kept them at peace. The Communists retained effective control over their north China base, to which they added new areas taken over by their guerrilla forces. The two rivals for power made a fragile partnership; the truce was short-lived.

War with Japan gave them a common enemy. In the summer of 1937 full-scale war between Japan and China began. No one yet knows exactly how the military conflict started in the area of Beijing, where Japanese troops were stationed. The most likely explanation appears to be that Communist and anti-Japanese Nationalist troops started firing on the Japanese. In turn, Japanese generals decided to crush the Chinese forces and to turn China into another "client state" of Japan. Major Japanese offensives began that year in the northern and central coastal regions of China. The Japanese troops pushed farther and farther into China in an effort to crush Chiang's forces.

The Chinese Republic could not match the military might of Japan. By 1939 the Japanese controlled the principal coastal areas of China, where they set up "puppet" regimes with Chinese collaborators. Chiang had to retreat far into the interior, placing his capital in the mountainous city of Chongqing (Chungking). His armies were

poorly equipped and poorly led. He had retained control of his state, but only by hus-
banding his forces and placing strict controls
on the offensive operations of his troops. He
remained suspicious of the political ambitions of his generals and chose to hold what
territory he could by defensive fighting,
avoiding bloody and futile attacks on the Japanese. He feared the Communists as well,
in their own way more successful than his
forces defending Chinese territory and people against the Japanese.

The Communist guerrilla forces spread
into large rural areas of central and northern
China behind the Japanese lines. By 1941
their Eighth Route Army totaled 400,000
men and held areas with a population of 44
million. That year the Japanese attempted to
wipe out the Communist insurrection, applying to the guerrilla areas the simple, brutal
policy of "burn all, kill all, loot all." The
Communists suffered severely, their army
declining to 300,000, but their war continued. The Japanese occupation forces
could not wipe out the Communist movement, nor could their armies destroy the Nationalists. On the other hand, neither Communists nor Nationalists by themselves could
expel the enemy from China. They had to
have help from outside.

The only ally who could provide that assistance was the United States. Soviet Russia
had given military aid since 1937, but when
Germany attacked in mid-1941 even those
supplies ceased. The U.S. government supported diplomatically the Nationalist government. President Roosevelt praised the
"magnificent defense of China" and made
possible Chinese purchases of military
equipment despite neutrality laws banning
aid to foreign belligerents. Beyond this modest support he could not go. Until 1941 trade
between the United States and Japan continued, including vital iron and petroleum.
Isolationism in America bred distrust of all

foreign wars; a growing naval conflict with
Germany turned the attention of the United
States toward the war in Europe. Until some
event in the Pacific forced the United States
into war with Japan, the Chinese had to fight
alone.

THE RISE OF THE JAPANESE EMPIRE

Japan underwent significant and far-reach-
ing political changes in the years between the
two wars. From a democratic regime it became militaristic; its foreign policy shifted
from international collaboration to expansionism. The conditions leading to militarism had their roots deep in Japan's political and cultural past, but the immediate
cause of the decline of civilian rule lay in the
economic collapse of the early 1930s. The
global depression was directly responsible
for the failure of Japanese democracy and
the beginning of Asian war.

Japanese Democracy

In the 1920s the country appeared set on
the path of peace and prosperity. The reforms begun in the years following the Meiji
Restoration of the 1860s had had time to become firmly established. In scarcely more
than a generation Japan had developed a
"mature" industrial economy equipped with
the most productive industrial technology
and organized to compete on the global market. The formula for success combined Western skills and capitalist methods with Japanese commitment to hard work and
savings and a high rate of government investment. Giant corporations (derisively
termed *zaibatsu*—"financial cliques"—by
their critics) permitted a few powerful business leaders to control production in key industrial sectors and gave them an influential
voice in political affairs. Obliged to import

vital raw materials—especially petroleum and iron—manufacturers turned their industrial skills to profitable ends, exporting much of their output to foreign lands and thereby paying without difficulty for further food and mineral imports.

The First World War had been a boon to growth, since Western competition had dwindled. Japanese businessmen moved into foreign markets once controlled by Western firms. Textile exports doubled, and so did the size of the Japanese merchant marine. Foreign earnings built up so rapidly that Japan ceased being a debtor country, for the first time owning more foreign investments than its own debts to foreign creditors (the United States was the only other country with similar war profits), and its gold reserves increased six times. The population grew to over fifty million, and the standard of living, though still far below that of Western societies, gradually improved.

These prosperous economic conditions strengthened the democratic institutions of the country. The political reforms, copied largely from British and German models, gave Japan the appearance of a Western constitutional regime. In the 1920s, new electoral laws introduced universal manhood suffrage. By then the power of the legislature (Diet) was similar to a Western parliament. The Japanese regime, though it resembled a Western cabinet system, had certain unique characteristics. Behind the scenes power lay in the hands of a few individuals: party leaders, advisers to the emperor, and military leaders. The key decisions of cabinet appointment came from the advisers to the emperor; cabinet ministers only then turned to their parties for support in the Diet. Political parties relied on the financial backing of the giant corporations, whose large campaign contributions made deputies and cabinets careful to heed the wishes of the business elite. Finally, the military retained control over their own operations and periodically assumed "autonomy of command" to take action regardless of the government's policies. In effect, the political system consisted of a delicate balance between elite rule and popular democracy, between business interests and military expansionists.

In the 1920s the balance swung toward party rule and economic interests. Since the 1890s Japan had built up a small overseas empire, extending from Korea and southern Manchuria through small occupied areas in China south to Formosa. Its navy possessed bases in the East and South China seas, where it was the dominant naval power. In the war its military forces had seized German concessions in China, and in 1918 they occupied eastern Siberia. But a large army and strong navy represented a heavy and unproductive burden on the economy, and foreign conquest provoked the opposition of Japan's most important trading partner, the United States.

Economic interests and foreign trade both pushed Japan's cabinets in the 1920s to curtail expansionism and to cut back expenditures for the military. The Japanese representatives at the Washington Conference of 1921–22 had good reason to agree to limit the Japanese navy to almost one-half the size of either the British or American navies and to withdraw Japanese troops from parts of north China and from eastern Siberia. In exchange, they obtained Western promises not to fortify new military bases in the Far East and international recognition as the major power in the Far East (see Chapter 3). Subsequently the Japanese cabinet cut drastically the size of the army and the military budget. For the time being Japanese imperialism was halted.

As long as the world economy expanded, the Japanese government and business leaders could restrain the military by arguing peace, not war, best promoted the country's interest in East Asia. Political leaders looked to the needs of the industrial economy and the urban population, ignoring social ills and the farm poor. Their motto might have been borrowed from one American president at the time, who argued that "the business of politics is business." The 1920s were good years for most Japanese, in spite of the terrible Tokyo earthquake of 1923 which killed 130,000 people and caused enormous property damage. Industrial production doubled and exports boomed, with 40 percent going to the giant U.S. market. Another 25 percent went to China, particularly to the relatively prosperous region of Manchuria where Japan established close economic ties and encouraged Japanese migration. The giant corporations expanded their operations to such an extent that they represented probably the largest economic empires in the world; one employed almost one million people in Japan and another million overseas and controlled hundreds of individual companies. The urban population grew to include almost half the country's inhabitants and real wages of workers rose by about one-half. In economic terms Japan enjoyed good times in those years.

Depression and Militarism

The world depression put an end to Japanese prosperity, to civilian rule, and to peaceful foreign relations. The economic and social signs of hard times appeared in all areas of Japanese life. Exports, a key indicator of Japanese economic success, fell to 50 percent of their 1920s level. The U.S. market no longer absorbed an abundance of imports, and the 1930 U.S. tariff cut the market still further by raising rates on Japanese products by 25 percent. The workers' living conditions worsened, as wages fell by one-third by 1931. Farm incomes declined even

more severely as rice prices fell to below production costs and silk prices collapsed. One-half of Japan's rural population worked as landless laborers; their living conditions, precarious in the best of times, became tragic.

These grim economic trends brought out the old weaknesses of civilian government and revealed new opposition to democratic rule. The close ties between party leaders and business interests discredited their policies when economic decline set in. The small circle of powerful political figures around the emperor, like the men around Hindenburg in Germany in 1932, were less inclined to back civilian rule. Old class antagonism between rural and urban poor and the wealthy revealed itself in popular support for the army, a traditional escape from poverty.

The influence of the military and the attraction of expansionist policies grew once again to provide old answers to the economic crisis. At the same time, movements closely resembling European fascism appeared in the country, glorifying war and imperial conquest and condemning democratic leaders for corruption, for selling out to the *zaibatsu* and for betrayal of national interests. Fanatical patriots turned to assassination of political leaders whom they judged "traitors" for opposing military conquest. Japanese militarism drew its strength in the 1930s both from traditional sources and from new mass support for authoritarian leadership and imperialism. In those conditions the political pendulum swung back to military domination.

The Japanese invasion of Manchuria in 1931 revealed how powerful military leaders had once more become. Crowds welcomed the news of conquest; the government abandoned any effort to limit the military operations. It defended the action—no war was officially declared—before the League of

Nations, to whom China had appealed for support. When the League formally condemned Japan for aggression and called on its members to enforce sanctions as provided in the League Covenant, the Japanese government withdrew from the League. The United States refused to collaborate in League actions but announced that it refused to recognize the conquest, a violation of Japan's treaty commitments. The gesture was theatrical and futile, a measure of the weakness of U.S. policy. Later the Japanese government renounced the limitations it had accepted at the Washington Conference on the size of its navy. The peace settlement of the 1920s in the Far East collapsed even before that in Europe. Manchuria, renamed Manchukuo, became in 1933 another puppet state within the Japanese Empire.

Militarism gradually took over Japanese political life. Civilian government never completely disappeared, becoming rather "window dressing" for imperialist policies. Political violence remained a tool of ambitious officers and fanatical patriots. Their attacks reached a peak in 1936 when young officers mobilized over a thousand troops in an attempt to overthrow the civilian government. The military leaders decided to oppose the insurrection, preferring to work through the cabinet and, in their own way, respecting the forms of constitutional rule. The rebellion was suppressed, its leaders executed. In 1937 national elections showed that a majority of the voters supported the civilian parties opposed to military rule. The wishes of the people had no influence on the government, however. Power had passed out of the hands of the parties into those of the generals. Civilians continued to run important ministries. In debates on foreign policy they spoke out in favor of peace and compromise. Yet their voices carried less and less influence in policymaking. In late 1941 General Tojo became prime minister, a post he

held for the next four years. The military ruled Japan.

This new direction in Japanese policies and leadership was already clear in 1936. The term "militarism" best defines the new ruling coalition of army generals and naval admirals, backed (reluctantly, it seems) by Emperor Hirohito and supported by the great corporations producing Japan's war arsenal. The defeat of the 1936 officers' uprising ended attacks by revolutionary officers on civilian government. Instead, the spirit of militarism spread through public life in a campaign glorifying discipline, order, and sacrifice for the fatherland.

This militaristic regime differed greatly from the political leadership of the 1920s, yet the changes came slowly and without great fanfare. It did resemble in some respects Italian fascism, yet lacked the essential traits of a charismatic dictator and one-party rule. The Japanese people obeyed their new masters and responded loyally when called upon to sacrifice their lives and their wellbeing for the sake of their country and their emperor. Patriotism was a powerful bond among Japanese. So too was respect for military valor. The two together constituted the cement which held together the population under the new military regime.

Japanese Imperialism

The expansionist foreign policy had taken shape as well by 1936. Its objective was the creation of a "pan-Asianist regional order" under Japanese leadership.[1] It entailed both the economic control of the Chinese market and of the natural resources of Southeast Asia and the military domination of the entire region, on land and on sea. Japanese

[1]Akira Iriye, *Power and Culture: The Japanese-American War, 1941–1945* (Cambridge, Mass., 1981), p. 34.

leaders emphasized publicly the benefits of their plan for the other countries. They explained later that they sought a "Greater East Asia Co-Prosperity Sphere." Asians, with Japanese assistance rid of their Western oppressors, would aid one another in a vast enterprise of free trade and economic development.

In reality, the principal goal was the expansion of Japanese political and economic might. The plan offered the Japanese army and navy a vast territory, never clearly defined, for conquest and glory, but stressed Japan's strategic interests and, up to a point, the limits to Japan's means to wage war. This program did not seek domination of all Asia and the Pacific, but it did risk conflict with both the Soviet Union and the United States, great powers directly affected by the Japanese plans for an enormous East Asian sphere of influence. Most dangerous of all, this policy expanded the powers and encouraged the ambitions of the military until at a certain point the government lost control of the forces of war. The military leaders' ambition for imperial conquest failed to take account of the limits to their country's real power; after ordering them in 1945 to accept surrender, Emperor Hirohito observed that they "had placed too much significance on spirit and were oblivious to science." By then, they had reduced Japan to ruins.

The first step toward Pacific war came in 1937 with the Japanese invasion of China. No decision to conquer Nationalist China was made by the Japanese government. The move by field officers to defeat Chinese forces started in motion a process of military mobilization and offensive operations organized and led by the army generals. They would accept nothing less than Chinese capitulation. By 1939, they had conquered all the major populated areas of China, as far south as the border of Indochina. They created in these areas puppet regimes, adminis-

tered by Chinese collaborators, resembling their Manchukuo regime.

Yet they failed in their principal objective, which was to force Chiang Kai-shek to surrender and himself to become their puppet. They could not dislodge the remnants of his army from their refuge in the interior of China, where Chiang clung to his position of Nationalist leader and head of China's patriotic war against the invader. The Japanese invasion of China provoked Chinese nationalist resistance among the masses in the occupied areas, many of whom participated in or supported Communist guerrilla operations against the Japanese. The Japanese retained control of the cities and rail lines, but found they could not dominate the rural population in the countryside despite brutal repression. The Japanese military were caught in an endless war.

Their solution to the dilemma was more war. They were encouraged by German defeat in 1940 of the Netherlands and of France, and the isolation of Great Britain. Late that year Japan joined Germany and Italy in the Tri-Partite Pact, a defensive alliance which strengthened Japan's war party. Western colonies in the Pacific and in Southeast Asia became a tempting prize to the militarists. Since the 1860s the French had ruled the area they called Indochina, on the southern border of the Chinese Republic. They had developed its food and mineral resources—especially iron ore in the north, rubber in the south—and maintained a small military force to control the population. The area was strategically located, for it provided the one line of supplies from the West to Chinese Nationalist areas.

A second area, the Dutch East Indies, was valuable particularly because of its oil fields. Since the early twentieth century, it had become a major center of world petroleum production, owned and exploited by the corporation Royal Dutch-Shell. This vital resource made the East Indies a prize possession to whoever controlled the archipelago. There too, the Indonesian peoples were dominated by Europeans, and some among them were already prepared to support an anti-imperialist, anti-Western revolt. The defeat of France and the Netherlands in 1940 left these colonies defenseless.

Eager for conquest and determined to end China's resistance, Japanese generals in 1940 moved troops to occupy northern Indochina. Their immediate goal was to cut off supplies from that region to the Nationalist Chinese. The larger objective of domination of all Southeast Asia tempted them still further the next summer. In mid-1941 their forces seized all of Indochina. Militarily the operation proved a simple matter, for the French authorities immediately capitulated. Diplomatically, the move proved the greatest mistake the Japanese military made.

The Japanese conquest of Indochina finally began U.S. resistance to Japanese expansion. By then, the balance of power in all East Asia had shifted toward Japan. Roosevelt considered aid to Great Britain in its war with Germany the principal U.S. priority, moving naval forces from the Pacific to the Atlantic in early 1941 to form the Atlantic fleet. The U.S. army units in the Philippines were isolated and weak. Great Britain, desperately fighting German air and naval attacks, had no forces to spare for a Pacific war. At a time of impending war with Germany, a conflict with Japan might place the United States in the middle of a global, two-front war. Realism suggested acceptance of Japanese conquests; Stalin did just that in signing a neutrality pact with Japan early in 1941.

On the other hand, the U.S. internationalist policy of the 1920s dictated opposition to Japan's flagrant violations of all the treaties signed in those years. Only U.S. dip-lomatic, economic, and (potentially) military power stood in the way of Japanese domination of all East Asia. The U.S. navy had begun a program to expand its forces, but more ships in the Pacific would not be ready until 1942. Since Japan's attack on China, some of Roosevelt's advisers had urged him to place an economic embargo on shipments of vital raw materials to Japan, a serious step since the Japanese economy—and military—depended on these supplies for the war effort. Until 1941, however, Roosevelt had resisted the move for fear of Japanese retaliation. There existed good reasons both for appeasement and for resistance to the Japanese.

In 1941 Roosevelt chose the policy of resistance, forced to take action finally by the Japanese conquest of southern Indochina. Japan's troops were in position to attack Western colonies throughout Southeast Asia. That summer, Roosevelt approved a new trade policy to oppose Japanese expansion. The United States placed a total embargo on all exports to Japan, including petroleum. Dutch authorities in the East Indies ended their oil sales to Japan was well. The U.S. secretary of state declared that his country would not lift the embargo until the Japanese "acts of agression" had ended. He demanded that Japan withdraw, not only from Indochina, but from China as well. Japan had to abandon its conquests to obtain the vitally needed raw materials.

The Japanese military rulers had to face the consequences of their reckless expansionist policies. The oil embargo on Japan cut petroleum imports to 10 percent of their previous level. Japanese officials warned that their entire oil reserves would run out within two years unless new foreign supplies were found. The Japanese naval commanders proposed one solution: invasion of the Dutch East Indies. This step would succeed only if accompanied by the defeat of British and American Pacific forces, however. The Japanese political leaders made one last effort to avoid war by seeking an agreement with the United States to lift the embargo in exchange for Japanese withdrawal from all Asian areas except north China, but the U.S. government would not compromise. The Japanese military had already laid plans for a new, combined naval and land offensive against American, British, and Dutch colonies and bases in the Pacific. On December 7, 1941, their attacks began, bringing world war to East Asia.

SUMMARY

In the two decades following the end of the First World War, Asian nationalism transformed the relations between the Western imperialist powers and the peoples of the principal Asian lands. It took different forms in different countries. The Indian National Congress, after long years of political struggle, won from the British the promise of self-government for the entire subcontinent. Whether the land would in fact remain united depended primarily on the relations between Muslims and Hindus, already in serious conflict. The rise of the Nationalist party of Chiang Kai-shek brought a superficial appearance of national unity to China and ended finally the most humiliating Western controls in the country. There, too, the future of the country rested partly on the outcome of an internal conflict, pitting Communists against the Nationalist regime. It also depended upon resistance to Japanese expansion. Japanese military leaders were able to mobilize the forces of their new nation-state for a war of conquest, in which both Asian peoples and western empires were the victims.

Although the Western empires were vanishing from Asia, the influence of the West remained strong. We cannot understand the new directions taken by these Asian lands without keeping in mind the impact of Western models of political and economic change. Asian nationalist leaders did not seek a return to the conditions of the past. Even while resisting Western domination they looked to the West for ideological and practical guidelines in constructing independent states. Only a few idealists such as Gandhi rejected industrialism, valued by most leaders both for its promise of an end to poverty and for an escape from their countries' dependence on Western capitalism. Soviet socialism held out the promise of freedom and equality for Asian Communists, and the Soviet state provided support for anti-imperialist movements in countries such as China. The Japanese borrowed Western political institutions in reforming their country. Nowhere did the results imitate the model. Mao evolved his own version of revolutionary Marxism. Japanese democracy, and later militarism, reflected the unique political culture of that country. Resistance to the West challenged imperialist domination while drawing inspiration from the Western political and revolutionary experience. The world was drawing closer together, in peace and in war.

RECOMMENDED READING

Indian History

MICHAEL EDWARDES, *British India, 1772–1947* (1968)

PERCIVAL SPEAR, *India, A Modern History* (rev. ed., 1972)

STANLEY WOLPERT, *A New History of India* (second ed., 1982)

Chinese History

*Jean Chesneaux, Françoise Le Barbier, Ma-
rie-Claire Bergère, *China: From the 1911 Revolution to Liberation* (1978)

John Fairbanks, Edwin Reischauer, and Albert Craig, *East Asia: The Modern Transformation* (1975)

James Sheridan, *China in Disintegration: The Republican Era in Chinese History, 1912–1949*
(1975)

Benjamin Schwartz, *Chinese Communism and the
Rise of Mao* (1951)

Jonathan Spence, *The Gate of Heavenly Peace: The
Chinese and Their Revolution, 1895–1980* (1981)

Japanese History

Herbert Feis, *The Road to Pearl Harbor: The Coming of the War Between the United States and Japan*
(1950)

Edwin Reischauer, *Japan: The Story of a Nation*
(rev. ed., 1974)

Memoirs and Novels

*André Malraux, *Man's Fate* (1934)

Ved Mehta, *The Ledge Between the Streams* (1984);
also *Daddyji* (1979)

Han Suyin, *The Crippled Tree* (1965)

chapter 6

THE SECOND WORLD WAR: THE GLOBAL CONFLICT

The Second World War came closer than ever in human history to uniting the peoples of the world in one vast, terrible, human endeavor. Countries from every continent were involved in the conflict, whose battlefields were scattered around the globe. Heroism was no longer the sole privilege of soldiers in battle. Guerrilla war and resistance movements in countries occupied by the Axis powers sustained there a spirit of war and kept alive visions of a better life to follow liberation. For the first time armies opened their ranks to women, not yet warriors but no longer merely protectors of the home and temporary workers. The scope of death and destruction extended throughout the civilian population. New military technology restored mobility to armies and made military aircraft the key element in naval battles and the means to carry the war far behind the front lines. At the end of the war, one single explosive device revealed the ca-

pacity of atomic energy to lay waste an entire city. Human ingenuity put in the hands of statesmen and their military commanders fantastic powers of destruction.

German and Japanese victories in the first stages of the war destroyed the old balance of power and put at these nations' disposal the peoples and resources of vast empires. The effect of their conquests marked deeply the population within those areas, obliterating old frontiers and overturning established governments. The Nazi New Order in Europe and the Asian empire of Japan differed enormously, since each projected onto subject lands the power and political culture of the conquerors. In their search for supporters among the conquered peoples, they both manipulated the rhetoric of ideology. The Nazis cultivated the European fascist movement, while the Japanese proclaimed their backing for anti-Western nationalism. Their success in winning help added a new term to

our language of war—"collaborators"—
those who chose to assist the occupying German or Japanese enemies against the Allies.
The legacy of Axis victories included both
great military empires and militant ideologies of combat.

The diversity of the principal Allied countries was greater still than that of the Axis
powers. The governments of Great Britain,
the Soviet Union, and the United States
fought common enemies, but their objectives
and even their manner of conducting the
war revealed very different perceptions of
global relations and political order. The
great war leaders of these states—Roosevelt,
Churchill, and Stalin—found a common language only by emphasizing the short-term
goals of war, summed up in the demand for
"unconditional surrender" of the Axis states.
As the tide of battle turned in their favor,
their discussion of the postwar world revealed how far apart were the objectives of
Stalin, deeply suspicious of the Western capitalist states, and those of the Western leaders. Although later critics pointed to the
shortcomings of their wartime diplomatic
agreements, it is important to remember
their successful collaboration in the last years
of war. In the end, however, the defeat of the
Axis states replaced the borders of their empires with a new boundary dividing the lands
freed by Soviet troops and those occupied by
the Western Allies. The peace, like the war
that preceded it, bore little resemblance to
the First World War.

THE EMPIRES OF GERMANY
AND JAPAN

The first phase of the European war, from
1939 to 1941, saw a series of rapid German
military victories followed by the creation of
a German continental empire. Assured of
the neutrality of the Soviet Union, German

troops easily defeated Polish forces by the
end of September 1939. Britain and France
had declared war on Germany but were incapable of offensive military operations to save
Poland. Carrying out its part of the secret
agreement with the Nazi state, the Soviet
Union seized eastern Poland. Hitler had
nothing to fear from the Russians. Consequently, he was able to direct all his forces in
the spring of 1940 against the Western
states. In another "lightning war," Germany
occupied all of western Europe except Sweden, Switzerland, and Spain, defeating
France in six weeks. Great Britain fought on
alone, a beleaguered country relying on its
navy and air force to prevent a German invasion. Its new prime minister, Winston
Churchill, promised a battle to the end, "on
the sea, on land, and in the air." The Battle of
Britain, waged that fall and winter in the
skies over England, left the Royal Air Force
the victors and discouraged Hitler's plans for
conquest of his last foe. Still, Britain remained in a desperate situation—its shipping attacked by German submarines, its
fleet severely damaged, its communications
with its Asian empire threatened.

German domination of Europe grew with
Italy's entry into the war on its side; later
small states from Central Europe joined.
The third Axis power, Japan, signed a defensive pact late that year with the fascist
states. The German conquests in Eastern and
Western Europe made the Nazi state the
most powerful military empire in the Western world. Churchill's only hope for victory
was the eventual help of the other two great
powers in the world, the United States and
the Soviet Union.

U.S. Neutrality

Gradually U.S. isolationism weakened as
German power grew. President Franklin
Roosevelt had never shared the revulsion

felt by many Americans at U.S. involvement in the First World War. He had begun his political career a supporter of Wilson's domestic and war policies and had been active in the war effort as secretary of the navy. He shared the belief, first defended by his elder cousin Theodore Roosevelt in the early 1900s, that the United States had to take an active role in world politics. Like Wilson, he considered Great Britain a valuable ally whose defeat in war would constitute a disaster for the United States. He was not as ardent an internationalist as Wilson, however. He appears to have judged collaboration among the leaders of great powers more important to peace than international forums like the League. A skillful politician and public figure, he learned from Wilson's tragic defeat the necessity to heed the wishes of Congress and the American voters in reconciling attainable and desirable objectives in foreign policy. Until the last years of the 1930s, his attention was directed to domestic reform and the political struggles arising from his New Deal program. Foreign affairs constituted a secondary matter until European conflict once again intruded into American life.

The first year of war in Europe forced Roosevelt to confront the consequences of American isolationism. The initial reaction of the U.S. Congress to the outbreak of war in 1939 was to persevere in the policy of noninvolvement in European affairs. It had previously passed neutrality acts banning sale of U.S. military supplies or the use of U.S. shipping in trade with any warring countries, an isolationist policy whose only immediate effect had been to cut off supplies to the enemies of the Axis powers. Roosevelt formally declared the United States neutral in the 1939 war.

As German military power grew, however, he spoke out more and more frequently against isolationism and in support of the British. He feared the strategic threat to U.S. security, especially after German victories in Western Europe in 1940. He argued that "if Great Britain goes down, the Axis powers will control the continents . . . and will be in a position to bring enormous military and naval resources against this hemisphere." He instituted peacetime conscription in 1940 to begin the expansion of the army, and in early 1941 created the Atlantic Squadron, the first U.S. naval force in the Atlantic since 1918 (made up largely of ships taken from the Pacific fleet).

Early that year, he obtained the approval of Congress to provide armaments to Great Britain on the Lend-Lease Program (though no "lending" at all was involved and payment was never expected). In the spring of 1941, the United States extended its war zone far into the North and South Atlantic to permit its naval vessels to protect shipping for Britain from German submarine attack. The United States was headed toward an undeclared naval war with Germany.

Yet all that time Roosevelt lacked sufficient political backing for war in defense of Great Britain. In the presidential elections of late 1940, he had to repeat his commitment to keep the United States out of "foreign" conflicts. His most successful speeches on international affairs discussed the war in Europe in idealistic terms. Roosevelt himself abhorred nazism and believed deeply in democracy. Yet his measures directed against Germany were based primarily on considerations of security and power. The American public understood far more readily, however, the rhetoric of internationalism.

To win support for his policies, therefore, Roosevelt emphasized the threat that nazism posed to "religion, democracy, and good faith among nations." He pledged U.S. support for a "world founded upon four essential human freedoms": religion, speech, security, and freedom from want. Roosevelt, like Wilson before him, talked of the European conflict in terms which portrayed it as a crusade for democracy, not a war for U.S. national security. In the summer of 1941, he obtained Churchill's approval for the Atlantic Charter, which committed both states to "a better future for the world" following the "final destruction of Nazi tyranny." The charter did not constitute a military alliance, however. A majority in Congress still opposed war on Germany. Isolationists like Charles Lindberg promoted the idea of Fortress America to be defended with 100,000 airplanes. Other Americans considered the growing danger of conflict with Japan of greater concern to immediate U.S. interests. The British had to fight on without the United States.

The German-Soviet War

The Soviet Union became their first important ally. Although it had collaborated with Germany in the 1939 defeat of Poland, the two states were ideological enemies and rivals for power in Eastern Europe. Stalin took full advantage of the secret agreements signed in 1939 with Germany. Soviet troops moved into Eastern Poland that fall, and in the summer of 1940 the Soviet Union annexed the Baltic states. To the north, a short Soviet-Finnish war in the winter of 1939–40 forced Finland, despite prolonged and heroic fighting against the Red Army, to cede its eastern region to the Soviet Union. These military operations enlarged Soviet territory (but did not improve its defenses, as 1941 proved) in the western areas where Stalin anticipated war with Germany would come.

At the same time, Stalin attempted to delay the conflict by appeasing Nazi Germany. He accepted a Soviet-German trade agreement providing for Soviet shipments to Ger-

many of vital raw materials, including petroleum, goods important to the German military buildup. The Soviet Union carried out the agreement to the letter. In addition, Soviet border forces in the west were ordered to do nothing to provoke the German army, whose generals Stalin thought the principal "warmongers." The Soviet dictator dismissed as "British provocation" reports in the spring of 1941 from Soviet spies and from Great Britain of a planned German offensive against the Soviet Union. He could not imagine that Hitler, still at war in the west, would attack his country that year. Because his word was law, the Soviet Union was caught unprepared for the greatest military offensive in history.

Hitler's decision to attack the Soviet Union revealed the extent to which he was obsessed with "Bolshevism" and consumed by the dream of making Germany ruler of the European continent. Strategically, it made no sense, for Germany remained at war with Great Britain and was receiving vast amounts of Soviet raw materials under the trade agreement. Militarily, it confronted Germany with the largest land army in the world, backed by a productive industrial economy. Yet none of these concerns swayed Hitler. His fanatical hostility toward Communism was as great as that toward the Jews. In the fall of 1940, he ordered that the vast resources of the German Empire and its European allies be mobilized for another "lightning war" against Russia. It was to be waged along a two-thousand-mile frontier with over four million soldiers spearheaded by ten thousand tanks and supported by five thousand planes. Plans called for victory in three months. On June 22, 1941, Germany invaded the Soviet Union.

The attack succeeded initially beyond the Germans' greatest hopes. Within two weeks Soviet frontier defenses were crushed and German tank forces had penetrated deep

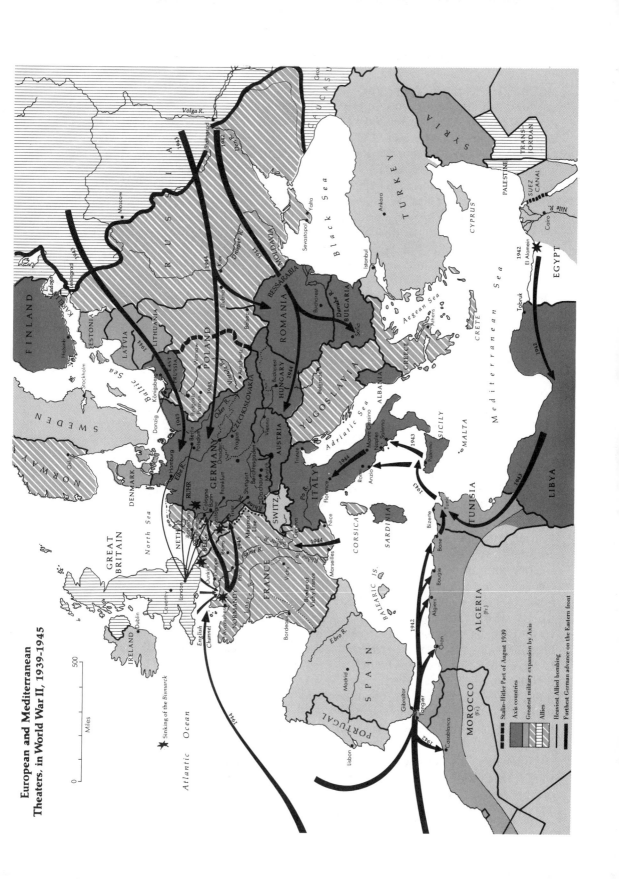

European and Mediterranean Theaters, in World War II, 1939-1945

Miles

Stalin–Hitler Pact of August 1939
Axis countries
Greatest military expansion by Axis
Allies
Heaviest Allied bombing
Furthest German advance on the Eastern front

★ Sinking of the Bismarck

Atlantic Ocean

NORWAY
SWEDEN
FINLAND
KARELIA
Oslo
Stockholm
Helsinki
Ladoga
Baltic Sea
Leningrad 1943
Moscow
Volga R.
Stalingrad
R U S S I A
GREAT BRITAIN
IRELAND
Dublin
Coventry
London
North Sea
English Channel
DENMARK
NETH.
BELG.
RUHR
Hamburg
Berlin
Potsdam
Danzig
Königsberg
EAST PRUSSIA
Warsaw
Auschwitz
POLAND
Białystok
LITHUANIA
LATVIA
ESTONIA
Minsk
Smolensk
Kiev
Dnieper R.
Don R.
CAUCASUS
GERMANY
Cologne
Bonn
Essen
Frankfurt
Stuttgart
Berchtesgaden
Munich
Elbe R.
Dresden
Prague
CZECHOSLOVAKIA
Vienna
AUSTRIA
Oder R.
Breslau
Posen
Budapest
HUNGARY 1944
MOLDAVIA
BESSARABIA 1941
ROMANIA
Bucharest
Danube R.
BULGARIA
Sofia
Sevastopol
Yalta
Black Sea
Istanbul
Ankara
TURKEY
SYRIA
TRANS- JORDAN
PALESTINE
SUEZ CANAL
Cairo
Nile R.
EGYPT
El Alamein 1942
Tobruk 1942
LIBYA
CYPRUS
Mediterranean Sea
CRETE
Aegean Sea
Athens
GREECE
ALBANIA
YUGOSLAVIA
Belgrade
Trieste
Adriatic Sea
ITALY
Florence
Rome
Monte Cassino
Anzio
Naples
Solerno 1944
Palermo
SICILY
MALTA
SARDINIA
CORSICA
BALEARIC IS.
SPAIN
Madrid
PORTUGAL
Lisbon
Gibraltar
Tangier
MOROCCO (Fr.)
Casablanca 1942
ALGERIA (Fr.)
Oran
Algiers
Bougie
Bône
Bizerte
Tunis
TUNISIA 1943
FRANCE
Vichy
Border of Vichy France
Marseilles
Nice
Genoa
SWITZ.
Maginot Line
Bordeaux
Ebro R.
Garonne R.
Rhône R.
Rhine R.
Saône R.
Paris
NORMANDY
Dunkirk
Calais
Compiègne
Po R.

into Russian territory. Along the way they captured hundreds of thousands of Red Army prisoners. Stalin, after days of shock and depression when he ceased to function as leader, took over the reins of power again in early July. He ordered Soviet soldiers to stand fast against the German offensive and in a radio broadcast (his first) begged the Soviet people, whom he addressed as "comrades, brothers and sisters, dear friends," to make every sacrifice in that "Great Patriotic War." Patriotism was the force on which he counted to win the support of the people. The mechanism of the police state was there to punish those who did not heed his call. Soldiers who shirked their duty and who appeared to have surrendered without good cause were judged traitors. He refused to make any effort to save the life of his eldest son, taken prisoner by the Germans that summer when his fighter plane was shot down. He made no allowances in that war for human weakness, pity, or compassion.

The German offensive continued until late fall. By October, all of western Russia had fallen. Leningrad was besieged, Kiev had been captured, and German troops were nearing Moscow. The Russian losses were enormous, totaling perhaps two million casualties, and most Soviet tanks and aircraft were destroyed. Yet the Red Army found new reserves, drawn from the Far East where war with Japan no longer threatened. In addition, bitterly cold winter weather had become its ally, slowing the German advance. In December, Soviet troops launched a successful counteroffensive, the first defeat suffered by the Germans in the Second World War. The German "lightning war" had failed, but the front lines were far inside Russian territory.

Hitler was possessed by the spirit of total war. Although deeply committed militarily on the eastern front and under no diplo-matic obligation, he linked the European and Asian wars by declaring war on the United States three days after the Pearl Harbor attack. His action ensured that Roosevelt's hope to join Great Britain in the European war came true. In the west, the attack on Great Britain included submarine warfare around the British Isles and frequent bombings of British cities. In North Africa, General Rommel's divisions came to the aid of Italian troops fighting the British in Egypt. In early 1942 Rommel's forces began an offensive intended to seize the Suez Canal and to establish German satellite states in the Middle East.

The eastern front remained the principal European battlefield. Military operations extended along a front from the Arctic Circle southeast to the shores of the Black Sea. The Germans and their allies maintained one million troops on that front; the Soviet combat forces, weakened by the defeats of 1941, numbered over two million and their size was growing. The ferocity of fighting left no room for compassion. Many of the Soviet troops taken prisoner in 1941 died of starvation and cold, left with little or no care by the Germans. German security forces shot whoever they suspected of belonging to or sympathizing with the Communist party. The German blockade of Leningrad sought to starve the city into surrendering, but Soviet leaders would not consider giving up the city, that winter a frozen wasteland without food or heat in which hundreds of thousands of its inhabitants died of starvation.

In a last effort to achieve victory against the Soviet Union, Hitler ordered his generals to prepare in the summer of 1942 an attack from central Russia toward the Caucasus mountains and the Caspian oil fields, south of which lay Arab lands where he hoped Rommel would be victorious. The plan, baptized Operation Blue, exhibited a visionary concept of war so far beyond German capabilities it bordered on the insane. Yet when it began, German fighting ability, coupled with the weakness of the Red Army, achieved the initial objectives. By September German units had reached the Caucasus while others had attained the edges of the city of Stalingrad, on the lower Volga River. They had not, however, destroyed the Soviet armies of southern Russia, most of whose troops had retreated beyond the Volga. Victory remained elusive, yet Hitler would settle for no less against his hated enemy.

The city of Stalingrad acquired for him symbolic importance. He chose to make its capture, though not originally an important objective, the goal of the offensive. The war of movement became a war of street fighting in a city far to the east of the main German front. The battle of Stalingrad dragged on into the winter.

The German Empire

By the end of 1942 almost the entirety of the European continent had fallen under the domination of Nazi Germany and its allied states. From the shores of the Atlantic Ocean as far east as central Russia, from the Arctic Ocean to the Mediterranean Sea, a German New Order reigned. It relied in part on the collaboration of allied states and of political movements sympathetic to Nazi Germany. Until 1943 Fascist Italy constituted Germany's most important ally, its troops fighting in North Africa, the Balkans, and Russia. In France, a small group of French political leaders collaborated with the Germans, who left them a state in southern France with its capital in Vichy. Most French people in the first years of defeat were resigned to German domination. Similar collaborationist regimes existed in the Netherlands and Norway.

In Eastern Europe, some states had allied with Germany as soon as or before the war began. Rumania, Bulgaria, Hungary, and Finland aided the German war effort. Conservative nationalists, bitter enemies of Soviet Russia, hoped to share in the spoils of a German victory. Fascist parties provided collaborators in the German administration, and volunteers for the SS divisions from other countries appeared in increasing numbers. National and political hatreds dividing Eastern Europeans helped the Germans as well. Many Ukrainians assisted Germany as police, administrators, and soldiers in order to fight the Communists, who had inflicted great hardship on them before the war. In Yugoslavia, the Nazis encouraged Croatian nationalists to join them with the promise of an independent Croatia after the war. In no case did this collaboration include more than a small minority of these national groups. Opposing them were resistance forces fighting the Germans in the underground and in forested and mountainous areas and providing assistance to the Allies. Still, the collaborators served the Germans well in helping to control occupied Europe.

The dominant characteristic of the German New Order was exploitation of the conquered lands. All Europe lay at the disposal of the Nazi leaders. French agriculture helped to feed German armies and to sustain a comfortable standard of living in Germany. While French people lived on meager rations, German food supplies remained abundant. The industrial production of occupied Europe augmented German economic resources and supplied military equipment to German armies. Many major enterprises, such as the Skoda metallurgical firm in Czechoslovakia, were taken over by Nazi administrators. German expropriation set the stage for nationalization after the war. Finally, the German authorities considered the working population of Europe to be available for their needs. German workers had to serve in the armed forces. In their place the

Nazis deported laborers from other countries to work in miserable conditions on German farms and in factories. From the Ukraine over a million men and women were transported to German lands, from Czechoslovakia over 300,000, from France 1 million—in all 5 million forced laborers. Germany turned the conquered populations into its subject peoples.

This repressive policy hit with greatest brutality the Polish nation and the European Jews, judged "subhuman" by Nazi racist ideology. Poland once again ceased to exist, much of its western territory incorporated in Germany and the Polish inhabitants forced to abandon everything to move to the east. The central region became simply the Government-General, an area open to exploitation by German businessmen provided with Polish forced labor. Another 1.5 million Poles worked in Germany. Polish intellectuals were arrested and shot. The economic resources of the area went to Germany, leaving Poles, in Goering's words, only the "absolutely essential for the maintenance at a low level of the bare existence of the inhabitants."

These racist policies reached their most inhuman level in the extermination of the Jews of Europe. Nazi anti-Semitism constituted a powerful bond among all party members and found supporters among people in Eastern Europe, where the bulk of Europe's Jews lived. Hitler's obsessive hatred of the Jews and his control of the "SS state" placed in his hands the fate of the Jewish population. Before the war he had introduced racial policies in Germany, stripping the Jews of citizenship, ostracizing them, forcing half of the 300,000 German Jews into emigration. German conquests in Eastern Europe in 1939–41 placed approximately 5 million Jews under German control. Hitler sought a way to eliminate them from all Europe. Forced resettlement in ghettos began

in 1940, but he found the slow death there by disease and starvation unsatisfactory. When German troops invaded Soviet Russia, they were followed by special SS death squads who executed hundreds of thousands of Jews. Yet these methods appeared to him insufficient to make Europe "free of Jews."

His solution was genocide, the systematic mass extermination of an entire people. He proposed the policy, termed by Nazi leaders the Final Solution, in 1941. Its implementation began in 1942. His instrument for this insane policy was at hand—the SS organization, whose members were sworn to absolute obedience to his orders. The Jewish population of all Europe was to be shipped in trains of cattle cars to special camps in Poland. These were extermination camps, organized according to the same standards of industrial efficiency as slaughterhouses for animals. The trains, arriving usually at night, poured out their loads of men, women, and children, most of whom were immediately herded into special sealed buildings to be killed by poisonous gas and then incinerated in enormous ovens. All that was left were mountains of clothing, gold teeth, hair, and other items taken from the victims. A few prisoners survived for a time to work as forced laborers, only to be killed in their turn.

When reports began to reach the West in 1942 of the existence of these camps, they aroused at first disbelief even among Jews. Allied leaders refused for long to believe the accounts. Then, in the face of mounting evidence, they issued public warnings to Germany. Their priorities of war took precedence, however, over efforts to save the Jews. Until late in the war, no Allied bombing raids were directed against the facilities or rail lines of the camps.

The Final Solution remained in operation to the end of the war. The last German Jews to be taken were First World War veterans, who left with their medals still believing they were headed for "resettlement" in the east. What little Jewish resistance broke out proved futile; the 1943 uprising of the remaining inhabitants of the Warsaw ghetto constituted an act of hopeless, heroic desperation. By the end of the war four to five million Jews had been exterminated, the victims of insane Nazi racism and the moral cowardice of Germans. Historians still debate the circumstances and causes of this policy of genocide, a phenomenon so complex and terrifying that it defies adequate explanation. Germany's New Order tore apart the old Europe, its peoples and its states. Nothing could return the continent to its previous condition.

The Japanese War

Pressed onward by the need for the petroleum of the East Indies and drawn by visions of a great victory in the eastern Pacific, the Japanese war leaders set in motion on December 7, 1941, their plan of military conquest. It called for a series of surprise attacks by Japanese naval aircraft to destroy the Pacific fleets of Great Britain, at Singapore, and of the United States, at Pearl Harbor. Subsequently Japanese land forces would invade the Philippines, the British Southeast Asian colonies, and the Dutch East Indies. The attack on Pearl Harbor put out of action the bulk of the U.S. Pacific fleet, missing only the three aircraft carriers on maneuvers at the time. Japanese planes the same day sank two British battleships, the sole naval protection for the fortress of Singapore. For the next year the Japanese navy controlled the Pacific Ocean from the Aleutian Islands south to the Coral Sea near Australia.

Naval victories opened the way for the military offensives of the Japanese army. The great British fortress of Singapore fell to a surprise attack in February 1942. The surrender of the garrison eliminated British rule in Southeast Asia and left the Japanese with 90,000 prisoners, many of them Indian soldiers. That spring Japanese troops completed the conquest of the Dutch East Indies. In May, the last American forces in the Philippines surrendered in the single greatest military defeat ever suffered by the United States. Japanese treatment of the captured Western troops was brutal. This happened not as a result of racism, but because the Japanese military code considered defeat and surrender so great a humiliation that only suicide could efface the loss of honor; prisoners lacked military valor and were often treated like slaves. Japan quickly proceeded to take over Thailand, Malaya, and Burma, where its army prepared to attack British forces in eastern India. In half a year it had conquered a territory with 140 million people, destroying the Western empires in Southeast Asia.

The Japanese government ruled these areas with occupation forces backing nationalist political leaders ready to collaborate with the conquerors. Throughout Southeast Asia anti-imperialist movements administered their lands in place of the vanquished Westerners. The Dutch East Indies became Indonesia, whose administration was led by the Indonesian nationalist Sukarno. Burma became a model Japanese satellite, receiving formal independence in 1943. Throughout the Philippines the Japanese found influential political leaders from the land-owning elite ready to collaborate in governing the population. Indian prisoners of war, taken when Singapore fell, were offered the opportunity of forming an Indian National Army to fight on the Indian front. The Japanese promised that their victory would bring independence to India. Thousands of Indian prisoners volunteered, knowing that their new enemies were their old comrades in arms. The promise of national independence and the military triumphs of 1942 won for Japan the collaboration of nationalists from every conquered land.

China remained the major prize and the most difficult conquest. The Japanese regime had planned to create puppet governments there similar to those in Korea and Manchuria. Following its occupation of the coastal regions of northern and central China, it supported collaborationist regimes in both regions. The central Chinese puppet state, located in the former capital of Nanking and led by former leaders in the Chiang's Nationalist party, claimed for itself the mantle of true Chinese nationalism by virtue of its opposition to the West and its "friendship" with Japan.

The continued defeats of Chiang's forces led even some of his own military commanders to defect to the Japanese-supported state. In 1942 several generals with about one-half million troops joined the Nanking regime. The latter's army grew in size to attain almost one million soldiers before the end of the war. It assisted the Japanese in their operations both against Chiang's army and against the Chinese Communist guerrillas. In this respect the war in China constituted another chapter in the civil war which had followed the fall of the empire in 1911.

The Japanese plans for a Greater East Asia Co-Prosperity Sphere extended over this entire conquered area. China along with Indonesia, the Philippines, Burma, Thailand, and Indochina were all to participate "through mutual cooperation" in an "order of common prosperity and well-being based on justice." The promise never came true. War held first place in the Japanese priorities; the resources of its territories, like those of German-held Europe, were put to the use of the Japanese military. The petroleum of Indonesia fueled the Japanese navy and food supplies went to the army and to the Home Islands. This economic exploitation alienated the population and fueled resistance movements which sprang up in every country. Later, trade among the East Asian lands dwindled when the American submarine war on Japanese shipping made the sea a battlefield and isolated the various countries one from another. The war against the Allies, not "co-prosperity," was the dominant feature of Japanese occupation policy.

Despite impressive victories, the Japanese military had failed to achieve their principal objectives. By mid-1942 the U.S. Pacific fleet had recovered sufficiently to launch its own attacks on Japanese naval forces. In China, Japanese campaigns against Communist-held regions did not end the guerrilla war, nor were new offensives against the Nationalist armies successful in forcing Chiang's surrender. The sufferings of the Chinese people, caught in the middle of these conflicts, were terrible; millions died of disease and starvation. One-half of Japanese overseas forces were tied down in the war against the Nationalist armies. The Japanese plan to dominate China did not come true. Neither the German military triumphs nor the great conquests of the Japanese gave these states the final victory their leaders had sought.

THE FORMATION OF THE GRAND ALLIANCE

The states opposing the Axis came together slowly into one global alliance. The Western Allies and the Soviet Union were unlike one another in many respects. They fought on distant battlefronts; they pursued separate war aims; their political systems were the product of opposing ideologies. These differences created barriers to understanding and were the cause of serious disagreements. Gradually, though, through meetings of foreign ministers and international conferences they agreed upon a set of common objectives. These goals set the guidelines for military collaboration and for the postwar reconstruction of Europe and East Asia.

The United States and the Allies

With the entry into the war of the United States, the global conflict found a central focus. Decisions made in Washington were very influential both to the course of the war in Europe and Asia and to the elaboration of diplomatic aims of the allies. This situation was the result primarily of the global military presence of U.S. forces and of the economic aid provided by the United States to its allies. In the first place, the United States came to possess the greatest array of modern armaments of any belligerent. The U.S. fleets in the two oceans constituted the largest number of fighting vessels ever to sail under one flag. The naval program begun by Roosevelt in 1940 produced quick results, replacing in 1942 the ships sunk at Pearl Harbor even while expanding the Atlantic fleet. Only the United States had access through its naval forces to the shores of every continent and island where the war was fought. The U.S. air force grew to surpass in size that of Great Britain, and by 1943 the combined forces of the two states controlled the skies over Germany. In the Pacific, the planes of U.S. aircraft carriers overwhelmed the carrier-based planes of the Japanese and sank most of the Japanese carriers. Only on land was the U.S. army outnumbered by another ally. The Soviet Red Army constituted the largest land army in the world, a fact of crucial importance for the ultimate fate of the states of Eastern and Central Europe.

The second reason for U.S. wartime leadership lay in its enormous economic resources. After remaining partially unused throughout the depression, factories and farmland began full operation when war production began. The nine million unemployed in 1940 found jobs, and business boomed. Mobilized for the war effort, the U.S. economy equipped not only its own military on land, sea, and air, but also provided great quantities of supplies to its allies. Roosevelt had started a program of military assistance to Great Britain even before the United States entered the war. This Lend-Lease aid began to go to the Soviet Union shortly after the German invasion of Russia.

When the United States became a belligerent, all previous political obstacles to economic aid vanished. The only barriers were the consequence of the war itself. Help reached the Chinese Nationalists by air throughout most of the war, as long as Japan controlled Burma. As a result China received only a small amount of wartime aid, about $1.5 billion. Similarly, access to the Soviet Union was impeded by German submarines and air force. The most direct, northern route around Norway to Murmansk was also the most dangerous. Ultimately the path taken to ship massive aid to Russia passed through Iran, whose territory was occupied jointly by the Soviet Union, Great Britain, and the United States. Roads and railroads were built from the Iranian coast to the Soviet border. This route did not operate fully until 1943, when supplies began to pour into Russia, providing that country with $11 billion in aid, principally food, aircraft, and military vehicles. The single greatest recipient, though, was Great Britain. Together with the Commonwealth countries, it received $30 billion in Lend-Lease supplies.

The large amount of aid reaching Great Britain was due to U.S. military priorities as well as to the proximity of the British Isles. The United States could not wage a two-front war with equal force both in the Pacific and the Atlantic. In the first months and years of combat the United States had to mobilize for war, to build a new standing army, to expand its merchant marine and navy, to develop a modern air force. In the Atlantic in the winter of 1941–42, its convoys could barely cope with the German submarine attacks. Most serious of all, its Pacific fleet was inferior to Japanese naval forces. The United States had to choose a major front. Roosevelt made the decision that the Pacific forces would have to fight and hold where they could, retreat elsewhere.

The war against Germany received first priority. The Atlantic fleet had to keep supplies flowing to Great Britain. The shared interests and objectives of the two states had for half a century formed a working diplomatic partnership, which had become a wartime alliance once already in 1917–18. Churchill and Roosevelt had begun forging new ties even before Pearl Harbor. The aims of the governments diverged in certain important areas. While the U.S. leaders championed the cause of independence for colonial peoples everywhere, including India, Churchill sought to retain as much imperial territory as possible. His country was weak, however. Although Great Britain was assisted by the entire British Commonwealth, even the economic and military aid of countries such as Canada and Australia could not compensate adequately for Britain's defeats of 1939 and 1940. Relying on U.S. wartime collaboration, Churchill had to acknowledge Roosevelt's leadership.

Both the United States and Great Britain depended heavily on the military contribution of their Soviet ally. Until 1944, only the Red Army stood between German and victory on the European continent. Without an eastern front, the Western Allies would confront the bulk of German forces when they attempted their European invasion. The U.S. government judged the alliance with the Soviet Union indispensable also for military victory in East Asia, where large Japanese armies controlled the key central and northern regions of China. The Red Army appeared to them the only military force in position to defeat Japan in Manchukuo and north China. In both the European and Asian wars, the Soviet Union was an extremely valuable ally.

Yet the U.S. and British governments could do little to take the enormous burden of fighting off the Red Army until Allied invasion forces crossed the English Channel and opened a major front in northwestern Europe. Stalin continually reminded his Western allies of this fact, begging them in 1942 to open a western front to relieve his armies retreating once again before the German offensive. Roosevelt responded sympathetically to the appeal, only to agree finally with Churchill that their military lacked both the naval power and infantry forces capable of staging a successful cross-channel invasion. In that year the Soviet Union had to continue fighting alone in Europe.

In the first two years of the alliance, the Western Allies made only small-scale efforts to share the burden of fighting with Russia. Their principal campaigns were centered on the Mediterranean area. They began with the invasion of North Africa in November 1942, a sideshow of particular interest to the British in regaining control of the Near East. The next spring, Allied forces invaded Italy, opening a new front still far from the main theater of operations in northern Europe. Their economic aid was even more modest, for convoys carrying Lend-Lease shipments through the Arctic Ocean were damaged so heavily by German attacks that they were suspended for the summer months.

In that situation, a diplomatic gesture acquired special significance to prove to Stalin that the West valued the Soviet alliance. The United States and Britain promised in early 1943 not to accept any peace terms from Germany except "unconditional surrender." The real meaning of the declaration was that under no circumstances would the two powers negotiate a separate peace with Germany. Obtaining Stalin's agreement to the policy signified to them that Russia would do the same, even without a second front in the west. This agreement for complete military victory in Europe represented a bond of trust, less important ultimately to the Grand Alliance than economic aid and military campaigns, yet significant still in the indispensable collaboration among political leaders.

Latin America and the Wartime Alliance

The alliance spread quickly to Latin American countries. Their relations with the United States determined whether their governments chose to join in the war against the Axis. Some declared war on Germany because they valued their ties with the United States and shared Roosevelt's democratic ideals, others because their leaders found it in their own interest to back the Yankees.

In the first three decades of the twentieth century, U.S. leaders had dealt with these states often in an arbitrary, forceful manner. Possession of the Panama Canal had made the Caribbean an area of strategic importance. A naval force and a Marine battalion were available where intervention was judged desirable. Cuba had lived under U.S. military occupation for a few years, and had at times had U.S. advisers set its government's financial policy to pay back foreign debts. At the time of the First World War, President Wilson had twice sent troops into Mexico in opposition to military rulers. Democracy could not be imposed at the point of a bayonet, however. The Mexican revolution ended with the triumph of democratic, nationalist forces, determined to assert their country's diplomatic and economic independence from their powerful neighbor. Intervention in all its forms aroused anti-Ameri-

can, anti-imperialist nationalist opposition. In the late 1920s the United States ended its policy of intervention and pulled its Marines out of Nicaragua, the last country under occupation, in 1933.

The real test of U.S. readiness to let the Latin countries run their own affairs came later in the 1930s. Roosevelt expanded nonintervention into what he called the Good Neighbor policy. Mexico put that neighborliness to the test when it nationalized U.S. oil wells and refineries, promising reimbursement later for the property loss. Outraged U.S. business interests condemned the Mexicans for their "socialist" acts, calling them "Reds" and urging U.S. military intervention to return the property. Mexicans supported their government against the new threat of Yankee imperialism. Roosevelt honored his commitment to nonintervention by negotiating the issue with the Mexican government. No U.S. troops or naval forces threatened Mexico; no U.S. diplomats encouraged political opposition to the Mexican regime. In return, a conservative Mexican government joined in 1942 the Grand Alliance, as did other important Latin American states such as Brazil and Venezuela.

Real equality did not exist in the relations between the United States and Cuba. That small Caribbean island-state joined the war against Germany for reasons differing somewhat from those of Mexico. Cuba's giant neighbor to the north was the dominant force in Cuban economic and political life. When the U.S. ambassador refused in 1933 to recognize a new Cuban left-wing political leader, this act alone was sufficient to encourage Cuban officers to seize power themselves. The head of this Cuban military government was Fulgencio Batista, one-time sergeant of the Cuban army.

In the years that followed Batista proved a skillful and powerful leader. In his relations with the United States, he adopted the position of what was called a "client politician," that is, acceptance of U.S. diplomatic and economic interests in return for U.S. diplomatic backing and economic advantages. Cuba, like many other Latin American countries, relied for the well-being of its population largely on the export of one principal commodity—in its case, cane sugar. Since the United States was the major market for these products, the state of its economy and the trade policies of its government were of vital importance to countries such as Cuba. In good times, their laboring population found work at poor pay, while great landowners and merchants became wealthy. Batista accepted these inequalities, and the U.S. government rewarded his loyalty by providing a guaranteed market (at above-world-market prices) for the bulk of Cuban sugar. The Cuban economy grew rapidly, and Batista, confident in his popularity, introduced in 1940 a democratic constitution and was himself elected president.

When the United States entered the Second World War, Cuba immediately declared war on the Axis powers. Its naval vessels joined in Caribbean patrols; it became an important center for U.S. naval and air operations in the Caribbean and mid-Atlantic, operating from the naval base in Guantanamo Bay. Batista's standing among Cubans was never higher. Even the Cuban Communist party (speaking more for Stalin and the Grand Alliance than for themselves) called him "the people's idol, the great man of our national politics." Nationalist resentment at U.S. power remained muted and beneath the surface of political life. Latin America appeared far removed from the international conflicts of Europe and Asia, and from the revolutionary movements emerging in Asian colonial lands. In those years the Caribbean and Central American countries remained securely within the U.S. sphere of influence.

The Soviet Union and the Alliance

The Soviet Union was a vital yet mysterious member of the Grand Alliance. Its importance lay in the six million men mobilized in 1942 in the Red Army, the only large force fighting the German army then and for the year to come. Western statesmen realized from the start that the U.S.S.R. would occupy a dominant position in Central Europe when Germany was defeated, creating a new balance of power on the continent. The greatest mystery for Westerners surrounded the international objectives pursued by the Soviet Union.

That state was ruled by a Marxist regime supporting the Communist International, publicly extolling world proletarian revolution. Yet Stalin had in the previous decade conducted Soviet foreign policy on the principle that whatever was in the interest of Soviet territorial security and power had first priority for world communism. He used the Soviet-German nonaggression pact of 1939 to expand Soviet territory in Eastern Europe and made known later to the Allies his determination to retain those lands. He protected Soviet territory and its sphere of influence in East Asia by signing with Japan the 1941 neutrality treaty, which he carefully respected. Revolutionary expansion played no part in these foreign dealings. In appearance the Soviet Union was a revolutionary communist regime; its policies were those of a great power. In both respects it constituted a troubling presence in the coalition.

Soviet objectives since the outbreak of war with Germany in mid-1941 concentrated on the defense of the country. The war had begun with disastrous military defeats and the loss of most of western Russia and the Ukraine. In this crisis the country mobilized for total war. Stalin took direct control of political and military affairs, assuming the positions of chairman of the Council of Commissars and of the Defense Council. He followed closely the actions of his generals and the reorganization of the nationalized economy. His dictatorial powers obliterated the distinction between political and military leadership; later they permitted him to adjust military operations to diplomatic interests of state.

The apparatus of the police state remained in place, its energies during the war directed to stiffening the will of the population to fight. Its arbitrary powers of arrest were directed against suspected collaborators and traitors as well as against those who dared criticize Stalin. (For having written to a friend about Stalin "the bandit chief," a front-line artillery officer named Alexander Solzhenitsyn was arrested in the midst of battle in early 1945 and sent off to prison.) The prison camps remained in place, though their inmates at times were ordered to the front on suicide missions. Deserters from the Red Army were shot; soldiers who escaped German encirclement individually were considered potential enemy agents and arrested. Stalin's demand that the people of his country "must fight to the last drop of blood" became the overriding feature of Soviet life.

The war required the mobilization of all the economic resources of the country. German victories in 1941 had deprived the Soviet Union of some of its most important industrial areas and most productive agricultural regions. When possible, factories were disassembled and shipped to eastern areas before the Germans arrived. The process was time consuming and of little help in the first year. The Siberian industrial economy proved its real defense value in that period. The Red Army was poorly equipped still in 1942, but the new armaments it did possess came from the eastern factories. People had to survive on the meager food supplies remaining; many were hungry and

in some areas famine set in. Food aid from the United States began to appear in that year; at times the one meat dish available to civilians came from a can from "Amerika" bearing the unusual name of "Spam."

The population responded with extraordinary patriotic fervor, though the sentiment was not universal. People in the western regions seized by the Red Army in 1939 and 1940 welcomed the German invaders; non-Russian nationalities in the southern Soviet areas provided a sizable number of collaborators for the Germans. Among the Russian population, though, the war against Germany became a national cause for which they were prepared to sacrifice their well-being and their lives. The population of the blockaded city of Leningrad endured the inhuman conditions of hunger and cold in a spirit best described as collective heroism, though over a million lives were lost before the Axis siege was lifted in early 1944. When German forces reached Stalingrad in the fall of 1942, the city became a battleground in the midst of which many of the city's inhabitants were trapped. The Great Patriotic War, as the Russians called the war with Germany, demanded and received mass support.

The greatest sacrifice came from the front-line soldiers. The Red Army lacked in the first two years of war sufficient military equipment and skilled officers to match the powerful German army (many of the older, experienced Soviet officers had died in the police terror). This weakness had been particularly apparent in the first summer of fighting, when military defeat and encirclement of whole armies led soldiers to surrender in enormous numbers, many dying in German camps. It remained the case in 1942 as the German offensive swept through southern Russia to Stalingrad. Soviet generals replaced the missing armaments by demanding suicidal heroism from their soldiers. By war's end, Soviet military dead had reached ten million. The experience of those cruel years served as a crucible in which communism and Russian nationalism were fused into a new Soviet political culture.

In these desperate circumstances Soviet authorities promoted the formation of anti-Nazi guerrilla forces wherever possible throughout Europe. Communist parties in the occupied areas were ordered to organize resistance, whose military operations were intended to divert German troops and thus to weaken the German war effort in the east. In Eastern Europe, and in France and Italy as well, Communist resistance groups became powerful armed movements. They proved most successful in the Balkans. In Yugoslavia, Tito, leader of the Communist party, organized a guerrilla army able to take control gradually of most of the mountainous regions of the country, though only at an enormous cost of casualties and hardship for themselves and for the civilian population.

These Communist resistance forces fought both to defeat Germany and to prepare for social and political revolutions in their countries after the war. The real revolutionary zeal of the Communist international movement was found among these anti-German insurgents. They took up arms for their nation against the foreign oppressor, and for communism. Their revolutionary commitment sprang from their communist faith, but it also found strength in their nationalist hatred of the Axis enemy and of collaborators. They fought alongside (and sometimes against) other anti-German guerrilla forces, whose political ideals ranged from conservative nationalism to socialism. To Stalin, the role of the guerrilla forces was to assist in the defense of the Soviet Union. To make clear that world revolution was not his objective, in 1943 he disbanded the Communist International.

Soviet military operations began to achieve some measure of success in the battle of Stalingrad. After stubbornly defending at great human cost a small area of the city on the very banks of the Volga River, the Red Army launched in November 1942 a counteroffensive to encircle the German forces. Two months later, the remnants of the German army surrendered. The Red Army lost probably half a million men in the battle, but the Germans lost as many. The German retreat returned the front only to central Russia, however. In the summer of 1943 the eastern front still lay deep in Russian territory. The battle which decided the outcome of the German-Russian war occurred that summer on the plains around the city of Kursk. Hitler attempted one last major offensive, the biggest tank battle in the entire Second World War. This time, the Red Army was prepared in equipment, troops, and competent generals. In the end, the Soviet military machine proved mightier than the German army, beaten and in full retreat. By the late fall, the German withdrawal had reached western Russia. Victory was at last becoming for the Soviet leaders a tangible reality.

The High Point of the Grand Alliance

In those conditions of new-found military strength Stalin was ready to negotiate a real diplomatic alliance with the Western powers. At the conference of Teheran that fall, he met for the first time with Churchill and Roosevelt. The Western leaders for their part were finally able to make the firm commitment of a second front in France in the spring of 1944. That conference marked the high point of good relations among the allies. The three leaders formulated there the basic terms of their Grand Alliance, focusing on three important objectives. First, they repeated their intent to pursue the war against Germany to total victory. Following German

Leaders of the Great Powers: Stalin and Roosevelt at the Teheran
Conference, 1943. (*National Archives*)

surrender, the country would be divided
temporarily into occupation zones. Policies
of demilitarization, denazification, and reparations payments would be imposed on the
German population.

Second, the Western leaders accepted Stalin's demand that the Soviet Union retain its
new western lands. Informally, they also
agreed that Poland, having lost eastern territory to the Soviet Union, would receive
German lands along its western border.
They reluctantly accepted Soviet territorial

annexation and new Polish frontiers for the
sake of the alliance, though in doing so they
ensured a new postwar Soviet sphere of influence in Central Europe. Third, the Soviet
Union consented to enter the Asian conflict
following victory in Europe. Roosevelt,
heeding the advice of his military, was convinced that only the aid of the Red Army
would end quickly the war against Japan.
Stalin's promise of military assistance constituted for the U.S. president a major
achievement, for which he was ready to pay a

high diplomatic price. The Grand Alliance had become a reality.

The great battles of 1944 made its power apparent to Allied and Axis states alike. In June the combined naval and land forces of the Western Allies opened a front on the Normandy coast of France. After weeks of fighting, American armored columns were able to begin a rapid offensive through central France, capturing along the way several hundred thousand German prisoners. In August, Allied forces liberated Paris, an operation ensuring control of the city to the Free French coalition (rivals of the French Communist leadership) and also consuming valuable war materiel intended for the drive to the Rhine River. The hope that Allied armies would be able to penetrate German territory that fall was frustrated by the failure of the British offensive through Belgium and the Netherlands. Germany had suffered a major defeat in the West, but the war remained still outside German territory.

In the East it suffered as overwhelming a defeat as the Normandy battle. Stalin assisted the Allied invasion by ordering a major Soviet offensive that June along the entire Central Front, then in western Russia. Hitler's instructions to the German army were to fight without retreat, a hopeless task but one that his general obeyed. The result was that the Red Army was able to defeat and to encircle most of the German military forces on that front, approximately 300,000 men. The destruction of the Central Front opened the Soviet path to Poland and to eastern Germany. By August, its advance divisions had reached the outskirts of Warsaw.

The approach of the Red Army triggered an uprising in that city by the underground

The Opening of the Western Front: Normandy Beachhead, June 1944.
(*National Archives*)

non-Communist Polish National Army, hoping to capture the city before the Russians reached it. Then the Red Army stopped. For months it remained east of Warsaw while a German division slowly repressed the uprising and destroyed the city itself. Only in January 1945 did the Red Army resume its offensive there. Historians still debate whether the Soviet halt was a military necessity or political expediency. It is certain that German annihilation of the Polish National Army forces in Warsaw ended the principal obstacle to Soviet political domination of Poland. Stalin fought the war for Soviet power, not for the national liberation of neighboring countries.

These great military victories triggered the collapse of the Axis alliance. Even earlier, one of the Axis powers had capitulated. The Allied landing in southern Italy in 1943 had finally inspired Italy's generals to come out in opposition to the Fascist state and to Mussolini. They and most of the Italian people had no desire to pursue further a hopeless, destructive war. With the help of the Italian king and even Fascist politicians, they succeeded in mid-1943 in removing Mussolini from power and in signing an armistice with the Allies. Immediately afterward, however, German armored divisions occupied the country and replaced the Italian troops in the front lines. The fighting in Italy, never an important theater in the war, dragged on for another two years. Nazi Germany more than ever provided the real force in the Axis coalition.

Its remaining allies disappeared in 1944. The military advance of the Russian forces led the leaders of small Eastern European states to abandon the war. Finland capitulated, ceasing its conflict with Russia but preserving its core territory. Rumania and then Bulgaria surrendered as Red Army forces penetrated the Balkans. Finally, the Hungarian state attempted to end hostilities, only to have German divisions seize control and turn their land into a battlefield against the advancing Soviet troops. By 1944 the German air force could no longer protect the country from continual Allied aerial bombardments. Massive British and American bomber attacks using explosive and incendiary bombs turned some cities to ruins, with the loss of hundreds of thousands of German lives. The "fire storms" caused by these attacks were as destructive as the first atomic bomb explosions. The worst occurred in early 1945 when the city of Dresden was bombed with losses estimated between fifty and eighty thousand lives. Despite Nazi fanaticism and the grim determination of German troops, Axis defeat was by then inevitable.

In those circumstances a small group of German generals finally broke their oath to Hitler and organized a conspiracy to remove the Nazis from power. They had fought as professional soldiers, not as Nazi fanatics. These officers sought to save their country from ruin at the hands of the Nazis. Their hope was to sign a separate peace with the Western powers to prevent Red Army occupation of Central Europe or, failing that, to surrender before Germany itself was reduced to rubble. The German conspirators recognized the war was lost, but that Hitler would never capitulate. In July 1944, they attempted to assassinate their commander, but the bomb they planted only wounded him. Their conspiracy failed, and they were captured and executed by the SS. The war continued, for Hitler and his Nazi followers preferred death in battle to defeat.

GLOBAL SPHERES OF INFLUENCE

By early 1945 the course of the war had made obvious that the fate of Europe rested in the hands of the Allies. It had also revealed the profound differences between the Western leaders and Stalin in their plans for peace. The future of European states depended in large measure on the policies of the victorious Allied powers, working either together or separately. The Grand Alliance promised cooperation both for war and for the peace to follow. More important than agreements among the Allies, however, was the movement toward Central Europe of Soviet and Western armies, behind which occupation authorities began reconstruction. While new Allied plans were laid for a common future for Europe, a kind of partition of Europe had already begun to emerge.

American Postwar Plans for Europe

Among the Western statesmen, Roosevelt had the greatest potential influence in laying the foundations for postwar Europe. The American political system placed the formulation of foreign policy in his hands alone, though it left to Congress and the voters the decision to allocate the funds needed for foreign ventures. An astute politician who had lived through the hopes and the deceptions of Wilson's internationalist policies, he anticipated that U.S. wartime influence would not extend into peacetime. The American people, through their elected representatives, would demand an immediate return to prewar conditions—the demobilization of U.S. troops and the end to foreign aid. In these circumstances the best Roosevelt could achieve would be a peace that was self-enforcing, that is, one that did not require permanent U.S. military commitments.

His plans relied upon two new developments. For one thing, he and his advisers looked to the restoration of an international economy based on free trade and a stable financial system. The United States had already taken the initiative in 1944 to organize, at the Bretton Woods Conference, institutions which would end the economic chaos and conflicts of the depression years. One of these was the International Monetary Fund, which, operating primarily with dollars, would ensure that trading states would be able to borrow funds to sustain imports and economic development. For the first time the U.S. government was taking a direct hand in organizing international trade and finance. U.S. leaders hoped to create the conditions for stable global economic expansion after the war, of benefit to the war-torn countries and to the American economy as well.

The second project Roosevelt promoted consisted of the restoration and expansion of the system of nation-states, whose independence would be assured by the Great Powers. He assumed that American isolationism was dead, and sought to replace it by a foreign policy of support for nationalism and collaboration among the victorious Great Powers. In his speech to Congress after his return from the 1943 Teheran Conference, he made clear how much importance he attached to a new postwar spirit of cooperation. "Britain, Russia, China and the United States and their allies," he declared, "represent more than three-quarters of the total population of the earth. As long as these four nations with great military power stick together in determination to keep the peace there will be no possibility of an aggressor nation arising to start another world war."

He referred to their collaboration as the work of Four Policemen and insisted that these states be granted special powers in the Security Council of the new postwar international organization, to be called the United Nations. It required wishful thinking to imagine Nationalist China capable of becoming the "policeman" of East Asia; only Roosevelt's deep optimism (and the euphoria of wartime cooperation) justified his hope in continued agreement with the Soviet Union. The alliance had to endure; he saw no other hope for a real peace.

National self-determination would, he hoped, settle the internal problems of new leadership and policies. In spirit, his new global policy resembled his Good Neighbor policy toward Latin countries: both recognized the importance of independent nation-states, and both assumed that the interests of powerful large states were compatible with those of neighboring small states. In a world torn apart by bitter struggle with organized resistance forces claiming political leadership, his faith in self-determination confronted serious difficulties. Where Soviet forces and Communist parties were in control, it was doomed to fail.

As Allied forces moved toward Central Europe the key role of occupation authorities became evident. France was the most important country liberated by the Normandy invasion. It had lost all real independence during the war, its economy in the service of the German war machine, its people subject to German exploitation. As the years of occupation passed, opposition to the Germans grew and underground resistance forces spread. Among these, the Communists constituted the most powerful group, but alongside them fought others, some socialist, some liberal Catholic, others simple committed patriots, gathered together in the Free French movement. Its leader was General Charles de Gaulle, a traitor to his army in 1940 when he refused to accept the armistice with Germany and fled to London. By 1944 his dedication and eloquence in the cause of French freedom had placed him at the head of the noncommunist forces resisting the Germans.

De Gaulle had much greater difficulty obtaining the recognition of Roosevelt, to whom "national self-determination" meant the choice of new leadership by free elections, not by self-proclamation. Yet his movement represented the major noncommunist political force in France, committed to free democratic government. This agreement on basic political principles, plus the popularity of de Gaulle among the French people and Resistance forces, finally earned him after Liberation the diplomatic backing of the Western Allies. The resistance forces also accepted his leadership, but he in turn had to agree to their demand for substantial internal reforms in what they hoped would be a new France. The reformist parties and groups active in the Resistance, including the Communists, enjoyed the support of the great majority of French people. They joined together in a coalition, reform government in which leaders of the Communist party were invited to participate. The Communists (with Soviet encouragement) agreed to cooperate and, in a manner consistent with the principle of national self-determination, France recovered its independence.

Stalin's Postwar Plans

While the Western leaders judged this procedure of democratic reconstruction suitable everywhere in Europe, Stalin accepted it only where it suited Soviet power politics. His objectives and methods of building peace differed fundamentally from those of Roosevelt. The difference lay in the use of power. While the U.S. authorities set out to create a new world order which would not require U.S. international intervention, the Soviet leader proceeded to deploy his military power to ensure diplomatic or political domination in the areas around the Soviet Union liberated by the Red Army. Stalin honored still the "law" of power politics to "respect only the strong" and retained his suspicious view of the "capitalist jungle." The war against Germany had temporarily allied capitalist states and Communist Russia, but in his opinion the fundamental antagonism between the two social systems remained. In his world view, applied even more ruthlessly in his dealings with fellow Communists, no one could be trusted of his or her own free will to work for the common good. He recognized only political and military power.

By these standards, he had to respect the might of the Western Allies, especially the United States with its undamaged, productive economy, great navies, enormous air power. Russia, bled dry and strained to the utmost to support the Red Army, was no match. For that very reason, however, he assigned first priority to the strengthening of the Soviet international position. Even before the war was over, Soviet scientists had begun work on nuclear weapons (spies in the United States had passed on word of the development of an American nuclear bomb). Of immediate importance to Allied relations, Stalin judged indispensable the creation of a Soviet sphere of influence around his country.

By 1943 he had begun to assemble the political and diplomatic parts of a postwar protective "buffer" zone on the Soviet western borders. Its essential condition was that the small neighboring states accept Soviet diplomatic hegemony. The Czech government-in-exile in London understood the future shape of Central Europe. It proposed to the Soviet Union diplomatic agreements by which the Czechs accepted Soviet international leadership in exchange for their internal freedom. Stalin agreed to the proposal. When the Red Army liberated Czechoslovakia, it passed control over to this government, which proceeded to recreate a parliamentary democracy and coalition gov-

ernment. In 1945, Stalin looked for diplomatic recognition of Soviet power, not Communist revolution in Czechoslovakia. He applied this "Czech model" in his peace treaty with Finland, whose leaders preserved their country's independence and democratic institutions at the price of accepting its place in the Soviet sphere. Realism, not communist ideology, dictated these agreements.

Where Communist forces enjoyed substantial power Stalin was prepared to accept their rule on the condition they too submit to Soviet leadership. Yugoslavia had by 1945 come under the control of Tito's Communist guerrilla forces. From their mountain bases, they proceeded to occupy the country following the passage of the Red Army. Implementing their revolutionary plans, they immediately set up a one-party dictatorship modeled on the Communist regime in Russia. At Soviet insistence, they accepted economic agreements providing cheap raw materials from their land for the reconstruction of the Soviet Union. Among Tito's aides were two agents of the Soviet secret police. Stalin and Tito cooperated so long, and only so long, as the Soviet leader believed his revolutionary Yugoslav comrade did not challenge Soviet dominance in the Balkans.

Events in Poland revealed most clearly to the West Soviet aims in Eastern Europe and provoked the greatest controversy among the Allies even before war's end. A Polish government-in-exile in London claimed the right to recreate the Polish nation-state. The Soviet leaders began negotiations with the London Poles, then broke off talks when in 1943 Polish officials requested an investigation of reports that Soviet secret police had in 1940 massacred thousands of Polish officers captured in 1939. That the reports were true mattered not at all to Stalin. To him, the Polish request damned their government as disloyal and unreliable, unfit to govern in the

Soviet sphere. From that moment he set about forming another Polish regime out of the remnants of the Polish Communist party, most of whose leaders his police has executed in the Great Terror. When the Red Army reached Polish territory in 1944, the Soviet occupation authorities immediately began eliminating the remnants of the non-communist Polish Home Army. At the end of the year, they established the Polish Communists in a new provisional government, from which the London Poles were excluded. The U.S. and British governments protested this mockery of national self-determination in Poland. In that country, Soviet influence extended into the very political life of the nation.

When the Allied leaders met at Yalta in February 1945, they had to discuss the future peace as well as the end of the war. Agreement on the disposition of German lands once the Nazis were defeated posed no problem; zones of occupation for the four European powers (including France) had emerged out of discussion the previous year. Berlin was also divided among the Allies forces, though the city itself lay within the Soviet zone which included a large eastern region as far west as the Elba River. Regardless of where troops from east and west met at war's end, these zones set the limits to the area they would subsequently occupy.

The issue of war in East Asia also brought no serious disagreements. In exchange for a Soviet offensive in Manchuria and Korea, Stalin requested Japanese territory (Sakhalin, the Kuril Islands) and concessions in northern Chinese territory (the same as those the Russian Empire had possessed until the Japanese victory in the 1904–05 war). Roosevelt promised to obtain agreement to these concessions from Chiang's Nationalist government, becoming once again Stalin's collaborator in redrawing the boundaries of

other states to satisfy Soviet territorial demands. Even the question of Soviet participation in the United Nations did not create serious problems, probably because Stalin concluded that Roosevelt's project, though useless to Soviet interests, posed no real threat. To this extent the Grand Alliance continued to function effectively.

Its limits were apparent when Poland was discussed. Roosevelt asked for Soviet acceptance of the principle of national self-determination and democratic elections. Although Stalin did agree to the Declaration on Liberated Europe promising free elections, the statement left so many holes for Soviet evasion that, as one of Roosevelt's advisers told him, "you can drive a truck through it." Soviet domination in Poland could not be shaken by diplomatic declarations. But Roosevelt asked for no more, so important to him was Soviet collaboration in the war against Japan. Historical debate continues on the failure of the United States to ensure a free Poland at the Yalta Conference, which some critics later called a "sell-out" to the Russians. Yet the imposition of a Soviet-backed Communist regime in that country was probably not negotiable; it revealed to what extent Stalin was prepared to ignore Western protests to create a Soviet sphere of influence in that area.

He assumed that the Western powers would lay claim to their own spheres, and took steps to make sure that Western Communists did not create difficulties. He ordered the Communist resistance leaders in France and Italy to give up their arms to the Allied armies, effectively depriving those parties of the possibility of a successful insurrection. By his understanding of power politics, that area fell in the sphere of the West, and Communists there had to bend to Western "bourgeois" democracy. The revolutionary hopes of some Communists there mattered less that good relations with the West, which brought his country Lend-Lease aid and deferred at least for a short time that conflict which he believed the capitalist states would one day begin again. When Roosevelt talked of "a world of peace" and great power collaboration, Stalin understood hegemony and spheres of influence. There could exist no real meeting of minds or permanent understanding between statesmen of such differing views.

The two armies proceeded that spring to defeat the remaining German forces. German generals kept the bulk of their troops in the east in an effort to halt the Soviet offensive. By April, Western armies were advancing rapidly through central and northern Germany. Churchill, foreseeing already competition with the Soviet Union over European spheres, urged that Western troops occupy Berlin and Prague, politically important cities far within areas designated for Soviet liberation. Eisenhower, supreme allied commander, refused to alter his military priorities to make room for political calculations. In April Roosevelt died, replaced by his Vice-President Harry Truman, an inexperienced former senator from the Middle West. The only course of action open to the new president was to follow Roosevelt's guidelines. The European war ended in May with Soviet troops in Berlin. That July, Western forces pulled back to allow the Soviet army to occupy its full zone. Carrying out their part of the occupation agreement, Soviet authorities opened to Western troops access to western Berlin, to become the Western-controlled area of the city. Demilitarization and denazification started, and arrangements for the imposition of reparations began in all areas of the defeated land. The German state had ceased to exist. What took its place depended on the four occupying powers, for the time being cooperating still as Allies.

The Defeat of Japan

The war in the Pacific followed a very different course. It continued until the end to be primarily a naval war. In early 1945 the British finally launched an offensive into Burma from India, which remained firmly under their rule. The opposition to the war of the Indian National Congress had failed in all its objectives. In 1942 Gandhi had demanded that the British "Quit India!" that is, give it immediate independence, to obtain Congress cooperation in the war against Japan. His decision proved a disaster for his party, whose leaders spent the rest of the war years in jail while the Muslim League collaborated with the British. The Indian Army continued to fight loyally, even when it found itself in combat against fellow Indian soldiers, captured by the Japanese, who had chosen to collaborate in the Indian National Army. The Indian civil service performed its duties as expected. Operating from India the British planned ahead for reconquest. The supreme commander of Southeast Asia, Lord Mountbatten, prepared for offensives to retake the lost British colonies. Before his forces could proceed beyond Burma, military events elsewhere brought the war to a sudden end.

The U.S. naval offensive had begun in 1943. The previous year U.S. naval forces had, in battles in the Coral Sea and west of Hawaii near Midway Island, thwarted Japanese plans for the destruction of U.S. military power in the Pacific. Instead, the Japanese fleet suffered serious losses, especially to the aircraft carriers which proved the decisive weapon in that far-flung war. Within a few months the U.S Pacific fleet was superior in numbers and power to the Japanese ships. Gradually U.S. naval and marine forces moved westward back across the Pacific, "island hopping" to establish ports and airbases closer and closer to Japan. In

1944, they dominated the seas as far west as the Philippine archipelago, permitting army divisions under General MacArthur's command to reconquer that country. MacArthur's next objective was Japan itself, where bitter fighting was expected before the Japanese surrender. By the end of 1944, the U.S. air force controlled the skies over the islands and operated from bases close enough for massive bomber attacks of Japan.

In those conditions Japanese cities lay open to the same "fire storms" which had destroyed several German cities. In the spring of 1945, Tokyo itself was consumed in a raging fire provoked by incendiary bombs, leaving nearly 100,000 people dead. That summer most Japanese urban centers were in ruins and the economy of the country was collapsing. Maritime commerce had been destroyed by U.S. submarines, depriving the military of vital raw materials. The Japanese war cabinet began in July to consider peace negotiations, though military leaders defended war to the death to protect the honor of their country and their emperor. The cabinet hoped for continued Soviet neutrality and for Soviet mediation to obtain from the United States essential peace conditions, principally the protection of the emperor. It was misguided on all counts, however, for Stalin was preparing for Asian war and the United States adhered to its demand of "unconditional surrender."

The U.S. war in the Pacific was in its own way total war. Hatred of the Japanese was high, particularly when stories of Japanese treatment of Allied prisoners of war appeared. The fanatical refusal of Japanese soldiers to stop fighting in the face of hopeless odds further strengthened the decision to eliminate the enemy. That destruction was intended to come in part through massive land offensives, by the Soviet Union in north China and by the United States in Japan. It was already under way as a result of the bombing raids by the U.S. air force, which acquired in the summer of 1945 a weapon of unimaginable power.

American development of the atomic bomb had first begun out of fear Germany would acquire the bomb. Germany's defeat and the successful testing of the bomb in July 1945 presented the U.S. leaders with a difficult decision. A weapon of unprecedented power was available, not to deter its use by the enemy, but to destroy an opponent defenseless against air attack and fighting a land war to the death. The U.S. government chose with little hesitation (only some of the scientists advising restraint) to drop the bomb on Japanese cities, previously targets for equally destructive fire storms. On August 6 one bomb obliterated the city of Hiroshima, its buildings and its population; a second destroyed Nagasaki on August 9. The world had entered the age of nuclear war.

The Soviet land war against Japan ended almost as soon as it began. On August 8, the Red Army invaded Manchuria. Stalin had respected to the letter his agreement with Roosevelt to begin war in Asia three months after the hostilities ceased in Europe. Japanese forces were overwhelmed by the Soviet invasion, which swept down Manchuria and into Korea. Despite inevitable defeat, a week elapsed before the Japanese war cabinet accepted surrender, bowing to Emperor Hirohito's decision that "the unendurable must be endured." Would the war have ended so quickly without use of the atomic bomb? With hindsight historians now conclude that it would have, sparing the Japanese people the horrors of nuclear destruction. At the time, however, American military experts foresaw a continuation for many months of all-out war. In that light, American leaders looked upon the atomic bomb as one more weapon of total war to achieve absolute victory.

The War and Asian Nationalism

The defeat of Japan left open the future of East and Southeast Asia. Japan in its entirety became a part of the U.S. Pacific zone of occupation, whose forces were under the command of General MacArthur. The Soviets had no share of that enemy territory. They did divide with U.S. troops the Korean peninsula, held by Soviet occupation troops in the north and by U.S. forces in the south. China presented a problem of far greater magnitude and complexity. The withdrawal of Japanese armies led immediately to the collapse of the puppet states in Manchuria and eastern China. Communist forces occupied large rural areas and numbered almost one million men. The Communist party was a stronger political movement than ever before.

Nationalist China remained confined to its mountainous western region. Yet the U.S. government had resolved to make Chiang and his Nationalist regime its East Asian "policeman." It undertook at the end of the war to build up this weak ally, supplying the Nationalist regime with transportation and supplies for the occupation of all China. The Soviet Union backed this policy, in public and privately. Late that year it signed a ten-year friendship treaty with the Nationalists, recognizing Chiang as China's legitimate ruler. In private, Stalin told the Chinese Communists to abandon their guerrilla war and to form a coalition government with the non-Communists (like those already in existence in France and Italy). A Chinese Communist revolution had no place in his calculations. His short-term policy placed China within the U.S. sphere of influence.

In the vast area of Southeast Asia, no real political power remained. The allied commander of Southeast Asia, whose headquarters was in India, had too few forces to occupy too great a territory. Temporarily Ja- panese troops, nominally prisoners of war, served as police under the command of a handful of Allied administrators. What was to follow? The empires of France and the Netherlands had collapsed at the beginning of the war, but the defeat of Germany had brought back to power leaders in those countries hoping for a restoration of some imperial possessions. The Japanese had strongly encouraged national independence in Southeast Asia and had themselves humiliated and humbled the former white rulers. Anti-Japanese resistance forces, including a strong Communist underground in Indochina, sought to organize new states. Even India confronted a political crisis when the release of the National Congress leaders raised immediately the cry for independence. Indian soldiers who had fought for the Japanese against the British were greeted as heroes when they returned home. The end of the Pacific war marked the beginning of an era of national revolution in Asia.

SUMMARY

The Second World War completed the work, begun in the previous war, of the destruction of Western empires. Hitler's pursuit first of continental and then global power led him to wage total war in Europe, conquering Western states which once ruled great empires, reducing the mighty British Empire to an embattled island fortress. The rise of the Japanese Empire continued that process, beginning first with the seizure of Chinese lands and then with the conquest of Western-controlled territories and the defeat of Western forces. The defeat of the German and Japanese empires left great areas of the world a vacuum of power, in many places scenes of terrible human misery and bitter hatred. In Europe, nearly fifty million civilians and military died in the war (twenty million in the Soviet Union alone), a grim measure of appalling destruction. Dominating the world were two great powers, each with its distinct political system and each with its own plans for a new global order. They collaborated in the war but had by war's end already disagreed on important issues of peacemaking.

Out of the passions and hardship of war emerged hopes and dreams of a new world to be built on the ruins of the old. These visions were carried forward principally by the resistance forces. The survivors of concentration camps and the millions of displaced persons sought for themselves little more than a place gradually to rebuild their lives after years of chaos and misery. The destruction of war paradoxically called forth a collective desire in the underground movements to remake society on new foundations. The hope for progress did not die, though in the midst of the war the numbers arrested, tortured, and executed were so great the effort appeared often hopeless.

This mixture of despair and of revolt, of compassion and solidarity, appeared to Albert Camus, French intellectual and member of the Resistance, all the more extraordinary, like the heroic struggle of one city against a devastating attack of the bubonic plague. His novel *The Plague*, completed just after the war, conveyed symbolically the highest ideals of the Resistance, in which people risked their lives merely to be "on the side of the victims," content to have the freedom to die so that humanity might ultimately live in a better world. Resistance movements, some with revolutionary hopes, took much of their strength from that vision born of despair. Great expectations for political change constituted one heritage of the war; conflict between the Great Powers was another.

RECOMMENDED READING

War in Europe

*ROBERT DEVINE, *Roosevelt and World War II* (1969)

JOHN GADDIS, *The United States and the Origins of the Cold War, 1941–1947* (1972)

RAOUL HILBERT, *The Destruction of the European Jews* (revised ed., 1985)

JOHN KEEGAN, *Six Armies in Normandy: From D-Day to the Liberation of Paris* (1982)

VOYTECH MASTNEY, *Russia's Road to the Cold War: Diplomacy, Warfare, and the Politics of Communism, 1941–1945* (1979)

GORDON WRIGHT, *The Ordeal of Total War, 1939–1945* (1968)

War in Asia

HERBERT FEIS, *The China Tangle: The American Effort in China from Pearl Harbor to the Marshall Mission* (1953)

BARBARA TUCHMAN, *Stilwell and the American Experience in China, 1911–1945* (1972)

JOHN TOLAND, *The Rising Sun: The Decline and Fall of the Japanese Empire, 1936–1945* (1970)

Memoirs and Novels

*PRIMO LEVI, *Survival at Auschwitz* (1961)

*THOMAS KENEALLY, *Schindler's List* (1982)

VASILY GROSSMAN, *Life and Fate* (1985)

chapter 7

THE COLD WAR, 1945–1953

The making of the peace to follow the Second World War posed enormous problems, far greater than those that confronted the statesmen in 1919. The war had torn apart the lives of millions of people, had destroyed or undermined political and economic institutions of many countries, and had overturned the old balance of power. The human scale of suffering defied imagination, and its impact was felt throughout Europe and East Asia. The political disorder at war's end called for new solutions, and the leaders of the wartime resistance movements were prepared to take power to introduce extensive social and economic reforms. Nationalist parties in lands freed from Japanese occupation demanded more forcefully than ever before leadership of their peoples. In those tumultuous years, reform and revolution dominated political life in Europe and Asia.

The vacuum of power left in Europe after the collapse of the Axis states opened the way for the United States and the Soviet Union to take the lead in the reorganization of European relations. In Eastern Europe, reconstruction proceeded in large measure according to the wishes of Soviet authorities and the political goals of Communist parties. In Western Europe, severe economic shortages and fears of Soviet domination combined to make these countries diplomatically and economically dependent on the United States. Political and human conflicts added to diplomatic insecurity to complicate enormously the peacemaking. Latent images of a global Communist revolutionary conspiracy reemerged in the West, replacing the idealized wartime picture of a loyal Soviet ally. In the Soviet Union, official pronouncements revived the image of the capitalist-imperialist threat in place of praise for the Western democratic allies. On both sides, the reappearance of these adversary terms indicated the breakdown of wartime good relations and became obstacles to further agreements for postwar peacemaking.

The new conflict between the Soviet Union and the United States produced its own grim vocabulary. The term Iron Curtain came to symbolize the political and diplomatic barriers dividing Communist and non-Communist countries in Europe. The overwhelming military and economic superiority of the United States and the Soviet Union in their respective spheres earned them the label of "superpowers." The expression "Cold War" captured the ominous character of the antagonistic relations between the two sides, never actually at war but still mobilizing their forces in anticipation of a new conflict. The invisible front lines were located in political and diplomatic areas of dispute between Communist and U.S.-backed states. This global confrontation presented U.S. political leaders, little experienced in power politics and global relations, with complex questions. What was the nature of the conflict? Was the threat communism or was it Soviet power? What areas constituted a vital interest to the United States and where ought U.S. support be directed?

The U.S. response to these new circumstances was a peacetime strategy of foreign involvement in the diplomatic and economic reconstruction of Europe and Asia. Baptized "containment," it set the guidelines for U.S. diplomatic and political policies for the years ahead. A local war on the Korean peninsula, launched by the Communist regime of the north, accelerated a new U.S. armaments program directed against the Soviet Union. The Cold War fueled an armaments race between the two superpowers, each preparing to defend itself against attack from the other side. Although the acute phase of hostility ended in the mid-1950s, the failure of postwar peacemaking and the continued U.S.-Soviet rivalry in later decades gave a warlike character to the relations between the superpowers.

THE COLLAPSE OF THE GRAND ALLIANCE, 1945–1947

Reform in Western Europe

In Western Europe, postwar reconstruction came under the leadership of parliamentary democracies. Backed by the large majority of the population, coalition governments introduced new policies of full employment and extensive social welfare for the people. The terrible destruction of war created the conditions for ambitious reconstruction, not just of the physical framework of industrial economy, but also of the human relations in a more humane society. Labor obtained a greater voice in industrial affairs. Women became active political leaders and new family policies provided state support for child care. The term used to describe the new economic conditions in countries such as Great Britain and France is "mixed economies," referring to the intermingling of nationalized (i.e., state-owned) enterprises and private businesses. Expensive in the best of times, these reforms exceeded the financial resources of their still impoverished populations. Yet political leaders could not back down. They believed deeply in social justice for their people, whose demand for a "new deal" created pressure for quick action. In those early postwar years, the governments in Western Europe were less concerned with Soviet power than with rebuilding their own countries.

In Great Britain, the end of the war marked the beginning of momentous political and social changes under the leadership of the Labor party. During the war it had collaborated in a national government and had prepared a plan for sweeping economic reforms and new social policies for the post-war period. It called on British voters in 1945 to "face the future" by supporting its plan for democratic socialism. In the national elections that year, it overwhelmed the Conservative party, led by Winston Churchill.

The Labor party took power at a critical time, for the war had resulted in the death of a million Britishers and had caused tremendous property loss, both to foreign investments and to domestic capital. One-third of the merchant fleet was sunk. Exports had shrunk at a time when Great Britain had great need of imported goods. Lend-Lease aid from the United States ended in 1945. A year later the British government had to ask Washington for a $4 billion loan, most of which paid for food and fuel imports and for protecting the British pound, losing value rapidly against the dollar. By the winter of 1946–47, the British government faced such a serious budgetary crisis that it could no longer pay both for its domestic reforms and for its foreign imperial obligations in India and the Middle East. It chose to renounce its great power ambitions, passing strategic responsibilities to the United States. Domestic interests came first.

The "future" which Labor offered the British laboring classes promised a "national minimum" standard of living to all citizens. The cabinet planned to achieve this goal by passing the most extensive welfare program of any democratic country. The reforms included comprehensive health care at state expense, guaranteed assistance to all in need of food and shelter, an ambitious program of state-constructed low-cost housing, and the opportunity for an advanced education for all talented youth. To pay for these expensive reforms, taxes went up on businesses and income tax rates rose for the well-to-do. Rationing remained in effect until 1947 to ensure that goods in short supply were fairly distributed. Labor's reforms brought to the British people more social justice and less inequality than ever before in their history.

The second important area of Labor reform was nationalization. The Labor leaders accused British capitalists of exploiting labor, preventing the economy from producing at its full capacity, leaving large numbers of workers unemployed—all for the sake of profit. They set out to end the "domination of capital" by nationalizing major British enterprises. The central bank, coal mines, electricity, railroads, and civil aviation were all made state property, their former owners compensated by long-term state bonds. The government planned new investments for these industries, its goal to guarantee a job to all British workers even if the enterprises were unproductive. Job security and the end to private ownership, not economic efficiency, was the purpose of these reforms.

Through the democratic parliamentary system, the British voters had permitted the Labor party to enlarge enormously state responsibility for social welfare and to limit capitalist free enterprise. One direct result was a great expansion of state involvement in the affairs of individuals and society. The result did correspond closely to Labor's plan for democratic socialism.

Plans for social and economic reform were equally extensive in both Italy and France, where wartime resistance movements formed the new political leadership in postwar parliaments. Both constitutions created cabinet government, making the presidency a ceremonial position (and leading in France to the resignation of Charles de Gaulle, sympathetic to the reforms but unwilling to play the game of parliamentary politics). Heading their governments were coalitions of liberal, socialist, and Communist parties. The Communist vote in both countries represented nearly one-fourth of the electorate, most of whom voted not for Communist revolution but for democratic and social reform. Communist leaders backed the reform programs of the French and Italian governments and accepted ministerial positions, though they remained rivals with the socialists for the support of the working masses and spoke out against the United States and in favor of Soviet foreign policy. The growing rivalry between the superpowers became in this manner a source of political conflict in both countries.

The reforms undertaken by the Italian and French governments resembled in many respects those of the British Labor government. They nationalized important industries, including the major banks and the production of energy (coal, gas, and electricity). They also introduced costly welfare reforms for health and old-age care. The French reform policies differed from those of the British, however, in emphasizing productive investments to modernize the economy. A planning commission, under the guidance of a talented, farsighted economist named Jean Monnet, suggested the means to put to most efficient use the state's new economic powers and financial resources. Railroads were electrified and labor-saving machinery introduced in industry. Workers, if deprived of their old positions, received help to retrain for new work. In the judgment of the government, the French people would benefit through greater efficiency and faster economic growth. Its social priorities offered less security but ultimately greater prosperity than the British economic policy.

Conflict over coalition politics and social policies ended the short era of political collaboration between Communist and democratic parties. Communist support for labor strikes in mid-1947 and their bitter attacks on the other coalition parties created a political crisis, resolved by the resignation of the Communist ministers and the formation of new cabinets. Socialist and liberal parties welcomed the expulsion of the Communists, whom they deeply distrusted and whom U.S. leaders, proposing to these countries economic aid, wished removed from power. In both countries, political leadership shifted to moderate parties. The time of radical reforms had passed.

These new governments preserved the system of mixed economies, continued to promote rapid economic growth, and governed without the large Communist vote. Reconstruction from war came slowly and living conditions remained difficult. Economic shortages and disappointment among the people at the slow pace of reform ensured to the Communist parties a large protest vote. Once in opposition, the Communists launched a massive popular campaign in favor of more socialist reforms, accusing the moderate cabinets of a "sellout" of the people and of "subservience" to the "U.S. imperialists." Opponents of the Communists accused them of taking their orders from Moscow, feared by many Europeans because of Soviet military power and its communist ideology. In those countries hostility toward Communist parties threw up political barriers as divisive as the Iron Curtain beginning to separate East and West.

Conflict in Germany

The acute problems of reconstruction of Central Europe brought together in one area the human, political, and diplomatic conflicts which were leading to permanent partition of postwar Europe. The hatred of other Europeans toward Germany extended beyond nazism to the Germans themselves. Throughout Eastern Europe the new governments forcibly expelled in 1945–46 most Germans who had not already fled. The total number of refugees probably exceeded ten million, most of whom sought refuge in the western zones of Germany. At the same time, the millions of forced laborers taken into Germany during the war sought to return to their homelands or to emigrate to a new country. The Jewish survivors of the extermination camps looked to Palestine; many Ukrainian and Russian deportees sought a new home in the West. These destitute peoples were concentrated in Central Europe, their care the responsibility of the United Nations and of the occupying powers, also obliged to help the inhabitants of the ruined German cities to survive hunger and cold.

In 1945, the priorities of the victorious Allies placed the destruction of old Germany before the reconstruction of a new state. The wartime agreements included the dissolution of the Nazi movement, demilitarization, and an unspecified amount of reparations. The Allies quickly disarmed and disbanded the German army. Denazification led to the arrest and interrogation of thousands of Germans in all zones, although many Nazi officials, including Gestapo and SS members, disappeared into the refugee population. The most prominent Nazis were put on trial in Nuremberg in the winter of 1945–46. Accused of "crimes against humanity," all were found guilty by an international tribunal and most were executed.

The first serious East-West disagreement arose over issues of reparations. The Soviet authorities began in their eastern zone to take apart entire factories for shipment to their own country and confiscated state possessions and the belongings of civilians for "war booty." They demanded that Western authorities deliver large amounts of German industrial property as well. In the spring of 1946, the impoverishment of the German economy and growing suspicion of Soviet policies led the Western powers to refuse to ship additional goods from their zones. This conflict over the economic spoils of war revealed the importance each side attached to Germany, becoming less and less the enemy and increasingly a front line between East and West. The zones were becoming territorial divisions.

In these circumstances, U.S. authorities decided in 1946 to alter their German policy from punishment to reconstruction. This sudden change resulted both from their growing awareness of Soviet power in Central Europe and from the economic burden of occupation. The cost of administering the zones grew as German living conditions worsened. A barter economy, in which cigarettes were the most commonly valued medium of exchange, provided the essential items for those Germans with anything at all to trade. The cost of supplying the Germans in the American zone with minimum food, clothing, and heating—$700 million in 1946—made restoration of German economic production a necessity. The British government, faced with near bankruptcy later that year, agreed to the new objectives.

In early 1947, the British and Americans united their two zones into one economic unit, joined by the French zone later that year. The Western governments proceeded to implement a new economic policy for the reconstruction of that part of Germany under their control, disregarding the vehement objections of Soviet occupation authorities who continued their policy of shipping German goods to their country. That year the U.S. government declared that "an orderly and prosperous Europe requires the economic contribution of a stable and productive Germany." One-fourth of the country was excluded from that new policy. Translated into plain language, the new Allied policy effectively partitioned Germany and marked the end of cooperation with the Soviet Union.

The paths of eastern and western Ger-

many diverged more and more. In the east
the Soviet authorities had in 1946 forcibly
incorporated the Social Democratic party
with the German Communist party and dis-
possessed all large landowners, distributing
the land to small farmers. Elections continued to be held but the Communists,
backed by the Russians, controlled the territory. In the western zones, Communists
were an insignificant force, opposed bitterly
by most Germans who identified the Communists with the Russians. In free provincial
elections in 1947 the important parties were
the Social Democrats (defending socialist reforms and favoring a unified, neutral Germany) and the Christian Democrats (strongly backed by Catholic voters and supporting
free enterprise capitalism and resistance to
Soviet power). Allied foreign ministers met
in 1947 to attempt to write peace treaties for
the Axis countries. They could only agree on
a treaty for Italy, never partitioned into
zones, where the Soviet leaders hoped the
Italian Communist party would continue to
play a key role in coalition politics. Germany,
divided into occupation zones, represented
for both Soviet Russia and the Western
powers a position of strength neither would
concede.

Who was responsible for the failure of
German peacemaking? Historians tend now
to assign responsibility to both sides, rejecting the theory that either consciously sought
partition. Stalin may have looked forward to
a united German state under Soviet influence; failing in that objective, he resolved to
keep hold of his eastern zone. The Western
Allies sought a united democratic Germany
outside Soviet control; when that goal appeared threatened by Russian political
moves, they fell back on the unification of
their zones. Partition came by default, a
product of mutual hostility, and the new, unstable balance of power in Central Europe.

Conflict in Iran, Turkey, and Greece

Farther to the southeast, the end of the
war had left three states internally divided
and confronting Communist opposition.
Greece, Turkey, and Iran shared a common
past experience of dependence on Western
states, primarily Great Britain. At the beginning of the century, Iran had ceded exploitation of its oil reserves to a British oil company. During World War II, it had been
occupied by British, American, and Soviet
forces. The British had forced the Iranian
ruler to abdicate in favor of his son, Reza
Shah Pahlevi, whose policies they could more
easily control. At war's end British and
American forces left, but Soviet troops remained in their northern zone. The Russians
permitted a Communist political movement
there to organize a separatist state, potentially the core of a new Iranian Communist
government. Following U.S. protests in 1946
to the United Nations, Stalin agreed to withdraw his troops. He apparently judged the
area of minor strategic importance in the
global competition with the West. In that
country diplomacy resolved the dispute, restoring the prewar frontier between Communist and non-Communist areas. As a result, the Iranian regime remained in the
Western sphere, its oil assured to the British.

To the west of Iran, the Turkish state
stood alone at the end of the war, having
remained neutral in the conflict. Stalin, who
had in the course of the Second World War
annexed land in both Asia and Europe lost
by Russia at the end of the First World War,
demanded in 1945 the "return" of territory
the Ottoman Empire had taken from Russia
in 1918. In addition, he sought control over
maritime commerce through the straits between the Black and Mediterranean seas (a
objective earlier of the tsarist state). The
Turkish government refused to negotiate,

and Soviet troops moved to the Turkish frontier. An old conflict began again, now a part of the global partition of spheres between the superpowers.

Great Britain sent military aid to the Turks to strengthen their resistance. Following the British came the Americans, first in late 1946 with a naval task force (to become the next year the Sixth Fleet) in the eastern Mediterranean and then, after British aid stopped in 1947, with economic and military assistance. In this manner the U.S. government made known to the Soviet Union its support for Turkey by means not only of diplomatic communications but also of a "language of force" which relied on naval power and economic aid. Gradually the shape of a new American policy was emerging, whose objective was resistance to Soviet expansion and whose means were U.S. diplomatic, military, and economic support for states close to the Soviet Union.

The conflict in Greece was of a different nature. When German troops withdrew from Greece in 1945, a civil war broke out between Greek Communist forces, active in the resistance, and the conservative, monarchical government backed by Great Britain. The Greek Communists pursued a revolutionary policy, similar to that of the Yugoslavs, for the formation of a Communist dictatorship and a socialist society modeled on Soviet Russia. The conservative Greek monarchy had the backing of non-Communist resistance forces and the British, whose troops had occupied the country following German withdrawal. The British government sought to protect its imperial interests in the Mediterranean, fearing that a Communist revolutionary regime would threaten its control there. A Communist military insurrection in late 1944 failed, largely because British troops intervened in the fighting. After a one-year truce, the Greek

Communist leaders resumed revolutionary guerrilla war.

Britain, unable to continue its military and economic aid to the Greek government, turned to the United States to protect its strategic interests. In early 1947 the U.S. government agreed. By extending aid to Turkey and to Greece that year—a policy baptized the Truman Doctrine in the United States—it enlarged its own sphere of influence to the eastern Mediterranean. Its objective of national self-determination, here as well as in other regions, was receding in importance, giving way to a new policy that emphasized the defense of strategic areas around the Soviet Union. Out of these regional diplomatic and political conflicts emerged the strategy later called "containment."

The U.S. Policy of Containment

In the two years following the end of the Second World War, the American government became aware that its wartime expectations for a postwar settlement in Europe were unrealistic. Before his death in early 1945 President Roosevelt had approved a few concrete plans for the new era to follow the war. His successor, Harry Truman, had carried out in all essential features these policies. He had participated in the foundation in 1945 of the United Nations, in which peacekeeping responsibilities were assigned to a security council. There Soviet and American delegates, along with the other permanent members (essentially Roosevelt's Four Policemen), shared the power to initiate policies and also to veto measures of which their states disapproved. Borne of the same hopes as the League in 1919, the United Nations became by 1947 another victim of the Cold War, paralyzed by the Soviet-U.S. antagonism. A second policy carried out by Truman was the destruction of Nazi Germany. By 1946 it had fallen apart as a result of the conflicts between Soviet and Western authorities over economic policy. Although in that year the two superpowers still managed to settle certain disputes, principally that in Iran, the U.S. policy of collaboration with the Soviets was proving incapable of providing agreements satisfactory to U.S. leaders.

The issue causing particular concern to Western European governments was the political reconstruction of Eastern European states. They had hopes for a postwar settlement in which occupation forces would withdraw to permit democratic elections and the restoration of independent states, but Soviet supremacy in Eastern Europe stood in the way of a return to the independent nation-states of the 1920s. A second trend heightening their concern was the manipulation of democratic procedures by Eastern European Communist parties, clearly intent on weakening other political parties and ensuring their own political domination. Both diplomatically and politically, the fate of Eastern Europe lay in Soviet hands.

Winston Churchill attempted in 1946 to arouse U.S. concern about these trends. Speaking as a Western statesman, he warned in a speech in the United States that across Europe had fallen an Iron Curtain dividing Communist and non-Communist lands, an image calculated to appeal to a U.S. public vaguely aware that "communism" threatened "democracy." Soviet economic weakness and the demobilization of the bulk of the Red Army were unknown features of a state that appeared monolithic and dangerous by its very size and by the revolutionary ideology its leaders preached. Churchill's aim was U.S. involvement in European affairs in support of a new policy taking into account the political and diplomatic in-

stability caused by Soviet might and Communist power in Eastern Europe.

His call for help came at a time when U.S. diplomats in Moscow were proposing a new policy toward the Soviet Union. The most influential spokesman was George Kennan, stationed in the Moscow embassy since 1944 and opponent of continued reliance by the United States on internationalism and conciliation to resolve disputes with the Soviet state. His views, laid out most forcefully in a lengthy report in February 1946 (published one year later), minimized the importance of communist ideology in Soviet foreign policy, which placed "Soviet power" first. He did not believe either that Soviet policy was "adventuristic," for it avoided "unnecessary risks." It was however deeply hostile to the United States and to any international settlements promoting stability and peace not in Soviet interests.

Kennan proposed that the U.S. government state its opposition to further Soviet expansion and prepare to use its diplomatic influence and economic resources to back up its policy. He believed that the Soviet leaders, though indifferent to "the logic of reason," were "highly sensitive to the logic of force" and would "withdraw when strong resistance is encountered at any point." Kennan proposed a strategy of "containment" to deal with the Soviet Union: resistance to expansion by diplomatic means backed by force, to be followed by negotiations when the Soviet Union was prepared to make concessions. His assessment appeared to fit well Soviet postwar diplomacy in places such as Iran and Germany and his proposals coincided with the new directions taken by U.S. leaders to oppose Soviet expansion in countries such as Turkey. Kennan's containment strategy became official policy in mid-1947.

Before this could happen, it had to meet the approval of the U.S. Congress. Public life in America was dominated in the postwar years by domestic interests, principally the enjoyment of a good life after the shortages of wartime. Demobilized soldiers returned to peacetime jobs while women, under pressure from public opinion and management, left their wartime work to become again housewives. The economy boomed, and foreign conflicts appeared distant affairs. Isolationism remained a strong force in the country and in Washington. Truman made his public appeal for a new global policy, not on the basis of strategic interests but, in the spirit of Wilson and Franklin Roosevelt, for the good of "free peoples" threatened by "aggressive movements that seek to impose upon them totalitarian regimes." Why did he use this crusading language? The answer lay in the need to win public and congressional backing for containment, for Congress had to consent to over half a billion dollars in foreign aid, an unprecedented request. Once again, U.S. foreign policy appeared to be seeking a "world made safe for democracy."

In concrete terms, the new policy sought two diplomatic objectives. One was to strengthen particular states of strategic importance to the West and in need of outside economic and military assistance. In March 1947 President Truman formulated publicly a new policy of foreign aid to the Greek and Turkish governments, the first country challenged by Communist insurrection, the other by Soviet diplomatic and military pressure. This Truman Doctrine, intended to protect a Western sphere of influence, appeared in public to be part of an anticommunist crusade, not at all what diplomats such as Kennan sought. It did win public support, and the funds were voted quickly.

The second objective was the economic reconstruction of Europe (extended also to Japan). Speaking in mid-1947, the secretary of state, George Marshall, proposed that the United States for the first time in its history offer foreign aid to lands devastated by war. That year the economic recovery of Western Europe was advancing rapidly but at such a high cost it could not continue without outside help; at the same time, the poor living conditions of the population there contributed significantly to social unrest, an important factor in the electoral strength of Communist parties. Both Japan and Western Germany, though just two years previously treated as enemies, appeared in 1947 important "front-line" areas along the borders of the Soviet sphere.

The immediate goal of the aid was economic recovery. The larger aim was to encourage the stabilization of economic conditions in independent states within a global economy. Marshall proposed that the United States provide large sums of financial aid as well as economic supplies to those governments ready to meet certain conditions, chief among which was the requirement that they coordinate their efforts and make public their financial and economic needs. The Bretton Woods agreements of 1944 had already set up the framework for a system of trade and finances. This Marshall Plan committed the United States to the expansion of the global industrial economy and to the improvement of economic conditions of distant countries without any specific diplomatic demands or expectation of repayment. These new policies turned the United States away from isolationism toward involvement in the international affairs of Europe and Asia.

Although the funds were not approved until mid-1948, the offer received immediate support from all Western countries. The Soviet Union and its satellites refused—on Soviet orders and after Poland and Czechoslovakia, both under Communist leadership, had first accepted. The Marshall Plan was not overtly anticommunist; the Truman

Doctrine was. Together, they altered the very basis of relations with the Soviet Union, however, for they brought the economic resources and potential military might of the United States to bear on areas where the line between Soviet and Western spheres remained unclear. The refusal of Marshall Plan aid by Eastern European states made clear that Europe was split in two. The United States constituted the major power in the West; the Soviet Union controlled the East.

Postwar Stalinist Russia and the New Soviet "Empire"

At the end of the Second World War, the Soviet Union was second only to the United States in military might and headed an international communist movement more powerful than ever before. Its victory over Germany had given its leaders a dominant role in those areas where the Red Army had triumphed. That conflict had also terribly weakened the country. Historians generally agree now that these two contradictory features—Soviet international strength and internal weakness—constituted factors of equal importance in Soviet postwar policy.

The position of power permitted Soviet expansion, limited by the strategic needs of the Soviet Union and Stalin's recognition of U.S. military might. Recovery from the devastation of war called for massive Soviet investments, requiring economic exploitation of the Soviet sphere as well as the continued sacrifices of the Soviet people. Stalin had accepted the alliance with the Western Allies in return for their assistance in the war, their economic aid, and their agreement to the establishment of a Soviet sphere of influence along his country's borders from the Arctic to the Pacific oceans. His policy after the war proceeded along the paths laid out during the war. His determination to expand Soviet

power was as great as before. For a few years after the war, he anticipated that the capitalist states would recognize his new sphere of influence. Collaboration with the West was important to him for its immediate benefits.

Although Stalin does not appear to have had any master plan for Soviet expansion, he did have certain minimum objectives, including recognition of new Soviet territory annexed in 1939 and 1940 and diplomatic domination in the states along the Soviet frontiers in Europe. Soviet policy was expansionist within these limits. It produced a new balance of power in Europe and Asia and confronted the Western states with the necessity to reconsider their wartime policies. Stalin's ambitious foreign objectives were in part opportunistic, dependent upon the readiness of the West to accept Soviet expansion and its reluctance to resist.

In the period between 1945 and 1947, Stalin had to take account of the political strength and revolutionary militancy of foreign Communist parties seeking to expand their influence, some by political maneuvering, others (in China and Greece) by insurrection. Yugoslavia's leaders backed Communist insurrection in the Balkans, despite occasional warnings from Stalin that they should avoid provoking conflicts with the West. Although Western observers at the time imagined that Stalin commanded all and had planned everything, we now know that he gave only general guidance between 1945 to 1947 to his aides and to the foreign Communists. Crucial to all his actions was his determination to protect his country's new-won position of strength in international affairs.

The war had caused great suffering among the Soviet people and at the same time aroused among many the hope for a better, more humane order in their country. The losses in life were so great no one has

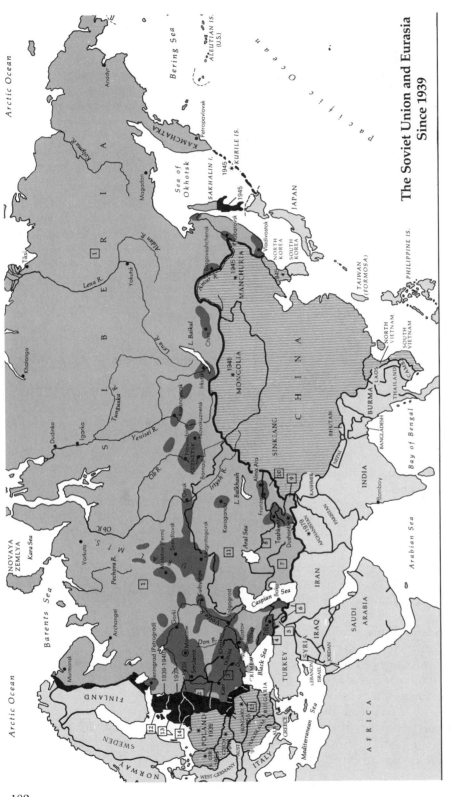

The Soviet Union and Eurasia
Since 1939

□ Areas annexed since 1940

▦ Other communist countries

★ Soviet interventions invasions, and occupations since 1939, excluding pursuit of German armies in World War II

SOVIET SOCIALIST REPUBLICS

1. Russian Soviet Federated
   Socialist Republic
2. White Russia
3. Ukraine

4. Georgia
5. Armenia
6. Azerbaidjan
7. Turkmenistan

8. Uzbekistan
9. Tadjikistan
10. Kirghiz Republic
11. Kazakh Republic

12. Estonia
13. Latvia
14. Lithuania
15. Moldavia

▨ Industrial areas (in U.S.S.R.)

ever been able to calculate them accurately; the figure of twenty million civilian and military dead, commonly repeated now, provides merely a measure of suffering. Large areas of western Russia were devastated, the cities reduced to rubble, the countryside stripped of its livestock, the mines flooded. So scarce were food reserves that when the 1946 harvest failed, a new famine swept the eastern regions, and the Soviet government had to request Western food shipments (provided by the United Nations).

Recovery required manpower, after a war in which one-half of the draft-age men had either died or were seriously wounded. Soviet troops, eleven million strong in 1945, were rapidly demobilized to provide labor for reconstruction. The Red Army declined to three million in 1948, far smaller than fearful Western observers believed at the time. Stalin ended hopes in 1946 for better living conditions for the Soviet population, however, when he proclaimed rapid growth of heavy industry the first priority. Industry was power, and it came before material comfort of the population. Collectivization of all arable land remained the basis of Soviet agriculture, permitting the Soviet state to drain the resources of the farms. Industrial growth did begin again, but at great cost to the population.

The lands occupied by the Red Army or dominated after the war by the Soviet Union had to provide resources for Soviet economic reconstruction. East Germany alone furnished before reparations ended approximately $5 billion in agricultural and industrial supplies; Manchurian factories were dismantled and shipped back to the Soviet Union before the Soviet troops withdrew in 1946, leaving Nationalist and Communist Chinese alike with an industrial wasteland. The European states within the Soviet sphere had to agree to the creation of "trade corporations," under Soviet control, which

extracted from these countries raw materials such as coal and services such as shipping at prices far below cost. The Soviet authorities practiced a policy of economic exploitation, regardless of whether the country was a former enemy, such as Germany, or an ally, like Poland or Yugoslavia.

The political influence of the Communist parties in the Eastern European countries grew in the years after 1945. Until 1947, however, it did not become so great that they had dictatorial powers. Stalin baptized these states "people's democracies," thereby indicating that he did not judge them fit to in-

Stalinist Peace Propaganda: Poster "For Peace, For a People's Democracy," approx. 1949. (*National Archives*)

stitute at that point Soviet-type socialist reforms. Noncommunist parties continued to exist, but their actual freedom of political action dwindled when the police, under Communist control, arrested their leaders. Multiparty elections took place, but Communists held the key government positions. The press remained relatively free. Social and economic reforms introduced in those countries partially nationalized economies and state-organized social welfare, similar in many respects to the policies applied in Western Europe.

Did Stalin plan in 1945 and 1946 to impose immediately one-party Communist dictatorships throughout Eastern Europe? The meager evidence available suggests that he did not. Poland was firmly under Communist rule, despite U.S. demands that free elections permit the Polish people their own choice of leadership. Czechoslovakia on the other hand remained a free parliamentary democracy, with a Communist at the head of the cabinet (his party received the largest vote, though not a majority) and a non-Communist president. Political conditions varied from country to country; the common trait was Soviet diplomatic domination.

Soviet Hegemony and Yugoslav Resistance

The new U.S. containment policies of 1947 brought a swift reaction from the Soviet Union. Stalin appears to have read these initiatives as a warning of a heightened danger of imperialist aggression. He responded by drastically strengthening Soviet domination over the states in his sphere and by mobilizing other Communist parties for political opposition to the West. Late in 1947, Soviet leaders organized a meeting of European Communist parties ostensibly to create a new international organization, the Communist Information Bureau (Cominform).

Its real purpose was to make clear Moscow's view of East-West relations and to mobilize the Communist parties and states within and outside the "socialist camp." Reviving the rhetoric of war, the principal Soviet speaker called for opposition to the Marshall Plan and to the "expansionist and reactionary policy" of the United States. He warned that a new "struggle against the U.S.S.R." had begun. His message was clear: Communists and Communists states had again to rally to the defense of the "socialist motherland." The formulation of the Truman Doctrine and the creation of the Cominform signaled the beginning of the Cold War.

The mobilization of international Communist support for the Soviet Union entailed three new developments: (1) the imposition of strict Soviet controls over Communist parties and governments, (2) the elimination from power of non-Communists in the Eastern European countries, and (3) new efforts by Communist guerrilla forces to seize power and the establishment by Communist insurgents of their own revolutionary regimes. The last policy affected most particularly the Greek and Chinese Communist forces. The Chinese, already engaged in fighting the Nationalists, expanded their offensive to destroy Chiang's regime. The Greeks regrouped in the north and proclaimed the formation of a Greek Communist government. The most dramatic result of Stalin's Cold War policy in Eastern Europe came in Czechoslovakia. In February 1948, the Czech Communist party forced the democratic parties in the coalition government out of power, destroying parliamentary democracy and forming a single-party dictatorship.

The increased Soviet control over foreign Communist parties, proceeding secretly, left no room for any "national independence" among Communist leaders. In Yugoslavia, the effort failed. In that country, the Yugoslav Communist leaders understood national independence to be the fundamental condition of their revolution. Tito had protested in 1946 that his state was not part of anyone's "sphere of influence," though he did explain later that of course he did not have the Soviet Union in mind. The Yugoslav Communists were revolutionaries, publicly committed to Communist dictatorship and supporters of the Greek Communist guerrillas. They were also nationalist in their unwillingness to accept Soviet domination. When Stalin attempted in early 1948 to replace Tito with a compliant Yugoslav leader, he found that his agents in the Yugoslav leadership were powerless against a united Yugoslav party leadership. Failing in his secret maneuvers, he made the conflict public. In the spring of 1948 the Soviet Union withdrew its economic and military advisers, a warning of Moscow's displeasure.

That summer the Cominform expelled the Yugoslav party from its membership, accusing Tito of confusing Soviet international policy with "the foreign policy of the imperialist powers" and of "boundless ambition, arrogance, and conceit." Its real goal was the overthrow of Tito. Stalin privately boasted that "I will move my little finger and Tito will fall." Instead, the party rallied around Tito. For the first time, Stalin had been defied by a nationalist Communist state in an unequal conflict Western observers compared to the Biblical contest of David and Goliath.

By the winter of 1947–48 nothing remained of the Grand Alliance. Negotiations had ceased and had been replaced on both sides by public denunciations. The United States launched a massive program of economic aid to Europe, coupled with military aid to Greece and Turkey. Stalin remade the Soviet sphere of influence into a virtual Soviet empire. Actual military conflict did not occur, but the talk was of war between the superpowers. From the perspective of several decades, we can now conclude that Stalin

never intended a military offensive against the west. To that extent Western fears were exaggerated. He did however make use of the international position of strength acquired in the German war to expand and enlarge the diplomatic and political domination of his country around its borders. He thereby contributed most of all to the failure of the peace.

Western fears of Soviet military aggression played a part as well in the growing hostility between East and West. American leaders magnified Soviet military might far beyond its real level and argued that it, plus Soviet communism, was proof of Soviet aggressive intentions. Partly because they needed to win American support, partly because they mistook Soviet power politics for revolutionary communism, they mobilized for global struggle against communist expansionism. They refused to use the "logic of force" as a means to negotiated settlements, as Kennan had proposed, rejecting real compromise for fear of "appeasement." Out of this impasse would emerge military alliances and the arms race.

THE COLD WAR IN THE WEST

The Partition of Germany

The first open conflict between the United States and the Soviet Union occurred in Germany. It originated in the new Allied policy toward the western German zones, joined in 1947 into one economic unit. This union formed part of a larger plan to revive the West German economy, still suffering from the destruction of war, from serious shortages of food and other vital goods, and from an inflation so serious the German mark had ceased to have real value. No longer were economic policies formulated for all Germany; negotiations with the Russians had broken down. The Western Allies' ultimate objective was the creation of a new German state (including their areas of West Berlin), and to achieve this, they were prepared to disregard the wartime agreements on German occupation. In the spring of 1948 the Western occupying powers announced the issuance of a new German currency for their zones, an important step toward an independent West Germany which they decided would be formed in 1949.

West and East had split in the middle of Europe. The West was in the process of rebuilding a new Germany. Although cut off from the eastern German lands, this western state had a population of fifty million and an industrial base to become a major economic power in Europe. Supported by the United States, it became a front-line region. The Western occupation forces no longer protected the Allies against Germany; they protected the German areas they controlled against the Soviet Union. U.S. intelligence services formed networks of agents to penetrate the east, recruiting former Gestapo supposedly skilled in anti-Communist espionage. In late 1947 one of these new secret agents was Klaus Barbie, a former Gestapo officer wanted for mass murder in France, described by the Allied list of war criminals as a "dangerous conspirator, brutal character, very cruel." New enemies made U.S. officials forget past crimes. The Cold War called a halt to denazification.

The Soviet authorities continued to oppose the unification of western Germany. They warned publicly of the revival of German militarism, probably more a propaganda move than a real fear. Of more immediate concern to Stalin was the emergence of a Western "imperialist bloc," including a unified West German state. Economic hardship, social discontent, and political divisions in the Western German zones were for him a far more desirable state of affairs. To stop

unification required blocking the currency reform, and to do that, Stalin launched the Berlin blockade. When the new currency first appeared in June 1948, Soviet troops stopped all rail, road, and canal traffic along the three corridors from the western zones through their zone into west Berlin, with 2.5 million inhabitants. They cut off electric power from East to West Berlin. Their aim was not to seize Berlin, which was only a pawn in the larger campaign to block the formation of a united Western Germany. The means was hunger and cold imposed on West Berliners, completely dependent on supplies from the West.

In instituting the Berlin blockade, however, Stalin did not take into account the capabilities of modern air transport (the Soviet state had little of its own). The Western powers decided to keep supplies moving along the air corridors, which the Soviets could not block without an act of war. The airlift worked; at its peak that winter one plane arrived every two minutes in Berlin. The blockade failed, and Soviets officials finally opened the roads to Berlin in May 1949. Neither side had used military force, for both did not wish to provoke a new war and sought to keep the conflict within political and diplomatic limits. Yet the blockade heightened greatly the Western fears of war. Stalin's clumsy policy had succeeded only in accelerating the unification of the western zones and the formation of a Western military alliance.

The German Federal Republic came into existence in 1949. Its constitution was written by Germans under Allied supervision. It was the work principally of Konrad Adenauer, leader of the Christian Democratic (CD) party, imprisoned by the Nazis and strong supporter of German collaboration with the West. It gave West Germany a federal structure under parliamentary rule (similar to Weimar democracy). In the first national elections of 1949, the Christian Democrats became the largest party and Adenauer the chancellor of the new Federal Republic. A sizable minority of Germans backed the Social Democratic party, opposed to the western alliance and in favor of neutrality. Throughout the 1950s, however, Adenauer continued to receive the support of a majority of voters.

Gradually the West German state recovered its full sovereign powers. In 1951 Adenauer gained full control over German foreign policy. Finally in 1955 his state entered the Western military alliance and obtained the right to form a German army. A nationalist and conservative, he would not accept the legality of the new western borders of Poland, far within old German lands, or recognize the new East German regime formed by the Russians (the German Democratic Republic). His state represented in his opinion the real Germany, and he refused to acknowledge the permanent partition of the German lands.

Western European Recovery and Unification

In the late 1940s and early 1950s Western Europe experienced a remarkably rapid economic recovery from the war. The Marshall Plan went into effect in mid-1948. By 1952 it had supplied over $10 billion in financial and economic assistance to Western Europe, the largest shares going to Great Britain ($3.2 billion), France ($2.7 billion), and West Germany ($1.5 billion). Each government chose the appropriate use of the aid. In Britain it helped to rebuild old industries. In France, it provided the means for modernizing French industry and transportation. The West German government used the funds to support a free enterprise system (called the "social market economy"), in which the state encouraged capitalists to reinvest their prof-

its and relied on workers to accept low wages and long hours. The result was what came to be known as the "German economic miracle." In 1952 German production had climbed to 50 percent above the prewar level.

By then, Western European economic growth averaged 5 percent a year (the lowest rate was in Great Britain, the highest in Germany). This growth came with large imports from the United States and increased trade among the European states. The economies of Europe and the United States were becoming increasingly interdependent. Gradually they adapted to the new system of international monetary exchange, conducting foreign trade in dollars and relying on U.S. economic growth to assure the prosperity and stability of what was becoming a global economy. The U.S. formula for economic aid to promote political stability and industrial expansion among the European states proved a remarkable success.

With economic recovery came plans for a new political and economic association among European states. The old dream of a federated Europe had revived after the horrors of war. The proposal for economic unification came from Jean Monnet, the head of French planning and former financier, who had become a close aide to the French government. He understood that a unified Europe could be reached only in stages and judged economic cooperation a practical step in that direction.

Monnet suggested in 1950 the formation of a common market for iron, steel, and coal among those European states which agreed to abolish among themselves all tariffs on those products. They would create a supranational commission, that is, a governing body whose policies no member state could veto, to coordinate production and wage plans among all the enterprises in this economic sector. This European Coal and Steel Community became reality in 1952 by an agreement among six governments of Western Europe (Italy, West Germany, France, and the Benelux countries—Belgium, the Netherlands, and Luxemburg). The Labor government of Great Britain refused to join, clinging still to the dream of British "splendid isolation" and suspicious of the important role business interests would play in the Community. Although political unification remained a dream, the Coal and Steel Community represented a historic event in the relations among European states. It marked a first step toward the integration of Germany—though only the western part—into an association of Western nation-states, previously its bitter enemies.

Support among Western Europeans for economic unity was strengthened by the relative loss of power of European states in comparison with the superpowers. Individually these countries were weak and vulnerable to pressure from the Soviet Union, whose troops and satellite states extended into the heart of Europe. To meet this threat, unification of Western Europe constituted a long-range goal. In the immediate circumstances, European leaders looked to military alliances for protection. Their first move in this direction came with the formation in early 1948 of a defense alliance, the Brussels Pact, among Great Britain, France, and the Benelux countries. Their larger aim, though, was to obtain U.S. collaboration in an alliance linking both sides of the North Atlantic.

Containment and Military Alliances

By 1948 the U.S. government had moved beyond its containment policies of military and economic aid to consider the rebuilding of its own military arsenal. Western European leaders encouraged this policy to overcome, in George Kennan's words, "their own military helplessness" and their "lack of confidence in themselves." In the United States, military conscription began again. U.S. foreign commitments expanded enormously in 1949 with the creation of a collective security pact among all countries of the North Atlantic area—all the major states of Western Europe as well as Canada—to form the North Atlantic Treaty Organization (NATO). Collective security entailed the commitment of each member to assist in the defense of the others against any aggression. In real terms, the presumed enemy was the Soviet Union, and the principal weapons with which to defend NATO was the U.S. nuclear arsenal. Containment was becoming militarized, and tied to the armaments race.

The Greek state, a member of NATO, received large amounts of U.S. military supplies in its war on the Communist guerrillas who controlled the north. Outnumbered by the regular Greek army and deprived after 1948 of Yugoslav support, the insurgents gave up the struggle in 1949, fleeing to Soviet satellite countries and taking thousands of Greek civilians with them. Western military and economic aid was probably the decisive factor in preventing that country from becoming a Communist dictatorship and Soviet satellite.

Primarily diplomatic, political, and economic in the 1947, the U.S.-Soviet rivalry came increasingly to be dominated by the military balance of power and the development of new nuclear weapons. In the context of the Cold War, scientists became warriors and laboratories the key places where possible future wars were planned. Neither side envisioned this armaments race to be the means to launch an aggressive war, for each feared above all the potential power new weapons would give the other. This logic was as true in the Soviet Union as in the United States. In 1949 the Soviet Union exploded its first atomic bomb, which had been under development since the war. We know now that the Soviet Union had already begun research on its own hydrogen bomb. The destructive capacity of this weapon exceeded by a thousand times that of the atomic bomb; its purpose could only be to deter nuclear war, an unthinkable catastrophe for civilization. In those years Soviet scientists set out as well to develop ballistic missiles, capable of carrying nuclear weapons in a matter of minutes from Russia to the United States and a greatly improved substitute for long-distance bombers, of which the Russians had very few. But each new Soviet step, though intended to deter attack, heightened pressure in the United States for new armaments in a cycle which appeared endless.

Deeply suspicious of Soviet intentions, the U.S. government at the time of the Korean conflict began an intensive program to expand the entire armed forces and began development of a hydrogen bomb. Convinced of the aggressive intent of Stalin, they believed U.S. security lay only in military superiority over the Soviet Union. In Allied countries near Soviet borders, the U.S. built air bases for its Strategic Air Command, whose bombers were in position to attack the Soviet Union. Military preparedness came by the early 1950s to dominate U.S. Cold War policies. Tragically, both Soviet and U.S. leaders could find no other way to ensure their countries' ultimate protection than to apply nuclear power to military use. Their Cold War policies turned the "logic of force" into a race to develop ever more deadly nuclear weapons.

The containment strategy in those years was redefined by U.S. leaders to include the formation of military alliances with countries near the Soviet Union. They offered the inducement of foreign aid in the form of armaments to strengthen the military forces of allied countries. These global anti-Soviet policies extended through the Middle East and Asia. The United States signed alliances with a number of states individually, including the Philippines and Taiwan. In the 1950s, the U.S. and British governments each organized military alliances in these regions: the South East Asia Treaty Organization (SEATO) included states extending from Pakistan to New Zealand; the British set up the Baghdad Pact, including Turkey, Iraq, and Iran. The most visible effect of these alliances was the distribution of armaments to dictators and democratic governments alike and the formation of a vast U.S. sphere of influence.

Even Latin America, far from the Soviet Union, was included in the early 1950s. The exaggerated fear among U.S. leaders of a global Communist revolutionary conspiracy created visions of possible Cold War conflicts wherever Soviet or Communist influence made itself felt. The Latin Communist movements had increased somewhat their backing among urban workers, but nowhere did they approach the strength of the European Communist parties. Still, the U.S. government set out to obtain Latin backing for its Cold War policies, sponsoring the formation of a regional organization, the Organization of American States, which included most Latin countries. It used its influence to encourage these states to sever diplomatic relations with the Soviet Union and to outlaw their Communist parties. The strategy of containment was extended worldwide, though it was not always clear what or who was being contained.

Stalin's Empire

In Eastern Europe, Stalin controlled through his ambassadors and secret police officials the small Communist countries on Russia's western borders. They had become "satellites," that is, states for whom decisions on leadership and key policies were made in Moscow. All appeared in the years after 1948 miniature replicas of Stalinist Russia. Their leaders ruled with the same dictatorial power as Stalin, employing similar repressive police methods. In some countries, little "show trials" were held of leading Communists who had fallen from favor, often accused of "national deviation" and "Titoism." These mockeries of justice repeated the experience of the Soviet trials of the 1930s. All the accused confessed their guilt, and most were executed.

The Soviet socialist model was applied by force to the Eastern European populations. Industry and commerce were nationalized. Peasant farmers were forced to sell their produce to the state at low prices. State plans set ambitious targets for industrial growth, achieved at the cost of miserable living conditions for the population. The Stalinist literary style of "socialist realism" was imposed on intellectuals, who had to glorify Soviet socialism and Stalin's "genius." A gray uniformity colored public life, forced into the Stalinist mold.

Of all Eastern European states, only Yugoslavia escaped Stalinist domination. The expulsion of the Yugoslav Communist party from the Cominform in 1948 was followed by the political and economic isolation of the Yugoslav state. Its trade with all other Communist states ceased and Soviet and East European states ended diplomatic relations. For a year Tito continued to claim his fidelity to Stalinism and to Soviet socialism. Beginning in 1949, he slowly took Yugoslavia's foreign and domestic policies far from the Stalinist model. He joined the leaders of newly independent Asian states in founding the so-called "nonaligned movement" of countries refusing to join either western or Soviet military alliances. He accepted economic, then military aid from the United States, which was ready to forget past quarrels and Yugoslav communism to weaken the Soviet bloc. Tito still fixed his hopes on the creation

of a socialist society, but his reforms ended Yugoslav imitation of Stalinist dictatorial socialism. Yugoslavia embodied a more democratic, nationalist form of communism, a model which other Eastern European Communists sought to imitate in the years after Stalin's death.

Despite Tito's public defiance of Soviet hegemony, Stalin chose not to invade Yugoslavia. Although Red Army forces surrounded Yugoslavia and made threatening moves, they never attacked. We can only speculate on the reasons for their inaction— perhaps Stalin anticipated prolonged Yugoslav resistance, perhaps he was determined not to risk a war with the United States. In matters of European security, the dictator pursued a very cautious policy. Tito's revolt did not disrupt Soviet domination elsewhere along its border. Although the Soviet Union possessed after 1949 nuclear weapons, it remained militarily inferior to the United States, possessing a few long-range bombers and only a Coast Guard to protect its shores. Whether through prudence or fear, Stalin pursued a foreign policy of domination but not aggression.

The Soviet leader was growing old. In 1949 he celebrated his seventieth birthday, receiving so many gifts from within the Soviet Union and around the world that they filled an entire warehouse. He continued to rule with dictatorial powers, feared by even his subordinates within the ruling party committee, the Presidium (formerly called the Politburo). His successor, Khrushchev, remembered later how Stalin could "without warning turn on you with real viciousness." His suspiciousness remained acute.

In that empire of fear no one's position or life was secure. Police terror had once before, in the late 1930s, been used against party leaders Stalin distrusted. In 1952 Stalin appears to have decided to end the career (and the life) of Lavrentii Beria, the second

1 the country.
f supporters
the winter of
loctors' plot,"
of party offi-
elf in "trea-
ntly had even
fficials to be-
ad the chance
w Great Ter-
ldenly ended
th brought to
rrible period
lew era in the
twar world.

: in East Asia
: from that in
rrender, oc-
States moved
Asian main-
inchuria and
thern half of
States. Else-
inese troops
e by the first
1 China and
ed resistance
ssume an ac-
considerable
oth through
struggle and
eping social
evolutionary
by Stalin's or-
on-Commu-
war quickly
juntries they
termined to
Indochina,

French military forces returned in strength
in 1946 and immediately attacked Communist centers of strength. The Communist
forces and their nationalist allies retreated to
the countryside, beginning a guerrilla war
which, with interruptions, was to last thirty
years.

In China, the Communists' political rival
was Chiang Kai-shek, successor to Sun Yat-
sen, president of the Nationalist Republic
and "generalissimo" of Nationalist armies.
Having survived the war, Chiang resumed
his efforts, begun twenty years before, to
unite all China under his rule. Allied with the
United States during the war, he continued
to rely on American help in the enormous
task of postwar reconstruction of a land of
over 500 million people who had endured
eight years of war.

Knowing little of Chinese political conditions, President Roosevelt had laid plans to
rely on Chiang to play the role of "policeman," ensuring the peace settlement in
East Asia. These optimistic—and unrealistic—objectives guided U.S. Asian policy
in 1945. President Truman gave the Nationalists military, political, and economic assistance. He sent fifty thousand Marines to
the northern coast of China and provided
planes and ships to transport part of the Nationalist forces, which numbered three million, into regions being evacuated by the Japanese. In addition, he made available to the
Nationalists military supplies worth $1 bil-
lion left from the war with Japan. In no other
war-torn country did the United States become so directly involved in the task of postwar recovery.

The real burden of rebuilding the Chinese state lay in the Nationalists' hands. It
proved a task they could not handle. Behind
a facade of power, the Nationalist state was
weak. Chiang's government was incapable of
administering the country in an efficient
manner. Nationalist generals given com-

mand over newly reoccupied provinces conducted their affairs like warlords, interested above all in enhancing their own power. They did little for the people. The inefficient Nationalist state and expensive army proved an obstacle to economic recovery. Exorbitant government spending fueled rapid inflation, which, begun during the war, became ruinous in the years afterward. The most serious weakness of the Nationalist regime was its inability to win the confidence of the Chinese people. Corruption and abuse of power discredited its claim to nationalist leadership. Its failure to implement land reform for the peasantry deprived it of popular support among the masses of the population.

U.S. assistance included participation in the political negotiations between the Nationalist government and the Chinese Communists. Extending to China the principle of national self-determination, General George Marshall traveled to the headquarters of the two contenders for power to obtain their agreement to a coalition government. The Communist claim to an important role in the rule of their country rested on their expansion during the war years, at the end of which the Communists controlled areas in central and northern China with over fifty million people and possessed an army of one million. The U.S. China policy had the help of the Soviet Union. Stalin, who considered

The Leaders of Revolutionary China: Negotiations in Yanan, 1945, with General George Marshall (far right, Mao Zedong; far left, Zhou Enlai). (*Phillip Sprouse Collection/Hoover Institution Archives*)

China part of the Western sphere of influence, signed in 1945 a ten-year friendship treaty with the Nationalist government (and in exchange obtained Nationalist acceptance of Soviet "concessions" in Manchuria). At the same time, he instructed the Chinese Communists to agree to the U.S.-sponsored coalition government. He later recalled that, when a Chinese Communist delegation came to Moscow in 1945, "we told them that we considered the development of the uprising in China had no prospect, and that the Chinese comrades should join the Chiang government and dissolve their army." The combined pressure of the superpowers appeared to succeed in bringing together the former enemies. In January 1946, the Nationalists and Communists signed a cease-fire and began discussions to form a joint government.

The agreement quickly collapsed. Political intervention by the superpowers proved incapable of effacing the bitter rivalry between the two parties. The United States could not force Chiang to put aside his deadly hatred of the Communists. The Soviet Union had no means to impose on Mao Zedong the dissolution of his peasant army and the abandonment of his liberated areas, twin elements to the policy on which he had based his revolutionary faith ever since 1928. Fighting between Nationalist and Communist troops began again at the end of 1946 over the perennial issue of territorial control. Manchuria was the prize, occupied by Soviet troops until 1946. Their withdrawal began a contest between Nationalists and Communists to take over that once-prosperous region.

In the battle for control of Manchurian cities, the Nationalists had the initial advantage. The Communists, less well equipped and fewer in number, had to retreat to the countryside to resume guerrilla war once again against their old enemy. In late 1946 the United States abandoned efforts to bring the two sides together. General Marshall declared impossible an agreement between, in his words, "the dominant reactionary group in the [Nationalist] government and the irreconcilable Communists." By late 1947, the Communist forces were two million strong and had succeeded in cutting off north China from the central regions. Only force of arms would decide the victor.

Communist Victory in China

That conflict constituted one of the greatest wars of the twentieth century. On one side was the Nationalist state, with over three million troops equipped with U.S. military supplies. In appearance still the dominant political force in the country, its strength was in reality declining. The weaknesses apparent in 1945 had become more serious. The army was poorly led and, with the exception of several crack divisions sent to Manchuria, made up of conscripts who deserted at the first opportunity. The population was increasingly hostile to the Nationalist government, incapable of assuring public order and of preventing the collapse of commerce and industry. When forced to choose, more and more Chinese turned to the Communists.

The Communist forces were fewer in number in 1948 than the Nationalists, but the balance was beginning to shift in their favor. Social, political, and military factors explain the increasing power of the Communist movement. The party leadership, under Mao Zedong, proved effective and skillful in mobilizing popular support and in forming a military and political organization capable of governing large areas of the country. The Communists had to rely on their own resources, for no aid came from the Soviet Union. They fixed their own political objectives, paying polite attention to Stalin's recommendations but never obeying him blindly.

Although their armed conflict with Chiang had begun in 1946, Stalin's new militant policy for the international Communist movement in 1947 appears to have encouraged their revolutionary struggle to defeat the Nationalists and to take control of all China. They revised their agrarian policy to promote radical reform. Farms of landlords and wealthy peasants were confiscated and the land redistributed among poor peasants. In the Communist areas, the exploitation of hired labor ended, and all peasants were assured a modest amount of land. A new revolutionary order was emerging in the Chinese countryside, and Communist support among the peasantry grew correspondingly. Mao had proclaimed ten years before that "political power grows out of the barrel of a gun"; that gun was held in the late 1940s by peasants who believed that they were fighting for their own land as well as for a liberated Chinese nation.

The Communist party cadres enforced these reforms ruthlessly, sometimes brutally. Still, they proved effective administrators capable of maintaining order in the "liberated areas." After decades of war, firm and orderly rule appealed to many Chinese. Another factor behind the growing strength of the Communists was military leadership. The commanders of the People's Liberation Army (PLA) had, after years of guerrilla fighting, learned to command massive army groups in battles increasingly resembling a regular war. They proved far superior to Nationalist generals. Although the Communists too conscripted peasants into their armies, their soldiers (among whom were increasing numbers of Nationalist deserters) remained disciplined, increasingly confident of victory, and convinced of the justice of their cause. The power of the Chinese Communists lay principally in their morale and leadership, not in numbers.

The struggle turned into all-out civil war

in early 1948. The best Nationalist troops had gone far to the Northeast in 1946–47 to occupy Manchuria and to defeat the Communist forces there. The lines of communication between those forces and the main Nationalist areas were stretched dangerously thin, depending on the rail lines connecting the cities which they controlled. The vulnerability of the Nationalist forces became apparent by early 1948. In the previous two years, they had failed to defeat the Communists' Manchurian forces, the United Democratic Army of the Northeast under the command of Lin Biao. While Nationalists' attention had been directed to the north, Communist troops had seized control of large rural areas in central China.

The Communist strategy in 1948 shifted to the conquest of Manchuria. In the spring of 1948 Communist armies blockaded Nationalist garrisons throughout the region. In mid-1948 they began the systematic destruction of the best troops the Nationalists could field, cut off from the bulk of Chiang's forces in China. By the end of 1948 the Nationalists had lost thirty divisions. Half these forces had simply deserted or surrendered without fighting. All Manchuria lay under Communist rule, and panic was spreading among Nationalist troops elsewhere.

In early 1949, the balance of military forces between the two sides was about equal. The U.S. government had done as much as possible to help the Nationalist government with economic and military aid. President Truman refused to send U.S. troops to fight in place of Chiang's demoralized army. The Communists, unaided by the Soviet Union, obtained most of their arms from American supplies captured from the Nationalists. The U.S. government protested the Communist offensive, and Stalin may have warned the Chinese comrades to show caution—to no avail. In the Chinese civil war, no outside powers could control the conflict. In the winter and spring of 1948–49, the PLA launched massive military offensives all through north and central China. One Nationalist army, surrounded in the capital city of Beijing, surrendered in January with the loss of half a million troops. Farther to the south, Communist forces numbering 500,000 attacked in late 1948 the main defensive line protecting Nationalist areas in central China. By February 1949, the defenses there were breached and the Nationalist armies destroyed. Between the spring and fall of 1949, Communist armies moved south across the Yangze River and into southern China. That summer, entire Nationalist armies, generals as well as troops, deserted to the Communists. By the fall of 1949, no important areas of resistance remained.

In October 1949, the Communist leadership proclaimed in Beijing the formation of the Chinese People's Republic. The most populous country in the world, land of the world's oldest civilization, had passed under the rule of the Communist party. A successor state had taken power, ending the long period of disorders in China following the fall of the Chinese Empire in 1911. The Communist leaders did not, however, consider the civil war at an end until they captured the island of Formosa, where Chiang and remnants of his Nationalist forces had fled. The PLA began to prepare for an amphibious invasion of the island, planned for the summer of 1950. Nothing appeared to stand in its way.

In those early months of Chinese Communist rule, the United States was not yet prepared to treat Mao's regime as an enemy. The U.S. government had that winter specifically excluded Formosa from its Asian area of "vital interests." Seeking to define clearly the region of the Far East it was prepared to defend, it outlined a "defense perimeter" extending as far east as Japan and omitting all

lands on the Asian continent (including Korea) as well as Formosa. From South Korea to the Philippines, new Asian nationalist regimes obtained U.S. economic and military aid. Early in 1950, the U.S. government agreed to supply aid to the new non-Communist Vietnamese regime, largely a French creation to win the backing of anti-Communist Vietnamese in the war with the Vietnamese Communist guerrillas. Still, these anti-Communist policies did not appear in late 1949 to exclude recognition of the new People's Republic of China. Secret talks began that winter between Chinese Communist leaders and the United States in preparation for the possible opening of diplomatic relations.

At the same time Mao Zedong was working out his state's relations with the Soviet Union. He traveled to Moscow in the winter of 1949–50 on his first trip outside China to begin lengthy and difficult negotiations with Stalin. The Chinese Communists requested a military alliance, economic assistance, and the end to Soviet concessions on Chinese territory. These Soviet-controlled areas included a port and railroad in Manchuria and a large area of Chinese Central Asia. The Chinese were requesting in effect the end to Soviet imperial domination in East Asia. Chinese and Russians shared a common Marxist-Leninist ideology, and Mao revered the wisdom and achievements of the Soviet party. However, though the Chinese desperately needed help rebuilding their war-torn country, they sought as well recognition of their new revolutionary nation-state.

For his part, Stalin persisted in treating China, even though Communist, in a manner resembling Russian tsarist policy toward the Chinese Empire in the early twentieth century. He apparently distrusted the Chinese Communists, whose independent behavior must have reminded him of the Yugoslav Communists. We may well believe

Mao's later statement that "Stalin feared that China might degenerate into another Yugoslavia and that I might become another Tito." Finally, Stalin certainly was concerned at the possible weakening of the Soviet sphere of influence in East Asia, which extended from Central Asia through Mongolia to North Korea. Alongside the Chinese leaders in the negotiations were Communist representatives from these lands. The negotiations dragged on for two months.

In the end, Stalin agreed to a military alliance and to loans (though less even than the loans made to the East European satellites). He agreed as well to withdraw Soviet forces from Manchuria in a few years. In exchange, Mao had to recognize the independence (under Soviet protection) of Mongolia and to tolerate the existence of a special autonomous region in Manchuria under a Chinese Communist leader taking orders from Moscow. Between these two enormous Communist states relations remained in public "fraternal" and the Chinese honored Stalin's ideological leadership. Yet Communist China did not join the ranks of Soviet satellites.

The Korean Conflict

Besides Mongolia, the only other Soviet Asian satellite was North Korea. Partitioned in a wartime agreement between the Soviet Union and the United States, the northern half of the country was ruled by the Korean Communist party, whose leaders proclaimed their objective to be the unification of Korea. In the south, Korean nationalist politicians set up a new regime under the leadership of Syngman Rhee. He governed his turbulent state with dictatorial powers and vowed that national unification would be his doing. In the years after 1947 both sides warned that they were prepared to seize by force the other half of the peninsula. The U.S. government, as opposed there as in China to becoming directly involved in civil war, took Rhee's talk of war seriously. In 1949, it withdrew most of its troops and left the South Korean army with only defensive weapons while continuing to supply economic assistance. Japan constituted the new forward post of the United States in the Cold War in Asia.

In those conditions, Stalin apparently decided to make the Korean peninsula the Soviet forward post. Korea was the only state partitioned after the Second World War where Soviet and American occupation forces were not present to guarantee the artificial frontier dividing Communist and non-Communist rivals. With the example of the Communist conquest of China in mind, the North Koreans set about planning their own "war of liberation." They could take no action without the approval of the Soviet Union, source of their military supplies. Sometime in the spring of 1950 Stalin gave his backing to the North Korean plan to conquer the south.

Just why he decided to take the risk of becoming indirectly involved in an Asian war against a small state aided by the U.S. remains unclear. Having had to recognize the independence of the Chinese Communists, he may have sought to strengthen his Korean satellite. The Chinese leaders did not support a military conflict in Korea, for they had made the conquest of Formosa their first priority. Stalin may easily have anticipated as well that the United States would make no major effort to defend South Korea, which it had not included in its strategic defense area. The fighting would not involve Soviet forces, only Koreans. Since South Korea appeared an easy target, he made the one reckless military decision of his entire political career. In late June 1950, North Korean troops invaded South Korea. Another local war had begun.

It became a part of the Cold War two days later when the U.S. president declared that his country would defend South Korea. This sudden reversal of U.S. policy was due to two factors. First, the U.S. leaders realized that a communist Korea would extend the ring of Soviet satellites to within a short distance of Japan, kingpin of U.S.–East Asian defenses. More important, U.S. failure to resist the Communist offensive would have conveyed a message throughout the world that the policy of containment hid military weakness, reviving memories of the 1930s appeasement policies toward Nazi Germany. Having emphasized the military dimension of containment, the United States had to prove its readiness to resist Communist military expansion promoted by the Soviet Union.

The Korean fighting quickly turned into a full-scale U.S. war. After Communist forces had routed the South Korean army, the United States had to send troops from Japan to fight the North Koreans if it was to stop the Communist offensive. The U.S. government appointed General MacArthur commander of the forces in Korea. He fought under the United Nations' flag when the U.N. Security Council (minus the Soviet representative, away protesting the failure of the United Nations to seat Communist China) approved the defense of South Korea against "foreign aggression." MacArthur's own ambitious battle plan included the ultimate destruction of communism in the Far East, in China as well as Korea. The U.S. government lent some support to that idea when in July it reversed its decision not to defend Formosa, sending naval forces of the Seventh Fleet into the Straits of Formosa to block Chinese Communist troops preparing to invade the island. Suddenly, the front lines of the Cold War extended around Communist China. Having made the mistaken judgment that China and the Soviet Union were united in Communist revolu-

tionary expansionism, the U.S. government was taking actions whose effect would force China to join forces with the Soviet Union.

U.S. objectives in the Korean conflict did not become clear until late that fall. General MacArthur made U.S. policy until then. His immediate goal was an overwhelming military victory and the capitulation of North Korea. He began a counteroffensive in September, forcing the North Korean army to retreat far to the north. Instead of letting only South Korean forces pursue the enemy into North Korea, he ordered U.S. forces to carry the war to the very borders of China. The U.S. government had already learned of Chinese warnings of military intervention if U.S. land forces approached Chinese territory. It could not halt MacArthur, however, who disregarded the Chinese messages in his pursuit of the Communist enemy.

As a result, Communist China entered the war as well. In November, 300,000 Chinese troops attacked U.S. forces, quickly overwhelmed and forced to retreat back into South Korea where the front soon stabilized in the region of the old border. The bloody war dragged on, in which the United States suffered over 100,000 casualties and the Chinese nearly 1 million. China and the United States had become enemies. In 1951 the U.S. government dismissed MacArthur from his position of commander-in-chief, an American "Caesar" whose dreams of military victory were out of touch with the limited objectives of Cold War military strategy. The U.S. government sought only to protect South Korea, refusing to use its nuclear weapons in a war not for conquest but for containment of North Korea.

The Korean action remained thus a limited conflict, a series of bloody, inconclusive battles of no benefit to either side. It confirmed Stalin's prediction of capitalist war on the socialist bloc and forced Communist China to rely on the Soviet alliance and to

New War in Asia: U.S. Counteroffensive against North Korean Forces, September 1950. (*National Archives*)

accept Stalin's leadership. Responsible for the outbreak of hostilities, he apparently prevented a compromise settlement. In 1951 the first peace negotiations began, only to stall over minor issues of prisoner repatriation raised by the Communists. Stalin probably was responsible for the continuation of the war for two more years, in the course of which North Korean cities were destroyed by intensive U.S. aerial bombardments. Shortly after his death in 1953 the prisoner issue no longer mattered to the Communist nego-

tiators, and an armistice was signed. Stalin had forced China to depend on his country for military aid and support, and at the same time had provoked the West to begin rapid rearmament. The United States moved new military forces to Europe, tripled its defense budget, and accelerated the construction of air bases around the Soviet Union. More than any other Cold War conflict, the war in Korea heightened the danger of a new world war and deepened the division of the globe into rival armed "camps."

SUMMARY

The Cold War did not represent in either Europe or Asia a permanent settlement to World War II. Stalin's determination to create a diplomatic and political sphere of influence along the Soviet Union ensured a partition of Europe that followed the approximate line of farthest advance of the wartime armies. It appears certain that he did not plan further wars after 1945; by his logic of "respecting the powerful," the military and economic might of the United States forbade any risky actions. Berlin was blockaded, not seized by Soviet troops. Only in Korea, where no American troops were stationed, did he authorize a Communist military offensive.

Stalin had only limited influence over Communist revolutionary movements, which emerged in Europe and Asia out of social and political conflicts of prewar and war years. Bitter fighting pitted Communists against non-Communists in all these lands. We realize now that these movements were not all subservient to the Soviet Union. The hostility of the Chinese Communists toward Western imperialism was profound yet they appeared ready in the months after their conquest to deal peacefully with the United States. Stalin, whose very nature seemed marked by deep suspicion of any independent leader or state, made ruthless power politics the basis of his policies. In these circumstances, Tito's nationalist revolt suggested the possibility of the emergence of other independent states under Communist leadership.

Western fears of Soviet attack resulted from several factors. They were partly the fruit of anticommunist hysteria, partly the result of a false image of Soviet might at war's end, partly a reaction against brutal Communist political domination of Eastern Europe. We know now that weakness, not strength, dictated Soviet exploitation of those countries. Eastern European satellite states lost all independence, so feeble and exploited they might have been annexed to the Soviet Union had Stalin not preferred to leave their rule to his Communist puppets. The discontent of their peoples was repressed, but only temporarily.

The rapid recovery of Western Europe was due partly to the dynamic new leadership of these countries, partly to massive U.S. economic aid. By contrast to the grim uniformity of Communist lands, the West enjoyed extensive freedom to experiment with new state reforms while still protecting individual liberty. Yet fear of Russia undermined hope in the West. The erroneous expectation of Soviet military aggression transformed the U.S. containment strategy from its original diplomatic and economic policies into a reliance on rearmament and military alliances. These efforts in turn provoked further Soviet military expansion. Lacking any other means of communicating their determination to fight if attacked, each side developed new arms in what became an endless race to preserve peace by preparing for war.

RECOMMENDED READING

The Cold War

*RICHARD BARNETT, *The Alliance: America-Europe-Japan, Makers of the Post-War World* (1983)

COLIN BROWN AND PETER MOONEY *Cold War to Détente, 1945–1980* (1981)

JOHN GADDIS, *Strategies of Containment: A Critical Appraisal of Postwar American National Security Policy* (1982)

ALAN MILWARD, *The Reconstruction of Western Europe, 1945–1951* (1984)

JEAN SMITH, *The Defense of Berlin* (1963)

DANIEL YERGIN, *The Shattered Peace: The Origins of the Cold War and the National Security State* (1977)

Soviet Foreign Policy

HUGH SETON-WATSON, *The East European Revolutions* (third ed., 1961)

ROBERT SIMMONS, *The Strained Alliance: Peking, Pyongyang, Moscow, and the Politics of the Korean War* (1975)

*ADAM ULAM, *Expansion and Co-existence: Soviet Foreign Policy 1917–1973* (second ed., 1974)

Memoirs and Novels

*WOLFGANG LEONHARD, *Child of the Revolution* (1981)

*ALEXANDER SOLZHENITSYN, *The First Circle* (1976)

*HEINRICH BÖLL, *Billiards at Half-Past Nine* (1973)

chapter 8

EAST ASIA IN THE POST-IMPERIALIST ERA

In the years following the end of the Second World War, internal reform and revolution replaced international war as the principal agent of change in East Asia. Wars in Indochina and Korea brought foreign intervention, but they remained local conflicts. Slowly the foundations of economic and political life were reconstructed, in most cases so different from conditions in the age of imperialism that East Asia appeared after the war to have entered a new era of economic development and state building.

The frontiers dividing nation-states remained those boundaries drawn by Western imperial powers. China never recovered its outlying dependencies of Mongolia and Korea in the north, or Indochina in the south, yet the Communist state retained by negotiation and force of arms the bulk of its territory and population. It, alone among the ancient Asian empires, did not break

apart into smaller nation-states. The Communists reformed the Chinese state and society, raising China once again to the rank of a major power. Japan too, though defeated in war, did not suffer partition. Under U.S. occupation, new reforms eliminated all visible traces of the period of militarism and restored parliamentary rule and a capitalist economic system closely modeled on Western institutions, yet adapted to Japanese culture. Japanese recovery, though slow to start, soon made the country one of the most productive, prosperous industrial nations of the world.

The emergence of new states in Korea and in Indochina was deeply influenced by the wars in which Communists and non-Communists, each backed by superpowers, struggled for control of their lands. The settlement of the Korean conflict left that country permanently partitioned between Communist and non-Communist states, like Germany a reminder of the Cold War. In Indochina, on the contrary, the war lasted far longer and had a very different outcome. For three decades, civil war and foreign intervention tore apart the former French colony. In the end, the military triumph of the Vietnamese Communist party made it the ruling force throughout that land, separated from its neighbors by the borders drawn by the French in the nineteenth century. The existence of these frontiers was one visible sign of the permanent impact of the West on East Asia.

The Soviet Union and the United States were a constant and important presence, both by the influence they exerted and by the opposition they encountered, in the evolution of the East Asian countries. Chinese Communists depended in the early years of their revolution on the Soviet Union for ideological inspiration and military support; when they turned against Soviet domination, the conflict produced a profound alteration in the Asian balance of power. The United States played a key role in the reconstruction of Japan, both as occupying power and as a source of economic aid until the Japanese economic "miracle" became in turn a model for American industry.

The outcome of the wars in Korea and Indochina each in their own way revealed the limits to U.S. power in the area. The 1953 peace settlement in Korea retained the partition and left the south under U.S. protection. In Indochina, a similar U.S. effort to protect a partitioned non-Communist state failed. South Vietnam was not remade into a strong, stable state, and the Vietnamese Communists would not renounce their ambition to take control of all Indochina. To understand the evolution of those states, we must pay attention both to internal political forces in each country and also to the policies of the two superpowers, whose global ascendancy made post-1945 world history in some measure a product of their actions.

JAPAN THE INDUSTRIAL GIANT

In August 1945, the Japanese imperial government surrendered unconditionally to the Allies, accepting American military occupation and the imposition of peace terms decided by the Allies. The defeat was complete, both militarily and psychologically. The Japanese people heard their emperor in his first radio broadcast accept in his name the surrender and the loss of independence, a humiliation "unendurable" and "insufferable" but nonetheless inescapable. For years to come, Japan was under the control and at the mercy of the Allies. It, like Germany, had to start anew.

The Reconstruction of Japan

The treatment accorded the two defeated states differed greatly, however. In the first place, Japanese occupation was the affair of the United States. The U.S. navy and air force had played the key role in the defeat of the Japanese Empire. American military forces alone occupied the country following the surrender. General Douglas MacArthur, U.S. Army commander-in-chief in the Pacific theater, became the supreme commander for the Allied Powers in Japan. He held absolute power in that country and was accountable only to the U.S. president. The territory he governed remained intact. The Soviet Union requested a separate occupation zone; MacArthur refused, and no Soviet occupation forces reached Japan. An Allied council had nominal authority to oversee MacArthur's work; in fact, it merely approved now and then policies the supreme commander had decided upon. Japanese occupation was a U.S., not an Allied, affair.

Late in 1945 Stalin complained that the Soviet general on the Allied council there "was treated like a piece of extra furniture," but his protest was half-hearted. He accepted the fact that Japan was in the U.S. sphere of influence.

The fact that the United States exercised such extraordinary control over Japan led to a second important feature of the Allied occupation. A central Japanese government carried out the orders of the supreme commander, unlike in Germany where no national government existed at any time during the occupation. The symbol of Japan's unity remained the emperor, who had not ruled the country for centuries but who had continued to be treated as a semi-divine person. When MacArthur assumed his post of supreme commander in late 1945, the emperor made a brief, ceremonial call, placing himself at the mercy of the victors. His purpose was to assume "sole responsibility for every political and military decision made and action taken by my people in the conduct of war" and to be judged for their conduct. Although the U.S. government had decided to punish Japanese "war criminals," MacArthur resolved not to hold Hirohito responsible and retained the position of emperor. Japan maintained its political unity and its imperial monarch, under American orders.

Nuclear Wasteland: Hiroshima, December 1945. (*James Watkins Collection/Hoover Institution Archives*)

The country over which MacArthur assumed command was in ruins. Total Japanese casualties numbered nine million; all major Japanese cities had been destroyed—most by massive U.S. bombing raids, Hiroshima and Nagasaki by single atomic bombs—and millions of civilians were homeless. The merchant marine had lost almost all its ships. Most of the textile factories and coal mines had ceased to function, and food production had fallen by nearly one-half. To add to the miseries, over six million Japanese who had lived in overseas imperial territories had fled or were forced to return to Japan. The destruction went much deeper than life and property, however. The respect for military authority had vanished with the humiliating defeat, and national pride and deference to the old elite were undermined by American domination of the Japanese state and people.

This psychological response to surrender played an important part, albeit difficult to define, in the success of the American occupation. The most unusual aspect of the adaptation of the Japanese to the conquerors was their readiness to cooperate in the building of the new order imposed by the Americans. It reflected, in the opinion of one Japanese historian, a deep-seated hope that "something can be done" despite the terrible destruction, and a widespread conviction that Japan's "path to future greatness lay in absorbing America's technological civilization."[1] The victors, in other words, held the key to recovery. Reinforcing this attitude was the enormous respect General MacArthur enjoyed among the Japanese. His imperious manners, disliked by many Americans, symbolized to the vanquished the traditional "way of the warrior," displayed with remarkable American informality. Although he

traveled daily in an open car to his headquarters, at no time in his six-year reign was he the target of an assassination attempt. The emperor had publicly accepted American rule and demonstrated his willingness to collaborate in the occupation; the Japanese people did the same.

During their years of occupation, the U.S. authorities imposed a series of fundamental political reforms on the country. These included a new constitution, the introduction of universal suffrage, legal protection of women's rights, and the expansion of the entire educational system. Least effective was a purge of over 200,000 former officers and politicians implicated in the war. As in Germany, many individuals subject to purge vanished temporarily, only to emerge in new positions of authority when the United States turned to reconstruction. The purge included as well the trial and conviction of war criminals, although death penalties went to only a handful. Among the condemned were General Tojo, held guilty of launching the war, and the military commander of the Philippines who had defeated MacArthur in 1942. Many Japanese, little aware of or concerned about the brutality of Japanese treatment of defeated peoples, found the principles applied in these trials to be a conqueror's justice. In historical perspective, the trials reveal to what extent Americans still believed in the Wilsonian philosophy of an international code of war; within a few decades, the United States, caught in new and ugly wars, was no longer able itself effectively to enforce these standards.

The principal political reform introduced during the occupation consisted in a new constitution. It drew heavily on the British cabinet system and was not substantially different from Japanese parliamentary democracy of the 1920s. A popularly elected parliament held sovereign power, choosing the cabinet headed by a prime minister. Mac-

---

[1]Masataka Kosaka, *A History of Postwar Japan* (Tokyo, 1972), p. 35.

Arthur took direct responsibility for the constitutional reform. He presented the Japanese government with the document he expected them to approve. When translated into Japanese, its passages sounded to one Tokyo newspaper commentator "exotically like American English." He also insisted that it include an introduction stating that "never again shall we be visited with the horrors of war through the action of government." No other constitution in the world made pacifism a political principle, another indication of the extraordinary circumstances of U.S. military occupation. Despite its "exotic" aspects, the constitution still fitted well the expectations and past democratic practices of Japanese citizens, becoming with relative ease the fundamental law of the land.

The U.S. occupation reforms were intended to restructure Japanese economic and social life by weakening the power of big business and landowners. They touched agriculture, industry, and labor. Most important and enduring were the changes in rural property holding, so extensive they resembled the initial land reforms in Communist China and earned MacArthur the reputation of a "radical." The American occupation authorities ordered a sweeping redistribution of farmland, taken from absentee landlords paid a price so low that their land was in fact confiscated. Over one-third of all Japanese arable land was transferred to five million farmers, previously tenants without their own land. They became afterward a major conservative political force in the country, supporting the new order which had given them their own farms.

U.S. efforts to encourage small business and labor proved much less successful. The spirit of these reforms resembled Roosevelt's New Deal policies of the 1930s, but it did not take hold among the Japanese business and political elite. An industrial reform broke up several of the giant economic firms, the *zaibatsu*, blamed by Americans for Japanese militarism. The U.S. occupation authorities passed laws with the express purpose of "tearing down the concentration of economic power," to be "redistributed peacefully" among small enterprises. Although many companies disappeared, large Japanese business firms reemerged within a few years and came to dominate once again the country's industrial economy. In addition, new laws protected and encouraged labor unions for factory workers and state employees. It led however to a labor militancy unexpected by the reformers. In postwar conditions of shortages and inflation, workers turned to socialist and Communist union organizers and activists. Many unions came under the control of the Communist party.

Continued labor unrest, manipulated by Communist labor leaders, produced bitter strikes and economic shortages in 1947 and 1948. When the unions threatened a nationwide general strike, MacArthur intervened in Japanese public life, forbidding the action. By then U.S. authorities had decided to emphasize economic order and discipline for the sake of rapid recovery. They sided with Japanese management and withdrew their support for labor unions. This conservative social policy set the pattern for Japanese capitalism in the decades to come. In sum, the U.S. occupation installed in Japan a type of democratic, free enterprise system which evolved into political and economic practices closely resembling those in effect in the 1920s. The partial success of these reforms was due to Japanese cooperation and to the compatibility of the new order with institutions introduced earlier by the Japanese themselves.

The new Japanese political leadership, apparently subservient to the occupation authorities, in fact had an important role to play in the introduction of this new order. Japan had a strong socialist movement, though split into several parties, and the labor unions attracted millions of members on promises of fundamental social improvements. These groups proposed socialist reforms far more extensive than the measures introduced by the American authorities. They had only a brief period in power, however.

In the 1947 elections, the Socialist party received the largest vote—still only 25 percent of the total—and assumed control of the cabinet. Socialist leaders encountered the opposition of the Communists (who obeyed Stalin's militant Cold War policies) and their labor unions, a conflict that seriously weakened the cabinet's political authority. Equally damaging to Socialist rule was the opposition of the U.S. occupation officials, increasingly hostile to left-wing politics. As in Germany, U.S. leaders judged political conservatives best suited to Cold War policies. Socialist reform faded in Japan by early 1948, the victim of the weakness of the Socialist party, of Communist agitation, and of U.S. occupation policy. Political power shifted to the conservatives, organized principally in the coalition of the Liberal and Democratic parties (soon to become one party), whose leader was Shigeru Yoshida.

Yoshida, backed by the U.S. authorities, became the dominant force in Japanese politics for the next years. Dissension among the left-wing parties assured the Liberal-Democratic coalition control in parliament and leadership of the cabinet. The goals of the conservatives were on the one hand to encourage Japanese business interests, and on the other to hasten the end of U.S. occupation. The pressures of the Cold War led the U.S. authorities to rely increasingly on Yoshida, prime minister after 1948, to assist them in their new policies.

In a major policy change (paralleling that in Germany), the United States concluded that Japanese demilitarization no longer constituted its major objective. MacArthur set out in 1948 to make Japan a "self-supporting nation" capable of resisting Soviet pressure from abroad and Communist political agitation from within. Using his occupation powers, he ordered in 1949 that the Japanese government cut its expenses drastically to promote economic growth. Yoshida cooperated, for the budget cuts ended socialist reforms and were supported by Japanese business and financial leaders, key supporters of his party. He also assisted in the creation of an anticommunist labor union movement and in the purge of Communists from administrative and union jobs. The new industrial unions cooperated with management, which held down wages and increased investments (a formula for recovery applied also by the West German government with the encouragement of the United States).

Yoshida's collaboration made him a valuable ally for the United States; it also advanced the political fortunes of his party and the conservative program it supported. By the early 1950s the entire labor union movement had declined, torn by battles between Communists and non-Communists and weakened by the new U.S. occupation policies. The primacy of business interests, the weakening of labor, and conservative political rule by Yoshida's Liberal-Democratic cabinet remained the dominant trends of Japanese internal politics in the decades ahead.

Independent Japan and the West

The question of relations with the United States represented the most important and controversial political issue in postwar Japan. Once the enemy, Japan became in the Cold War years an important ally of the United States. The outbreak of war in Korea and U.S. intervention turned Japan into a major

Far Eastern base for the U.S. military. Its geographical position on the eastern borders of the Soviet Union made it a desirable location for air bases for the U.S. Strategic Air Command, and its ports provided harbors to the U.S. navy. In these conditions the United States decided in 1951 to end the occupation. The reforms had gone into effect; Japanese political leadership was in the hands of conservatives. The peace treaty that year left Japan in possession of its main islands. It lost the Kuril Islands and Sakhalin to the Soviet Union. Formosa belonged to China again, and Okinawa was occupied by the United States. Japan began reparations payments to countries conquered during the war (except China). Although bitter memories of Japanese occupation remained in other Asian lands, in Japan the population behaved as though they had entered a new era in the history of their ancient kingdom.

What policy was Japan to pursue in the power struggle between the Soviet Union and the United States? Some Japanese nationalists hoped to restore Japan to a position of independent East Asian power, protected by its own military forces and free to set its own course between the superpowers. Antimilitarists and pacifists, on the contrary, urged the neutralization of their country, which they argued should take no part in the Cold War and should refuse the presence of any military, either its own or American, on its territory. Prime Minister Yoshida chose a compromise between these two sides. In the U.S.-Japanese Security Treaty of 1952, he accepted a military alliance with the United States, permitting U.S. military bases in Japan and leaving his country (like West Germany) under the protection of the U.S. "nuclear umbrella." He adhered to Cold War policies, of which the most controversial among Japanese was the U.S. opposition to diplomatic and economic relations with Communist China. He refused, on the other hand, to give in to repeated requests from the U.S. government that Japan rearm beyond the minimum level of its self-defense forces. His country remained a "disarmed" state, able to devote its energies and resources to economic growth.

The issue of the U.S. alliance aroused bitter controversy in Japan throughout the 1950s. The Security Treaty set the terms of this uneven alliance between the mightiest military power in the world, the United States, and its former Asian enemy. Opposition to its terms came principally from the Socialist party and from a very strong pacifist movement which became prominent in 1955 at the time of the commemoration of the nuclear destruction of Hiroshima and Nagasaki. In 1959, when the treaty was being renegotiated, political opposition and street demonstrations grew so violent that the government was for a time paralyzed. This was the most acute crisis which Japan's parliamentary regime had confronted since the war. In the end, the Japanese public turned against the violent tactics of the opponents to the new treaty, which was ratified virtually by force in parliament that year. In return, the conservative prime minister bowed to opposition to his authoritarian handling of the crisis by resigning. Parliamentary democracy had survived through a peculiarly Japanese combination of force and diplomacy.

The 1950s represented the time of transition for Japan from postwar recovery to a period of phenomenal economic boom in the 1960s and 1970s. In the decade after the war, the effects of destruction of property, military defeat, and the loss of empire created conditions discouraging to economic enterprise. Lacking foreign markets and shipping, uncertain about the future, Japanese businessmen remained reluctant to begin real reconstruction of the economy. In addition, they feared the consequences of worker unrest and U.S. economic reforms.

By the early 1950s both these issues had been solved to the satisfaction of Japanese industrialists and bankers. The political conservatism of Yoshida and the ruling Democratic-Liberal party protected and reassured investors; the labor movement subsided. Beginning in 1950, massive U.S. purchases of goods for its troops in Korea gave a strong boost to the Japanese economy. The U.S. government permitted Japanese goods unrestricted entry into the American market, and its economic assistance, comparable to the Marshall Plan aid going to Europe, made investment funds available for the modernization of the Japanese economy.

These conditions laid the foundation for the Japanese "economic miracle." Per capita national income reached the prewar level in 1956. At about the same time food rationing finally came to an end, though Japanese families still had to content themselves with a very modest standard of living. Surplus wealth went primarily into economic expansion; the Japanese put in savings an average of 20 percent of their income (in the United States, only 7 percent was saved in the early 1960s). Industries went heavily into debt, using the savings of the Japanese people to invest in new products, new machinery, and the formation of commercial organizations for expanded foreign trade. By the late 1950s the economy was growing at the extraordinary rate of 10 percent a year; national income doubled every seven years. No Western capitalist country had ever matched that rate of expansion.

Foreign observers pondered the "message" of the Japanese miracle. Some pointed to the political commitment of the conservative government to help industry with credits and guidelines for the development of products, a sort of free enterprise planning system. Others emphasized the superior educational level of the Japanese, highly trained and able to adapt easily to a new industrial era of complex technology. Still others underlined the favorable international conditions, including U.S. free trade and technology and the rising demand for products in Asia and the West. Taken altogether, these factors provide important clues to the emergence of Japan, a quarter-century after defeat, as one of the most prosperous countries in the world.

New industries sprang from the enterprise of Japanese businessmen and their ability to use Western technology to make reliable, inexpensive products. The story of some of these entrepreneurs reveals one key to the "miracle." In the late 1940s a young Japanese mechanic, Sochiro Honda, began to make motorcycles at a price far below Western imports. By the end of the 1950s his firm was the largest maker of motorcycles in the world, with markets throughout Asia and in the West. Electronic inventions in the West opened up a new consumer market for television; in 1958 a Japanese electronics engineer started a small firm with $500 and seven workers to make some of these electronic items. His firm, Sony, became within a decade one of the principal world producers of television equipment. Recognition of new opportunities and quality work were important factors assuring the success of Japanese entrepreneurs offering new products for consumers in the expanding global economy.

Individual initiative combined in Japan with the old techniques of giant corporate management and government support. The enterprises, called by the Japanese "business communities," brought into one firm banking, transportation, and sales operations, with branches extending into Asia and the West. Their employees and workers, grouped in "company unions" with guaranteed lifetime employment and high wages, represented the "aristocracy" of the labor force. They were far better off than those workers in small business where labor was poorly paid and unemployment a constant threat.

These giant corporations competed among themselves, yet all benefited from government help. The aid they received came principally from the Ministry of International Trade and Industry. It took the responsibility to forecast future international developments in trade and industry and to set economic objectives for business. Government control over foreign exchange and over licensing of foreign technology permitted it to guide development to the areas it judged most desirable for economic growth. It practiced a form of "guided capitalism."

As in the 1920s, Japanese political stability and economic success depended on foreign sales and access to Western markets. Export was a vital necessity to the country. Three-fourths of all the energy consumed came from imports, increasingly petroleum from the Middle East. "Export or die" remained a guiding principle of government policy. The United States continued to provide the single largest market, taking one-third of Japanese exports. Gradually investors from Japan began, with their new wealth, to purchase banks, factories, and other enterprises in the United States. They collaborated with American businessmen and instructed American workers in new labor-management relations and methods of production. Japan had lost its political dominion but in its place had acquired a vast economic empire. Its government refused to play a role of Asian "policeman" for the United States and persisted in keeping military expenses low. One of the last political reminders of its defeat vanished when in 1970 it regained possession of the island of Okinawa. The war and Japanese militarism had become by then a distant memory.

MAO'S CHINA

Maoism and the Communist Dictatorship

The Chinese Communist party undertook after 1949 the monumental task of transforming the Chinese state and society and of remaking the outlook and values of the vast Chinese population. The leadership of Mao Zedong, the object by then of a semireligious "cult" resembling that of Stalin in Soviet Russia, gave to Chinese communism and to the policies of the new Chinese state unique characteristics we call Maoism. Two reflected the peculiar path to power which Mao had chosen, namely, the special revolutionary role of the peasantry and the importance of the People's Liberation Army in revolutionary war. The third, the product of Mao's own prominence, sanctified both his leadership and his interpretation of Marxism-Leninism.

Ever since the 1920s Mao had encouraged the peasantry's special contribution to the Communist march to power. The experience of those years gave him confidence in their revolutionary zeal. He judged them capable of heeding his call for the construction of socialism with the same energy and dedication they had shown during the struggle against the Nationalists and the Japanese. The hope he placed in the masses emerged in a folksy tale he told in 1946, a simple allegory of his vision of the difficulties confronting his party and of the means to revolutionary progress. The obstacles—imperialism and feudalism—took the guise of "two mountains," whom a "foolish old man"—his party—sought to remove. What to skeptics appeared impossible did not pose an insurmountable difficulty to him, however, since "the masses of the Chinese people" were, under proper party inspiration and guidance, capable of "miracles" as great as moving mountains. This idealized faith in the potential fabulous powers of the mobilized masses remained with him throughout his years in power and inspired extraordinary—and ultimately disastrous—experiments in socialist revolution.

The second key element in Maoism was the importance he attributed to the People's Liberation Army, in his opinion an integral part of the Communist movement. It had been the spearhead of the party in the seizure of power. Its discipline and dedication set the model for the whole revolutionary vanguard, of which it was in some respects the elite. Mao conceived of the PLA as a revolutionary political and military organization, far superior to an ordinary conscript army. No earlier Communist movement had placed such heavy responsibilities on its military organization in the struggle for political power.

Finally, Mao himself encouraged the study of his own writings to provide a unified body of revolutionary wisdom. He had organized during the war years a massive indoctrination program called the "rectification campaign." It consisted of the obligatory study of a body of writings, largely his own. All party members and PLA soldiers had to learn the texts. The message consisted of two principal lessons: (1) the revolutionary ideology of Marxism-Leninism had to be adapted to Chinese conditions, and (2) Mao possessed the creative knowledge to discover the Chinese path to proletarian revolution and to lead the party in its conquest of power. This campaign belittled (without specifically saying so) the Russian communist model of insurrection.

Its most important feature was the emergence of the cult of Mao. By the end of the war, his followers were praising him as "not only the greatest revolutionary statesman in Chinese history, but also its greatest theoretician and scientist." His preeminence in the Communist movement resembled that of Confucius for China's old gentry-scholars. Maoism promised to his followers that the Communist revolution, joining the party and the army and supported by the peasant masses, would lead to the great resurgence of China dreamed of by so many Chinese since the fall of the empire. While attacking Confucianism and feudalism, the new Communist regime was deeply and permanently influenced by the Chinese political culture.

The Chinese Communists conceived of their country's immediate future primarily in the form of Soviet socialist institutions. During their first years in power, they idolized the achievements of the Russian Communists and looked to the Soviet Union for their model of political dictatorship and economic revolution. They considered at that time that the Soviet Union had successfully achieved a socialist society. In doing so, its leaders had uncovered the correct policies which China had to follow on its own road to socialism (not even the Russians claimed then to have found the key opening the door to the Marx's highest stage of human development, the communist society). Mao declared on his visit to Moscow in the winter of 1949–50 that Soviet collectivization, nationalized industry and planning were "models for construction in New China." While the Japanese were in those same years reconstructing their state and economy on the basis of Western democratic and capitalist institutions, China set out to imitate Soviet socialism.

The Chinese leaders encountered enormous problems implementing their revolutionary plans. They had extensive experience governing comparatively small areas during their years of guerrilla war. Suddenly they found themselves ruling a land larger than the continental United States with a population approaching 600 million.

Among them were many who had been on the side of the Communists' enemies. Political convictions and self-interest had incited many Chinese to work with the Nationalists, while others had collaborated with the Japanese. Added to these political divisions were profound social differences among the population. Poverty and illiteracy characterized the peasant masses. In the cities, some capitalist trade and production existed, but the industrial sector of the economy was still very small. China remained an impoverished country, severely damaged by a decade of war, whose new leaders dreamed of building a socialist society of abundance and equality. The revolution had a great distance to go, and some of its leaders, especially Mao, were very impatient.

The formation of new political institutions came first. The ruling organs of the new state copied the Soviet "democratic" system. When the new constitution went into effect in 1954, it gave the Chinese state a National Assembly, chosen by popular election, whose responsibilities included selection of the president of the Republic and of the Council of Ministers, charged with the conduct of state affairs. Behind this democratic facade lay, as in the Soviet Union, the monopoly of power of the Communist party. All candidates to elected political positions had the advance approval of party authorities.

The Communist party itself followed the Leninist principle of centralization of rule in the hands of a Central Committee and a Politburo, whose chairman was Mao Zedong. He also held the positions of president of the Republic and head of the People's Liberation Army. Taken altogether, these responsibilities confirmed his preeminence over the state and the party. His authority was uncontested in those years. Like Lenin (and Stalin, whose power and eminence Mao admired), he set policy guidelines in all areas of state and party action. To the extent that any man could exercise supreme power in so enormous and complex a country, the fate of China lay in his hands. Around the great square in Beijing were hung the portraits of the intellectual giants of revolutionary Marxism, beginning with Marx and Engels, then Lenin and Stalin, and finally Mao. This image of the "apostolic succession" of the Communist movement elevated Mao to the rank of world leader.

Making a Communist revolution on the ruins of the oldest civilization in the world presupposed the purging of enemies and the elimination of rival ideologies. The Communists therefore set up a state administration with the repressive powers to rid the country of political and class opponents. Their measures for the "repression of the enemy classes" began with a purge of the population conducted by the army, the courts, and the secret police (the National Security Forces). A law against "counterrevolutionaries" in 1951 encouraged mass meetings and public denunciations of anti-Communists. No one knows the numbers arrested and sentenced; moderate estimates mention one to three million executions.

The guidelines to punish crimes followed as well a "policy of benevolence" which relied on public humiliation and ideological re-education to correct social and political abuses. The party singled out for particular attention bureaucratic corruption (the "Three Anti's" campaign against authoritarianism, indifference, and bribery) and public abuses of wealth and power (the "Five Anti's" campaign against fraud, bribes, tax evasion, theft of state property). In addition, educated Chinese had to learn the fallacy of their old beliefs and the correctness of Marxism-Leninism-Maoism in a thought-reform campaign which required public self-criticism of ideological errors. Diversity of political belief and action was no longer tolerated. By their own special methods, the Chinese Communists enforced a monopoly of power over their country's political life and thought.

Major reforms altered Chinese society as well as the state. New agrarian laws were introduced in 1950. They included the confiscation of the land of landlords and rich peasants. Almost half of China's arable land changed hands in the next two years, at the end of which every peasant family possessed at least a small plot of land. China had never experienced so massive a shift of wealth. The land remained for the time being the property of individual peasant farmers who worked it for their own benefit. Like the NEP policies of Soviet Russia in the 1920s, which the Chinese leaders were closely imitating, these reforms deferred socialist collectivization until later.

The social reforms undertaken in those years constituted an unprecedented effort to end the subjugation and "bonds" which had characterized earlier Chinese society. The attack on old China included among its targets the traditional family, bastion of Confucianism and ancestor worship. The Chinese Communists championed the principle, defended by the Western socialists since the nineteenth century, of the equality of rights of women. Applied to Chinese society, it required the abolition of the old marriage practices, including infant and forced marriage, concubinage, and infanticide. Divorce became legal as did abortion. The practice of footbinding, symbol of women's subjugation, was finally wiped out, a relic of that "feudal" past the Chinese were asked to put behind them. The family law of 1950 challenged the customs of centuries.

These social reforms became effective only after massive propaganda campaigns and new edicts drove home the message that the revolution would not spare the family. In those years the regime propagated birth control methods to limit the rapid growth of the population. Other Communist social policies included a ruthless campaign against drug addiction, wiped out within a few years, and against illiteracy, which slowly diminished. Political dictatorship and sweeping social reforms brought the power of the new state and of the party into the personal lives of the Chinese population. In the process, the party introduced an appreciable measure of equality into Chinese social relations.

These reforms became the foundation of the new Communist regime. They went into effect with apparent ease, although the private thoughts and habits of so many millions of people could not be altered overnight. After Mao's death, drastic changes occurred in economic policy, but the transformation of China accomplished in the early revolutionary years was substantial and permanent. A Communist dictatorship had embedded itself in China, adapting in the decades to come to the old political culture but never permitting a return to the past, either in public or private life. The reforms also prepared the way for the mobilization of the population for the great socialist revolution ahead. The experience apparently deepened Mao's conviction that the Chinese masses could achieve extraordinary feats of social progress. When the war in Korea finally ended in 1953, he began preparations for the great transformation of his country. He was encouraged in these plans by remarkable political changes occurring at that time in the Soviet Union.

Maoist China and Soviet Socialism

Stalin's death in early 1953 opened a new period in Soviet relations with China. His heirs confronted serious problems in domestic and foreign policy, some the result of the oppressive weight of his police empire, some coming from his search for absolute power in and around the Soviet Union, and some emerging from new developments for which he was himself in part responsible. They had to decide among themselves how to rule the country without permitting the reemergence of one-man dictatorship and police terror, agreeing finally on a form of "collective leadership" in which one man, Nikita Khrushchev became for several years the principal policymaker (see Chapter 11). They began a process of "destalinization," first secretly then publicly condemning the crimes Stalin had committed. In doing this, they challenged the legitimacy of one-man leadership in a Communist state. Mao, whose position in China resembled somewhat Stalin's, believed their actions excessive and their judgment faulty.

At the same time, they revised substantially Soviet foreign policy. These changes included the improvement of relations with the West, concessions to the other Communist states, and new agreements with independent neutral states in Asia and Africa. They broke the isolation in which Stalin had forced their state, partly out of concern to avoid nuclear war, partly to expand Soviet diplomatic influence in the postimperialist age. The new policy toward the United States, termed "peaceful coexistence," accepted the possibility of good relations with the "imperialist camp." Their military might, in their opinion, made unlikely an attack from the West. It also heightened the danger of accidental nuclear war unless Cold War tensions were reduced. The Chinese leaders were prepared to cooperate in the effort to end the Cold War conflicts, for their country had for three years been at war with the United States in Korea. They were suspicious, on the other hand, of "peaceful coexistence" with the American imperialists, who protected and armed their Nationalist enemies in Taiwan (Formosa).

The post-Stalinist era began a brief period of close collaboration between the two leading Communist states. Both governments were eager to bring the Korean and the Indochina wars to an end. The reasons which lay behind their decision are hidden in the secret records of Kremlin and Beijing deliberations. They undoubtedly knew of the threat by President Eisenhower's new administration to increase its military effort in Korea and may also have heard the rumors (spread intentionally) that it was considering the use of nuclear weapons. They were aware that the Soviet Union remained militarily much weaker than the United States despite possession of its own atomic bombs. The Chinese were particularly eager to end the stalemated conflict in Korea, for the war deferred domestic economic development by draining manpower and resources to a war which brought the Chinese no benefits and heavy casualties (including one of Mao's sons). In the spring of 1953, the demand by Communist negotiators for the forced repatriation of all Communist prisoners in Allied hands, including those who preferred not to return to North Korea or China, was dropped. That summer, the Korean conflict finally ended.

The armistice agreement left in place the Korean enemies whose rivalry for rule of the peninsula had created the conflict in the first place. After three years of fighting, the North Korean Communists ruled a country whose cities were in ruins and whose industrial economy had barely survived American bombardments by borrowing underground. They depended more than ever on Soviet aid, though they still vowed some day to "liberate" the south. In the southern half of the country, the state was ruled by Syngman Rhee, a virtual dictator after the years of war. He governed a land deeply scarred by battle and as dependent on U.S. economic assistance and military protection as his northern enemies were on Soviet backing. The end of that war left no side the victor, but did remove one conflict which risked escalating into a global nuclear war.

The following year, the Chinese and Russians again collaborated in ending another war along China's borders which involved the Western powers. The Chinese Communists had begun in 1950 to provide military aid to the Vietnamese guerrillas fighting the French. The war did not lead to Communist victory, however, and by 1954 the United States was becoming increasingly involved in support of the anti-Communist Vietnamese and the French (see the discussion under "Indochinese War and Vietnamese Communism" later in this chapter). That new "war of liberation" threatened in its own way the progress of the Chinese revolution. The French government, no longer prepared to pursue a conflict it could not win, agreed to negotiations in Geneva in 1954. Representatives from Communist China and the Soviet Union participated, alongside Vietnamese delegates and the French. Acting together, they persuaded Ho Chi Minh, leader of the Vietnamese guerrillas, to accept the partition of Vietnam, leaving only the north in Communist hands. It was not an agreement to the liking of the Vietnamese Communists, but, lacking Chinese and Russian help to continue the war for the conquest of all Vietnam, they had to agree. To pursue their internal reforms, the Chinese Communists became partisans of political, not military conquest of power by revolutionary forces. Like the Soviets before them, they placed highest priority on the needs of their own revolution.

In those years the Soviet leaders were prepared to help them in their ambitious plans. Mao did not make public his misgivings about public attacks on Stalin or about "peaceful coexistence" with the United States. These disagreements were less important than Soviet diplomatic concessions and economic aid. The new Soviet leaders publicly acknowledged China's rank as an equal in the "socialist camp." They renounced the special concessions Stalin had demanded, withdrawing entirely from Manchuria (and abandoning their Chinese Communist ally in that region, who quietly disappeared). They agreed to expand their economic aid, providing China in the following five years with machinery, credits, and technical assistance worth billions of dollars. The next few years were a "honeymoon" in the relations between Soviet Union and China.

Peace in Korea and Indochina and improved relations with the Soviet Union constituted the essential international conditions for the "socialist transformation" of China. The Russians had waited eight years for recovery under the New Economic Policy before initiating major economic reforms. Mao allowed only five years, believing fervently in the ability of the Chinese masses under his leadership to build socialism. He, like Stalin, looked forward to a social and economic transformation of his country so profound it would represent a "revolution from above."

Following the Soviet example, the Chinese leaders adopted the principal institutions of socialist revolution—command planning, collectivization, rapid industrialization of the state-controlled economy. In 1955 they introduced their first Five-Year Plan for economic development. That same year, Mao, in the spirit of Stalin's 1929 collectivization campaign, ordered the rapid replacement of private farming by collective farms. He claimed to see a "new upsurge in the socialist mass movement throughout the countryside." Calling for a class war of peasants on wealthy farmers, he launched a campaign for collectivization on the Soviet model. Although serious opposition to this abrupt rural revolution existed among the party leadership, Mao's authority was sufficiently great to override the objections from his colleagues.

The end of private farming permitted the socialization of ownership of the land and also the exploitation of agricultural wealth to promote rapid industrialization. In 1955 the state nationalized all private commerce and industry, the former owners allowed to remain only as employees or managers. Aping the Russians, the Chinese leaders introduced strict controls on peasant consumption to turn agricultural production to the benefit of the cities and the industrial population. By 1956 the entire Chinese economy was under state control. Mao expected miracles of socialist development, pointing to the Soviet experience to justify his claim. "The Soviet Union's great historical experience in building socialism inspires our people," he wrote that year, "and gives them full confidence that they can build socialism in their country." Never again did Mao refer in such glowing terms to Soviet socialism.

In fact, it appears that Mao had by then serious doubts regarding the revolutionary potential of his party, the benefits of Soviet-type industrialization, and the wisdom of the new Soviet leadership. This transformation is masked in the revolutionary rhetoric of his public pronouncements, yet we have good reason to conclude that his search for a new, unique Chinese path to socialism began that year. What provoked his dissatisfaction with his earlier plans?

In the first place, industrialization was producing in his country results which he had not anticipated. The Five-Year Plan had launched the rapid expansion of Chinese industry, but the price was high. Workers, technicians, and factory managers in the urban areas began to earn more and to live more comfortably than before, encouraged to increase their productivity by rewarding those who worked well with higher wages and other benefits—called by the Soviets "material incentives." However, the conditions of the Chinese peasants on their collective farms remained miserable. Industrialization produced more, not less, inequality. This trend ran contrary to Mao's deeply held conviction of socialist equality. Social justice, not productivity, was his objective. His slogan of "walking on two legs," launched shortly afterward, emphasized the need to develop agriculture as well as industry and to help the peasantry as well as the townspeople.

In the second place, imitation of the Soviet policies undermined Mao's own leadership, for it strengthened the power of moderate party leaders. These men (including Zhou Enlai, chairman of the council of ministers, and Deng Xiaoping, who became in the late 1970s Mao's successor) emphasized orderly change, rational economic policies, and strict limits on arbitrary leadership. They had objected to his abrupt decision for rapid collectivization in 1955. In the course of 1956 they attempted to restrict his power within the party leadership. They took inspiration from the new attacks on Stalin, accused publicly by Soviet leaders of fostering a "cult of the personality" which strongly resembled Maoism in China. Mao appears never to have doubted that he remained, as his admirers called him, the Great Helmsman of the Chinese revolution and that his opponents were in one form or another enemies of true communism.

Finally, Mao appears to have come to the conviction that the new Soviet leadership was no longer inspired in its domestic or foreign policies by a correct understanding of Marxism-Leninism. In the spirit of the Protestant church reformers challenging the Catholic papacy at the time of the Reformation in Europe, he came to believe that he grasped better than they the ideological truths necessary to lead humanity to salvation in a communist society. In later years he damned Khrushchev for allowing a form of capitalism to undermine the Soviet economic system and for permitting a corrupt bureaucracy to take power. He also objected to the eagerness of Soviet leaders to maintain good relations with the United States, which to him was the principal obstacle standing in the way of the victory of the "socialist camp." We cannot appreciate the bitterness of the impending conflict between the Soviet Union and China without keeping in mind the importance to both sides of the communist ideology. United until then in one secular "church," their dispute led each party to damn the other as heretics. The origins of this great schism in the "socialist camp" lay in Mao's determination to lead his country along a unique Chinese road to communism.

The Great Leap Forward

The Maoist revolution began with public criticism of the existing conditions in Communist China. Mao's first step consisted in making clear that all was not well in his country. He did so by mobilizing the intellectuals, from whom he could hope to hear strong criticism of inequalities and injustices among the people and of policies of his party opponents. In 1957, the new campaign began under the banner of images of "a hundred flowers" blooming and "a hundred schools" contending to promote "socialist culture." Mao confidently predicted that Marxism in China had nothing to fear from such frank discussion, for "Marxists need to steel and improve themselves."

Criticism focused largely on abuses by officials in the state and party organizations, and on hardships created by the industrialization drive, all mistakes Mao blamed on his colleagues and their misguided policies. By late 1957 he had taken back into his hands the reins of party leadership. Having let intellectuals reveal the "contradictions"

caused in Chinese society by the introduction of Soviet-type socialist reforms, he allowed the party to repress the outspoken critics. The Hundred Flowers wilted quickly in late 1957, replaced by Mao's Great Leap Forward toward communism.

His conviction of the leading role of China in world revolution was revealed to the Soviet leaders late that year. In November 1957, he traveled to Moscow to join in the celebrations of the fortieth anniversary of the Bolshevik Revolution. The Soviet leaders had many reasons for celebration, among them the launching earlier that year of the first artificial earth satellite, *Sputnik*. The Soviet Union had succeeded as well in its drive to build intercontinental ballistic missiles.

In a speech to the assembled delegates of the world Communist movement, Mao made clear his conviction that the socialist camp had to prepare for war. Imperialism (meaning the United States) would in his opinion never allow the Communist countries to develop and to triumph peacefully. In concrete terms, he expected the Soviet military to deploy their nuclear missiles to defend China from U.S. aggression. If nuclear war came, he was sure China would survive. Mao considered Soviet military support for his country to be more important than "peaceful coexistence." Soviet and Chinese national interests were beginning to diverge seriously. His statements at the anniversary celebration uncovered his profound belief that he, best of all Communist leaders, understood the future direction of revolutionary world struggle.

This conviction inspired his new social and economic policies. He had proclaimed in Moscow that "the East wind prevails over the West wind." In one sense, he suggested that socialism would inevitably triumph over capitalism. In a deeper sense he may have meant that the Chinese way to communism was the correct path. In early 1958 he set out to prove that this was true. He based his hopes on the assumption that the Chinese masses were capable of such prodigies of work, of such superhuman efforts and of such radical improvements in their collective institutions that their will power and his leadership would bring to China in a few years both abundance and communist egalitarianism. He wrote that the "600 million people of China" were like a "clean sheet of paper" on which "the newest and most beautiful pictures can be painted." He asked that they assist him in a Great Leap Forward. By implication, he suggested that communism would come more quickly in China than in Russia.

In concrete terms his vision required that the old methods of socialist construction be either abandoned or seriously modified. Rational economic planning had to end, for it was worthless and harmful. He argued that in a year Chinese workers and peasants could by their own efforts raise economic production by 100 percent, could complete enormous dams and flood control projects, and could transform collective farming into communistic farming. He proposed the creation of rural communes, relatively few in number and grouping up to 100,000 peasant households. They were to be organized on egalitarian principles, with no special benefits to good workers and no separate garden plots or private houses. Families would organize their lives collectively with meals and child care provided by the commune.

The focus of economic activity in China shifted to the countryside. Mao believed that the new communes would be so effective that millions of farmers could leave to work on great construction projects. Farm laborers themselves would produce consumer goods, even their own iron in small blast furnaces. As a result of his utopian faith in the collective labor of the Chinese peasantry, the priority assigned industrial production van-

ished. Industrial funds were cut back and supplies diverted to the communes. Mao wrote just before the campaign got under way that "there is no difficulty in the world" the masses cannot overcome "if only they take their destiny into their own hands." Since mass work was required, more Chinese were needed, and birth control had to end (it did not return until twenty years later when the country's population had grown by another 300 million). The Great Leap Forward revealed Mao's extraordinary revolutionary populism and utopianism.

The reality was near disaster. The worst consequences resulted from the radical reorganization of agriculture. Peasant farmers lost incentive to work, were taken from their farming for great irrigation and flood prevention projects, and spent long hours in political indoctrination meetings. Agricultural production in 1959 and 1960 declined seriously, and hunger again spread through the Chinese countryside. We still do not know the full extent or the exact causes of the famine that occurred in the early 1960s. Despite severe rationing and the decision in 1961 to import large quantities of grain, millions (some estimates suggest fifteen million) died as a result of hunger and disease provoked largely by Mao's disastrous experiment in mass mobilization. Industrial production fell, then stagnated in the early 1960s. Only in 1965 did it recover to its pre-1958 level. Mao's dream had seriously damaged Chinese economic development and undermined the well-being of the population whose salvation he claimed to seek.

These critical conditions permitted Mao's opponents in the party leadership to end the Great Leap Forward. They publicly criticized "guerrilla methods" in politics and put the blame for the country's ills on an unnamed "dead ancestor," who could only be Mao. Yet this reversal of policy did not lead to his removal from office. Mao's authority as Great Helmsman of the Chinese revolution ensured his protection from attack. In late 1959, the commander-in-chief of the Red Army criticized Mao for causing suffering among the Chinese and destroying the Soviet alliance. For having spoken out, he himself was forced to resign, replaced by Mao's close ally, Lin Biao. Still, for a few years Mao had to suppress his dissatisfaction with the course of his country's social revolution. His vision of egalitarian socialism no longer set policy, and he became a "venerated ancestor" among the party leadership.

His revolutionary policies hastened the breakup of the Sino-Soviet alliance. Many issues divided China and Russia by the late 1950s. Disputes over territorial questions and differing policies toward the United States were bound to strain the ties between the two most powerful Communist states. In addition, Mao challenged the authority of the Soviet leadership by his Great Leap Forward policies, which promised to take the Chinese right over the heads of the Russians and to place Mao at the forefront of the world Communist movement. In 1960 Mao accused the Russian Communists of betraying Leninism and selling out the cause of world revolution. Khrushchev in retaliation stopped all Soviet assistance, refusing help in Chinese nuclear development and breaking the economic aid agreement. Within a few weeks all Soviet technicians left, and factories being built by the Russians stood abandoned.

The "Second World" of Communist countries split apart as a result of the growing Soviet-Chinese dispute. China was isolated, supported only by a few Communist parties and governments. To Soviet leaders, good relations with neutral Third World countries became as important as their relations with China. At about the same time as their quarrel erupted with China, they agreed to sell arms to India. These two Asian giants had been unable to settle a territorial dispute along their Himalayan frontier. In 1950 Chinese troops had seized the kingdom of Tibet and later began building a strategic highway into that land from the northwest. The Indian government refused to cede the territory and threatened to move its own troops there. Although isolated, the Chinese leaders prepared for war. The Sino-Indian dispute ended in 1962 in brief border war in which Chinese troops defeated Indian forces and occupied the disputed area (see Chapter 9). The Soviet Union remained neutral. The Sino-Soviet alliance had collapsed. Its disappearance began a fundamental and long-lasting change in the Asian balance of power.

The Great Cultural Revolution

The years between 1960 and 1965 were a period of temporary calm before a new and even more violent revolutionary offensive by Mao and his supporters. The agricultural communes relaxed their egalitarian rules. The recovery of agriculture required a large investment of state funds, allocated in those years according to pragmatic criteria of need and productivity. Although powerless to prevent these changes, Mao refused to compromise, condemning his colleagues for their "bourgeois" spirit contrary to true communism. He promoted his ideals—and his "cult"—in a little red book entitled *Quotations from Chairman Mao*. Its distribution was assured by the People's Liberation Army, under Lin Biao's control. To make it available to the entire Chinese population and to foreign supporters, one billion copies were printed.

Its principal audience in China came largely from the country's youth, among whom admiration for the Great Helmsman was deep and unquestioning. Mao encouraged their "socialist education" in his thought and their support for his ideals. In his mind there emerged a picture of an ongoing conflict in China between forces of evil—his enemies—and of good—the masses, the army, and the students. Chinese youth constituted in his view a revolutionary class whom he intended to throw into a new "class struggle." His immediate objective was to end the "counterrevolutionary restoration" of those he called a new exploiting "bourgeoisie"—well-paid professionals, intellectuals, and party bureaucrats. In a manner recalling Stalin's Great Terror, he was preparing to institute a new class war against his own party and the educated elite of his country.

The decade of turmoil which began in 1966 had no parallel in the history of previous Communist revolutions. It involved both the Chinese state and society, destroying party institutions and patterns of rule; reorganizing education, industry, and agriculture; and demolishing the relics of traditional culture. So chaotic were conditions that the full story remains obscure. In 1966, Mao was still the revered leader of his people, able to mobilize supporters among the students, workers, and soldiers to participate in his new Cultural Revolution. That year he made clear who the enemies were, warning that "the bourgeois agents who have infiltrated the party, the government, the army and all sectors of cultural life constitute a gang of counterrevolutionary revisionists. At the first opportunity they will seize power and substitute the dictatorship of the bourgeoisie for the dictatorship of the proletariat."

Mao's principal weapon in this class war was a mass movement to promote what he called the Great Proletarian Cultural Revolution. His ultimate goal was nothing less than the destruction of the old party leadership and the creation of a new revolutionary regime, consisting of "revolutionary mass organizations," running a country rid of greedy bureaucrats, profit seekers, and ego-

tistical intellectuals. His fantastic plans for a new revolutionary order relied on the three features of Maoism he had created before the revolution: mass mobilization, military combat, and faith in his own leadership. We still do not know how he managed to win sufficient backing from party leaders to begin a campaign which they must have known threatened their policies and their power. Somehow, in 1966 he obtained from the ruling party committees approval for the creation of a special committee to organize and lead a Great Cultural Proletarian Revolution. This organization launched a propaganda campaign in mid-1966 calling on all 700 million Chinese to "destroy the old world." The first recruits for the Cultural Revolution came from the student youth. That fall all regular university and high school studies ceased (the interruption lasted nearly ten years). Students had better things to do than learn, for Mao called them to lead his new revolution.

The Red Guards constituted the revolutionary organization of Chinese youth. Their appearance coincided with Mao's reemergence at the head of the Cultural Revolution, an event symbolized by his much-publicized swim of the Yangze River in July 1966. Supposedly covering 15 kilometers (about 9 miles) in one hour, his physical prowess conveyed a message of political as well as physical rejuvenation (he was 73 years old). That August, he gathered together one million Red Guards youth at the Gate of Heavenly Peace in Beijing, appearing before them just as the sun rose in the east. His message was simple: "Destroy the old and construct the new." That fall and winter violence swept the country as these self-proclaimed revolutionaries organized mass demonstrations, attacked "counterrevolutionaries," imprisoned party officials, and destroyed old monuments and shrines of China's past. Centers of resistance emerged when party officials mobilized their own supporters to oppose this "children's crusade."

At the same time, Mao ordered workers to destroy the vestiges of capitalism in the factories by ending unequal wage scales favoring the skilled and productive workers and by taking control of the factory from the manager. These Maoist workers formed committees for revolutionary combat and class struggle. They constituted the second wave in Mao's offensive against "counterrevolution."

Little still is known of the tumultuous events in the ten years that followed. Serious disorders accompanied the attack on party officials and factory administrations. Rival groups of Red Guards fought for leadership and battled too with worker organizations claiming to defend the "true" Maoist line. Punishment for "class enemies" included public humiliation, exile to the countryside, imprisonment, even death by beating. Cities like Canton and Shanghai experienced such violence it resembled civil war.

In these conditions, units of the People's Liberation Army began in 1967 to intervene to enforce public order and to settle the conflicts. Mao authorized the army to "supervise" the economic and political affairs of the provinces. He introduced in this manner a third force in his revolution. The army commanders did not seek to militarize the Chinese state. Instead, they organized revolutionary committees grouping representatives of workers, students, and the military in a very disorderly and unstable coalition. They replaced the old regional and city party committees, a prime target in the Cultural Revolution. The guiding principle of action of these committees consisted of the "three loyalties": loyalty to the "person, the thought, and the policies" of Mao Zedong. Maoism constituted the very essence of the Cultural Revolution.

Mao's revolutionary regime proved incapable either of governing the country effectively or of establishing new institutions for socialist revolution. The PLA became by default the backbone of political rule throughout the country. At a party congress held in early 1969, the head of the PLA, Lin Biao, second only to Mao in political power, proclaimed that the Great Cultural Revolution had triumphed. The reality appears to have been extraordinary turmoil. PLA provincial military commanders represented the sole remnants of political authority in the country. The tasks of industrial construction, training of professionals, and scientific research had all been abandoned in the upheaval. Hundreds of thousands of scientists, specialists, and teachers were forced to seek "reeducation" by assuming menial tasks in agricultural communes. Even the peasants, untouched by political turmoil, felt the impact of the Cultural Revolution in their work. All manifestations of "capitalism," including private plots of farmland and pay incentives for higher agricultural productivity, disappeared again from the communes. China had entered a period of "permanent revolution" from which it did not emerge finally until Mao's death in 1976.

Relations with the Soviet Union became so strained in those years that war appeared likely. Mao's supporters treated the Soviet Union as if it had become the principal enemy of China. They condemned the Soviet party bureaucracy, calling it a "bourgeoisie" who had completely abandoned the world socialist revolution and who exploited the wealth of the country for their own sake. The Soviet embassy in Beijing was attacked and burned by Red Guards. The Chinese press published maps claiming most of eastern Siberia to be rightfully part of China (these lands had belonged before the nineteenth century to the Chinese Empire). Chinese border troops attempted to occupy small areas along the frontier. The result was pitched battles with Soviet forces in 1969, and sporadic violence all along the border that year and the next. The Soviet leadership seems to have concluded that Mao was as dangerous and aggressive as Hitler had once been. They clearly believed the threat of war with China was very serious, for they moved large military forces, including nuclear missiles, to their eastern region bordering China. The conflict between Russia and China became a "new cold war."

The End of Maoism

Gradually a reaction against internal turmoil and foreign danger brought an end to the period of revolutionary zealotry of the Great Cultural Revolution. Once again Zhou Enlai, the chairman of the council of ministers and the most influential moderate party leader, resumed his role in policy making. The process by which power changed hands again remains unclear. The mystery is greatest surrounding the first and most dramatic incident in their recovery, the fall of Lin Biao, head of the PLA. In August 1971, an official communiqué stated that Lin had tried to seize control of the government. Failing in his attempt, he and his military advisers had fled by plane in the direction of the Soviet Union, only to be shot down over Mongolia by Soviet fighter planes. Whatever the real events might be, Mao's strongest supporter was dead. In 1972, the Red Guards were formally dissolved, most of the members sent to work in the countryside where they could no longer be Maoist revolutionaries.

In the late 1970s, the Maoist revolutionary order was dismantled. Mao himself died in 1976, honored for his role in conquering China, but no longer judged the Great Helmsman of Chinese socialism. The funeral of Zhou Enlai, who died the same year, was the occasion for demonstrations and a remarkable outpouring of grief, a public statement revealing both the pain and suffering which the Maoist radicals had caused and the eagerness in the country for new, moderate policies. Mao's successors heeded the call for a new beginning for Chinese socialism. They abandoned all that was left of the Maoist revolution.

In the late 1970s and early 1980s, the new party leadership, headed by Deng Xiaoping, introduced new policies which substantially altered the entire social and economic system of Chinese socialism. Education, science, and technology became a high priority. The new economic reforms set up what is called a type of "market socialism," that is, a combination of state ownership of industry and guidance of agriculture, along with private enterprises and incentives to reward efficiency and productivity. Collectivized farming was reorganized so thoroughly in 1978 that the new system resembled a form of private farming. Chinese farmers, attracted by the promise of consumer goods, proved so successful in growing crops that by the mid-1980s China had a surplus of food for export. The new leaders also abandoned the Soviet method of command planning, allowing enterprises to work for profit, inviting foreigners to open their own factories in certain areas, and authorizing private stores to compete for customers.

In these conditions, what remained of Chinese socialism? The leaders made clear that the dictatorship of the party was immutable and that Western political liberties had no place in their vast country, whose population exceeded one billion in the early 1980s. The power of the state was directed to such tasks as enforcing a Draconian policy of birth control, in theory limiting families to one child only. The party still asserted, as Lenin had long before argued, that it possessed the wisdom to organize and lead the people to socialism. But no one claimed to know what a real socialist society was or when communism would emerge in China.

Important changes took place in Chinese foreign policy as well. Mao's dream of world proletarian revolution gave way to a recognition of the necessities of Chinese national security. The Soviet Union presented a serious threat to China, far greater than that posed by the United States. Secret talks initiated in 1971 by the Chinese premier, Zhou Enlai, led in the spring of 1972 to the visit of President Nixon to Beijing. The United States remained the leading capitalist state, yet its naval and nuclear might counterbalanced that of the Soviet Union. At the very least, improved relations with Washington gave the Chinese Communists the assurance that war with the United States was avoidable. Immediately afterward, Japan and China, once bitterest of enemies, resumed diplomatic ties, and the Japanese began developing their trade with China. In the world of the 1970s, the Chinese Communist state no longer based its foreign relations on the ideals of a crusading revolutionary movement. It remained a supporter of socialist states in the Third World, but emphasized above all its own vital interests of security and economic development. In the new pattern of global relations of the 1980s, it was one of the major powers of East Asia.

INDOCHINESE WAR AND VIETNAMESE COMMUNISM

Like China, the land the French imperialists named Indochina experienced decades of war between Communist forces and their allies, on the one hand, and nationalist enemies and foreign powers on the other. Un-

like China, however, it lacked one dominant ethnic group and political culture. The French had created one colony of many peoples, among whom the Vietnamese and the Khmer had the two largest populations (and were bitter enemies). It was divided as well by competing religious groups, with many Buddhists but also an important new Catholic community. Like China, its economy was based primarily on agriculture, with many large estates owned by a few wealthy landowners and worked by a poor peasant population. It resembled many other colonial lands in the fact that, by the middle of the twentieth century, its peoples were prepared for nationalist and social revolt against imperialist rule.

The political conflict in Indochina began at the end of the Second World War. In Indochina, the center of the struggle lay in the populous coastal region known as Vietnam. It provided the recruits for the Vietnamese Communist party, whose founder and leader was Ho Chi Minh. He, like Mao Zedong, believed absolutely in the inevitability of global proletarian revolution, one part of which was the fight against imperialism in his land. He honored the leadership and wisdom of the Russian Communists, but, in this also resembling Mao, he and his party represented an independent revolutionary party in the world Communist movement. The immediate objective of the Vietnamese Communists was the conquest of all Indochina.

Their principal enemy at the end of the Second World War was France. In 1945, the new French state had begun to reestablish control over its former empire. During the war Japan had occupied Indochina with the help of Vietnamese collaborators. In a gesture of defiance of the Allies, the Japanese commander had before surrendering in 1945 proclaimed Indochinese independence. The withdrawal of his forces permit-

Mao   Lin. Chou . CCP .
total victory   Chiang-Taiwan

store some form of French imperial domination, in 1946 they attacked the Communist-occupied areas in Vietnam and quickly moved their troops into the inland regions of Cambodia and Laos. The Communists and their nationalist allies retreated to the countryside, where they, like their Chinese comrades to the north, resumed guerrilla war.

The French Indochina War and the Partition of Vietnam

In its first years a French colonial war, the conflict in Indochina became a part of the Cold War when the U.S. government intervened in 1950 on the side of the French. In the previous years, the war had not gone well for French forces. They had tried to obtain the backing of nationalists there by creating in 1949 the independent states of Vietnam, Cambodia, and Laos, yet they attracted few active supporters and had to bear the principal burden of the bloody fighting. French generals promised quick victory against the guerrilla forces of their enemies, but could not end the insurrection. Their standing army, made up of both Vietnamese and French soldiers, occupied key urban areas, but the countryside lay beyond their control.

There the Vietnamese Communists set up their own rule, much like Mao's "liberated areas" in Chinese rural areas in the 1930s. They were the only strong nationalist movement and found support from other anti-French groups. Then as later, they dominated the guerrilla movement, appropriating the symbols and mystique of anti-imperialist nationalist resistance for their own "war of liberation." Their resistance forces grew in strength among the Vietnamese population both because they promised to eliminate economic exploitation and social inequality and because of nationalist backing. They expanded even more when the Communists triumphed in China. The

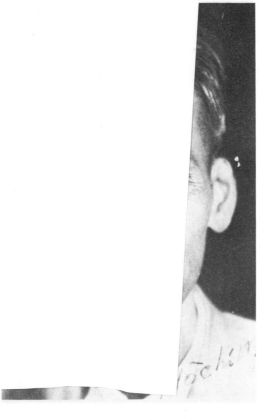

Vietnamese Communist Leader Ho Chi Minh. (*David Barrett Collection/Hoover Institution Archives*)

ted the Vietnamese Communists, the principal anti-Japanese resistance force, to claim leadership of the Republic of Vietnam. Prepared to negotiate with the postwar French government, Ho traveled to Paris in 1946. Had an agreement been reached there, Indochina would have very soon become a Communist country.

French imperialist dreams stood in the way, however. While talking of eventual freedom for Indochina, French officials and military commanders there were absolutely opposed to Communist rule. Resolved to re-

Chinese leaders opened the border to provide military supplies to Ho's forces. That increased aid ensured the failure of French efforts to repress the Communist insurgents.

In 1950 the U.S. government finally became actively involved in the Indochina war. It changed its view of that conflict, judged previously a French effort to restore an outdated empire, when it decided that Indochina was part of the global battle between the Free World and communism. Disregarding evidence of the independence of the Vietnamese Communist party, the U.S. government concluded that a Communist victory in Indochina represented a strategic threat to the stability of all Southeast Asia and would constitute a victory of global Communist forces. That was a misguided, and ultimately tragic decision. The reasons lie partly in anti-Communist political forces within the United States, outraged at the "loss" of China and so dedicated to a crusade on communism they paid no attention to the human and material cost of intervention in Indochina. They also lie partly in the hysteria generated by the Cold War fear of Stalin, assumed to be conducting a global plan of conquest (North Korea's aggression appeared proof of this theory). As a result, the French found an ally, and the United States found itself in the eyes of many Vietnamese the new Western imperialist invader.

Beginning in 1950, the United States began to provide France with military and economic aid for the war in Indochina. In return, it demanded of the French that they finally suppress the Communist guerrillas. Not only was the French army unable to do so, but in the attempt it suffered a major military defeat. By 1953, its forces were overextended by its campaign to wipe out the Communist insurrection throughout the country. It could not protect its mountain fortress of Dienbienphu, encircled by the Communists. The surrender of the fort and

its ten thousand troops in early 1954 ended the French efforts to retain control of Indochina.

That year, a new French government concluded that their forces could not win the war. Like the Chinese Communists before them, the Vietnamese Communists proved capable of sustained, costly fighting in pursuit of their goal of national liberation. Although their losses were heavy, they continued the struggle thanks to the readiness of so many Vietnamese to sacrifice their lives and well-being to defeat the foreign enemy. It was a lesson learned by the French at great human cost; later the United States would learn it at even greater cost, both to the United States and to Indochina. The French people were by 1954 unwilling to continue the fighting. Their army had suffered 100,000 casualties in a war draining the wealth of the French economy for control of a distant country of no vital importance. The glories of imperial dominion no longer attracted them. Although the French army still occupied much of Indochina, the government in 1954 accepted to negotiate with the Vietnamese Communists.

At that point the U.S. government expanded even further its involvement in Indochina. It was one of the participants at the Geneva conference which negotiated the end of the war. Representatives from the Communist and non-Communist Vietnamese governments and France were there, as were delegates from Communist China and the Soviet Union. Peace in Indochina was an international affair. The French and American negotiators sought a partitioned Vietnam, limiting the Communists to the northern half where their centers of strength were located. Although they had forces in the south as well, the Communist delegates found no support for the formation of a large Communist state even from the Soviet Union and Communist

China. The Russians and Chinese, determined on a quick settlement to the war, assured Ho Chi Minh that he could achieve unification easily without further fighting. His forces, still the only strong, organized political movement in the country, would easily take over all Vietnam in the elections planned for 1956 to end partition. Ho accepted the temporary partition of Vietnam, and in 1954 the French Indochina war came to an end.

State Building in North and South Vietnam

The Eisenhower government was determined to prevent Communist seizure of the south. The new policy was the work of the U.S. secretary of state, John Foster Dulles, whose foreign policy turned containment of Soviet power into a campaign to defeat Communist movements in any country outside the "socialist camp." Although U.S. officials warned that South Vietnam had a slim chance to survive, he brought out of exile a nationalist leader, Ngo Dinh Diem, to become ruler of the new state. U.S. agents from the Central Intelligence Agency (CIA) began to organize the hunt for Communists in the south and U.S. military advisers took over the task of forming a new army. U.S. economic and military aid poured into the country; by 1960, South Vietnam had received over $1 billion in American assistance, which became vital to the very functioning of its state and economy. Dulles's determination to create a noncommunist state in the place of a French colony turned the United States into the "nation builder" of South Vietnam. The result was the emergence of a U.S. political satellite under "client" nationalist leaders who could not survive without American support. In President Kennedy's words, South Vietnam was "our offspring."

That effort at creating a non-Communist

Vietnamese state represented an audacious gamble, probably doomed from the start. In a land divided by political rivalries and with no strong institutions or outstanding non-Communist nationalist leader to guarantee the stability of a new political order, the problems of nation building under the best of circumstances would have been daunting. Nearly one million refugees fled from Communist rule in the north, most of them Catholics fearing Ho's political dictatorship and Communist repression of religion. Most of the southern Vietnamese were poor peasants, reluctant to support either the Communists or the Diem regime for fear of persecution by the other side. Diem gave them no reason to risk their lives for him. He chose to ally with the wealthy landowners of the country, who opposed any expropriation of their land for redistribution among the peasantry. Diem, despite U.S. requests for reform, heeded their wishes.

His main interest lay in strengthening his personal power, threatened principally by the Communist underground movement (called the Vietcong) in the south. With U.S. encouragement, he refused to hold the elections on Vietnam reunification, scheduled for 1956, knowing that the Communists possessed still the means to manipulate the voting to ensure their own victory. Instead, he built up his police and army, used primarily as instruments for internal repression. They proved effective in weakening the Communist party, over half of whose members were dead, in prison, or had moved to the north. His goal for Vietnam was an authoritarian, conservative state protecting landowners and business and subsidized by the United States. A similar political formula had worked in South Korea, far more integrated for centuries and independent after 1945. Diem lacked sufficient support among the Vietnamese and, most important, confronted a dynamic Communist revolutionary movement opposed to what it called the "Western imperialists and their puppets."

After 1954, the Communist government of North Vietnam rapidly introduced the fundamental institutions of a Soviet-type regime. It formed a single-party state, eliminating all political opposition. With Chinese and Soviet socialism as its model, it forced the peasant farmers into collective farms, disrupting agricultural production and, by its own admission later, allowing the use by party and police officials of brutal repressive measures against the rural population. Ho Chi Minh pursued his "revolution from above" with a fanaticism equal to that of Stalin and Mao.

At the same time, he continued to work for unification of first Vietnam, then all Indochina, under his leadership. The Chinese and Soviet comrades had urged political methods, not insurrection, to take control of the south. Diem's refusal to hold elections and his repression of the southern Communists forced Ho to change his tactics. In 1959, he called once again for "armed struggle" against Diem's regime. Communist cadres returned south along the secret "Ho Chi Minh trail" built on Cambodian territory, bringing supplies and new directives. The Communists' first target was local rural officials, on whose shoulders rested the stability of Diem's new regime. Political assassination and intimidation spread in areas where the Communist underground established new bases of operations. The weakness of the South Vietnamese state quickly became apparent: peasants preferred collaborating with the Communists, who protected those who helped them; Diem's officials feared for their lives (in 1960 twenty-five hundred were assassinated) and retreated into fortified camps. By the end of that year the Communist insurrection had spread widely, and U.S. officials were warning that Diem's state was

in "serious danger." U.S.-sponsored nation building had not succeeded.

The revolutionary conflict pitting the Vietnamese Communists against the South Vietnam regime soon became a U.S. war. The authoritarian rule of Ngo Dinh Diem could not heal the bitter internal conflicts between Buddhists and Catholics, who constituted the political elite on which Diem, himself Catholic, relied to remain in power. Most South Vietnamese army recruits did not fight with the same commitment as the Vietcong or the North Vietnamese forces, for whom the battle to "liberate the south" represented a nationalist revolution against Western imperialists and their "puppets" as well as a socialist revolution. The new Communist insurrection, begun in 1960, benefited both from its support among southern enemies of Diem and the United States and from the readiness of North Vietnam to commit all its resources to a national struggle which Ho Chi Minh, head of the Communist party, had begun in 1945. Supplies for the guerrillas came partly from captured government materiel, partly from North Vietnam. Central leadership and party cadres came south to aid and direct the southern Communists. A conflict still among Vietnamese, the fighting was in 1960 essentially a civil war which the Communists were close to winning.

U.S. Intervention in Vietnam

Why did the U.S. government choose to become directly involved in that war? Two factors were decisive, one connected with the Korean war, the other with events in Cuba. On the one hand, opposition to Communist China had become a central feature of U.S. Asian containment policy. U.S. leaders believed—mistakenly—that the fighting in Vietnam represented another step in global

Communist aggression. If not stopped in Indochina, they feared that other South Asian states would fall to Communist insurrection "like a row of dominos." The new Kennedy administration judged the South Vietnam civil war not a local conflict, but part of a major struggle in the Cold War to prevent, in the words of one U.S. official, "China's swallowing up Southeast Asia."

This apprehension at further Communist expansion was deepened by the Cuban revolution (see Chapter 11). Fidel Castro had transformed his country by the early 1960s into a Soviet-type socialist regime, accepting Soviet economic and military aid and in 1962 even welcoming (temporarily) Soviet nuclear missiles on Cuban territory. The transformation of the Cuban revolution in those very years into a Communist regime backed by the Soviet Union heightened the determination of the new U.S. president, John Kennedy, to resist another Communist insurrection in a state backed by the United States.

Overly confident in the ability of the United States to dominate the course of internal conflicts involving Communist forces, he and his advisers imagined that greater military and economic assistance would assure Diem's victory. This conviction and the readiness to rely on U.S. military power led one U.S. senator later to judge his government guilty of the "arrogance of power." A decade later the justification for intervention proved unsatisfactory to many Americans. In the face of dogged Communist resistance, the self-assurance vanished, and U.S. leaders finally concluded that China was not an enemy and perhaps might even become an ally. Until then, the United States poured more and more resources into the suppression of the Communist insurrection in South Vietnam.

U.S. intervention in the conflict came in two steps. In the first four years (1961–1965), it involved primarily increased military aid to South Vietnam, responsible for the actual fighting. That policy brought supplies necessary to double by 1963 the size of the Vietnamese army, trained by fifteen thousand U.S. military advisers. The political weakness of the South Vietnamese state proved more damaging even than the problems confronting the Vietnamese army. U.S. reliance on the Vietnamese regime proved misplaced, for increasing numbers of South Vietnamese were opposed to Diem's authoritarian rule. His political ambitions did not match the actual strength of his regime, and he appeared incapable of winning popular support and of reforming his corrupt state.

In 1963, the United States became even more deeply involved in the desperate efforts to create a viable South Vietnamese state. Vietnamese generals, with the tacit approval of U.S. officials, stepped into the internal political struggle. In a military coup, they seized control of the government and assassinated Diem (only a few days before President Kennedy's assassination in the United States). Their involvement in government, which the United States hoped would restore order, end corruption, and strengthen the Vietnamese ability to fight the Vietcong, only increased the internal decay of the Vietnam state. Within two years ten different generals briefly seized power in a self-destructive struggle for political leadership. The most serious consequence was the expansion of Communist-controlled areas, including by late 1964 entire provinces. Even the capital, Saigon, was encircled by guerrillas, while Communist cadres operated freely in the city. The South Vietnam government had lost any claim to Vietnamese national leadership. Unless the United States itself took drastic action, within a few months the Communist insurrection would succeed.

The perspective of "losing" South Vietnam appeared unacceptable to the U.S. government. President Kennedy's successor, Lyndon Johnson, was elected in 1964 primarily on a program of extensive domestic social and civil rights reform. Despite his sincere commitment to the Great Society which he promised Americans, he turned his attention to Vietnam, arguing that he could not become the "first president to lose a war." His advisers, exaggerating the strategic importance of Vietnam and the ability of U.S. troops to fight a guerrilla movement, guaranteed quick victory if the United States intervened directly in the war.

The U.S. Indochinese War

Persuaded by their arguments, Johnson set about organizing direct U.S. intervention in Vietnam but without a declaration of war. He expanded enormously the presidential war-making powers. On the basis of erroneous evidence of an unprovoked North Vietnamese naval attack on a U.S. destroyer, he obtained in 1964 congressional approval to send military forces into combat in Vietnam whenever he wished (the so-called Tonkin Gulf resolution). When coupled with the extensive covert operations of the Central Intelligence Agency, this resolution gave the U.S. president a greater role in global affairs than ever in U.S. history.

In early 1965, Johnson used those powers to order American combat forces into action in Vietnam, taking the crucial step of turning the Vietnam civil war into the U.S. Indochina war. For the second time since the end of the Second World War the United States entered a land war in Asia. The conflict did not resemble the Korean conflict, however. In guerrilla combat there existed no front lines. The enemy was everywhere, easily confused with the civilians. The only clear separation was that distinguishing Americans and Viet-

namese. The Indochina war posed problems the U.S. military had never confronted before.

The formula for victory included two separate operations. The U.S. objective remained limited, as in the Korean conflict, to the defense of the south. On the one hand, U.S. land forces were responsible, in collaboration with South Vietnamese troops, for the "pacification" of the south, that is, for the suppression of Vietcong guerrillas. At the same time, the U.S. leaders began aerial war against North Vietnam, which they believed was responsible for the insurrection.

U.S. air force commanders were persuaded that their air power could inflict such destruction on North Vietnam that the Communist leaders would ultimately have to accept an end to their uprising in the south for the sake of their own survival. The U.S. air force began the most intensive bombing campaign in its history. In the next eight years its planes dropped over one million tons of bombs on North Vietnam, which suffered probably 200,000 civilian casualties. U.S. analysts overlooked two important considerations, however, when they promised Communist capitulation. North Vietnam, an agrarian economy, did not offer targets vital to its economic life. Second, the government and people were prepared to endure enormous suffering in that war of national liberation. Not even Germany or Japan in the Second World War had experienced such massive air attacks. Yet at no time did the bombardment slow the movement of supplies south to the guerrillas or force North Vietnam seriously to consider abandoning the war.

The land war in the south failed as well to achieve its main objective. By 1968 the United States had over 500,000 troops in South Vietnam, nearly as many as the South Vietnamese army. To attempt to separate Vietnamese civilians from Vietcong guerrillas, it moved peasants into protected settlements and created "free-fire zones" where any inhabitants were judged Communist supporters. Assisting infantry operations, the U.S. air force conducted intensive bombing attacks in rural areas of South Vietnam. What effects did this massive U.S. military involvement have? The immediate result was to prevent an easy Vietcong victory. The Communist guerrillas lacked the equipment and numbers to defeat the combined U.S.–South Vietnamese forces. They attempted in early 1968 one major offensive to seize urban areas in the south (the Tet offensive), only to suffer a crushing defeat. Their military strength dwindled by one-third, from 300,000 to 200,000, as a result of the bloody battles.

The Vietnamese Communists could not win that war, yet they did not surrender. They were prepared to continue a prolonged struggle in the face of extensive bombings and despite the heavy loss of Vietcong and North Vietnamese forces, which by the end of the decade probably suffered over one-half million dead. Ho Chi Minh warned in 1966 that the war "may last twenty years or more." He mobilized his Communist state and called on the nationalist loyalties of Vietnamese to back the struggle against the "atrocious rule of the United States and their henchmen." After the losses of the Tet offensive of 1968, North Vietnamese forces assumed the principal role in the fighting. The Communist guerrillas dug hundreds of miles of underground tunnels, some 30 feet

Fighting the Unseen Enemy: U.S. Troops in Combat against Vietnamese Communists, approx. 1968. (*Official U.S. Navy photograph courtesy Freda Utley Collection/Hoover Institution Archives*)

below ground, to escape the massive U.S. bombardments. Many died, but more took their place. The United States could not end the insurrection.

The diplomatic, political, economic, and human price of U.S. intervention in the Vietnam war grew to the point it far exceeded the importance to the United States of victory. The most obvious result were heavy casualties among the South Vietnamese, helpless victims caught in the fighting between the two sides. As serious for Vietnam society was social disorder on a monumental scale, including the destruction of organized village life in many areas, the fall in agricultural production as a result of bombing and the use of herbicides to "defoliate" forested regions, and the influx of four million refugees to the cities. The human suffering of the Vietnamese appeared out of all proportion to the limited war aims.

The cost to the United States, though it had no common measure to Vietnam's hardship, was sufficient to question the very reasons for intervening. The total expense of air and ground fighting plus the aid granted the South Vietnam government raised the price of war to over $150 billion. Before war's end, the years of fighting left fifty thousand U.S. dead. Within the United States bitter political conflict arose when predictions of "quick victory" proved wrong. Many Americans recoiled at the brutality of the war, revealed to them by instant television coverage. The diplomatic price of U.S. intervention proved high as well, for the war deflected attention and resources from larger issues of great power relations, such as Soviet-American arms control and the worsening conflicts in the Middle East. The very continuation of the Vietnam war represented a defeat for the United States.

The combination of these factors forced the U.S. government in 1968 to turn once again to the policy of reliance on South Vietnamese armed forces. While peace negotiations began with the North Vietnamese government, the new Nixon administration started in 1969 to withdraw U.S. troops. "Vietnamization" meant passing responsibility for the war to the South Vietnam government, more dependent than ever on U.S. military and economic aid. It also brought one final effort to end the flow from the north of supplies, most of which passed through the neighboring neutral state of Cambodia. In 1970, after years of secret bombing, American infantry invaded that country, and the United States became the protector of an anti-Communist military government. Northern supplies continued to reach the south, however, and Cambodian Communist insurgents (Khmer Rouge) took over large areas of their country. The net effect of that invasion was to involve Cambodia directly in the war, beginning a second Communist war of liberation in which the United States was the imperialist enemy. Still the U.S. withdrawal continued, until by 1972 no combat troops remained.

The disappearance of U.S. forces doomed the South Vietnamese regime. The compromise peace settlement negotiated in 1972 between the United States and North Vietnam virtually assured a Communist victory. The Vietnamese Communists accepted the U.S.-backed government in South Vietnam, but the United States agreed not to demand the withdrawal from southern territory of North Vietnamese troops. The presence of these forces in the south gave the Communist leaders bases from which to launch a new offensive when the right moment arrived. The treaty was not signed until the U.S. government had overcome South Vietnamese opposition by secretly promising to intervene again if North Vietnam did attack. The promise proved worthless, however, after

President Nixon's resignation in 1974 following the Watergate scandal. The South

ssful
ıalist
ould
tion-

final
ham.
orces
y the
ıfter-
: for-
nam.
ed in
g the
-year
nded
try in
:volu-
come

ımese
inous
ed in-
t over
lution
price
devel-
'thou-
ghting

continued between Cambodia........ Vietnamese. The Communist triumph in Indochina was one more vivid example of the revolutionary force of the fusion of Communist ideology and anti-imperialist nationalism. It also revealed the limits to U.S. control over distant lands. The fate of Indochina had passed into Communist hands, but the defeat of the United States was in global terms limited and of secondary importance. The visit by the U.S. president to Beijing in 1972 represented the major diplomatic event in East Asia, not the fall of South Vietnam.

SUMMARY

War and revolution had profoundly altered the pattern of development of East Asian lands. Japan no longer possessed a great empire or was ruled by a militarist regime. Having occupied a vast area of East and Southeast Asia, it had to abandon all conquered territories. Its defeat opened the way to revolution and new state building in that vast area.

The internal transformation of East Asian lands depended in large measure on forces unique to each country. The victory of the Chinese Communists constituted the most important feature of postwar East Asia. Although Mao's dream of Chinese socialism brought the country two decades of political and social turmoil, Communist leadership remained firmly in place. The Vietnamese Communist victory in Indochina in many ways resembled the Chinese experience, for in both cases nationalist ambitions fused with Communist ideology to sustain a long revolutionary war. The gradual rise of a democratic, capitalist Japan, after U.S. occupation and under U.S. military protection, represented a return to the reform plans launched by the Japanese themselves in the late nineteenth century.

What then were the common characteristics of the history of that region? Behind the diversity of historical experiences we can discern a pattern which repeats itself, in different ways, in other parts of Asia, the Middle East, and Africa. In the first place, the aspiration for national independence emerged as a powerful political force, though one often disputed among several parties and resolved at times only by force of arms. Second, the objective of economic development became an integral part of political action and of popular hopes. Even Mao's utopian vision of communist equality ultimately was abandoned in favor of extensive reform for economic growth. Whether called "market socialism" in China or "guided capitalism" in Japan, the goal was raising production and improving the standard of living of the population. Even South Korea, permanently separated from Communist North Korea, managed to join the ranks of the so-called "new industrial nations" of the late twentieth century. Finally, East Asia became more, not less, involved in global affairs following the end of Western imperialism. The superpowers extended their rivalry into the region, and governments there looked to the West or to the Soviet Union for aid and guidance in their economic reform and for military support. Independence and global interdependence constituted two inextricable facets of the postwar history of East Asia.

RECOMMENDED READING

Communist China

JACQUES GUILLERMAZ, *The Chinese Communist Party in Power, 1949–1974* (1976)

ROBERT MACFARQUHAR, *The Origins of the Cultural Revolution* (two volumes to date, 1974 and 1983)

MAURICE MEISNER, *Mao's China: A History of the People's Republic* (1977)

SUZANNE PEPPER, *Civil War in China: The Political Struggle, 1945–1951* (1978)

STUART SCHRAM, *Mao Tse-tung* (1966)

HARRY SCHWARTZ, *Tsars, Mandarins and Commissars: A History of Chinese-Russian Relations* (1964)

Postwar Japan

AKIRA IRIYI, *The Cold War in Asia* (1974)

MASATAKA KOSAKA, *A History of Postwar Japan* (1972)

EDWIN REISCHAUER, *The Japanese* (1977)

Indochinese War

GEORGE HERRING, *America's Longest War: The United States and Vietnam, 1950–1975* (1979)

GEORGE KAHIN, *Intervention: How America Became Involved in Vietnam* (1986)

STANLEY KARNOW, *Vietnam: A History* (1983)

Memoirs and Novels

LIAN HENG AND JUDITH SCHAPIRO, *Son of the Revolution* (1983)

HENRY KISSINGER, *The White House Years* (1977)

chapter 9

NATION BUILDING
IN SOUTH ASIA

Within a few years of the end of the Second World War, the Western empires in South Asia had vanished. The Dutch left their colony of the East Indies, the United States gave full independence to the Philippines, and the British granted freedom to India, Burma, and Malaya. The political transition, coming in some cases after centuries of colonial rule, was abrupt, beginning a prolonged period of adjustment to the new conditions of independence. The Western states had maintained domination in the last resort by force of arms, but had also recruited and trained for military and administrative service increasing numbers of their colonial subjects. Their years of rule had led to economic investment for the extraction of raw materials needed in Western industry and for the development of manufacturing, and to the construction of railroads and ports for the movement of goods. In these and other ways the imperial period left its marks on social and political life in the new nation-states.

Anti-imperialist nationalism represented the most powerful political legacy of Western domination. Nationalist movements in all those lands combined two features, one being the opposition to Western political and economic imperialism, the other the affirmation of national identity uniting the people within each country. The presence of Western administrators and soldiers focused hostility on common enemies and the symbols of past oppression and exploitation. National identity, on the other hand, was not so easily created, for religious and social barriers still divided these societies. Throughout the area competing religions exercised a strong hold over large groups of the population, for whom protection of their community and religious practices remained a vital and often divisive issue.

The process of decolonization, occurring as well in other parts of the world, transformed global relations and opened up new possibilities for the internal development of these new states. The transfer of power came at times peacefully, at times after colonial war or in the midst of civil war. The leaders of these new countries had to undertake the complex task of nation building, which required the merging of religious, cultural, and social groups within one national culture controlled by one unified state. The temptation was great to turn to military force to maintain internal unity; as a result, democratic institutions created at the time of independence were soon replaced in many countries by authoritarian regimes.

Freedom brought with it a very distinct sense of fundamental differences between the newly independent lands and the rest of the world. The broadest definition of this uniqueness came from the Indian leader Jawaharlal Nehru, who sought a language to distance his country from those parts of the world where the Cold War dominated international relations. Decolonization had in his opinion created a new division of the peoples of the globe. Alongside the two "worlds" of capitalist (the First World) and communist (the Second World) states, there existed, in his view, a Third World of developing nations such as India. Many other leaders shared his view and supported a policy of "nonalignment" with either the Western or the Soviet bloc. These lands confronted acute problems of poverty and economic backwardness. Their efforts to raise living conditions and to stimulate economic growth relied in some cases on the free enterprise system of the West, in others on the central government controls resembling those which Stalin's Russia had first used. While looking often to foreign lands for aid and guidance, they adapted and altered these policies and institutions to suit their needs

and conditions. The rise of authoritarian regimes and the emergence of nonaligned states both constituted new trends in the postwar history of South Asia.

THE NEW ISLAND REPUBLICS

The history of the nations of Southeast Asia in the quarter-century after the war followed a common pattern. The first years were a period of decolonization, that is, the elimination of political ties to Western states and the first stages of nation building. The new regimes set out to define a new international policy in their relations with East and West, gathering to discuss common problems and policies even when they were deeply divided on the most desirable course to take. Their political development in the following decade was toward increasingly authoritarian rule, with small groups of leaders controlling elections through a state party, and remaining in power for long periods. Finally, economic growth became an increasing concern, where poverty retained its grip over both urban and rural masses while business or bureaucratic elites built up great wealth. Social unrest erupted at times in spontaneous uprising, giving support to guerrilla movements organized by revolutionary parties. Nation building constituted a complex, often violent, process.

Philippine Independence

The withdrawal in late 1945 of Japanese forces provided the opportunity for nationalist independence movements to take power throughout Southeast Asia. Liberation of the Philippines came with the return in 1944 of General MacArthur and U.S. forces, two years after their defeat by the Japanese. The U.S. government had before the war granted the Philippines self-rule in a political system, copied from the American institutions, with an elected president and legislature. Dominating the political life of the islands were powerful families, whose influence lay partly in their great wealth, partly in a patronage system of rule by which they built up a large following of political "clients." Japanese occupation had little effect on these social inequalities, but did spark a major peasant uprising directed both against the foreign enemy and against the great landowners, many of whom collaborated with the Japanese occupation forces.

After the war, the transfer of power to the Philippine people did not weaken the dominance of these political and social elites. The United States granted independence in 1946 to the new Philippine government. The first elected president had himself worked with the Japanese. His administration, like the preceding one, made no effort to punish collaborators. No nationalist revolution swept in new leaders or offered the peasant population a concrete plan for land reform. Independence came peaceably without upsetting the privileges and comforts of the Philippine upper classes.

Important features of the colonial past also marked the country's economic and diplomatic relations with the United States. The new Philippine regime joined the Western bloc in the Cold War, signing a military alliance and permitting the United States to retain its naval and air bases and in exchange receiving military and economic aid. It preserved the laws introduced by the United States which protected capitalist economic development. The islands depended as much as before on the United States for foreign trade. Special trade agreements permitted Philippine goods to enter the United States without tariffs. In return U.S. investors received special financial incentives to continue developing businesses in the new republic. Close ties existed between Philip-

pine traders and industrialists and U.S. bankers and manufacturers. Thus the interests of the Philippine government and businessmen were closely bound to those of the U.S. government and economy. Socialist experiments had no place in the new order.

Internal social and religious conflicts within the Philippines remained as serious after as before independence. The wartime peasant uprising in the main island of Luzon continued for years afterward. It received militant leadership from the Communist party after Stalin gave his backing in 1947 to Communist participation in wars of "national liberation." Initially successful in taking control of large areas of the countryside, the insurgents lost support when the Philippine government finally passed new laws to protect tenant farmers. It allowed Ramon Magsaysay, the dynamic and popular commander of the army, to organize effective resistance to the guerrillas. To induce peasants to abandon the rebellion, Magsaysay offered them ownership of their own land. He proved to be a charismatic nationalist leader, who was popular with the masses and whose formula of reform and repression was successful in ending the insurrection by 1951. Magsaysay subsequently became a reform president, who continued to work to alleviate the hardship of the poor classes of his country until his death in 1957. In those years his brand of nationalist leadership legitimized democratic rule and temporarily ended Communist revolutionary opposition.

Sukarno and National Liberation for Indonesia

In the East Indies, years of colonial war between Indonesian nationalists and Dutch forces followed liberation from Japan. Before capitulating in August 1945, the Japanese occupation authorities had encouraged nationalist collaborators to proclaim the independence of their country. No Allied troops reached the East Indies until weeks later. In the interval, an independent government of Indonesia appeared. It was the work of a remarkable nationalist leader, Sukarno, who had for the previous twenty years agitated against Dutch rule of the East Indies and preached a semireligious message of Indonesian nationalism. His Five Pillars of national liberation (democracy, internationalism, nationalism, social prosperity, and belief in God) were less important than his charismatic hold over the Indonesian people, who took inspiration from his promise of a mystical rebirth of Indonesia following independence.

Powerful opposition to the new regime appeared when Dutch armed forces reached the islands later that year. The leaders of the Netherlands opposed complete independence for the East Indies primarily in the hope of preserving their economic holdings and of exploiting that country's rich minerals and petroleum for the reconstruction of their war-torn land. For the next four years, they attempted to reestablish by force of arms some form of colonial rule over the islands. Indonesians, led by officers trained previously in the Dutch armed forces, organized guerrilla bands to fight the Dutch. War spread throughout the East Indies.

Sporadic fighting between the Dutch and Indonesian nationalists lasted until 1949. Through the entire period Sukarno remained the dominant figure in the resistance movement. His forces did not possess the military might to defeat the Dutch, which had ninety thousand troops in the East Indies. The Dutch, for their part, lacked the strength to end the nationalist insurrection and to reimpose their rule. The ultimate victory of Indonesian nationalism was due partly to the perseverance of Sukarno's forces, fighting for a cause they deeply believed in, and partly to American opposition to Dutch

imperialism. The U.S. government judged these colonial wars a relic of a bygone age of European domination and considered independence from colonial rule a progressive development, though on the condition that the Communists did not take control. In 1949, it warned the Dutch government that it could not continue Marshall Plan assistance as long as the Dutch pursued their war in the East Indies. Confronted with an endless war and the loss of vital economic aid, the Dutch government that year finally abandoned their colonial struggle.

In 1950, the independent unified republic of Indonesia came into existence. Its new constitution promised parliamentary democracy to the eighty million people of the vast archipelago, whose islands stretched across three thousand miles, and which was divided by great inequalities of wealth as well as by different languages and religious practice (though Islam was the predominant faith). Political parties representing the various peoples of the islands feuded among themselves, weakening their authority in a state unified only by its leader and by the nationalist liberation movement which the people had supported. Sukarno was the national hero of the independence movement and became the first president of the republic with great personal prestige. His stature rested not only on constitutional power and nationalist ideology, but also on his magnetic hold on the Indonesians, many of whom virtually worshipped him. In many respects, Sukarno was Indonesia.

In the British territories of Burma and Malaya, nationalist forces emerged from the war better organized and stronger as a result of their experience under Japanese rule. They did not encounter opposition to their demand of postwar independence, for the British Labor party, in power after 1945, included among its reforms the emancipation of all Asian colonies. Its goal was to hand over powers gradually and peacefully to democratic leaders already experienced in self-rule during the colonial period. After British troops moved back into Burma, Malaya, and Singapore, British authorities began negotiations to end imperial rule. In 1948 Burma and Malaya became independent states, though the latter retained close military ties with Great Britain. There, as in the island republics, Communist forces began in 1948 guerrilla insurrections. The British troops helped the new national governments to repress within two years the uprisings and to begin the process of nation building. Only Singapore, naval port and commercial center for all Southeast Asia (and largely Chinese in population), remained a British crown colony with local self-rule. It was the exception (like Hong Kong), a remnant of an empire surrounded by independent states.

The Cold War and Nonalignment

From the very start the new governments had to confront the Cold War conflict between the Communist countries and the West. Communist insurrections in the late 1940s, backed by an impoverished peasantry, presented the leaders with the threat of internal revolution. To put down the uprisings, they relied upon their new armies and on Western military assistance. Political conditions altered in the 1950s following the end of Communist guerrilla war and the emergence of new leadership in the Soviet Union and in the United States. President Eisenhower, elected in 1952, introduced what he termed a "New Look" in U.S. foreign policy, which included the extension of U.S. military alliances into the areas of new Asian nation-states. It revised the containment strategy against the Soviet Union to emphasize military pacts among states aligned with the West. The United States

sponsored the formation in 1955 of a regional alliance, the South East Asia Treaty Organization (SEATO), joined by the Philippine and Pakistan governments as well as by Australia and New Zealand. This policy brought global power politics into South Asia and obliged nationalist leaders to formulate their own position toward global competition between the superpowers.

The choice offered by the new Soviet leaders after 1953 was economic and military assistance in exchange for refusal to join the Western alliances. They abandoned Stalin's opposition to the "bourgeois nationalist" (i.e., noncommunist) governments of the newly independent Asian and Middle Eastern states. One indication of their new views of nationalist revolution in Asian lands was their opposition to further Communist insurrection, to be replaced by political competition for power. Their principal objective was to establish good relations with the nationalist leaders and to dissuade them from joining the Western alliances. The introduction of this Soviet world policy represented a significant innovation in Soviet foreign policy after Stalin's death, as important as peaceful coexistence and improved relations with independent Communist states. The new nation-states were courted by both the United States and the Soviet Union. Economic aid, diplomatic interests, and political ideology all played a part in their leaders' choice.

The first international conference of Asian and African states gathered in 1955 to discuss foreign policy for the newly independent states. Sukarno of Indonesia took the initiative of inviting all the new leaders to the city of Bandung. Coming at the time of new Soviet initiatives and Western efforts to extend military alliances through Asia, the Bandung Conference became a forum for debate on the Cold War among Asian and African leaders. It revealed the profound divisions among these states, some of which, such as the Philippines, allied themselves closely with the West, while others chose to remain "nonaligned," that is, to avoid alliances with either side.

Nehru was the most eloquent and influential spokesman for this "third way" between Western and Communist blocs. He argued strongly against becoming involved in "Europe's troubles, Europe's hatreds and Europe's conflicts" and warned of "some other great countries" (referring to the United States and to the Soviet Union) which "have got into the habit of thinking that their quarrels are the world's quarrels and that, therefore, the world must submit to them." His state had already extended diplomatic recognition to Communist China and had accepted economic aid from the Soviet Union. Although Nehru's initiatives were condemned by the United States, they proved to other Asian leaders that nonalignment represented a successful policy of peaceful relations with Western and Communist "worlds," and served as well the interests of their states. His way offered them an alternative to diplomatic ties to and dependence on the United States, promising them the stature of leaders of fully independent states and the possibility of economic assistance from both East and West. Among those at Bandung attracted by nonalignment was Sukarno.

Sukarno and Indonesian Nation Building

The Indonesian leader assumed in the mid-1950s powers so great he was a virtual dictator. His state, which had in theory functioned until 1957 as a parliamentary democracy, remained deeply divided by bitter political quarrels. Fundamentalist Muslims demanded that the state enforce Islamic religious practices; regional rivalries opposed the leaders of the various islands of his vast republic. Only the army constituted a strong institution of national unity, of which Sukarno had for long been the political symbol. The alliance between the two became in those years the foundation for authoritarian rule in Indonesia. Like many other leaders of Third World countries, Sukarno himself came to believe that the unity and welfare of his new state depended upon his strong leadership. In 1956 he declared to Indonesians that he had "dreamed" of "burying" the old constitutional order and of giving his people a Guided Democracy and a Guided Economy. His dreams translated into political dictatorship, state planning, and nonalignment. The next year, he took over control of the state; parliamentary democracy in Indonesia had come to the end of its short, disorderly life.

The leadership provided by Sukarno relied more on intuition and personal favoritism than on coherent policy. The government seized all Dutch and other foreign businesses and estates, nationalizing the great oil fields of Royal Dutch-Shell, but its management proved incompetent and inefficient. Sukarno accepted the economic assistance of Western and Communist countries, both competing for good relations with his state. The United States provided aid totaling nearly $1 billion by the mid-1960s; the Soviet Union contributed funds and technicians for major building projects. Much of the foreign assistance went to Sukarno's own personal schemes, including vast palaces and gifts to his personal favorites. The army grew rapidly, for his new policy also included the territorial expansion of Indonesia into areas controlled still by the Dutch and by the British. To win the backing of the many political factions in his country, he offered their leaders positions in the largest cabinet of any country in the world—one hundred ministers, who worked largely for their own personal benefit and wasted enormous sums of money on useless projects. Meanwhile, the county went deeper and deeper into debt, and foreign trade declined for lack of funds to pay for imports.

The Sukarno dictatorship brought with it his own "personality cult." He received the grand titles of Permanent President and Great Leader of the Revolution. He retained the trust and admiration of most Indonesian people, but his posters, slogans, and speeches hid serious weaknesses in his regime. He lacked his own strong mass organization and came to believe that the Indonesian Communist party, largest political movement in the country, would provide him that disciplined popular support. He became deeply hostile toward the West, blaming Britain for resisting his plans for seizure

of Malay territory and damning the United States for its Asian military alliances. His opposition to the West by 1964 became so strong that he renounced all Western economic aid and proclaimed his readiness to collaborate with Communist China (with whom the Indonesian Communists were closely allied).

Boasting that his country was "living dangerously," Sukarno declared war on "neo-colonialism" (shortened to NEKOLIM in his speeches) in all its forms. The blame he attached to supposed remnants of Western colonial rule was in reality a means to shift responsibility for economic mismanagement and diplomatic failures to Western states and away from his leadership. Behind his rhetorical sparring with the West, he appears to have been increasingly attracted by a gran-

Indonesian Heroes and Imperialist Devils: Indonesian Government Poster Entitled "The Five Pillars [of Indonesian National Liberation] Crush All Forms of Imperialism." *(Howard Jones Collection/Hoover Institution Archives)*

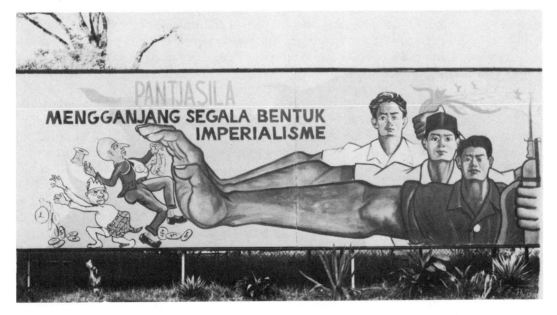

diose vision of a new Indonesian regime, in which he would ally with the Communist party to create a new party dictatorship freed from reliance on the military.

The encouragement he gave the Communists proved his downfall, for in doing so he became (wittingly or unwittingly) the center of a violent struggle for power. The Communists and army generals were bitter rivals. In 1965 the Communist leaders resolved to end the conflict by secretly organizing an armed uprising to seize control of the government. They seem to have believed that they enjoyed Sukarno's backing (though he was careful not to commit himself formally to their side). With the help of a few army units, in mid-1965 they began their insurrection by capturing and executing several of Indonesia's top military leaders.

The Communist uprising failed. The surviving generals, led by General Suharto, mobilized their troops and appealed to the population to join in resisting the "godless" enemies of the nation. The underlying hatreds and fears within Indonesian popular culture, stirred up by pressures of nation building, suddenly emerged, producing a terrible butchering of Communists, their supporters, and even of Chinese suspected of loyalty to Communist China. No one knows how many people died in the anti-Communist massacres; the most conservative estimates range from 200,000 to 300,000. Sukarno, no longer trusted by his generals, lost power in 1966 when General Suharto took over the government.

The new military dictatorship ended the experiment in a socialist Guided Economy. Western aid was once again accepted and foreign businessmen (mainly Japanese) welcomed. Indonesia remained a neutral, nonaligned country but became dependent on loans and aid from Japan and the United States to keep its economy from going bankrupt. What had caused the country these grave problems? Neither elected governments nor Sukarno himself proved capable of governing effectively, the politicians because of their lack of vision, Sukarno because his dream of Indonesia was completely removed from the political and social realities of his country. In the end, the army leaders used their repressive powers to enforce national unity and order. General disillusionment with Sukarno and the bloody destruction of the Communist movement removed any significant opposition to military dictatorship in Indonesia.

The Marcos Dictatorship in the Philippines

In the Philippines democratic government survived somewhat longer in the difficult period of nation building, but it too ultimately fell to an ambitious political leader. The combination of Western investment and massive U.S. aid in the 1950s and 1960s helped the country's economy to grow and to raise somewhat the standard of living of the urban population. Social conflict did not disappear, however. Power and wealth remained in the hands of the social elite. Rapid population growth and the poverty of much of the rural population stood in the way of any quick end to the acute social inequalities among the population.

In these conditions of misrule and social hardship, armed opposition to the Philippine government reappeared in the late 1960s. A new Communist insurgent movement, called the New People's Army, attacked government outposts and established control in isolated rural areas. It won the support of poor peasants as well as of intellectuals who despaired of their government's ability ever to achieve real social reform. An additional cause of instability arose from the antagonism between the Christian majority of the islands and Muslims living primarily in the south, where another center of insurrection challenged the power of the central government. Although the forms of democratic government remained in place, power was increasingly concentrated in the hands of a few political leaders and in the armed forces. These conditions opened the way for authoritarian rule.

The fragile popular consensus on which democracy depended was broken as a result of the pressure of violent social and religious conflicts and of the ambition of a power-hungry politician, Ferdinand Marcos. Elected president in 1965, he used his legal powers under the constitution and the peculiar informal network of power which political patronage and "family" connection provided him to expand enormously his authority in the country. By the end of his second term, political opposition to his authoritarian rule was widespread. Rather than give up office, Marcos in 1972 instituted a regime of martial law. With the backing of the army he arrested his political opponents and ended democratic government. Marcos turned his dictatorship into a source of private enrichment (some estimates later placed his total wealth at over $1 billion) and a means to maintain a powerful political machine. Power brought enormous benefits to him and to his followers.

His authoritarian government failed, however, to resolve any of the major problems confronting his country. His regime was incapable of repressing the Communist and Muslim uprisings, and was unable to improve economic conditions despite vast amounts of U.S. military and economic aid. Even the Catholic church joined his opponents in the early 1980s. In 1986 he had to flee the country when army leaders turned against him and joined the political opposition, by then close to popular revolt. His successor as president was Corazon Aquino, widow of a prominent opponent of the regime whose assassination in 1983 was probably engineered by Marcos's supporters. She promised to restore democratic rule and reunite the country, but the heritage of decades of political corruption and authoritarian rule posed enormous problems. These conflicts had weakened seriously the process of nation building in the Philippines.

The City-State of Singapore and Nationalism in Malaya

In the Malay peninsula, nation building could not overcome the hostility dividing the Muslim and Chinese populations. We can see in that one small region the conflicts occurring during decolonization in many other countries. While the political and economic interests of a political elite pushed in the direction of a state ruling a large and diverse population, the ethnic and religious antagonism dividing the masses of the people threw up major barriers in the way of political unity.

The most serious problems arose in the relations between Singapore and Malaya. The British ended finally their rule over the prosperous, largely Chinese city of Singapore in 1963 and convinced its leaders to join the Malaya Union to form the Federation of Malaysia. This new state constituted an artificial creation, not a unified land. The Muslim Malay people, largely peasant and lacking the skills of the Chinese, resented the prosperity of Singapore and were fearful that their Muslim religious practices and communal organization would suffer if they were ruled by Chinese politicians. Riots in the city of Singapore and political quarrels within the Malay government revealed the intensity of the hostility between the two groups. Malay leaders, fearing that the ethnic conflict would destroy the fragile unity of their young state, decided to expel the city from the federation. In 1965, Singapore was forced to form its own independent state, an island of only two million people.

Its isolation proved a blessing, creating the conditions for an economic boom which rivaled that of Japan. The island state relied upon capitalist enterprise, political authority, and international industry and trade to assure its economic welfare. The British had introduced self-rule through democratic elections. Gradually one party, the People's Action party, became the dominant political group. Anticipating a Communist insurrection in their city like that which occurred in 1965 in Indonesia, the Singapore government destroyed the Communist movement and outlawed its labor organizations. Essentially a one-party state, its leaders repressed labor unrest and separatist ethnic movements among its Chinese, Malaya, and Indian inhabitants. They promised instead full employment and equal protection for all national groups living among its cosmopolitan population. They invited foreign investors to take advantage of the island's industrious, cheap work force to develop oil refining and textile and electronic manufacturing. They opened the doors of the city-state to international banks and welcomed international commercial firms to use its port.

Singapore founded its prosperity on the global economic expansion of the 1960s and on its internal stability, assured by an authoritarian government. The result was a rate of economic growth above 10 percent in the late 1960s and, soon, a standard of living for its population second only, among Asian countries, to that of Japan. Economic conditions on the island were the envy of surrounding states. Militarily insignificant, its security depended largely on its vital role in the economic development of Southeast Asia. It too was a nonaligned country, seeking good relations with all countries, Communist and non-Communist, conducting financial and commercial affairs with whoever

had the means to pay. Although it resembled in size a city-state of Renaissance Italy, it contained within its borders all the dynamic economic forces propelling the global boom of that decade.

INDEPENDENCE FOR INDIA

Conditions within the Indian subcontinent at the end of the Second World War resembled those in the other South Asian lands. Nationalism represented a powerful mass movement among the population, which at the same time was divided by ethnic and religious conflicts, of which the most threatening was that dividing Muslim and Hindu communities. Poverty as terrible as that anywhere in Asia existed there alongside extravagant wealth. Autocratic princes still ruled over large areas, while in other regions democratic political practices were already well established. Over the subcontinent's 400 million people ruled the government of Great Britain, still in possession of what remained its greatest colony (see Chapter 5).

Indian Decolonization and Communal Conflict

The legacy of war in India differed from that of the other countries in South Asia in one vital respect. Japanese armies had never penetrated far into Indian territory. The British viceroy, the Indian civil service, and the Indian army remained the central forces in the united provinces while the six hundred princes who had accepted British rule continued to control their principalities. Only those Indian soldiers, who were made prisoner in 1942 and had accepted the Japanese offer to form the Indian National Army, had become collaborators against the British. Their welcome as heroes on their return to India in 1945 proved that resistance to the British overrode all other issues confronting Indians in the postwar years. The wartime demand by the National Congress that the British grant India independence had led to the imprisonment of the movement's leaders, replaced in the provincial and central governments by members of the rival Muslim League. Upon their release in 1945, Congress leaders renewed their campaign for the withdrawal of the British.

Both Congress and the League sought independence, but their goals were increasingly at variance. Congress leaders had vowed to preserve the unity which the British had given the subcontinent. They sought national independence and a democratically elected government respecting the rights of the entire population, regardless of religion or social rank. Special consideration to any religious community represented to men such as Gandhi a betrayal of their deepest belief in civic equality under a free Indian nation-state. This vision was challenged by the "communalism," that is, social isolation, of separate religious communities, which constituted the central feature of the life of most Indians.

The very existence of the Muslim League revealed the threat to Indian national unity posed by the defense of exclusive Muslim interests. Concerned solely to assure the well-being of the Muslim population, the League leaders argued that protection for India's 150 million Muslims required separate political representation. The half-century before 1945 had witnessed a rising number of violent incidents and riots opposing Hindus and Muslims. Every province mingled the two communities. No single territory was exclusively Hindu or Muslim. The population of Calcutta, largest and most industrial of India's cities and the capital of Bengal, was almost equally divided between these religious communities. Their very proximity was a cause of friction and political rivalry

when the prospect of self-rule raised the specter of majority and minority religious representation. National independence threatened to tear India apart.

The League preferred the gamble of partition to one unified nation-state. If the new Indian state, ruled democratically, gave all power to the majority, the League feared that the Hindus, regardless of the promises of National Congress, would abuse their powers and oppress the minority Muslims. What to political idealists appeared the best safeguard of individual rights seemed to the League majority oppression. Before the war it had sought special Muslim rights within a new India; in the postwar years, it made the demand for a separate Muslim nation-state its immediate objective. No such state had ever existed. The League proposed the name of "Pakistan," a word whose letters came from the principal Muslim provinces of northwestern India. The followers of the Muslim League were prepared after war's end to resort even to communal violence to prevent Indian national unification.

The end of the Asian war in August 1945 made the issue of Indian independence the first priority for British and Indian leaders. The British Labor government supported freedom for the subcontinent as firmly as for the other Asian colonies. Political weakness as well as socialist idealism dictated rapid liberation for India, whose rule placed a heavy financial burden on the impoverished British treasury. The country proved more difficult than ever to rule. Indian sailors on British warships in Bombay mutinied for several days in 1946 and flew the National Congress flag over their ships. Mass demonstrations and violence were a constant threat. The British hope was that new elections would produce an Indian leadership capable of negotiating with them the terms of independence.

When those elections were held in 1946,

National Congress candidates won a majority in nearly all the provinces, but the Muslim League received the support of most Muslim voters. Who then spoke for India? Congress and the League both agreed to negotiations with the British, but each on its own terms. Congress refused to recognize the right of the League to speak for a religious community, fearing that to do so would represent a fatal concession to partition. Mohammed Ali Jinnah, head of the Muslim League, demanded that Muslims be granted an equal voice alongside the Congress. In July 1946, he concluded that his party could not receive by legal means recognition to be the sole representative for India's Muslims. In those conditions, he called on his Muslim supporters to demonstrate by forceful means their political might to the British and to Congress.

The League's Day of Direct Action in August 1946 represented the real turning point in the history of postwar India. Jinnah proclaimed that "the only solution to India's problem is Pakistan," that is, partition of the Indian subcontinent into "Hindustan" and his Muslim state. To make clear that civil war was the alternative, he demanded of Muslims throughout India that they join in Direct Action, including strikes, meetings, and demonstrations. He and the other League leaders probably knew that rioting would accompany the demonstrations and that communal conflict would inevitably result. He accepted the possibility, saying: "We also have a pistol." The meetings did lead to Muslim-Hindu riots throughout the country. The tragic process of partition had begun.

Bengal was the scene of the greatest bloodshed, its capital city for several days torn by violence in what observers later called the Great Calcutta Killing. Perhaps six thousand people died in that city alone, most of them innocent inhabitants attacked by the rioters from both sides. British forces moved into the centers of rioting, gradually restoring order. Gandhi, horrified at the violence, set out on a personal pilgrimage through Muslim as well as Hindu areas of Bengal to restore peace and tolerance by his own personal example and teaching. Although he risked death at the hands of a fanatic, he too helped calm the population, but only temporarily.

Sporadic violence among religious communities continued throughout that winter and on into the next year. The Muslim League had at the cost of many thousands of lives proven that India could not remain one peaceful, democratic country. Either it would have to be ruled by a dictatorship—a possibility no one even considered—or it would somehow have to be divided.

It is easy to blame partition on the League. Nehru, himself without any deep religious feeling and cosmopolitan in his political ideology, hated the League and all it embodied. He considered the Muslim religious identity which the League cultivated to be "medieval," a dangerous anachronism in a "rapidly changing world" of industrialism, science, and nuclear power. He repeated assurances that other religious groups "have nothing to fear from the Hindus." After his visit to riot-torn areas of the Punjab that August, he expressed despair and "shame" that Indians should have betrayed the "great ideals that [Gandhi] had placed before us." He and the other Congress leaders persisted that year in working for a free and united India. Their cause was lost. The country was too deeply and bitterly divided. The Muslim League had encouraged, but not created, that bitterness and hostility. Religious and social divisions, not political manipulation by the League, decided the fate of India.

Frustrated and baffled by the impasse in negotiations, the Labor cabinet in February 1947 proclaimed that Britain would pull out of India within a year. It was prepared to leave even if no constitution or agreement had been created for the peaceful transfer of power. This statement was a declaration of defeat in the form of an ultimatum. The British government refused any longer to take responsibility for the escalating violence, recognized by one British official to be the "natural, if ghastly, process tending in its own way to the solution of the Indian problem." Jinnah had made his point. A new British viceroy, Lord Mountbatten, went to India that spring to make one last effort to achieve a negotiated settlement. He agreed that partition presented the only solution. The Muslim League, he reported, was ready to "resort to arms if Pakistan in some form were not conceded."

The Partition of India

This settlement still required the agreement of the National Congress, leader of the majority of India's population. It did not have the support of Gandhi, whose entire life and moral preaching had been dedicated to brotherhood and toleration. He had pursued national independence because he believed it to be the path to Indian spiritual rebirth. Acceptance of Pakistan meant recognition of communalism and the victory of religious intolerance. He considered the partition to be destructive and evil. On this issue Gandhi, apostle of nonviolence, became intransigent. "Even if the whole of India burns," he stated, "we shall not concede Pakistan, even if the Muslims demanded it at the point of the sword." He did not impede the settlement, however, allowing Nehru to assume leadership of Congress to take on his shoulders responsibility for Indian independence. That spring, Nehru concluded that partition was inevitable. In June 1947, Mountbatten announced to India and the world that the subcontinent would receive independence not as one but two states.

Partition cut through the fabric of Indian political, economic, and social life. The provinces with a substantial Muslim population would go to Pakistan, the rest to India. The leaders of two key provinces, Bengal and Punjab, acquiesced in partition of their own regions since their populations were so evenly divided among religious groups. The boundaries to separate the states were determined secretly by a British official. The partition left the Indus River valley in the west and part of Bengal in the east in the new Pakistan state, itself divided in two. Three-fourths of the subcontinent's population went into India, under Congress leadership.

The partition required the division of land, communities, economic systems, and the institutions of state administration and army. East Bengal's economy, dependent on the export of jute, lost its principal port and center of industry, Calcutta, which went to India. The vast irrigation system in the province of Punjab was disrupted since the frontier cut across river and canal systems. The Sikh community itself was split in two, with its holy city of Amritsar in India and its capital of Lahore in Pakistan. Millions of Hindus remained in Pakistan, and one-third of all Muslims were still in India. August 15 was set as the day of independence.

To add to the confusion, the six hundred princes of the subcontinent had to choose whether they would join their principalities to one or the other state. Neither the British nor Congress and the League were prepared to permit independent principalities, since their greatest fear was still further partition of the land into a collection of petty, feuding states. With considerable pressure from Mountbatten, almost all the princes accepted before independence to join the state in which their principality was located. No decision was reached on the important northern province of Kashmir, source of the Indus River and of the irrigation waters of Punjab. Its population was largely Muslim, its prince

Hindu. The large central principality of Hyderabad as well remained uncommitted, its Muslim prince dreaming of a place in Pakistan despite the fact that his population was largely Hindu. Two sources of conflict confronted the new states, one arising in possible disputes over these provinces, the other emerging from the still unknown reaction of Muslims, Sikhs, and Hindus when they found themselves after partition at the mercy of another community. The threat of civil and religious war was very real.

Nehru spoke to the Indian people on Independence Day, August 15. He proclaimed that "we are a free and sovereign people and we have rid ourselves of the burden of the past." Despite Jinnah's objections, his state kept the name of India. Even with partition, it was the second most populous country in the world. The removal of the "burden of foreign domination" represented in his eyes a great historic event, part of the liberation of colonial peoples in their move to equality with the Western nations. He had ambitious plans for dealing with the "great economic problems of the masses of the people," including increased production, redistribution of wealth, irrigation, and hydroelectric projects. First, however, the country had to "put an end to all the internal strife and violence." In Karachi, the capital of Pakistan, Jinnah spoke to his people, praying that "God Almighty give us strength to make Pakistan truly a great nation among all the nations of the world" and urging toleration for his country's Hindu population. That day the exact boundaries of India and Pakistan were made public, revealing the true dimensions of partition.

Centuries of British rule had created a legacy which shaped the new states from the start. British administrators had formed the Indian civil service, whose authority extended down to the level of village life of the peasants in the rural districts. The British

had trained an Indian army in Western military skills. Indian administrative and military personnel began immediately to serve in the new regimes and replaced the departing British officials. British officers still constituted the high command in the Indian army while others agreed to serve in the Pakistani armies. English had been the language by which many educated Indians communicated among themselves and acquired direct access to Western learning. It became the first official language in both states.

The constitutional origins of self-government lay in the Government of India Act of 1935, which created a federal state protecting regional rights. It established the principle of legislative control over the executive in a cabinet system of rule, modeled on the British parliamentary system. This constitution provided the basis of government for both Pakistan and India in their first years of existence. The era of British colonial domination passed on as well a valuable economic inheritance. The enormous Indian railroad network and the ocean ports, sinews of an industrial economy, became the property of the new states, as did the irrigation system and hydroelectric dams. The one legacy which did not endure was the unified state, partitioned into two by the irreconcilable differences between the Muslim League and the National Congress, between Muslims and Hindus.

The leadership of these states came from the political parties which had played the key role in the independence movement. In India, Nehru assumed the position of prime minister in a cabinet of Congress leaders. The provinces retained their laws and political leadership chosen in the 1946 elections. Both states became dominion members of the British Commonwealth. In India the executive position of governor general, the representative of Commonwealth authority, went to Lord Mountbatten, Nehru's personal choice. In Pakistan, Mohammed Ali Jinnah chose for himself the post of governor general, leaving cabinet affairs in the hands of his aides. Ultimately elections would permit the choice of delegates to constituent assemblies to write new constitutions. The formal transfer of power from the British state to India and Pakistan occurred remarkably easily, and the new leaders imagined that their populations would heed their calls for peace and accept the partition as the necessary price for their freedom.

Independence, Communal Violence, and War

Neither the British nor the nationalist leaders understood the intensity of communal loyalty among Muslims, Hindus, and Sikhs. As a result, they failed completely to anticipate the outpouring of fear and anger provoked by the announcement on August 15 of the new boundaries. Westernized leaders such as Nehru and Jinnah had built up a vast following among the masses, yet were separated from them by class and education. They did not heed the warning from Sikh leaders in the Punjab that "our swords shall decide if the Muslims shall rule" or note the rising numbers of Sikh men joining armed bands. Only Gandhi sensed the tremendous human tragedy that partition had precipitated.

The regions where greatest violence was likely to occur were the two partitioned provinces, Bengal in the east and Punjab in the north. Calcutta, capital of Bengal, had been the scene of the worst rioting in 1946. At the urging of Mountbatten and with the backing of the city's Muslim leader, Gandhi accepted to go there. He was prepared to place his own life in jeopardy to prevent blood from flowing again in the city. He went to live in the worst slums of the city, proclaiming a fast to death unless the leaders of the religious communities agreed to collaborate in keeping their peoples from rioting. So great was his moral authority that, almost single-handedly, he maintained peace in Bengal that month.

In the Punjab, however, violence erupted immediately. Rumors on both sides of the boundaries of atrocities committed on the other set Hindus and Sikhs against Muslims in Indian Punjab, while in Pakistan Muslim bands attacked Sikhs and Hindus. The fifty thousand troops Mountbatten had at his disposal could do little to stop the rioting. Terrified families and entire villages set out on foot or in trains to find refuge, the Muslims to Pakistan, the Hindus and Sikhs to India. They became the targets of roving bands of killers and of robbers. The violence spread to the Indian capital of Delhi, where Hindu refugees from Pakistan spread stories of massacre, rape, and looting by Muslims. In retaliation, Hindus attacked the city's large Muslim population. Mountbatten and Nehru, collaborating closely to prevent chaos from engulfing the country, had to call out the army to restore order there.

In the vast countryside, order was restored much more slowly. Perhaps one million Indians and Pakistanis died that year as a result of the hardship of flight or of mob violence. By mid-1948 an estimated five million refugees had arrived in India and perhaps an equal number in west Pakistan. Independence brought the worst civil strife in Indian history and left in its wake bitter hostility between the two countries. Nehru attacked the Muslim League as "fascist" and vowed never to let such religious fanaticism destroy the democratic and nonviolent principles of the Congress movement. Two years later he recalled in a sort of self-confession the anguish of those terrible months, when Indian leaders became "slaves of the events that inexorably unroll themselves before our eyes" and responded with "fear and hatred."

Even he resembled his people in his anger that fall.

Gandhi himself came to Delhi late in the year to continue his crusade for peace and understanding, directed toward the leaders of the two states as well as toward the two communities. He attacked fanaticism no matter who preached religious intolerance, Hindu or Muslim. He received all who wished to see and to talk with him despite rumors of plots against his life. On January 20, 1948, a Hindu political extremist shot him as he was going to prayer. Nehru grieved with his people, telling them that "the light has gone out of our lives and there is darkness everywhere." Gandhi died a martyr's death, another victim of the partition.

In late 1947 the Indian leaders turned to military force to bring Kashmir into their state. Its Hindu prince refused to make any decision until finally part of his Muslim population, aided by Muslims from neighboring Pakistan, rebelled and demanded he join Pakistan. That October, Mountbatten authorized the use of Indian troops to stop the Muslim attack and to occupy most of the province. Nehru denied that his state was an "aggressor nation" and claimed that the Pakistani invasion represented "aggression of a brutal and unforgivable kind, aggression against the people of Kashmir and against the Indian Union." In fact, both sides were guilty of aggression, turning to their armed forces for control of the vital Himalayan area.

War with Pakistan began when Jinnah sent Pakistani troops to try to expel the Indians. His troops failed to defeat the Indian forces, and an armistice ended the fighting, leaving Kashmir divided. Thus a final consequence of partition was to make Pakistan and India outright enemies. They remained in a state of hostility punctuated by two more short wars during the next three decades. Pakistan, the weaker state, sought military alliance and foreign aid from the United States to bolster its strength; India ultimately took military aid from the Soviet Union. Partition brought the Cold War to the subcontinent.

THE DEVELOPMENT OF INDEPENDENT INDIA AND PAKISTAN

Indian Nation Building

Gradually under Nehru's leadership a new Indian state took form. In the first violent months he, Mountbatten, and the head of the National Congress, V. Patel, ruled virtually as a military government. Yet the elements of a democratic state began to appear. The first task consisted of completing the incorporation of the principalities into Indian provinces under democratic rule. In exchange for generous allowances, almost all princes renounced their power peacefully. Only the Muslim prince of Hyderabad resisted, until finally Indian troops occupied his land in 1948 to "restore order" in what was officially called a "police action." The removal of the princes from power amounted to a sort of national revolution, achieved almost without force.

The second task in state building required the formation of an administration and army. Despite Congress's earlier criticism of Indians working for the British civil service and army, the new government accepted willingly their incorporation directly into the new Indian state. Indian leaders preferred the stability and efficiency provided by trained administrators and experienced military to the dangers of bringing in new state servants. A new government gave orders to personnel who served them as loyally as they had the British *raj*.

By relying on the personnel and institutions of the previous administration, the Congress leaders indicated their willingness to preserve at least some of the privileges and prestige of the old bureaucratic elite. In a symbol of the continuity with the British, they moved into the old imperial buildings. The enormous palace of the British viceroy, which Gandhi wanted used as a hospital for the poor, became the residence of the governor general (later the president) of India. Nehru occupied the luxurious mansion formerly headquarters for the British commander-in-chief. The new state displayed ostentatious power; the temptations of rule later led some in the Congress leadership, though not Nehru, to abuse their power. On balance, it is fair to conclude that the benefits of the English political inheritance greatly outweighed the ill. The ability of the Indian state to survive the turmoil of the accession to power in 1947–48 was due in large measure to the British-trained administration and army.

India's Leader: Jawaharlal Nehru. *(Embassy of India, Washington, D.C.)*

Great responsibility for the shape of the new state rested in Nehru's hands. His political authority was enormous; he shared with Gandhi the prestige of father of his country. To him, nation building had to include efforts to bring social and economic progress to India. Like Mao in China, he conceived of the struggle for national independence as a step toward material and spiritual improvement in the life of the people of his country. Unlike Mao, he rejected political dictatorship and ideological intolerance. His political ideal, as he told an American audience in 1949, was to find "some balance between the centralized authority of the state and the assurance of freedom and opportunity to each individual." The National Congress had from the start united diverse groups defending a variety of interests and creeds. It was divided between those favoring private enterprise and others (like Nehru) attracted by socialist ideals and state

intervention in economic affairs. The new state had to reconcile these diverging objectives; Nehru valued this diversity, accepting the compromises it forced upon him.

Agreement on basic political goals did unite all factions of the National Congress. Its principal aim was to develop in India a real democracy. In Asia only Japan had effectively adapted Western democratic institutions to its public life; it had the advantage of small size, a homogeneous population, and historical unity. Democratic government in India represented in practice an enormous gamble. It appeared to Congress leaders the best guarantee of tolerance and equal rights to all Indians regardless of religion, language, or caste. A third goal, one particularly important to Nehru, was the introduction of social reforms to promote the welfare of the people while still permitting free enterprise to develop. These three objectives—democracy, toleration, and partial socialism—pointed toward the transformation of one of the oldest civilized societies in the world. The task of the Indian leaders was formidable, and their means of action limited by the very democratic institutions and diversity they wished to protect.

The Indian Constitution went into effect in 1950. It preserved and extended the federal structure first introduced by the British in 1935. The states and the federal government were all ruled by responsible ministries, dependent on majorities in their legislatures to remain in power. The position of greatest importance was that of prime minister of the federal cabinet, empowered even to dissolve provincial governments (that is, to disregard federal separation of powers) if there existed a threat to the unity of India. Nehru occupied that office until his death. Political and civil liberties were guaranteed to all citizens. Voting was by universal suffrage. The first elections for regular legislative positions took place in 1951. Over 170 million citizens had the right to vote, over half of whom were illiterate. This enormous electorate made India, as Nehru later remarked, the "largest functioning democracy in the world."

Those elections proved a remarkable success. Political violence and corruption, though present, did not impede the free choice of candidates. Almost two-thirds of the electorate voted, selecting their representatives by pictures on the ballot when they could not read. Over half of the voters supported parties other than the National Congress. Still, it remained the single largest party, controlling the federal and most of the state (provincial) ministries. The greatest victor was Nehru himself. The campaign of the Congress party stressed above all his leadership. He symbolized the unity of the country; his prestige assured the party itself internal cohesion.

As a result, by 1951 Nehru's authority within India was enormous. Many years earlier, he had written for an Indian journal an anonymous portrait of himself, warning that "in this revolutionary epoch Caesarism [i.e., dictatorial rule like that of the Roman general Julius Caesar] is always at the door, and is it not possible that Jawaharlal [Nehru] might fancy himself a Caesar? Therein lies the danger for Jawaharlal and India." He might well have added that the danger existed in all the newly independent Asian and African countries. Sukarno of Indonesia did succumb to the temptation of Caesarism. Nehru's restraint was a key ingredient of Indian democracy.

Social Reform and Socialism

The introduction of democratic socialism constituted an important aspect of his program for independent India. His ideal was "a socialist pattern of society which is classless, casteless." His principal concern was the terrible poverty of much of the Indian population, among whom 40 percent were estimated in 1950 to have inadequate food for an active life. He did not attempt a campaign of expropriation of private property, however. Peaceful reform and tolerance of diversity forbade that path of reform. Instead, he conceived of an economy divided into public and private sectors (somewhat resembling the English economy after the Labor party reforms of the late 1940s). India's established industries remained in private hands, as did its farms and commerce.

Still, the Indian state played a central role in economic development. The state assumed ownership of major new industrial projects such as steel mills, of public utilities (gas, electricity), and of new irrigation projects. This development of India's "mixed economy" (part capitalist, part socialist) was guided by a National Planning Commission, responsible for decisions on state investments, agricultural development, transportation, and so on. Essentially, it was supposed to employ state funds to guide economic development in a manner best suited to improve the living conditions of the people. It relied on a mixture of Soviet planning methods, which Nehru admired, and the collaboration by India's capitalists and peasant farmers. Its most ambitious plan for rural development relied on the voluntary efforts of millions of villagers. The Village Development Program provided state funds to village committees for the construction of wells and of schools, for minimum health care, and other measures essential to fight poverty. Within a few years, 150 million Indians shared in the benefits of this program. Indian socialism excluded the use of compulsion and mass mobilization in economic development.

The first Five-Year Plan began in 1951. It emphasized the expansion of agricultural production, financing major irrigation and flood control projects. The aim was to make India self-sufficient in its food supplies. It also began the development of India's heavy industry, with the goal of providing the country with adequate industrial capacity to produce the essential factory goods needed for improved living standards and for industrial growth. At the start, foreign aid was indispensable. The country lacked the means to pay for these expensive investments. Neutrality proved a valuable foreign policy. Nehru permitted both Communist and Western states to share in India's economic plan. Three steel mills were built—one by Great Britain, one by the United States, one by the Soviet Union.

Planning worked well in those first years.

India's agricultural production climbed 3 percent a year, almost twice as fast as population growth. The second Five-Year Plan, though not as successful as the first, did maintain the economic expansion. Industrial production, the great hope of that plan, grew 6 percent annually, a rate which increased to 9 percent in the 1960s. The hope of freeing India from dependence on industrial imports was frustrated primarily by a population explosion of almost 2 percent a year (over ten million people). India could do no better than an annual increase of 1 percent per person in national income over ten years. Perhaps the best comparison is with China, where famine and economic stagnation followed the Great Leap Forward of the late 1950s. By contrast, India's moderate policies avoided social turmoil and steadily improved its economic condition, albeit at a "turtle's pace."

Nehru had made "equitable distribution" of wealth his second economic goal. This objective proved unattainable. A land reform in 1953 took farmland from absentee landlords to be redistributed among the peasant farmers, who also received new land put under cultivation through irrigation. Yet substantial inequalities of wealth and power remained, for prosperous farmers allied with local officials while the farm laborers, often from the untouchables, were without protection. In the Indian countryside, many peasants remained landless, while a small number (5 percent) held one-third of all the arable land. Their holdings, though not great (several hundred acres at most), constituted the principal source of the increased agricultural production. The Green Revolution of the 1960s introduced improved seeds and fertilizer, raising India's harvests at a rapid rate and bringing substantial profits to successful large farmers. Taking land from them meant reducing production. Equity and productivity did not go hand in hand.

Slowly improvements also came in health and education. Life expectancy among Indians rose (between 1950 and 1970) from thirty-two to fifty years, an indication of a higher (or less impoverished) standard of living for more Indians than ever before. Over those same years, literacy spread to nearly one-third of the population. So important did the state judge the diffusion of information among the population that it set up a national television network and provided villages television sets in some cases before schools. Despite these improvements, over one-third of the total population at the end of the 1960s remained impoverished. Many of the very poor abandoned rural villages to crowd into cities such as Calcutta, where half the population lived in poverty. A wasteland around a new pesticide factory near the city of Bhopal became a shantytown for some of these poor migrants, until an explosion in 1984 at the plant spread poisonous gases to kill thousands of the inhabitants. Urbanization in such conditions was not a sign of economic development, rather of the struggle to survive on the part of those millions of Indians still deprived of the benefits of the new wealth of the country.

Had India become a socialist economy? The country's factories and farms remained largely in the hands of private owners. The "public sector" of state-owned industries included only major economic enterprises. Socialism represented above all an ideal of shared wealth and a justification for state planning and partial nationalization of industry. Anything further would have required forceful revolutionary change, measures Nehru rejected as intolerable and alien to Indian life. He remained faithful to his ideal of "practical, pragmatic socialism which will fit in with the thinking of India and with the demands of India." In other words, Communist methods of class war and forceful expropriation remained unacceptable.

He would not attempt to wipe out "acquisitiveness" by violence. The socialist revolution he sought had to come through the cooperation of the Indian people.

During the same period the Indian government attempted to enforce fundamental social reforms. Nehru insisted that progress come in this area "through our own volition, as a result of our own experience," not "through any kind of force or pressure." Traditions and social custom changed very slowly, however. The constitution itself abolished the social category of untouchables and declared caste restrictions illegal. It posed the principle of social equality for all Indians regardless of religion, caste, or sex. To become effective, these reforms had to alter the customs of marriage and property ownership, bastions of caste exclusiveness and of the subjugation of women. Caste prejudices continued to divide the population, and the exclusion of the untouchables from society improved hardly at all despite special laws to protect them.

Eight years passed before the government obtained legislative approval of the basic laws establishing equality of right for Hindu women; it still did not attempt reform of Muslim practices for fear of violent opposition. The Hindu Marriage Act of 1955 and the Hindu Succession Act of 1956 established the legal basis for equality among Hindu Indians. The Succession Act gave women equal rights with men in inheritance and ownership of property; the Marriage Act declared polygamy and bigamy criminal offenses, permitted divorce, and made provision for alimony. Subsequently, marriage dowry was made illegal. Upper-class women in India did share to a great extent in the new opportunities for education, work, and equality in marriages. Among the remainder of the population, restraints and oppression remained in place. *Purdah* (female seclusion) was widely practiced, and marriage dowries for brides became more oppressive than before. Thus the position of women improved very slowly. Only by comparison with past conditions could one conclude with Nehru that these reforms instituted "justice" and "equality of status and opportunity" among Indians.

In one respect the government found that the divisions among Indians were growing greater. Regionalism represented a powerful force in a country separated by languages and cultures. Loyalty to ethnic groups inspired campaigns for the reorganization of provincial states, a new form of partition still within the federation but a cause of violence and rioting. Gradually, the government had to give in to these pressures. In 1956 several states disappeared, and new states, organized on the basis of a common language, took their place. This measure opened the door for further agitation among India's peoples, whose bond of unity still remained fragile. In later years, the most powerful movement for separate political recognition came from the Sikh religious community. A tiny but fanatical group of Sikhs turned to assassination of political leaders and indiscriminate murder of Hindus to force the government to concede a separate Sikh state in the Punjab.

Nehru had not created out of the enormous Indian population one nation in the full sense of the word. He had focused the attention of Indians on national problems and given them a sense of national pride. In that effort his personal contribution was crucial. Just how important he was to Congress and to India became apparent when he died in 1964. The leadership of the country passed for two years to a close colleague. Then, following the latter's death, the party turned to Nehru's daughter, Indira Gandhi. The choice revealed the appeal of the family itself to Indians as well as the political skill and ambition of Mrs. Gandhi. She gradually built up her own party organization and national following in the years that followed, winning a major victory in the elections of 1971. In principle, democracy continued to govern Indian political life.

Unlike her father, Indira Gandhi turned to authoritarian methods of rule to overcome political opposition. In 1975–76 she declared a state of emergency when her government lost political backing over the controversial issue of mandatory birth control. Widespread opposition forced her to return to constitutional rule. She resorted again in the early 1980s to arbitrary measures, including military repression, to put down Sikh agitation to obtain political recognition. The entire Sikh community united in opposition to her rule. She paid with her own life for these policies when a Sikh member of her own bodyguard assassinated her in 1984. In that crisis, the Nehru heritage determined the new leader of India. Her successor was her own son, Rajiv. In India, Nehru's personal charisma became a family heritage, endowing his daughter and then grandson with the symbolic majesty of national unity.

Nehru and Nonalignment

Decolonization meant to Nehru the opportunity for his state, like other former colonies, to free themselves from all forms of Western domination. He shared Sukarno's opposition to any form of "neocolonialism," that is, subservience to Western diplomatic or economic power, though he never turned the concept into a political slogan to justify defiance of all Western ties as did the Indonesian leader. Three obstacles stood in the way of his goal to make India an international center of peace and unity among Third World countries. One was the quarrel which divided India and Pakistan. The second was the problem of the Indo-Chinese frontier. The third was the campaign of the

U.S. government to form military alliances among these states. The first problem remained a constant preoccupation, worsened by a U.S. military alliance with Pakistan. The Chinese conflict, ultimately, proved the undoing of his foreign policy.

In the early years, the Sino-Indian border dispute did not appear serious. To the north of India, the mountainous land of Tibet had existed during the decades of Chinese civil war as a separate kingdom, claimed by China but ruled in fact by the Buddhist leader, the Dalai Lama. A long and very poorly defined boundary, established by the British a century before, separated India from China and Tibet. In 1950 Chinese Communist forces moved into Tibet. Nehru protested at first, and then advised the Tibetan leaders to cooperate with China, hoping to keep peace with his new Chinese neighbor.

The Indian government claimed large regions in the disputed, uninhabited territories in the Himalayas. Nehru did not attempt to confirm the boundary either by military occupation or by negotiations with the Chinese. Instead, India signed an agreement in 1954, the Sino-Indian Agreement, recognizing Chinese control of Tibet. Nehru chose to deal with the boundary dispute by ignoring it. In the meantime, the Chinese state began building a strategic road through part of the territory in question to link Tibet with the western province of Xinjiang (old name, Sinkiang). How could peace be preserved among the Asian states when they confronted intractable territorial conflicts? Nehru had no solution to that problem.

The other challenge to Asian unity arose from U.S. efforts to find military allies against the Soviet Union. Nehru became increasingly opposed to the U.S. Cold War strategy, judging it a greater threat to peace in South Asia than Soviet policies. When the Eisenhower administration set about forming a Southeast Asian military alliance,

Nehru concluded that this move represented a new form of imperialism, a "modern version of a protectorate." He did not believe that Indian democracy or security was threatened by the Soviet Union. His country had a long mountain chain to the north, an excellent strategic frontier. It needed foreign aid from all possible donors. The Indian government considered Pakistan its principal enemy. Nehru's lack of cooperation earned him the reputation of "crypto-communist" from Eisenhower's secretary of state, John Foster Dulles.

This single-minded American policy aroused Nehru's anger when the U.S. welcomed Pakistan in 1955 into the South East Asia Treaty Organization, providing it with military aid. To Nehru the U.S. measures were acts of power politics, providing India's enemy the means to launch a new war and sabotaging his policy of nonalignment. Indian national interests and Nehru's principles combined to make him a strong critic of U.S. containment policies.

Nehru slowly worked out his new foreign policy in the years following independence. In spirit it resembled the National Congress goals for a reformed India. It sought peaceful change through cooperation, with its ultimate goal the equitable distribution of wealth and well-being among all the peoples of the world. Within India, the National Congress had striven to unite groups with varying interests around one common goal, independence. India acted in world affairs in a similar manner, not allying with any power bloc but trying to serve as mediator and unifier among states. In a speech in 1949 Nehru stated that his country's objectives consisted of

the pursuit of peace, not through alignment with any major power or group of powers, but through an independent approach to each controversial or disputed issue; the liberation of subject peoples; the maintenance of freedom; the elimination of

SEATO

racial discrimination; and the elimination of want, disease and ignorance.

His ideals were those of a visionary who dreamed of an era of peace to come with the liberation of subject peoples.

To organize a group of nations adhering to his principles he relied on his prestige as Indian national leader and the influence of his large state. In the 1954 Sino-Indian treaty, the Chinese Communists supported his Five Principles: peaceful coexistence, nonaggression, territorial respect, nonintervention, and equality. To them the principles probably appeared a minor concession to the Indian leader in exchange for recognition of their conquest of Tibet. Nehru came away believing that they had accepted the Five Principles to guide their own policies (including acceptance of Indian border claims). He defended his policies before a larger audience at Bandung in 1955. The Afro-Asian Conference agreed with his goal that there should be "no dictation in the future" by powerful Western countries to the new Third World states. Differences divided them so deeply already, however, that the participants did not subscribe to his Five Principles, merely adopting a vague "Declaration on World Peace and Cooperation." To India the benefits of his policy were clear. In 1955 the Soviet leader, Khrushchev, came to India on a state visit and left behind a generous economic aid agreement. India became a leader among Third World nations, making no concessions to Western diplomatic pressure and without taking sides in the Cold War.

The Five Principles did not assure peace with China, however. The unresolved border issue and Chinese annexation of Tibet became a source of serious conflict. By 1958 the Chinese road between Xinjiang and Tibet was nearing completion. It was built through high mountainous regions (14,000–15,000 feet) where India had no frontier troops. A new issue arose following Chinese oppression of Buddhism in Tibet. In 1959, Mao's Great Leap Forward policies, which included in Tibet the persecution of the Buddhist church and seizure of church lands, provoked widespread resistance among the Tibetan people. Chinese troops repressed the uprising, and the Dalai Lama fled to India. There, Indians welcomed him as a victim of Communist persecution. The Chinese government accused India of "walking in the footsteps of the British imperialists and harboring expansionist ambitions toward Tibet." Chinese and Indian frontier forces moved closer along their long high-mountain frontier. Nehru confronted the fact that China, a "world power or would-be world power," and India had serious differences, so acute that "for the first time two major powers of Asia face each other on an armed border." Power, not moral principles, become the deciding factor in that conflict.

Neither side was prepared to compromise. China was isolated, but its army was well trained and equipped for mountain war. The Indian government, at odds with the United States over aid to Pakistan, turned in 1959 to the Soviet Union for military equipment, aid which both Russians and Chinese knew might be used in a Sino-Indian war. Nehru continued to claim that justice was on India's side, denouncing China's "unlawful" seizure of Indian territory. He would negotiate with the Chinese on the condition that they concede Indian possession of the disputed frontier regions. The Chinese government refused. Finally the Indian army began in 1962 to move troops into the remote western areas where the Chinese strategic highway was located. War had become unavoidable. China would not abandon its vital road link; India had chosen to support its claim to the frontier region with military force.

The Chinese knew that military superiority was on their side. Indian troops were still few in number and unprepared to fight at high altitude. In late October 1962, Chinese troops attacked along both the eastern and western borders. Everywhere Indian resistance collapsed. Within three weeks Chinese forces had destroyed Indian frontier defenses and were in a position in the east to invade the Indian lowlands. Nehru accused the Chinese government of violating "all principles which govern normal neighborly relations between sovereign governments" by a "deliberate cold-blooded decision" to invade India. Nonalignment provided no protection at a time of military defeat. Fearing a Chinese invasion of India, Nehru appealed for U.S. naval and air support. The United States agreed, moving ships from the U.S. Pacific fleet into the Bay of Bengal, close to one of the areas of fighting.

Then the Chinese troops withdrew. They had defeated Indian frontier forces and had established control over the territory around the Tibetan road. Their commanders sought no more. In the east they pulled back behind the original border and proclaimed a cease-fire with a twenty-mile neutral zone to separate the opposing sides. The war was over. Although no negotiations followed the end of the fighting, China had settled the border dispute by force of arms. Its army had fought and won a limited war for a specific territorial objective, applying a centuries-old Western principle of using war as a continuation of diplomacy by other means. India was powerless to alter the settlement.

The consequences of the war on Indian foreign policy obeyed another hallowed principle of power politics—"the enemy of my enemy is my friend." The Soviet Union and India shared a common enemy in Communist China. Consequently, increased Soviet military aid flowed into India. The United States, not to be outdone by the Russians, increased its economic assistance and began providing military armaments as well; total U.S. aid since independence reached over $8 billion by the late 1960s. The Chinese government for its part found in Pakistan a "friend" in opposition to India. No military alliance united the two states. Beyond the new-found good relations lay the vague possibility, however, that another war between India and Pakistan might find the Communist states themselves on opposing sides.

A border dispute did lead to another Indo-Pakistan war in 1965. The territory in question was itself of little importance. This fact revealed to what extent the two states still remained hostile, ready to fight at the slightest provocation. Communal violence sporadically broke out in parts of each country, bringing a protest from the other government. In 1964 Indian police had repressed demonstrations by Kashmir Muslims, and in retaliation Muslim mobs in East Pakistan massacred Hindus. This violence and a minor border dispute caused war to begin in 1965.

Although it led to only a few months of inconclusive fighting, in that time the new Asian balance of power became apparent. The Chinese government condemned India's "criminal aggression" and promised full support to Pakistan. The Soviet Union and the United States warned China not to intervene and called for a cease-fire. The superpowers both feared the dangers of a widening conflict. The Soviet government became peacemaker in the end, inviting both sides to negotiations in the Soviet Union. India and Pakistan accepted a return to the prewar borders. The war solved nothing. It did make clear that the Indian subcontinent too had its place in global politics, in which state interests, not the Five Principles, fixed policy and determined allies.

Islam and Militarism in Pakistan

That war represented a defeat for Pakistan. Hoping to conquer Kashmir, the Pakistani leaders had sent their best troops into battle against the Indian army. Military victory proved beyond the means of the smaller state, though it was by the mid-1960s a militaristic regime. The Muslim state had changed dramatically since independence. The first years had revealed the similarities and differences between India and Pakistan. In both states the 1935 federal structure and the cabinet system of rule provided the first elements of independent political life. But the Muslim League failed to sustain democratic rule. Its problems were enormous. Its leader, Jinnah, died in 1948. His successors were thwarted in their policies of nation building by deep internal social and cultural differences among Pakistanis and by the limited influence of the Muslim League itself among the population. The country was split in two. East Pakistan, with a unique Bengali language and culture of its own, was ruled from a great distance by West Pakistan.

Regional and tribal conflicts strained from the beginning the unity of the new nation-state. Only the Muslim religion provided a strong bond. The first constitution proclaimed Pakistan an Islamic Republic, the first state to lay down the principle that the Koran was the basic law of the land. Many Middle Eastern states with large Muslim populations imitated its example later. A shared Muslim identity was not sufficient, however, to bind together East and West Pakistan. After 1954 East Pakistanis rejected the political leadership of the Muslim League, preferring their own parties. As a result of political and social problems, prime ministers succeeded one another in rapid succession, six in the first ten years of independence.

In 1958 parliamentary democracy in Pakistan ceased to exist. The "Caesarism" of which Nehru had warned became a reality in the Muslim state. A general, Ayub Khan, seized power that year, proclaiming that he wished to introduce order and to set up Basic Democracy. The term masked a military dictatorship. He kept faithfully to the military pact with the United States, for the alliance brought his poor country massive U.S. aid— $4 billion between the late 1940s and late 1960s. He accepted the suggestions of American economic advisers to encourage individual enterprise and capitalist development, a strategy which brought economic growth at the price of further deepening the country's social inequalities. Military rule could not guarantee political unity. Pakistan's failure to win victory in the 1965 war worsened opposition, particularly from East Pakistan, more populous than West Pakistan and considered by economists the most impoverished area in the world. In the late 1960s it was under military occupation, its political leaders under arrest. Ayub Khan was replaced at the end of the decade by another general, but the change brought no improvement in the conflict between the Bengali Muslims in the east and the Pakistan government.

In 1971, the conflict became open war. That year Bengalis demonstrated and rioted against Pakistan rule. Repression by the army led millions of Bengalis to flee across the border into Indian Bengal, where they were welcomed. The Indian government decided to support the rebellion, partly to satisfy its own Bengal population, partly to weaken Pakistan. When Pakistani forces persisted in military repression, the Indian army invaded East Pakistan. Once again India and Pakistan were at war. This time, however, the fighting ended with Indian victory, both in the east and in the west. The peace settlement required that the Pakistan government withdraw from Muslim Bengal, which proclaimed its independence under the name of Bangladesh.

Pakistan itself remained with less than half the population of the prewar state. Its economy came to depend more than ever on U.S. foreign aid, whose benefits continued to flow primarily to the middle classes. Poverty and disease were severe among the lower classes, forcing many Pakistani men to leave their country in search of work. Remaining away, some for years at a time, in Europe and the Middle East, the "remittance" of their earnings sent back to their families came to represent a substantial part of Pakistan foreign earnings. The glory of independence waned, leaving behind only the original vision of a country uniquely Muslim. Political repression and economic difficulties were at least partially compensated in the view of many Pakistanis by their people's religious unity. Koranic legal and social regulations, enforced in theory by the state after 1978, gave the country the appearance of fidelity to Islam. Religion was still the most potent symbol of Pakistani nationalism.

SUMMARY

Did independence bring substantial improvements to the populations of the South Asian countries? The question, which we will also confront in examining other Third World regions, is both controversial and complex. On what grounds does one measure progress in the history of developing nations: political independence, freedom, economic growth, reduction of social inequalities, national pride? The best historical approach to this problem is perhaps provided by the issue of "neocolonialism," a term suggesting the continued existence of

Western economic domination after decolonization.

Neocolonialism was blamed by Sukarno for the failure of his country to establish stable government and to realize the great cultural and social achievements he had promised his people at the time of independence. He affirmed that vestiges of the colonial past were to blame for Indonesia's problems. Responsibility in fact appears to lie partly with the incompetence of the Indonesian state, partly with the monumental problems of social conflict and economic impoverishment of his country. In those conditions, his country could not avoid some form of dependence on the developed countries. In the Philippines, on the other hand, neocolonialism does describe accurately the situation in which a political elite, in power during many generations of colonial rule, continued to dominate the state, and in which the economic development of the country remained closely bound to economic interests in the United States. This dependence was increased by the Cold War military ties between the Philippine state and the U.S. government, more concerned to preserve its naval and air bases than with the politics of the regime receiving U.S. aid. Yet that land appears the exception, not the rule throughout the region.

The evolution of the Indian subcontinent following liberation from British domination reveals a pattern of development which "neocolonialism" does not help us to understand. A new Asian balance of power confronted India with a powerful eastern neighbor, whose successful military action in the Sino-Indian war dashed Nehru's hopes in the peaceful benefits of nonalignment. The Cold War penetrated the subcontinent when the United States became the ally of Pakistan, yet the initial conflict between India and Pakistan grew out of the unique

neocolonialism?

in multi-
combined
ı explosive
rol of state

ıterests in-
ficiently to
goals. The
ınce on In-
programs
ı multina-
ıequalities
l wealth of
associated
luctivity—
ion in the
ve invest-
d the new
ght we can
f change in
ough cost-
olutionary
ımmunism
the end,
ı states no
ınd social

JOHN HUGHES, *Indonesian Upheaval* (1967)

C. L. M. PENDUS, *The Life and Times of Sukarno* (1974)

STEPHEN SHALOM, *The United States and the Philippines: A Study in Neocolonialism* (1981)

AMRY VANDENBOSCH AND RICHARD BUTWELL, *The Changing Face of Southeast Asia* (1966)

Postwar India and Pakistan

*LARRY COLLINS AND DOMINIQUE LAPIERRE, *Freedom at Midnight* (1975)

MICHAEL EDWARDES, *Nehru: A Political Biography* (1971)

SARVEPALLI GOPAL, *Jawaharlal Nehru* (2 vols.)

PENDEREL MOON, *Gandhi and Modern India* (1969)

PERCIVAL SPEAR, *India, Pakistan and the West* (1965)

RICHARD WEEKES, *Pakistan: Birth and Growth of a Muslim Nation* (1964)

Memoirs and Novels

*V. A. NAIPAUL, *Voyage Among the Believers: An Islamic Journey* (1981)

*PAUL SCOTT, *The Raj Quartet* (1979)

tics in Indo-

chapter 10

WAR AND REVOLUTION
IN THE MIDDLE EAST
AND AFRICA

The history of the Middle East after 1945 is a story above all of war, revolution, and civil strife. More than any other region in the world, it became the arena of political conflict and great power rivalry. No one state dominated the territories once ruled by the Ottoman Empire. Its collapse in the First World War marked the first step in the political reordering of the Middle East. In the territories south of Turkey and between Iran and Egypt, the borders drawn by the Western powers to separate their "mandated" states divided a population largely Muslim in religion and Arab in culture and grouped within each land peoples of differing, often conflicting religious, ethnic, and social identity.

The roots of the instability of the region lie thus in the fragmented nature of these lands. The second stage in their development began in 1945 when decolonization brought full independence to all the Middle Eastern states. Nation building constituted there, as in other parts of the Third World, a major objective of new leaders, but only the Egyptian people were sufficiently unified nationally to provide a solid foundation for this process. Elsewhere, political life was dominated by the struggle among shifting factions within a small conservative elite. These leaders often praised "pan-Arab nationalism," but their support for this vague ideal of Arab unity did little to overcome the internal disunity of their states. They were unable to find a path to nation building.

To provide that unity, two important mass movements did appear in the decades after the war. Populist nationalism, best seen in Nasser's Egypt, was based on social reform and a strong national leadership, similar in many ways to Nehru's policies in India. Very different was the movement called Muslim fundamentalism, which appeared in lands in and beyond the Arab world. It sought within Islam itself a set of ideals to mobilize the believers in a Muslim nation, unified and disciplined. The Muslim Brotherhood had first taken this direction, but fundamentalism assumed a variety of forms in later years. One appeared as the state ideology of revolutionary Iran in 1979. Although the two movements did provide the bonds for state building, the political conflicts they provoked only deepened the disunity among Middle Eastern lands.

The violent history of the region was due to two factors outside the Arab community. The first was the presence in the midst of Arab peoples of Jewish settlers in Palestine, where they founded their own state of Israel. The inflexible opposition of Arab states to the very existence of this country led to four separate wars in the three decades following the Second World War. Pan-Arab nationalism came to mean essentially resistance to Western imperialism and also to Zionism, a symbol to Arabs of the illegitimacy of Israeli occupation of Palestinian land. The second external factor explaining Middle Eastern instability was foreign development of the region's petroleum reserves, found there in greater abundance and higher quality than anywhere in the world. The dependence of the industrial countries on this vital resource brought the pressures of the Cold War to bear on the oil-rich countries, leading to competition between the superpowers and to Western intervention in Middle Eastern affairs. More than any other region of the globe the problems of independence became in the Middle East a source of tragic conflict.

By contrast, the history of sub-Saharan Africa in those years focuses attention on the internal difficulties of nation building and economic development. Projected suddenly into the era of national independence, the leaders of these new states were handicapped by myriad problems, partly the result of the colonial experience of their lands, partly the consequence of poverty, of social and ethnic conflict, and of the economic backwardness among the peoples they ruled. In the southernmost African state, the colonial past remained a bitterly divisive presence as a result of the white supremacist policies of the descendants of the Dutch settlers, opposed with increasing violence by the African nationalist movements. South Africa experienced in its peculiar manner the divisiveness of communal conflict in the midst of the struggle for African political rights and national freedom.

DECOLONIZATION AND WAR IN THE MIDDLE EAST

The Conflict over Palestine

The end of the Second World War immediately brought out the long-standing conflict between Arabs and Jews in the British mandate of Palestine (see Chapter 3). By war's end, the other mandated territories—Lebanon and Syria, Iraq and Jordan—had received their independence, under constitutional monarchs (in the latter two) or elected parliamentary governments. No leaders enjoyed comparable authority in Palestine, where 1.2 million Arabs confronted 600,000 Jews, each side demanding political self-rule. Arab opposition to British occupation and Jewish migration had led in 1936 to a prolonged and bloody Arab revolt. As a consequence, when British forces had finally suppressed the insurrection, the British government laid plans for the possible partition of the territory. While the Zionist organization had welcomed the prospect of a Jewish nation-state, even reduced in size, Arab leaders were united in opposition and vowed to fight any grant of territory to the Jews. The prewar deadlock in negotiations for Palestinian independence raised, as in India, the prospect of civil war as two religious communities fought to control land each considered its own.

The Second World War deepened the conflict over Palestine. On the one hand, it brought independence to the Arab states, whose leaders were united only in their opposition to a Jewish state in Palestine. On the other, the reaction to the horrors of the Holocaust aroused greater support than ever before among Jews for their own nation-state and turned the Zionist commitment to that cause into a crusade. The war temporarily ended all discussion of future Palestinian self-government, Jewish migration, and partition. The British made the maintenance of order in Palestine their sole objective, virtually ending Jewish immigration. Yet those were the very years when Jewish persecution in Europe rendered the creation of a Jewish homeland in Palestine a matter of life and death.

The British government increased its domination in the region during the war. The vital importance of the Suez Canal, and of the region's petroleum, caused British forces to repress any signs of possible Arab collaboration with Germany. In Palestine, the Muslim religious leader, the grand mufti of Jerusalem, publicly announced his loyalty to Nazi Germany and fled to Berlin, where he made radio broadcasts to the Middle East calling for Arab revolt against the British. In Egypt and in Iraq, political leaders and some army officers appeared ready to welcome Rommel's divisions when his offensive in 1942 reached Egypt. To guarantee their control, British military forces forcibly installed leaders in both states who supported the Allies. Palestinian Jews welcomed the opportunity to join in the war against Nazi Germany, sending thirty thousand men to serve

in the British army. They later became the core of the Israeli army.

The Palestinian crisis erupted immediately following the war. The British government, caught between Palestinian Arabs and Jews and intent on keeping the support of the Arab states, refused to open the country to more immigrants. Jewish refugees scattered across Europe looked to Palestine for a new home and received the help of the Zionist organization. Desperate migrants sailed from Europe to the Holy Land in decrepit old boats such as the *Exodus*. Some ships sank before reaching their destination. Others were captured by the British, who placed the passengers in internment camps in Cyprus, prisoners again.

The Jews acquired a valuable—though half-hearted—ally when the U.S. government spoke out in 1945 in favor of Jewish immigration to Palestine. Some American political leaders were sympathetic to the cause of Jewish nationalism, and all—in particular President Truman—were under political pressure from American Jewish organizations to assist in the creation of a Jewish homeland in the Middle East. In 1945 Truman indicated his support for a plan for massive settlement of Jewish migrants in Palestine. U.S. involvement made the crisis an international affair.

Unable to transfer power peacefully to a Palestinian state, the British government turned to outside help. Palestinian Arab leaders all agreed that their land had to become one independent nation-state under the rule of the Arab majority. The Zionists, like the Muslim League in India, demanded special territorial protection for their people, who they feared would otherwise suffer persecution by the Arabs. To force London to heed their demands for immigration and self-rule, Palestinian Jews launched in 1945 a violent resistance movement, which included terrorist attacks against British officers and officials.

Abandoning their hopeless effort to bring the two sides together and resolved, as in India, to withdraw quickly, the British government declared in early 1947 that it was placing the fate of its Palestine mandate in the hands of the United Nations. This international body had to determine whether Palestine should become one state or two. The United States played the key role in mobilizing support for partition (backed also by the Soviet Union and its satellites to demonstrate their opposition to "British imperialism"). In November of that year a majority in the U.N. General Assembly voted in favor of separate Arab and Jewish states. As in India, the existence of two deeply antagonistic communities, each intent on defending its own national rights, had led to partition of the country.

This solution was unacceptable to the surrounding Arab countries. Opposition to a Jewish state had become a key test of loyalty to the cause of pan-Arab nationalism, and to the Palestinian people. An additional factor behind their decision to intervene in Palestine was the competition among Arab leaders for political influence in the Middle East and for control of the Palestinian territory. The king of Jordan hoped to annex the lands west of the Jordan River and feared Syrian plans for a Greater Syria encompassing all the land from Iraq to the Mediterranean. The Iraqi and Egyptian monarchs were rivals for leadership of the Arab countries. On only one point did they all agree—the Middle East had to remain Arab. This objective had brought them together in 1945 in a regional organization, the Arab League. They proclaimed its general purpose to be "coordinating policies" and "strengthening relations" among its members (Syria, Lebanon, Jordan, Iraq, Saudi Arabia, and Egypt); its specific goal was to prevent the formation of a Jewish state in Palestine.

The founder and leader of the League was Egypt, which was the largest and most powerful Arab state. Its population had grown rapidly, rising from ten million in the early century to sixteen million. The standard of living of the urban and rural masses had probably stagnated in those years, creating the conditions for bitter social unrest. A few industrialists, bankers, and landowners enjoyed great wealth; some were Coptic Christians, and many others were foreigners. This business and landed elite controlled political parties and stood in the way of any reforms to fight poverty and introduce social reforms. In those conditions of social unrest and political corruption, the Muslim Brotherhood grew stronger than ever before. Its membership after the war rose to over one million, and it (with considerable exaggeration) claimed to have a half-million Egyptians in its paramilitary force, the Phalanx. No political party possessed such mass support. Alone among all the political organizations in the country, it offered material support and spiritual guidance to the country's lower classes. Its Muslim fundamentalism appeared both in its efforts to use the Islamic creed as a guide to social reform and in its violent resistance to the idea of a Jewish homeland in Palestine.

Opposition to Palestinian partition constituted the sole political issue uniting the Egyptian masses and the state. In postwar years Egypt lacked strong national leadership. The Wafd party, the outstanding nationalist movement earlier, had discredited itself among Egyptians by its wartime collaboration with the British. The monarch, King Farouk, was isolated from his people by his nationality (he was Turkish) and by his incompetence as a ruler. He possessed great wealth, owned vast landed estates, and lived in great luxury, spending as much time on the French Riviera as in Egypt. He distrusted the leaders of parliament, who threatened his monarchical privileges, and feared the religious fanaticism of the Muslim Brotherhood. In Egypt as in the other Arab countries, the only cause capable of overcoming political disunity was the struggle to prevent the creation of Israel.

In the winter of 1947–48, Palestine was a land torn by civil war. Jewish and Palestinian military units fought one another for control of villages and towns as the British forces gradually withdrew to the coast. The Palestinians received arms from the Arab League; the Jews had to take their weapons where they could find them. The day after the last British troops left Palestine in May 1948, Jewish leaders proclaimed the formation of the state of Israel. Their dream had come true, but it was threatened by enemies within and surrounding Palestine. Egypt, Iraq, Syria, and Jordan immediately declared war on Israel and sent their armies to destroy the new state. The first Arab-Israeli war had begun.

Egypt took the lead. The Egyptian army marched off to fight its first war while volunteers from the Brotherhood's paramilitary forces joined the Palestinian Arabs. King Farouk ignored the warnings of his generals that the army was poorly prepared and equipped for war. He believed that Arab forces would quickly annihilate the outnumbered and ill-armed Jewish army. He, and most Arab leaders, underestimated the ability of the Jews to resist.

Surrounded on three sides by enemies, the Jewish forces fought for the survival of their new nation-state and for their faith. The Palestinians did not possess the same ideological-religious fervor, and many, fear-

War for Palestine: Palestinian Arab Irregulars, 1948. *(National Archives)*

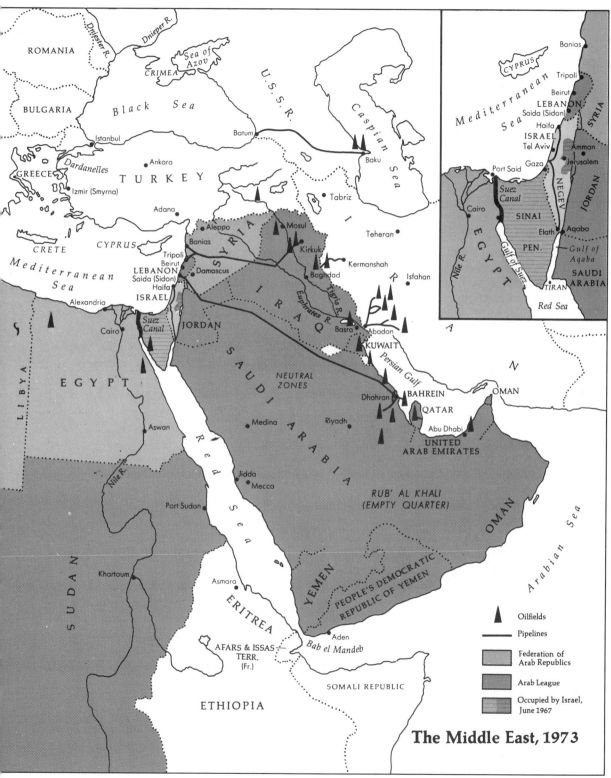

ROMANIA

BULGARIA

Black Sea

CRIMEA

Dnieper R.

Dniester R.

Sea of Azov

U.S.S.R.

Istanbul

Dardanelles

GREECE

Izmir (Smyrna)

CRETE

Ankara

TURKEY

Adana

CYPRUS

Mediterranean Sea

Batum

Baku

Caspian Sea

Tabriz

Teheran

Kermanshah

Isfahan

Aleppo

Banias

Tripoli
Beirut
LEBANON
Saida (Sidon)
Haifa
ISRAEL

Damascus

Mosul

Kirkuk

Baghdad

SYRIA

IRAQ

Euphrates R.

Tigris R.

Basra

Abadan

Alexandria

Cairo

Suez Canal

JORDAN

EGYPT

LIBYA

Aswan

Nile R.

Red Sea

Medina

Jidda

Mecca

SAUDI ARABIA

NEUTRAL ZONES

Riyadh

KUWAIT

Persian Gulf

Dhahran

BAHREIN

QATAR

Abu Dhabi

UNITED ARAB EMIRATES

OMAN

RUB' AL KHALI
(EMPTY QUARTER)

Arabian Sea

OMAN

Port Sudan

Khartoum

SUDAN

Asmara

ERITREA

YEMEN

PEOPLE'S DEMOCRATIC
REPUBLIC OF YEMEN

Aden

Bab el Mandeb

AFARS & ISSAS
TERR.
(Fr.)

SOMALI REPUBLIC

ETHIOPIA

Inset:

CYPRUS

Mediterranean Sea

Banias

Tripoli

Beirut

LEBANON

Saida (Sidon)

Haifa

ISRAEL

Tel Aviv

Gaza

Port Said

Cairo

EGYPT

Nile R.

Suez Canal

Gulf of Suez

SINAI PEN.

Elath

NEGEV

Amman

Jerusalem

JORDAN

Aqaba

Gulf of Aqaba

SAUDI ARABIA

TIRAN

Red Sea

SYRIA

Legend:

▲ Oilfields

— Pipelines

Federation of Arab Republics

Arab League

Occupied by Israel, June 1967

The Middle East, 1973

ing for their lives and their religion under Jewish rule, fled the Jewish-controlled areas. The fighting skill of the Jews was matched by only a few Arab forces. The Jordanian Arab Legion, led by English officers, seized part of the area on the right (western) bank of the Jordan River and part even of the city of Jerusalem, whose Jewish area for months was surrounded and under siege. Among the Egyptian officers, some, like captain Gamal Nasser, fought bravely, but his commitment was not matched by most of the army, badly led and badly supplied by the Egyptian government. Egypt lost all of the Negev Desert in southern Palestine. Lacking any coordinated strategy, the Arab forces conducted separate campaigns and could not prevent the Jews from occupying an area larger even than that granted by the U.N. partition plan.

Failure of the Egyptian offensives was the key to ending the war. In February 1949, the United Nations obtained agreement from all sides to an armistice. Israeli forces occupied the coastal region of Palestine, part of the Jordan River valley, and the Negev Desert to the Red Sea. Jerusalem was divided. The armistice line confirmed the partition of Palestine, and thus represented a victory for Israel. It emerged a small, oddly shaped state surrounded by enemies. The flight of most Palestinian inhabitants left the Jews a majority of the population. The new Israeli government began the process of constructing a Jewish nation-state and introduced socialist policies brought from Europe. It supported the formation, begun earlier by the first Jewish settlers, of collective farms, the *kibbutz*, whose members shared their meager crops as they struggled to make the desert fertile once again. The new state, a parliamentary democracy, welcomed Jews from any country and made Hebrew, the Biblical tongue not spoken for two millennia, the official language. It bore some resemblance to a theocracy, that is, a state whose laws and policies were inspired by a religious faith, yet at the same time it was a modern nation-state, providing the freedom and individual opportunity of a Western country. To many Arabs, it became the object of abiding hatred both because of the partition of Palestine and because of its "Western imperialist" character, which challenged traditional values and the Muslim faith. Surrounded by enemies, the Israelis had to arm their nation in anticipation of another war.

The defeat of the forces of the Arab League represented a deeply humiliating experience for all the Arab countries, discrediting political leaders. A constant reminder of the defeat was the presence of 750,000 Palestinian refugees, scattered throughout the Middle East but concentrated in Egyptian territory. The Palestinians received little help from the Arab states. A few were able to find a new place for themselves in other parts of the Middle East; most remained in miserable refugee camps under U.N. care, hoping for the day when Israel would no longer exist and they could return to their homes. In all respects the Israeli victory was a disaster for the Egyptian monarchy, unable to unite Arab forces and to organize and lead its army. The months of war proved a bitter lesson for army officers, who returned to Egypt convinced that the corrupt political leadership of their country had betrayed them, the Egyptian nation, and the Arab cause. Among this group originated the conspiracy which ended the monarchy and began a populist nationalist revolution in Egypt.

Political Revolution in Egypt

The leader of this secret opposition was Gamal Nasser. When a student before the

Second World War, he had been active in the nationalist movement which he hoped would "rebuild the country so that the weak and the humiliated Egyptian people can rise up again and live as free and independent men." Son of poor parents, he chose the career of an army officer both to improve his own life and to promote the cause of Egyptian nationalism. In the first years, army life brought him no glory and little opportunity to participate in nation building, but it formed the bonds uniting Nasser and other officers, including Anwar Sadat (his successor as ruler of Egypt), when they later did set about remaking Egypt. His real political career began after the Palestinian war, when he and his colleagues realized, as he wrote later, that "our battle was taking place in Cairo. We knew that we had to liberate our country first, in order to be able to fight." Believing themselves betrayed by the monarch and the parliamentary regime, they chose to rely on their own leadership and inspiration to restore Egyptian power and influence. Their military conspiracy sought a political revolution.

The constitutional monarchy was increasingly unpopular in the years after the war. Free elections in 1950 (the last multiparty elections until 1984) revealed to what extent parliamentary politics had become the affair of a small political elite. Few voters bothered to cast their ballots; those who did split their choice among several parties, leaving the Wafd with only 40 percent of the total parliamentary representation. The state was weakened still more by King Farouk's ambition to control the government. Anti-British nationalist policies constituted the only cause around which the new cabinet could mobilize popular support. In 1951 it began a campaign to force the British to withdraw their troops from the Suez zone. The British refused to negotiate, and the movement grew

increasingly violent. In early 1952 riots protesting British actions broke out in Cairo. The king dismissed the cabinet, took over rule, and called in the army to repress the rioting. In doing so, he sealed his own fate as well as that of parliamentary democracy.

The political chaos that year created the opportunity for Egypt's revolutionary officers to move into action. The officers were organized in a secret group calling itself the Free Officers, under Nasser's leadership. Founded in 1949, it grew to about a thousand members. When King Farouk ordered the army into Cairo to end the riots, its members finally set in motion their plans for a military *coup*, that is, the overthrow of the monarchy by military forces. In July 1952, they took over command of the armed forces with the help of General Naguib, a senior officer who shared their opposition to the monarchy. Army units surrounded the royal palace and forced the king to abdicate. On leaving the country, Farouk's parting words to the victorious insurgents were: "Your task will be difficult. It isn't easy, you know, to govern Egypt." With only vague plans for the future, they had begun Egypt's nationalist revolution.

The process of remaking the Egyptian state had only just begun. Few Egyptians regretted the departure of the Turkish king. There did still exist other contenders. Liberal parties sought to protect the constitution, as well as the interests of the capitalists and landowners who supported them. The followers of the Muslim Brotherhood looked forward to a regime to protect the Muslim religion from the corrupt influence of the West in a sort of Islamic republic. The officers were not, however, prepared to tolerate political diversity and dissent. Nasser referred sarcastically later to the "dispersed followers and contrasted remnants, chaos, dissensions, surrender and idleness" which they encountered in the months after over-throwing the monarchy. It is likely that they never seriously considered sharing the re-sponsibilities and privileges of rule.

Their response to the political confusion they encountered was to eliminate their rivals and to end parliamentary rule. They dissolved parliament and the cabinet, replac-ing them with a Revolutionary Command Council (RCC). It consisted of the leaders in the Free Officers conspiracy, under the chairmanship of Gamal Nasser. The council abolished the constitution and in early 1953 disbanded all political parties. Lacking a mass following, the liberal parties disap-peared from public life. The small Commu-nist party became the first target of outright repression, its leaders thrown in jail. Nasser proclaimed that "the Communists are agents who believe neither in the liberty of their land nor in their nation but only do the bid-ding of outsiders." The real crime of the Communist movement was to proclaim pro-letarian revolution to be the salvation of the Egyptian people. Egyptian nationalism was the cause which to the officers sanctioned their military dictatorship and promised the resurgence of their country.

The Muslim Brotherhood presented the Revolutionary Command Council with its most dangerous rival. The military leaders opposed the Brotherhood for two reasons. In the first place, they did not share the Brotherhood's goal of Islamic revolution. They were Westernized officers, for whom the Koran fixed religious belief and practice, not state policy. Second, the Brotherhood challenged their own political power. In January 1954, Muslim leaders began mass street demonstrations aimed at forcing the council to implement their plans for an Isla-mic revolution. The ruling officers seized the opportunity to arrest the Brotherhood lead-ership and to ban the organization, which, as in previous periods of repression, went un-derground. In October 1954, one of its members attempted to assassinate Nasser. The police asserted—though without real proof—that the Brotherhood sought to overthrow the new regime. Police repression worsened, and prisons filled with political prisoners. The revolutionary officers had defeated all their rivals for power.

Their new regime incorporated immedi-ately the objectives of pan-Arab nationalism. They reiterated their determination to pre-pare for a new war with Israel. At the same time, they took steps to strengthen the na-tional liberation movements under way in North Africa, the last area where Arabs lived under Western imperial rule. Arab na-tionalists from Tunisia, Morocco, and Al-geria, still part of the French Empire, found refuge in Cairo, where they received finan-cial assistance from the new government. The French government was not deeply committed to maintaining its rule in Moroc-co and Tunisia, to which it granted indepen-dence in 1956.

Algeria, on the other hand, presented a far more complex human and political prob-lem. The Algerian National Liberation Front, with its headquarters in Cairo, had called in 1954 for an Algerian insurrection against the French. It confronted resolute opposition from over one million Europeans of French culture and citizenship. They were deeply hostile to the Arabs and to Algerian independence. To defeat the Arab na-tionalist revolt and to protect the European settlers, the French government sent in hun-dreds of thousands of troops, some just with-drawn from Indochina. This new French co-lonial war lasted until 1962, when Algeria, last of all Arab lands, finally received its inde-pendence. Western empires had disap-peared from the Middle East, but Western interest in petroleum and the conflict over Israel continued to keep the West directly involved in Arab affairs.

NATIONALISM AND THE GREAT POWERS IN THE MIDDLE EAST

Iran and the West

On the eastern edge of the Middle East, the state of Iran was pulled into the Cold War soon after the end of the Second World War. Its strategic location on the Soviet border and its abundant petroleum reserves made it one of the first areas of serious conflict between East and West (see Chapter 7). The shah, constitutional monarch of Iran, drew from that experience the conclusion that the independence of his country and his own rule depended upon the protection and support of the West. Like other countries in the Middle East, the Muslim religion represented the single strongest cultural bond among the population, still closely bound to a patriarchal social order. The West appeared to them an alien presence, but to the shah, it offered diplomatic security and a model of economic development. He adhered to his pro-Western policies until his reign came to a violent end in 1979, when a radical fundamentalist revolution transformed Iran into an Islamic Republic.

The abundant petroleum reserves of Iran assured income to the state and direct Western involvement in Iranian politics. Its exploitation had been the work of the British Petroleum Company, which like the other international oil corporations, decided the rate of extraction and the price of the oil—and hence of the royalties to the Iranian government. The shah hoped to obtain greater control of this valuable natural resource, but only by negotiations with the Western states and oil companies. In his calculations, acceptance of exploitation of Iranian oil by Western corporations was compensated by protection from Soviet intervention and economic and political assistance for his regime.

There did exist a nationalist alternative to the shah's pro-Western policies. As in other Third World countries after the Second World War, a political movement emerged in Iran which sought to end the dependence of their country on the West. It appeared in the form of a coalition of political groups called the National Front, headed by a dynamic political leader, Dr. Mohammed Mossadeq. His program included state ownership of the oil properties and neutrality for Iran in the conflict between East and West. With strong backing from Iran's lower classes, Mossadeq in 1951 became prime minister. One of his first acts was to order the nationalization of Iran's oil wells and refineries.

His policy of confrontation presented the British government and the international oil corporations with the first challenge to their control over Middle Eastern oil, a loss of power they were determined to resist. British Petroleum obtained the support of all the other oil corporations for a boycott of Iranian oil, in effect declaring financial war on the National Front. The government confronted a serious economic crisis, worsened by Mossadeq's refusal to recognize the authority of the shah and his inability to preserve the unity of his National Front coalition. When the political conflict grew violent, the shah fled the country. Mossadeq's nationalist reform policies were leading the country into political revolution.

This Iranian affair, begun in a dispute over nationalization of oil, appeared to the U.S. government a Cold War conflict. In 1953, the new Eisenhower administration decided that containment had to include opposition to anti-Western regimes in strategic areas. It feared such states would be targets, in the words of one U.S. leader, of "Soviet pressure designed to accelerate Communist conquest." The Iranian Communist party (called the *Tudeh*) did support Mossadeq, though it did not dominate the National Front or dictate cabinet policy. But the very presence of Communists in the coalition suggested to U.S. leaders a Soviet conspiracy and appeared to justify U.S. intervention in the political crisis there. The U.S. Central Intelligence Agency sent covert aid, including arms, to the shah's supporters in the country. Popular demonstrations against Mossadeq and opposition to his rule by army leaders, secretly encouraged by U.S. agents, forced Mossadeq to resign in mid-1953. The shah returned to take power in what was in effect a U.S.-backed counterrevolution.

The shah fixed three principal objectives upon resuming his rule. The first was to keep firm control over the country. He purged the army of all dissidents and built up a police force to repress political opposition. He tolerated parliamentary politics but remained the power behind the government. Not a dictator in the full sense of the word, his rule remained authoritarian. His second objective was to restore cooperation with the Western states. He brought Iran into the Middle Eastern military alliance, the Baghdad Pact, alongside Great Britain, Turkey and Iraq. He accepted U.S. protection for his country and backing for his state, ultimately signing a defense treaty with the United States. In return the United States provided his country with large amounts of economic and military aid, more than went to any other state outside the NATO alliance. U.S. advisers helped to train his military, equipped with U.S. war materiel, and provided assistance in setting up his new police force. In global power politics, the shah aligned his country on the side of the West.

His third objective consisted in the transformation of Iran's society and economy. He ultimately called his plan a "White Revolution," combining political order (symbolized by the monarchical color white) and social revolution. The shah undertook a "revolu-

tion from above" to make Iran, in his words, "comparable to the most developed countries in the world." He introduced policies for the development of industry, for land reform to increase peasant holdings (including the expropriation of property belonging to Muslim religious societies), and for the establishment of civil law in place of Koranic law. Like Kemal Ataturk in Turkey, he sought to exclude Islam from Iranian public life and to break the social and cultural bonds of Muslim tradition. He forced into exile religious leaders who opposed his Western reforms. The most influential of these Muslim fundamentalists was the Ayatollah Khomeini, whose program, more extreme than that of the Muslim Brotherhood, included the transformation of Iran into an Islamic republic in which the Muslim religion and religious leaders would dominate the state and society.

The difficulties facing the shah's ambitious plans were great. He confronted serious opposition to his regime from groups demanding political liberty—largely students and educated professionals—and from religious leaders and their followers, principally the peasantry and poor urban classes, who demanded the preservation and strengthening of traditional Muslim laws and practices. To achieve his economic goals, he needed large sums of money. The major sources of these funds were Iranian oil revenues and foreign aid, both dependent on Western countries. He dealt with the political problem by police repression; he overcame his financial difficulties by collaboration with the West. Although he appeared a strong ruler, conditions within his country and in the international arena weakened his powers.

Upon resuming his rule in 1953, he returned ownership of Iran's oil properties to the international corporations. The oil embargo ended; once again Iranian oil flowed to Western markets. He insisted, however, on an increased share in the profits from the sale of his country's petroleum. His new agreement, plus expanding world petroleum demand, increased oil revenues from $22 million in 1954 to almost $300 million in 1960. Yet the Iranian government still had no control over the price set or the amount of oil produced, decisions made by the oil corporations to ensure that their production worldwide did not undermine prices. They kept oil prices low—still below $2 per barrel—to promote sales, leaving Iran and the other petroleum-rich countries with less revenue than they believed they should receive. During a recession in 1959 the oil corporations agreed among themselves to lower prices even more, a move taken without any consultation with the Middle Eastern states. The power of Western corporate leaders to make such crucial decisions represented even to an ally of the West such as the shah an unfair act of Western economic domination.

That action incited the major oil-producing countries to join forces. The shah turned to the king of Saudi Arabia, who had also begun an extensive program of economic development. The Saudi and Iranian governments shared common interests both in preserving their conservative monarchies and in resisting the oil corporations' exclusive control of their major natural resource and source of state income. They hoped that by combining forces, they could make the international oil corporations take their interests into account.

At their initiative, representatives of all the major oil-producing states gathered in 1960 to form the Organization of Petroleum Exporting Countries (OPEC). The immediate objective was to stabilize oil prices and to coordinate their petroleum policies to protect "their interests, individually and collectively." Behind this modest aim lay the au-

dacious goal of fixing levels of oil production and prices. While their organization had in fact little immediate impact on oil policy, the tremendous increase in Western demand for oil in the 1960s improved their economic situation substantially. By then petroleum use had risen so rapidly that it provided over half the West's energy supplies, so vital that industrial economies could not function without it. The Middle East possessed the best and most abundant oil supplies. In the late 1960s oil prices began a slow increase, rising to over $2 a barrel, and revenues going to Iran and Saudi Arabia reached nearly $1 billion. Although their policies were basically conservative, these two states had lent their political weight to a radical shift in the global economic balance of power. In the world of international finance and economics, these revenues and the possession of great petroleum reserves gave the OPEC countries new power and influence.

Nasser and the New Egypt

The Egyptian military leaders, lacking the natural riches of the oil countries but with great ambitions for social reform and international power, set out in a different direction toward what can be called populist nationalism. They had overthrown Egypt's constitutional monarchy in 1952 to end the reign of an incompetent and corrupt monarch, but also to undertake a nationalist revolution. They were convinced that they were the rightful national leaders, the "vanguard" as Nasser wrote in 1953 whose "mission had not ended." What policies should they adopt? They themselves had no blueprint, merely a vague set of "principles" formulated before they took over the Egyptian state. The Six Principles included the withdrawal of British troops from Suez, an end to "feudalism," reforms for "social justice," a "powerful national army," and a "sound democratic system."

These principles provided no practical guidance to neophyte military rulers divided among themselves on both the goals and political reforms of their revolution. General Naguib preferred a return to constitutional government, but Nasser believed the "mission" of the "vanguard," that is, the officers, was to carry on the revolution. In early 1954 the conflict broke into the open. Nasser's power over Egyptian military and police was sufficient to force Naguib's resignation. Proclaiming that the revolution was threatened by a return of the old order, Nasser placed officers in positions of control throughout the state. The military dictatorship became stronger and more centralized.

The militarization of the state and the disappearance of Nasser's only rival for leadership completed the Egyptian political revolution. In place of political parties the military leaders created a single movement, called in 1955 the Liberation Rally but given different names in the years ahead. It alone enjoyed freedom of assembly and the right to select candidates for elected office. Censorship was imposed on radio and the press, and labor unions lost the right to strike. A constitution was adopted in 1956 creating a National Assembly, but its representatives were chosen prior to election by the Liberation Rally and it had no real power. A cabinet replaced the Revolutionary Command Council, but it consisted of the same officers who had led the country since 1952. Nasser held the title of president of the Republic, in fact a benevolent military dictator committed to national revolution.

The goal of "social justice" included in the Six Principles led in the first years only to a modest land reform and to plans for the construction of a great dam on the Nile. Seizing the king's estates and cutting back on landlord property to two hundred acres (still quite large), the government in 1953 distributed the available land among medium and small farmers. The reform, though limited, did strengthen the support for the new regime among the influential rural families, who benefited most from the reform.

Nasser's most ambitious project was the damming of the waters of the Nile behind a new dam at Aswan, a structure so huge it would dwarf the pyramids. Plans for its construction foresaw such abundant water for irrigation that the arable land of Egypt would increase by one-third and hydroelectric power in a greater quantity than all the electricity then available in the country. A great source of pride to Nasser, it embodied both the hope for social betterment—populism—and the grandiose vision of a national revolution in Egypt. How could the dam be paid for? The Egyptian state lacked the necessary financial means. Like India, it could not sponsor major economic development without outside help.

The most dramatic international consequence of the military revolution was Egypt's defiance of Western policies and Nasser's emergence as nationalist leader among Arab peoples. At the Asian-African Conference at Bandung in 1955, Nasser attacked military alliances and the state of Israel, both representing to him aspects of Western imperialism. Following the example of Tito of Yugoslavia and Nehru, he proposed a policy of nonalignment for his country. He refused to join the Baghdad military pact with Turkey, Iran, and Iraq, calling the treaty (in terms which echoed Nehru's judgment of SEATO) a "modern version of a protectorate" and condemning its members for collaborating with "Western imperialism." His refusal seriously undermined his state's chances of substantial aid from the United States, the Cold War champion of alliances against the Soviet Union.

Egypt's conflict with Israel launched Egypt on its new policy. It remained in a state of war with the Jewish state. Yet the Egyptian army was still badly equipped and needed to import modern weapons which could be paid for only by foreign loans. The United States hesitated, concerned that aid might fuel a new Arab-Israeli war, but the Soviet Union was ready to help. In the Middle East as in Asia, the new Russian leaders were prepared to establish good relations with important states not members of Western alliances. Their offer of arms and financial credits presented the Egyptian regime with a tempting source of assistance.

In late 1955 Nasser announced that the Soviet Union had agreed to a long-term loan (to be repaid in cotton and rice shipments) to permit Egypt to buy from Communist countries fighter planes, tanks, arms, and naval vessels. He received the acclaim of nationalists throughout the Middle East for his action, concrete proof that his state was not subservient to Western powers. He judged the arms deal to be part of a policy of "positive neutrality," which to him included maintaining good relations with, and receiving aid from, both sides in the Cold War. With hindsight, his action appears a mild protest against Western domination. At the time, Cold War passions among Western leaders magnified the implications both of his aid to Arab rebels in French North Africa and of his arms agreement out of all proportion. Some in the West judged him a dangerous revolutionary and potential Communist ally.

The price of his arms deal with the Communist countries became apparent in mid-1956. He had begun negotiations in 1955 with the World Bank, largely financed by the U.S. government, for a major loan to begin construction of the High Dam at Aswan. He staked the prestige of his regime and of his own leadership on the mammoth project. Negotiations dragged on to July 1956. Suddenly the United States announced its refusal to participate in the projected loan; Great Britain soon after made the same decision. Their message was clear—Nasser's cooperation with Communist states had cost his state Western economic aid for the Aswan Dam. The decision represented a public humiliation of the Egyptian leader and a serious diplomatic blunder. In retaliation, Nasser seized the Suez Canal, a move which in turn led to war in the Middle East and economic recession in the West.

Suez and the 1956 War

The Suez Canal remained in 1956 an economic enterprise run and owned by Westerners, a symbol of Western economic imperialism and a valuable piece of property bringing substantial income to its owners. The last British troops withdrew from the Suez zone early that year. A tempting source of revenue, the Suez Canal Company also constituted to Egyptian nationalists such as Nasser a relic of the days of Western rule. In July 1956, he declared to an enormous crowd of Egyptians gathered in Cairo that his government had taken possession of the Canal Company. "Our pride, our determination, and our faith," he cried, had been challenged by the West. Nationalization of the canal proved that "this nation will not accept humiliation and degradation." If the imperialists did not approve of his action, they could "choke in their own rage." His defiance of the West had brought him and his country into direct confrontation with Western states, a move enthusiastically applauded by his people.

The Egyptian seizure of the Suez Canal incited the British and French governments to make one final effort to reassert their influence in the eastern Mediterranean. They believed nationalization a threat to their security, for the canal remained a vital pathway for strategic goods, especially petroleum, to

Western Europe and they were deeply suspicious of Nasser's nationalist ideology. Strategic and ideological reasons incited the two states to organize a reckless, ill-conceived invasion of the canal zone. They found a ready ally in Israel, whose economy suffered from the Egyptian blockade of its shipping through the canal and whose leaders feared another Egyptian invasion. The three states attacked in late October 1956. Israeli troops raced across the Sinai desert to the canal, while a British and French naval force and paratroopers seized the Suez ports and the entire canal zone. Militarily the operation was a complete success. Politically it failed, for Nasser, instead of being thrown out of power as the invaders hoped, became the national hero for the Egyptian people. Diplomatically the invasion proved a disaster.

Opposition came from all sides. The attack was condemned by almost the entire membership of the United Nations. The Soviet Union offered Nasser more military aid and warned Britain and France of its readiness to take "all measures" to protect Egypt. The U.S. government, angered at the independent Allied military action and intent on keeping good relations with Third World countries, condemned the invasion. It backed its opposition by immediately reducing economic aid to Great Britain and France and refusing to protect the British currency, losing value rapidly as panicky Britishers bought up dollars. Faced with universal diplomatic opposition and a major financial crisis, the British convinced the French and Israelis to withdraw. President Eisenhower had used U.S. economic power and diplomatic influence to defeat their intervention. Lacking U.S. support, the British and French were isolated and unable to continue the war. At that very moment the Soviet Union was sending troops into Hungary to crush a popular revolution seeking to free the country from Russian domination. The

Western states could do nothing to stop the Russian intervention. The superpowers had each in its own way demonstrated their international might.

The Suez crisis was Nasser's greatest triumph. He had defied the imperialists and had won. In the Middle East, his action revived the popularity of pan-Arab nationalism. To Egyptians he became their undisputed national leader, though his forces' only achievement in the war had been to block the canal with sunken ships, closing it to navigation for another year. A serious economic recession swept Europe as a result of the sudden end of oil shipments. In the peace settlement, Nasser was willing to accept a U.N. proposal for the stationing in Egypt of an international "peacekeeping" force. Its task was to patrol the Egyptian-Israeli frontier to prevent new terrorist attacks on Israel or a new Israeli invasion. The outcome of the Suez crisis gave Nasser the illusion of great power. His action earned him for a few years the standing of leader among Arab states and among nonaligned countries of the Third World.

Egyptian Socialism

The most enduring effect of the Suez war was the impetus it provided to state control over the Egyptian economy. Nasser called these developments "Arab socialism," implying that these reforms set a model for all Arab lands. Until 1956, the Egyptian economy had functioned along capitalist lines, allowing private ownership of banking, industry, and agriculture, welcoming foreign investment. The war brought the state new economic powers. The government suddenly, without any long-range plan, became owner of the Suez Canal Company, responsible for the operations of the canal. During the war Egypt took possession of foreign-owned and -operated enterprises in any way connected with France and Great Britain. These included many banks, insurance companies, industrial enterprises, and extensive landholdings. These nationalized holdings gave the government an important role in the small Egyptian industrial economy.

Thus the Suez crisis expanded the Free Officers' goal of "social justice" into a larger vision of "socialism." It took a form much like Nehru's economic policies. To provide the economic guidelines to operate the businesses and to enhance state powers over the Egyptian economy, the cabinet turned to economic planning. It created in early 1957 a National Planning Committee and approved later that year a Five-Year Plan for economic development. Foreign aid came from both the Soviet Union, which began construction of the Aswan Dam in 1960, and from the United States, which shipped food supplies to help feed Egypt's growing population. Nasser declared that the goal of the Egyptian revolution was "a cooperative, democratic, socialist society."

The economic role of the Egyptian state grew more significant still in the early 1960s. Explaining that socialism represented Egypt's future, Nasser ordered the government to nationalize all major industries and commercial enterprises and to take control of foreign trade. At the same time it instituted a second land reform, reducing to one hundred acres the maximum size of individual holdings. Again, as in 1953, this reform benefited most Egypt's small and medium farmers, whose family farms grew in size while farm laborers received little or no land. It did not constitute a rural "revolution," for only 20 percent of Egypt's arable land had changed hands. The state did win the strong support of a new rural "middle class," farmers whose well-being and prestige in their communities were due to state reform. Like India, Egypt became a mixed economy, with small commerce and farming in private hands, while major enterprises were state owned.

What did the Egyptian people gain from these reforms? In concrete terms, the economy in the 1960s grew at a per capita rate of 5–6 percent in the first half of the decade, slowing to 2–3 percent later (partly as a result of the disastrous 1967 war). Egypt began to produce large amounts of iron and steel, and increasing quantities of oil (only enough for internal demand). Yet the ideal of "social justice" held out a promise the state could not fully keep. Women were encouraged to enter the work force, yet (except for a well-educated minority) they were still bound by Muslim customary law to the patriarchal family. Employment in the countryside and towns could not keep up with the expanding population. Economic development could not cope with the widespread poverty of the lower classes. The population, already over thirty million, was growing at an annual rate of one million. To avoid social unrest, the state subsidized the sale of cheap food to Egypt's urban masses, for whom the city was a place of welfare, not work. Imported agricultural produce, provided in large measure by foreign aid, became the sole protection against famine.

Nasser's great project for the transformation of Egypt was the Aswan Dam. It was finally completed in 1970, forever ending the yearly flooding of the Nile. The reservoir—named Lake Nasser—stretched over three hundred miles upstream, impounding water used to generate hydroelectric power (10 billion kilowatt hours per year) and to irrigate year-round one-third more agricultural land. The ecological price was high, for the irrigation water carried disease through the canals and left deposits of salt on the land, no longer cleansed by flooding. The Mediterranean Sea began to erode the Nile delta, for silt ceased to reach the sea, and fish vanished from the nearby waters no longer enriched by nutrients from the river. The Aswan Dam illustrated vividly the vision and limits of Nasser's socialism; its planners could take pride in its role in Egyptian economic growth, but in achieving this goal, they permanently destroyed the natural balance between people and nature which had existed before.

Why did socialism, adopted years after the nationalist revolution, prove so attractive to Nasser and the Egyptian military government? It held out two rewards to them, one practical, the other ideological. It expanded the control of the state over the economy, permitting the regime to increase revenues for ambitious plans ranging from social welfare to a powerful army. At the same time, it reassured Nasser that his leadership was, in Marxist terms, historically progressive, and that his rivals, such as the monarch of Saudi Arabia, were remnants of a "feudal" past. Nasser was convinced that victory was on his side for, as he wrote at the time, "history cannot move backward." Reviewing in 1963 the sweeping reforms of the previous two years, he proclaimed that the triumph of Egyptian socialism was a "historical inevitability."

Nasser and Pan-Arab Nationalism

Egypt in the years after the Suez war became the center of pan-Arab nationalism and supported socialist movements in other Middle Eastern countries. From Cairo, the Voice of Arabs radio defended the cause of Arab unity and called for opposition to imperialism, feudalism (typified by Saudi Arabia), and Zionism (Israel). Nasser revived the vision of a great pan-Arab state to unite all "progressive" Arab lands, that is, states not ruled by conservative monarchs. He made one concrete step toward its realization when in 1958 he signed a treaty of union with the government of Syria. The Syrian government affirmed its support of a pan-Arab nation-state and backed Egyptian anti-imperialism, but its leaders had more practical reasons for joining Egypt at that moment. Confronted with serious internal religious and political opposition, faced with the threat of war with Iraq, they sought Egyptian protection of their regime. What appeared to be evidence of pan-Arab nationalism was in fact an affair of state.

As a result, the United Arab Republic (UAR) became an extension of the Egyptian state. Nasser became its president and Egyptian officers assumed important posts in Syria. The UAR proved a failure to its Syrian supporters. The breaking point came in 1961 when Egypt imposed its socialist policies on the Syrian economy. Discontent with the union brought together the Syrian army and business community. In September 1961, the army seized power and reinstated the independent state of Syria. Nasser considered at first sending Egyptian troops to invade Syria, then abandoned the idea. Keeping the title of UAR for Egypt alone, he blamed the failure of his political union on capitalist and imperialist enemies. Pan-Arab nationalism proved weaker than the needs and interests of political leaders of the various countries. Although he and other Arab leaders made gestures later of support for political unity, Arab nationalism never revived. The frontiers created by the prewar Western mandates remained in place; within each state, military and political factions struggled to take power and to rule the diverse peoples of their country. State building in those circumstances led to greater, not less, rivalry among Middle Eastern lands.

In that divided region, the conflict with Israel posed the most serious threat of war. Nasser took the lead among Arab states in proclaiming his opposition to the state of Israel. Time and again he spoke out for "liquidating the Israeli aggression on a part of the

Palestine land." His deeds in the ten years following the Suez war were not, however, warlike. He accepted until the mid-1960s the U.N. peacekeeping force along the Egyptian-Israeli frontier. Purely symbolic, its presence on the Egyptian side of the border absolved Egypt of responsibility to undertake a dangerous new war, one which the country could not afford and which his military could not win.

The likelihood of conflict grew when in the mid-1960s new centers of resistance to Israel appeared. One was the new, radical nationalist group which took control of the Syrian government in those years. The second was the Palestinian movement. Palestine refugees, scattered throughout the Middle East, were concentrated primarily in refugee camps in Egypt and Jordan. There, they had gradually formed new social organizations to help rebuild their lives, and also to begin a new struggle to recover their Palestinian homeland. In the early years they received financial aid from Arab leaders, who sympathized with their cause but placed first their own state interests. The Palestinians themselves had to overcome internal quarrels if they were to make Arab states pay real attention to their demands.

In 1964, they finally succeeded in obtaining the approval of the Arab League for the formation of the Palestine Liberation Organization (PLO). The principal political objective of the PLO was Palestinian "self-determination following the liberation of our country," that is, after the destruction of the state of Israel. Arab League backing was still half hearted. Other issues appeared more pressing to most League members, who hoped to exercise some moderating control over the Palestinians. No Arab leader dared call for a compromise settlement, since to do so would require recognition of the state of Israel. Hostility toward the very existence of a Jewish state in Arab land and the hope of

revenging the defeats of 1948 and 1956 encouraged talk of a "just" war.

The talk became action in 1966. The government in Syria decided that year on a policy of "revolutionary war" to defeat Israel and to "liberate Palestine." Its proclaimed goal was to support the Palestinians. Its larger objective, one Syrian leaders had dreamed since the fall of the Ottoman Empire, was to expand the influence of their state over the entire region to create a Greater Syria. The immediate effect of the new policy was to permit PLO guerrillas to launch raids from Syria on Israeli settlements. The Syrian leaders, following Nasser's example, turned to the Soviet Union for military and economic assistance in their ambitious plans.

Competition between the superpowers became in those years an additional factor in the Arab-Israeli conflict. The Soviet government was seeking more actively than before to widen its influence in an area previously dominated by the West. Accustomed to view the world in terms of competing ideological "camps," the Soviet leaders divided the Middle East into "reactionary" regimes closely tied to the U.S., and "progressive" states, such as Nasser's Egypt and the new Syrian government, which opposed "imperialism" and Zionism. They found justification both in their ideology and state interests to provide assistance to the states most vehemently engaged in the struggle against Israel. Egypt and Syria were eager to expand their military forces and could not obtain the necessary armaments from the United States. The Soviet Union was ready to help. In the mid-1960s it increased considerably its military assistance to both countries. If a local war resulted in which Israel was defeated, it indirectly would be a winner as well.

The U.S. government had had considerable success in extending alliances and establishing good relations with the states in the Middle East. It had signed military alliances with Turkey and with Iran and had signed economic aid agreements with several other states, including Egypt. Its diplomatic ties with Israel remained a central feature of its Middle Eastern policy. It had extended a formal assurance to protect the "right to exist" of the Israeli state and sent billions of dollars of military equipment and economic assistance.

Israeli leaders, remembering the diplomatic opposition of the United States in the 1956 war, trusted primarily their own military to ensure the security of their state. Israel's population of almost 3 million (2.5 million Jews and 300,000 Arabs) was very small by comparison with the surrounding Arab countries, and its territory, exposed to invasion on three sides, could quickly be overrun by enemy forces. Its military leaders therefore laid plans for a possible "preemptive attack," that is, a war of aggression on its Arab enemies, if they judged their territory threatened, either by terrorism or by Arab attack. The conflict between Israel and the Arab states fed on nationalist hostility between Arabs and Jews, Palestinian terrorism against Israel, competition for leadership among the Arab states, Israeli strategic fears, and superpower rivalry. It is no wonder the dispute defied diplomatic settlement.

The Six-Day War and Its Consequences

The Syrian decision in 1966 to promote "revolutionary war" and the terrorist acts of the PLO had in that conflict the effect of sparks falling in a keg of dynamite. PLO raids from Syria and Jordan on Israeli territory led to reprisals by Israel, which launched military attacks against PLO camps in both states. The Syrians called on Egypt for military support. Nasser could not avoid involvement. He had spoken too long and too fervently of the "liquidation of Israeli aggression" to back down. Of what use was

Egyptian talk of Arab solidarity, the Syrian leaders asked publicly, if Egypt kept the U.N. peacekeeping forces between its army and Israel?

In early 1967, Nasser abandoned his cautious policy. In May 1967, he ordered the U.N. forces to leave Egypt and closed the Gulf of Aqaba to shipping bound to Israel from the Indian Ocean. In the tense atmosphere of that spring, these steps signaled preparation for war against Israel. No evidence exists that he had ordered the Egyptian military to plan an invasion. The most likely explanation for his reckless action was his ambition to be leader of the "progressive" Arab countries, a role he could not sustain except by placing Egypt in a position to wage war. Although probably unintentional, Nasser's action constituted the fatal step in the actual outbreak of another Middle Eastern war.

Fearing a new Arab attack, the Israeli government approved the risky plans of its military for a preventive war on all its Arab neighbors. Two decades after the first Arab-Israeli war, the same enemies met once again in June 1967. The Arab states proved as poorly prepared as before, and the Israeli army and air force functioned with extraordinary skill and deadly precision. As a result, the Six-Day War was a resounding triumph for Israel. It turned into a military disaster for Egypt. That state was Israel's principal enemy, for it possessed the largest Arab armed force. Israeli planes destroyed in the first hours of war the entire Egyptian air force. In the next three days its armored columns occupied the whole Sinai peninsula to the Suez Canal. Its army then seized the west bank of the Jordan River and the rest of the city of Jerusalem from Jordan. Finally, it forced Syrian troops out of the mountainous border area known as the Golan Heights. It achieved these victories in six days. The defeated Arab states accepted a U.N. truce, leaving Israeli troops holding all the territory occupied during the war.

That war proved a turning point in the post-1945 history of the Middle East. In the following years, new forces emerged in the conflict with Israel and the West, and new trends set the pattern of international economic relations and internal political divisions. In a very real sense Arab political leaders and intellectuals confronted an ideological crisis. Nasser, the self-proclaimed progressive leader and hero of pan-Arab nationalism, was dethroned, his great army demolished. Arabs perceived that, in the words of an Arab historian, "a small state had displayed their historical inadequacy, had seized massive chunks of land, and had devastated the armies whose weapons and machismo had been displayed with great pride."[1] The old formula for nation building was discredited at the same time as the balance of power in the Middle East shifted toward new centers of diplomatic and political leadership.

In the search for new solutions, Egyptian leaders chose to abandon anti-imperialism and the fight against Israel to deal with their own internal problems. Nasser died in 1971, replaced by another former army officer and member of the Free Officer group, Anwar Sadat. Military aid from the Soviet Union rebuilt Egyptian military forces, which in 1973 launched its own surprise attack across the Suez Canal against Israeli forces. That so-called Yom Kippur war, though not a great military victory for Egypt, wiped out the dishonor of the 1967 defeat. It was settled only after the conflict threatened to involve the Soviet Union and the United States, each side seeking to protect its ally but quickly turning to diplomacy to avoid the danger of

nuclear confrontation. Like the Balkans before 1914, local war in the Middle East had become an international affair.

That war represented only the first step in Sadat's search for a new solution provoked by the crisis of 1967. In an audacious and risky reorientation of Egyptian foreign and internal policies, he turned his country toward the West. He concluded that Egypt's economic needs and diplomatic interests were best served by allying with the United States. In 1975 he broke all military and economic ties with the Soviet Union. The United States quickly took the Russians' place, providing vast amounts of financial and economic aid desperately needed by the Egyptian population. His third step, the most dangerous to him personally, was his decision to accept peace with Israel. Breaking with thirty years of Arab anti-Zionist policy, he recognized the existence of Israel, opened the Suez Canal to Israeli shipping, and signed in 1979 a peace treaty which restored to Egypt all the land lost in the 1967 war. His action outraged other Arab leaders and was deeply resented by many Egyptians.

His pro-Western solution to Egypt's problems included domestic reforms as well. He abandoned Nasser's comprehensive socialist program, introducing measures to encourage capitalist development, and allying with Egypt's wealthy, secular elite. He supported feminist measures (in which his wife took an active part) to expand the rights and opportunities of Egyptian women. His actions made him an increasingly controversial leader, particularly among Muslim fundamentalists. In 1981, he was assassinated by a group of army officers and soldiers, who believed that he had betrayed the Muslim faith and the Arab cause.

For a few years after the Six-Day War, the Palestinian movement carried on its own crusade against Israel. After 1967 the PLO had come under the leadership of young

---

[1]Fouad Ajami, *The Arab Predicament: Arab Political Thought and Practice Since 1967* (New York, 1981), p. 12.

radical nationalists, headed by Yasser Arafat, who hoped to make their organization the voice of progressive Arabs and the core of a Palestinian nation-state. With financial aid from the wealthy Arab oil countries, they set up their own army and laid plans for war on Israel by all means, including international terrorism. Their hopes were destroyed, however, by the opposition they encountered from all sides. In 1971, the king of Jordan sent his troops to force them out of his land, which had become the target of Israeli attacks. The survival of his state mattered more to him and his people than the liberation of Palestine.

The collapse of the dream of pan-Arab nationalism was apparent in the fate of the PLO. Instead of leading an Arab crusade, the PLO became a pawn in the power struggle among Arab states. It moved into Lebanon, where its effort to seize control of the southern part of the country broke the fragile balance among the Muslim and Christian groups which for decades had kept that small country an island of peace and relative prosperity. Lebanon came to epitomize the agony of an Arab land where nation building had failed and where foreign powers manipulated and encouraged internal armed forces in a struggle for power and territorial control. The PLO kept control of southern Lebanon until 1982, launching attacks on Israel. That year, the Israeli army invaded the country to crush the PLO forces. It too could not dominate the situation, finally withdrawing in 1984 to escape constant terrorist attacks from Muslim and PLO groups. Into the vacuum of power it left stepped a new foreign power, Syria.

In the new pattern of Middle Eastern politics which followed the Six-Day War, two new Arab leaders raised the anti-imperialist flag, behind which they sought to enhance their power and political influence. To the west, the oil-rich state of Libya came in 1969 under the rule of a military regime headed by Muammar Qaddafi. He used his state's great wealth to expand his army and to provide generous subsidies to radical Arab movements opposed to Israel and Western imperialism. Syria was the second state, it too controlled after 1970 by a military dictatorship under Hafiz Assad. Although the political rhetoric of both leaders resembled the populist nationalism of Nasser, their actions revealed that foreign power, not internal social reform, was their principal goal.

The objective of the Syrian leader was a Greater Syria, dominating the Middle East from the Mediterranean to Iran. This aim translated into an anti-Israeli, anti-Western policy, for the Jewish state and its U.S. ally constituted Assad's most powerful opponents. As in the 1960s, the Soviet Union supplied military and economic aid, for after the loss of Egypt it was eager to strengthen its ties with Syria. The Syrian army, bolstered by Soviet arms and military advisers, moved into Lebanon when civil war first broke out there in 1975. It gradually spread its forces through eastern and northern regions of the country and became in the 1980s the dominant foreign power in the country. In addition, Syrian agents secretly began to use terrorist organizations to attack Assad's enemies, principally Arabs opposed to his expansionist policies.

Thus Egypt's peace with Israel did not reduce the threat of war nor did it end the competition for influence in the region between the superpowers. The new regional powers adopted for themselves the anti-imperialist slogans which Nasser had first proclaimed. Israel remained in occupation of Jordanian and Syrian territory, prepared to wage a new war to prevent the creation of a Palestinian nation-state. Nation building in the Middle East left a permanent legacy of violence and war, a tragedy for Arabs and Jews alike and a threat to global peace.

UNIVERSITÉ DE MONCTON

À: 86 - 87 ✓

DE: 114 - 115 ✓

RE: 117 - 143   DATE:

153 - 154
170
191 - 199
201 - 232
233 - 259

MEMO
COMMUNICATION INTERNE

"Petroleum Power" and Muslim Fundamentalism in Iran

The importance of Middle Eastern petroleum became obvious to the entire world following the outbreak of the 1973 war. The extraordinary growth in demand for oil in all industrial economies during the 1960s placed these lands at the mercy of any international crisis which lowered oil production. By the early 1970s the governments of the oil-producing countries had obtained control over oil production, key to international petroleum prices. The 1973 war provided them the opportunity to prove their new power in world affairs.

To demonstrate support for Egypt in that war against their Zionist enemy, the Arab OPEC states declared an embargo on oil exports to the United States, Israel's only ally and source of military supplies. At the same time, they curtailed oil production. The latter action had drastic consequences, for it sent oil prices soaring in a few weeks to four times the prewar level and as a direct result caused a serious recession in Western economies. The embargo ended in 1974, but rising demand and strict production limits prevented a decline in oil prices.

A second blow to the global industrial economy came when another sudden price increase occurred at the end of the 1970s. As a result of the revolution in Iran, oil output there suddenly fell sufficiently to double world oil prices. All countries dependent on oil imports suffered. Although prices declined again in the mid-1980s (to their 1975 level), when production increased and de-

Major International Petroleum Movements, 1974. *(From* World Energy Supplies: 1950–1974, *United Nations, Series J, No. 20, 1977, Table 7)*

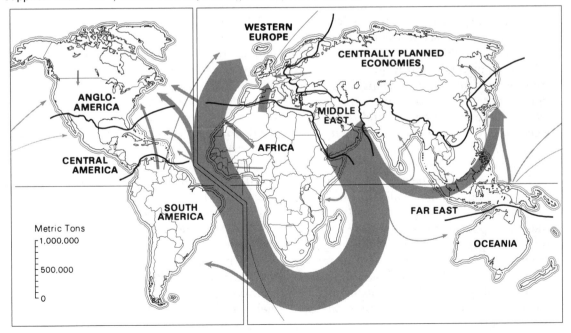

mand remained stable, the effect of OPEC policies left Western states painfully aware of their dependency on imports from Arab states. OPEC leaders had proven the power of oil as a potent weapon in international disputes. Unlimited access to vital raw materials such as petroleum, enjoyed by the West until the 1960s, had permanently vanished. A new global economic order was emerging, in which the developed nations were forced to share power and wealth with countries in possession of valuable resources.

The political implications of "petroleum power" were most apparent in Iran. The greatest triumph of Muslim fundamentalism came in Iran, where a revolution in 1979 ended the reign of the shah and led to the creation of an Islamic Republic, a "theocratic" state governed by the country's Shia religious leaders. The shah's plans for a White Revolution, predicated on oil revenues and the support of the West, had failed to take into account the strength of Iranian opposition to his reforms. Fundamentalist Muslim leaders decried the corruption of religious morality brought by the shah's Western reform. Socialists and nationalists alike were increasingly hostile toward his authoritarian methods of rule and the political corruption of his regime. Fueling the opposition were serious economic problems caused by grandiose and expensive industrial projects, which led to rapid inflation. By the end of the 1970s social and political conditions in Iran were ripe for revolution.

The central figure behind the revolutionary opposition was the Ayatollah Khomeini, a Muslim religious figure who had opposed the shah's policies for two decades. His inspirational preaching aroused mass support among the laboring population and among all those shocked by the impact of Western materialism and the decline of Muslim religious observances. An astute political leader, he mobilized the diverse oppositional

forces to demonstrate against the shah's reign. In late 1978, urban rioting had spread throughout the country, forcing the shah to order the army to repress by force the demonstrators. Bloodshed in the streets aroused even more massive protests, until in early 1979 the shah's police and army were powerless to defend the regime. The shah fled the country, which was now in the hands of Iranian radical and fundamentalist revolutionaries.

The overthrow of the shah's state in 1979 set in motion a revolution directed against American imperialism, blamed for Iran's ills, and dedicated to the creation of an Islamic republic modeled on the Koran's description of Mohammed's own state. This "flight to the past" represented in spirit a religious crusade, whose supporters were equally ruthless in dealing with Iranians and foreigners, Muslims and non-Muslims, whom they judged enemies of the true revolutionary faith. Iranian women had to return to the veil and seclusion as dictated by Shia religious custom.

Khomeini called for an uprising of the Shia faithful in neighboring Iraq, ruled by a military dictator of the rival Sunni Muslim persuasion. The Iraqi government, fearful of this dangerous revolutionary neighbor and eager to seize Iranian oil fields near their border, invaded Iran in 1980. It miscalculated, however, for the Iranian army, backed by the religious zeal of the new state, halted the offensive. The two states refused to stop the fighting, which neither side could win. As a result, the war dragged on, another center of Middle Eastern conflict.

Iran, once judged by U.S. leaders their strongest ally in the Middle East, suddenly turned into an enemy. The Islamic regime was violently opposed to all manifestations of U.S. power, symbol of the "devil" to Khomeini. In late 1979, Iranian militia invaded the U.S. embassy in Teheran and took sixty

American hostages, defying international law to humiliate the United States and to force the U.S. government to return the shah for trial. The Iranians did not agree to release the hostages until over a year later. That humiliating experience provided the most graphic evidence of the new revolutionary force of Muslim fundamentalism and of the collapse of Western domination in the Middle East.

DECOLONIZATION IN AFRICA

Last of all colonial areas, the lands of sub-Saharan Africa achieved independence in the 1960s. This vast political revolution came quickly and unexpectedly. Only in hindsight does it appear a part of the larger global trend of decolonization and nationalist revolution. Until the late 1950s the entire area, with the one important exception of South Africa, was governed by European states, principally Great Britain and France. At the end of the Second World War, the British had begun to lay plans for the liberation of their African colonies, which stretched along part of the Atlantic Coast and through East Africa. Even then, its most ambitious planners anticipated that liberation would come slowly. One colonial expert emphasized the economic and social obstacles which stood in the way of state building in the British colonies in Africa, pointing to "their ignorance and poverty, their disease and widespread malnutrition, their primitive cultivation and harsh natural conditions, their hopelessly inadequate revenues and need of services of every kind."

This catalogue of obstacles in the way of effective African rule failed to take account of two other factors, one the rise of African nationalism, the other the unwillingness of European states to enforce colonial rule when faced with determined independence movements. What one British statesman called a "wind of change" sweeping away empires made itself felt in Africa as well as in the Middle East and Asia. It inspired a small group of African nationalist leaders to demand freedom for their lands. They organized their own nationalist movements, strong enough in the years after the Second World War to reach out from the coastal cities into the rural areas, which were drawn into a market economy. Many of the nationalist supporters were army veterans who had fought in the war for the Allies, prepared for a new battle for independence. Contacts over the previous decades with the West through military service, through labor in Western-owned mines and factories, through education and travel, had broken down the isolation of the African peoples and created the conditions for African nationalism.

African Nationalism

Throughout Africa the Western powers encountered in the 1950s organized opposition to their rule. The colonies they governed consisted of territories which their first administrators had united within artificially drawn frontiers. The peoples in these areas were divided by tribal loyalties, by religion (principally Muslims, concentrated in northern areas, Christians, and animist groups in the south), and by language. The northern areas of Nigeria, most populous of all the African colonies, were controlled by Muslim tribal city-states, whose leaders had no contact with the other half of the population living along the southern coast. "We found," one Nigerian Muslim ruler wrote later, that "the members of the other regions might well belong to another world as far as we were concerned." The presence of white administrators and soldiers ruling these colonies became the symbol of imperialism, whose destruction provided the one common bond uniting African nationalist leaders and peoples.

The areas where strong movements against white rule first emerged in the 1950s were in the Gold Coast and in Kenya. In the latter colony, members of the dominant Kikuyu tribe organized a prolonged terrorist campaign against white settlers on their land. Their movement, which they called the Land Freedom Army but which Europeans termed the Mau Mau, looked to a political solution for their economic problems, for it supported a nationalist leader, Jomo Kenyatta, in his campaign to end foreign rule. Its greatest weakness, one apparent in other African colonies as well, was the unwillingness of other tribes to join the revolt. Still, the British needed four years to repress the violence. They sentenced Kenyatta to seven years in prison and resettled many of the Africans in fortified villages. The Mau Mau uprising constituted a serious revolt leaving a total of thirteen thousand dead among the blacks (both Mau Mau and British supporters) and thirty-three whites dead.

The most effective anticolonial movement, and the first to achieve its goal of independence, arose in the Atlantic coast colony of the Gold Coast (later to become Ghana). Its pattern of political agitation and the difficulties it confronted reveal important characteristics of African movements elsewhere in later years. It was the work of a young Western-educated nationalist leader named Kwame Nkrumah. A dynamic and skillful leader totally dedicated to freedom for his land, he began in the late 1940s to mobilize the support of his people against British rule. By then, a strong labor union movement had appeared in the colony's port cities, from which cocoa beans, the principal Gold Coast cash crop, were exported to the West. The inland areas where the crop was grown, inhabited by the once powerful Asan-

ti tribe, were linked with the coast by economic ties and shared many grievances against British rule. Nkrumah was able in 1949 to join these tribes, and others from the Muslim north, into one organization, the Convention People's party.

He promised that freedom would bring them an end to their hardships and a new era of progress and opportunity. "Seek ye first the political kingdom," he urged them, "and all else will follow." With these promises he mobilized his supporters to defy British laws, pointing to the example of Gandhi and the Indian National Congress. Those who served prison terms were honored by his party as Prison Graduates. The British government reluctantly granted the colony self-rule in the early 1950s, releasing Nkrumah from jail to become prime minister. Violence was avoided by political concessions on both sides. Still, Nkrumah demanded independence in a unified state. When the Asanti tribal leaders protested, fearing the rule of the southerners, the British revised their proposed constitution. For the sake of freedom, Nkrumah accepted the federal system but was determined to reunite the country under his rule as soon as independence came. Nationalist leaders such as he could mobilize a strong movement against the imperialist power, but their coalition of forces rested on a common enemy, not a shared political culture or a common program. Decolonization in Africa posed problems of state building more acute than anywhere else. In 1957 Ghana became free, with Nkrumah the leader of the first liberated colony of postwar Africa.

By the late 1950s the British and the French governments had both decided to end imperial rule as quickly as possible. They lacked the resources to govern their African colonies, whose freedom was demanded by nationalist movements there and was backed by the leaders of the newly independent

Third World countries as well as by the superpowers. Their defeat in the Suez war of 1956 had turned them away from imperial visions of power toward the immediate concerns of internal economic development and European unification. Thus African nationalist demands for independence met in later years with relatively little resistance from the Western states. Once a continent under the political domination of European imperial powers, Africa quickly reemerged an area with over thirty independent states.

Political Independence and White Resistance

The process by which liberation came depended in large measure on the policies of the imperial states. Great Britain followed the procedure which it had used in Asia of negotiating with nationalist leaders in each colony for the creation of constitutional, democratic governments. After Gold Coast independence came Nigeria, where the leaders of the various peoples agreed in 1960 on a federal government to keep unity among its thirty-five million people. In 1963, Kenya became an independent state under the leadership of Kenyatta. In all cases the new constitutional order was modeled on British parliamentary democracy, a Western import which the British judged best and which nationalist leaders considered a temporary measure by which to take over the reigns of government. Despite the speed of decolonization, the British and African leaders managed to cooperate and to maintain peace among the population during the transfer of power.

The French method differed from the British in one major respect. In 1958 the French government offered to all French African colonies both independence and French economic and political assistance in an association it called the French Community. The only alternative it proposed was independence outside the community and no French support at all. The policy was the work of Charles de Gaulle, French wartime hero, become in 1958 once again leader of France. His offer of aid through the French Community was an effort to maintain some ties between France and the African states, creating bonds which some African leaders condemned as "neocolonialism." Most nationalist leaders, however, judged it a helpful measure both to their new states, which lacked effective armies, and to their economies, whose development depended on the aid of developed countries. Each colony voted that year on the choice; the voters adhered in each area to the recommendation of their nationalist leaders.

All the former French colonies except one chose to join the community. They received economic aid, advisers and technicians, a monetary union with France protecting their currency, and permanent French garrisons in several countries on call in the event of political unrest. The moderate leaders of these new states were effective opponents of radical revolution, a danger to themselves as well as to the ties with France. They defended French economic interests and obtained French backing when political unrest threatened their rule. One African leader concluded later that "General de Gaulle is the greatest African of our time." His opinion revealed how highly he valued political stability, achieved at the cost of very little social reform. The aid France provided did bring those countries substantial benefits, among which political order was perhaps the most important.

In the largest of all the African colonies, the Belgian Congo, decolonization became on the contrary a nightmare of civil war and bloodshed. The area experienced for the first time violent anti-Belgian demonstrations in early 1959, organized by a small na-

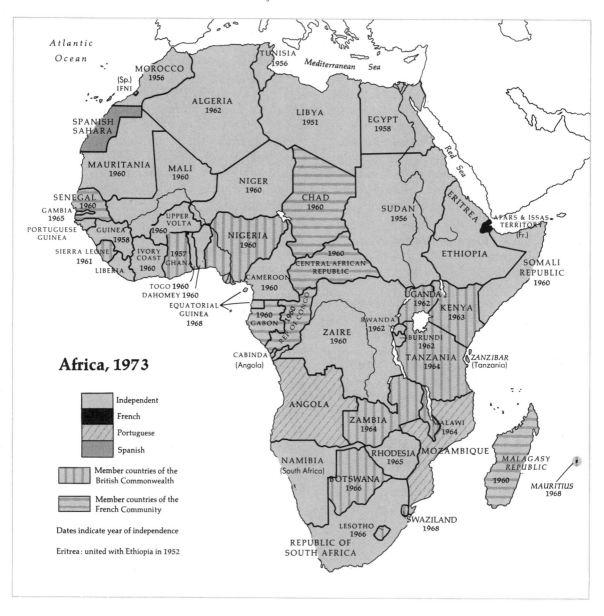

Africa, 1973

Independent
French
Portuguese
Spanish

Member countries of the
British Commonwealth

Member countries of the
French Community

Dates indicate year of independence

Eritrea: united with Ethiopia in 1952

tionalist movement supported largely by urban workers in the capital city. This sudden opposition was sufficient to convince the Belgian government, swept along by the "wind of change," to grant its colony independence immediately. With no preparation and without adequate leadership among the Congo nationalist leaders, the land was freed from Belgian rule in mid-1960.

The consequences were tragic for the new state and for its population, African and white. What little political organization existed in the country quickly collapsed. The Congolese army mutinied and turned on the white settlers, who began to flee the country. Tribal groups fought among themselves. The only political leader with a strong following, Patrice Lumumba, could not restore order in the army and refused any help from the Belgians. The disorders became outright civil war when the southern region of Katanga, rich in mineral resources and center of mining operations owned by Western interests, seceded from the new state. The United Nations agreed to send troops from member states to keep the Congo from complete collapse and anarchy. In the course of the fighting, Lumumba himself was captured and executed by Katanga forces. In 1965 a military leader, Joseph Mobutu, finally took over the government. By then the surviving white settlers had fled, the economy of most regions was in ruins, and thousands of Congolese had died in the fighting and rioting. The Congo (later to be called Zaire) had become a shell of a state.

The process of decolonization encountered serious opposition in those areas of the African continent settled by large numbers of European migrants. Backed by their governments and united in strong political parties, they had become the dominant force in their countries. The prospect of independence provoked strong resistance when it threatened their own rule and the security of their economic holdings. They looked to South Africa as a model for the type of white-dominated state they hoped to create.

In that southernmost country of the African continent, the British had granted self-rule in the Commonwealth before the Second World War. Politics was dominated by whites, although a variety of parties competed for power in a parliamentary system. The single strongest political movement was the Nationalist party, grouping most of the Afrikaners and a bastion of Afrikaner nationalism and racism. Although racial discrimination toward nonwhites was sup-

ported by most whites, racist prejudice was especially strong among the four million Afrikaners. The basis of their power in South Africa lay in their sense of themselves as the "chosen people," their cruel experience in the Boer War, and the determination of their political leaders to protect their domination no matter what the cost.

The economic wealth of the country, concentrated in gold and diamond mining, lay in the hands primarily of the English and other white immigrants. The Second World War had brought prosperity to the business interests of the country, dominated by the Anglo-American Corporation. Its holdings were so extensive that one-half of all the companies in the South African stock exchange were in its hands. The social consequences of economic development constituted a threat to the white segregation policies. On the one hand, laws excluding Africans and Coloreds (largely Indians) from contact with whites had grown increasingly severe. On the other, the needs of commerce and industry had drawn an increasing number of nonwhites into the urban economy, where they provided the mass following for the African National Congress (ANC). This organization emulated the methods and goals of the Indian National Congress, agitating peacefully for democratic freedoms and an end to segregation in all forms. Its growing influence, and the support it received from liberal whites, represented to Afrikaners a serious political danger.

In the late 1940s the Nationalist party triumphed in elections in which the principal issue was concessions to the growing African nationalist movement. The Nationalists proceeded in the next ten years to put in place a policy of absolute racial domination by the whites, which it called *apartheid*. All nonwhites were denied the right to participate in democratic government. Blacks did not even enjoy the right to free choice of residence, being forced to live in special settlements and permitted into urban areas to work as "guests" (the so-called "pass system"). Racial segregation excluded them from public life in the white cities and permitted their leaders only those powers the government judged necessary to keep order in the African settlements. The first confrontation between ANC supporters and the Nationalists occurred in 1960 at Sharpsville, in the course of which police killed over sixty unarmed demonstrators. Rather than seek to calm the discontent by easing segregation, the Nationalist government outlawed the African National Congress and imprisoned its leaders. The Afrikaners created a regime of white supremacy more ruthless than at any time in South African history.

The other sub-Saharan land with a large white population was the British colony of Rhodesia. There, 200,000 whites clung obstinately to their colonial privileges. To them British decolonization appeared to portend their abandonment to African rule. They had denied Africans equality of rights and had managed to keep exclusive power over the area as long as the British government protected them. Their leaders agreed to independence in 1965, but with laws written in such a manner that they retained control of the state. They banned the African nationalist parties and forced the African leaders to flee the country. Under pressure from the Commonwealth states, the British government publicly condemned these actions, demanding that Rhodesia gradually move to democratic majority rule. More important to the fate of Rhodesia, however, was the rise of guerrilla war led by African nationalists, who found protection and support from surrounding independent African states. The whites were too few and too weak to resist for long, conceding in 1980 the right of universal suffrage and participation

by the African nationalist movements in free elections. White rule ended in Rhodesia, renamed by its new African nationalist leaders Zimbabwe.

African State Building

During the 1960s the new African states proceeded slowly and painfully through the difficult process of state building. The experiences of the many countries varied greatly. Still, by the end of the decade, two trends had emerged. One was the appearance of authoritarian governments, most frequently under military rule, whose leaders replaced one another in forcible, sometimes bloody struggles for power. The other was the increasing impoverishment of the rural and urban population, growing rapidly and unable to obtain sufficient food even to sustain its earlier level of consumption.

Having been deprived of the experience of self-rule and confronting complex problems of political unification and economic development, the African states quickly abandoned the democratic constitutions adopted at independence. Power passed into the hands of a few ambitious leaders, backed by the military and accepted by most of the population. One West African politician, whose state was among the best ruled on the continent, explained that "in young countries such as our own, we need a chief who is all-powerful for a certain period of time. If he makes mistakes, we shall replace him later on." He offered his people political stability under strong central rule, and considered this the best they could hope for. The experience of other African states suggests that he was right.

In Kenya, Kenyatta remained in power for fifteen years until his death. He had no serious political rivals, for his authority as father of his country was enormous. His political party controlled the government; violence rarely disrupted public life, though one influential politician from a rival party was found assassinated, his murderers never captured. Kenya experienced orderly rule and relative prosperity, with white settlers living alongside their former enemies. The army remained small, and the press enjoyed substantial freedom to report on public events. Kenya represented the best case of independence with a stable government protecting a peaceful society.

In many other states, however, authoritarian regimes brought only instability and misrule. Ambitious politicians sought ever-greater power by manipulating parliaments and creating mass parties whose only purpose was to serve and to glorify their leader. Little or no freedom existed, and political prisoners filled the jails. Events after independence in Ghana illustrate this trend. Nkrumah had promised great changes when he took power. He set out to organize a socialist economy similar to that of Egypt, but he lacked the skilled personnel and the ability himself to use effectively the resources, including foreign aid, at his disposal. Economic conditions worsened, and the standard of living of the people declined. Proclaimed by his party Man of Destiny and Redeemer, he rewrote the constitution to entitle him to be president for life. His greatest ambition was to be leader of African nations. He promoted the Organization of African Unity and spent vast sums of money entertaining visiting African heads of state. Economic decay and political disorder led in 1966, nine years after independence, to his overthrow by Ghanian military commanders. The only disciplined national force, the army replaced Nkrumah's rule by a military regime. Ghanians welcomed his departure, destroying the statues and photographs which had glorified his exalted leadership throughout the country.

In most African countries, power changed hands frequently and by force of arms. During the 1960s there occurred in the thirty independent states a total of forty successful insurrections, the work of small groups of leaders and followers. Many others were attempted but failed. The decline of democratic rule among the African states appears most clearly in the fact that in no state was one government replaced by another peacefully through democratic elections. In such political disorder, the population turned for protection to their tribal leaders. Tribal power frequently determined the winners in the struggle for power; conflict among tribes became a cause of bitter civil war. The bloodiest of these was the war in Nigeria. During three years in the late 1960s the Ibo tribe fought to establish its own state, called Biafra. Outnumbered and besieged by the Nigerian army, the Ibo leaders abandoned the struggle only after their land was largely devastated and famine had decimated their people. Nigeria was reunified, but at a terrible price. State building became under those circumstances a desperate effort to hold together the meager remnants of unity. Authoritarian rule by strong leaders proved the most successful solution.

The second dominant characteristic in the evolution of these young states was economic decline. The population everywhere in the continent was growing as rapidly as in any part of the world (between 2.5 and 3 percent a year). Food production did not keep up with the need. In some areas, farmers chose or were forced to plant crops for export in place of food crops. Some states attempted to monopolize the export of cash crops, lowering the price paid for these crops to increase their revenues. The result was economic decay when farmers ceased growing unprofitable produce. In Ghana, the controls set up by Nkrumah and preserved until the early 1980s by the military rulers undermined the cocoa exports, which fell by almost one-half.

The most damaging development for agriculture, however, was the decision of leaders in most governments to introduce price controls to keep food costs low and thus ensure calm among the poor in their cities. In the name of "populism" or "socialism," they reduced prices for agricultural produce so drastically that farmers had little incentive to sell their crops. Many reduced or stopped raising food for market. Even before drought hit large areas in the 1970s, food production per capita was declining. The fall amounted to 7 percent in the 1960s and 15 percent in the following decade. Only foreign imports, provided largely by aid programs, prevented endemic hunger in some lands.

Instead of economic development, many African countries actually witnessed growing impoverishment. In the first quarter-century of its independence, the average national income per person in Ghana declined 1 percent each year. Only ten countries (out of more than thirty) managed to achieve substantial economic growth (over 2.5 percent annually) after independence. Industrial projects proved too expensive; imports exceeded in value exports and required extensive foreign loans. By the 1970s most African states could not pay back these loans and were virtually bankrupt.

In many countries the first generation of African nationalists, hopeful that state power and socialism would produce quick economic benefits, succeeded only in disrupting the existing relations of production and lowering the standard of living of the bulk of the population. The economic trend began to reverse itself finally in the 1980s, when new leaders began to encourage farm production by abandoning price controls and curtailing government expenses. But the experience of the first decades after independence had been terribly disappointing to those who expected that the end of colonialism would open a new, better age for the African peoples. Freedom meant power and prosperity for a tiny elite; for the others, it represented at best only the hope of better conditions to come.

"Intermediate Technology": New Cooking Stove in Mali, Africa, 1983. (*U.N. Photo 153352/Kay Muldoon*)

SUMMARY

Decolonization brought the Middle East and Africa into a new era of rapid political and economic change. Political leadership often passed into the hands of nationalists who resorted to the methods of authoritarian rule which Nehru had called Caesarism. They were attracted to socialist policies of nationalization and social welfare. Nationalism constituted the dominant ideology among all the new states, whether the leadership was conservative or revolutionary. Yet the apparent rapidity of historical change hid underlying cultural and social conditions which altered little if at all. The importance of the Muslim religion and customs in the lives of Middle Eastern peoples stands out in the recent history of that region. Communal ties there, and tribal bonds among African peoples, provided some measure of stability in turbulent times. In a period of such social turmoil and foreign conflict, it is remarkable that state building proceeded well enough to preserve the unity of the new states. The methods did not imitate the Western pattern of national democratic rule, but the reasons lay as much in the inadequacies of colonial rule as in the ambition of nationalist rulers.

In Middle Eastern lands, the most notable and tragic trend was the persistence of war and civil conflict. No single explanation can clarify the complex conditions behind this violent history. The existence of the state of Israel and the success of Israeli armies represented a central factor, for they maintained in the very heart of the region an image of "imperialism" which Arab nationalists everywhere refused to tolerate. In a deeper sense the West constituted a disruptive presence everywhere, visible in the intervention of the great powers in Middle Eastern politics, but apparent also in the socialist policies of Nasser and in the White Revolution of the shah of Iran.

These two leaders each in their own way challenged the domination of Islam, attempting to introduce a kind of secular nationalist faith to take its place. A similar process had occurred earlier in Western countries, sometimes accompanied by violent conflicts between church and state. There, secularization had triumphed. The extraordinary strength of Muslim fundamentalist movements and the rise of leaders identifying their states with Islam testified to the continued vigor of the Muslim faith. It often became the basis of Arab nationalism and sustained the prolonged hostility between Israel and its Arab neighbors. After the 1967 war, Israel in its own way appeared to some Muslims the proof that a united religious community could forge a strong nation-state. "Imperialism," on the contrary, symbolized a secular heresy. To combat this subversion of their nationalist faith and of Islam, some Muslims judged war and civil strife legitimate forms of combat. Their continued struggle for what they defined as national rights sustained the threat of new international and civil war.

RECOMMENDED READING

Postwar Arab History

RAYMOND BAKER, *Egypt's Uncertain Revolution Under Nasser and Sadat* (1978)

JEAN LACOUTURE, *Nasser: A Biography* (1973)

DON PERETZ, *The Middle East Today* (third ed., 1978)

ANTHONY SAMPSON, *The Seven Sisters: The Great Oil Companies and the World They Made* (1976)

P. VATIKIOTUS, *The History of Egypt from Muhammad Ali to Sadat* (second ed., 1980)

Israel and the Postwar Arab States

MICHAEL COHEN, *Palestine and the Great Powers, 1945–1948* (1982)

LARRY COLLINS AND DOMINIQUE LAPIERRE, *O Jerusalem!* (1980)

SAMI HADAWI, *Bitter Harvest: Palestine Between 1914 and 1967* (1979)

EDGAR O'BALLANCE, *The Arab Israeli War 1948* (1957) and *The Third Arab Israeli War* (1972)

Postwar Iran

SHAUL BAKHASH, *The Reign of the Ayatollahs: Iran and the Islamic Revolution* (1984)

AMIN SAIKAL, *The Rise and Fall of the Shah* (1980)

Postwar Africa

ERNEST HARSH, *South Africa: White Rule, Black Revolt* (1980)

MARTIN MEREDITH, *The First Dance of Freedom: Black Africa in the Postwar Era* (1985)

chapter 11

EUROPE AND LATIN AMERICA BETWEEN THE SUPERPOWERS

The decade following the Second World War was a period of recovery and renewal throughout the world. Gradually the wounds inflicted on economies and societies healed and new states appeared where old empires had once ruled. The new pattern of postwar global relations had emerged clearly by the early 1960s, so different from prewar years that it has been called "the second twentieth century." The rivalry between the superpowers slowly changed character after Stalin's death. Leaders of the two states met periodically and began to search for agreements that would reduce the danger of nuclear war. Yet at the same time, their competition for political and diplomatic influence spread until it encompassed all important areas of the world, from South Asia and the Middle East to Latin America. In all these regions, local conflicts became entangled in superpower relations. This trend gives to world history of this "second twentieth century" a special focus on events and decisions taken by a handful of people in Moscow and Washington.

Despite the unprecedented power of these two states, however, the course of events even in areas within their spheres of influence revealed the important role of popular aspirations and national leadership beyond their control. Europe and Latin America, each in its own ways, evolved in new directions reflecting the strength of particular cultural and social forces in those areas. The peoples in the Soviet satellites had the least opportunity to determine their own future, for Soviet diplomatic and political domination set severe limits to their independence. Yet no empire imposed from outside can maintain absolute control, a truth that even Central Europeans were able to prove in the decades after Stalin's death.

In Western Europe, two important trends marked the postwar years. Economic and political recovery opened new opportunities for cooperation among the states and the integration of their economies, breaking finally the centuries-old pattern of national conflicts. At the same time, the problems of social injustices and economic inequalities became an increasing concern to the population and, consequently, to political leaders. Public responsibility for minimum well-being of all the people became widely acknowledged, though disagreement continued on the extent of that responsibility. It became a priority for the Catholic church as a result of the decisions taken at the Second Vatican Council, which gathered Catholic leaders from the entire world.

Latin America was the region where Catholicism was most powerful. Poverty had long existed there alongside great wealth. Sharing some of the social and economic characteristics of the Third World, it was closely tied culturally to Europe. Movements for political revolution and for social justice, some inspired by Marxist socialism, others by the new Catholic social concern, encountered bitter opposition from political and social elites within these countries.

They also became the object of U.S. attention, for the Yankee state in North America had for a century considered the region to be in its diplomatic sphere of influence and American investors played an important role in the economy of Central and South America. A political revolution in Cuba in 1959 revealed that resistance to the United States could lead to superpower conflict. The Cuban revolution is important to an understanding of the "second twentieth century," for events in that one small island brought together nationalism, socialism, and nuclear confrontation between the Soviet Union and the United States.

EUROPE AND THE SUPERPOWERS

The Soviet Union After Stalin's Death

The Soviet Union and its European satellites evolved slowly in the years following Stalin's death in 1953. The institutions and policies by which he had dominated his vast country and the neighboring lands left a complex legacy. On the one hand, they had aroused a deep and abiding hatred toward Stalinism among subject nations and the millions of Soviets made victims of his system. His heirs in the Soviet Communist party feared the potential for widespread popular unrest, and themselves concurred on the necessity to end the terror. Yet they were determined to maintain the institutions of Soviet socialism put in place by the Stalin Revolution and were equally intent on preserving Soviet control of its satellites and on matching U.S. military power and global diplomatic influence. The evolution of the Second World of Communist countries after 1953 responded to these conflicting pressures and to the objectives of the new Soviet leaders.

Their most pressing problem was a new system of leadership. Concern for their own survival and influence motivated their decision to abandon Stalin's one-man dictatorship, which had weakened the Politburo (renamed the Presidium in 1952) and had given the secret police unlimited punitive powers, even over the party. They knew from their regime's early history of the method of collective leadership which Lenin had created and which had in those years made the Politburo the center of political power. In a decision that laid the foundation of stable party rule in the decades ahead, they agreed in 1953 to reinstate the Leninist practice of collective leadership. They thereby ensured that the small group (about fifteen) of Presidium (Politburo) members would be able to make the major decisions on state policy, and they chose from among their ranks the appointees to the two most powerful political posts in the country—one in the party (the first—or general—secretary of the Communist party)—and the other in the Soviet state (the chairman of the Council of Ministers). The man designated that year to head the party was Nikita Khrushchev.

For the next decade, Soviet foreign and domestic policies were shaped, on the one hand, by the goals of the collective leadership and, on the other, by the personality and aims of their new leader. Born in a poor peasant family, Khrushchev rose through the ranks of the Communist party in Stalin's years to become the head of the party and his country. He, like his colleagues in the Presidium, never doubted the fundamental truths of Marxism-Leninism—the superiority and inevitable triumph of socialism over capitalism, the necessity for Communist party dictatorship. Their attitudes and methods of rule were formed in the harsh environment of Stalinist Russia, through years of revolution and war. This political culture nurtured in them a suspicious, antagonistic view of the West, and the dogmatic conviction that they knew what was best for the Soviet people and for the "socialist camp." It is not surprising, therefore, that they believed it indispensable to preserve the essential institutions of Soviet socialism—collectivized agriculture, nationalized industry, central command planning.

On the other hand, the entire party leadership was determined to end Stalin's terrorist system. Its continued existence threatened their own positions and was contrary to Marxism-Leninism. They proceeded rapidly to remove from office and to execute for "crimes against the people" the head of the secret police, Beria. The laws authorizing terror were abolished, and thousands of Stalin's victims were released from jail or prison camp. This quiet "destalinization" did not proceed far enough for Khrushchev. In early 1956 he denounced at a party congress Stalin's "crimes" and the "cult of the personality." Russians opposed to all forms of Stalinism took encouragement when they heard of his speech, and satellite peoples took hope that they could end Soviet domination. In fact, the Soviet leaders still permitted the secret police (now called the Committee of State Security, or KGB) to repress political dissenters and were prepared to keep intact their "socialist camp," if necessary by force.

Khrushchev himself remained in power only so long as the collective leadership was in fundamental agreement with his policies. He undertook a series of economic and social reforms to raise the standard of living of the Soviet people, promising them in 1961 that they would attain "communism in our generation"—in ten years. He described a grandiose welfare state, offering its inhabitants free housing, schooling, transportation, and health care. To him, communism meant "collective consumption." The Western "consumer society" of private cars, stereos, blue jeans, and jazz records epitomized to him corrupt capitalism.

While his colleagues shared his hopes for Soviet socialism, they were not prepared to let him undermine their power and privileges. He came to believe that his reforms were obstructed by "bureaucratism," the disregard for the needs of the people by bureaucrats, in the state or his own party. He failed in his efforts to reduce their power, however, for bureaucracy constituted the essential institution by which Soviet socialism and party rule governed the country. Even his own colleagues in the Presidium finally turned against him. With the backing of Red Army generals (displeased that Khrushchev had curtailed military expenditures), they voted in 1964 to send him into "early retirement." They undid many of his reforms and ended public denunciation of Stalinist crimes, preferring political stability and bureaucratism to Khrushchev's idealism and reformist zeal. This collective leadership, among whom Leonid Brezhnev became the most influential policymaker, remained in power for the next two decades.

Soviet Foreign Policy and the Arms Race

The new direction given Soviet foreign relations by the post-Stalinist leadership remained basically unaltered throughout those years. It was marked by three important features. One was the willingness to improve relations with the United States while still competing for power and influence. A second was greater internal autonomy to Soviet satellites, still kept—if necessary by force—under Communist rule in the Soviet sphere. A third was a new global policy of assistance and closer relations with neutral and "progressive" Third World countries. India and Egypt benefited substantially from this last feature, as did Cuba in the 1960s.

Soviet leaders placed at the very core of their foreign policy the development of military forces capable of matching U.S. armaments. They devoted in the 1950s and 1960s increasingly large sums to the improvement of their armed forces, still inferior in numbers and quality to those of the United States. From their perspective, the armaments race meant achieving a destructive power comparable to that of their rival superpower. The Soviet Union had developed its arsenal of nuclear weapons more slowly than the United States. In 1960 it possessed still only two hundred nuclear bombs, at a time when

the United States had over six thousand. Khrushchev was determined to close that gap by developing a "monster" thermonuclear weapon (tested in 1961, it exploded with the power of over thirty million tons of TNT) and by using Soviet missiles to best advantage (including an attempt to place some in Cuba). The Soviet Union's launching in 1957 of the space satellite *Sputnik* publicized its space technology, but its military forces still in 1962 had four times fewer intercontinental ballistic missiles (rockets armed with nuclear warheads with a range of thousands of miles) than the United States. The Soviet Union's naval weakness became obvious in the Cuban missile crisis, when it could do nothing against a U.S. naval blockade of Cuba (discussed in the next section of this chapter).

Khrushchev's successors set out to end Soviet military inferiority and to achieve a relative military balance of power with the United States. An additional impetus to military spending was the appearance of a new and potentially dangerous enemy, China. In the late 1960s they moved forty-five Red Army divisions equipped with nuclear weapons along the Chinese frontier. One result of their military investments was the appearance in those years of a large, multiocean Soviet navy, with capital ships on all the major seas of the world. The Soviet Union also enlarged its nuclear arsenal, until in 1970 it included eighteen hundred nuclear warheads, fewer still than the American armed forces but sufficient in case of global war to annihilate the United States.

This grim numbers game, played by both sides, supposed that the possession of nuclear armaments represented the ultimate assurance the other side would not threaten the use of or actually use these weapons in the event of a serious conflict. It was vivid proof of the failure of postwar diplomatic relations between the two states. The nuclear arms race prepared for a war neither side sought or could win. This fact provided a compelling reason to both Soviet and American leaders to seek agreements on issues threatening nuclear conflict.

Stalin's heirs revealed that they recognized the importance of this issue by abandoning Stalin's ominous theme of "inevitable war" between capitalist and socialist systems. Instead, they proposed a new theory of "peaceful coexistence" (better understood in Western terms as "competitive coexistence"). It pointed to the need to begin regular talks with U.S. leaders, the first of which occurred in 1955 in Geneva when Eisenhower and Khrushchev met. The Soviet leaders sought means to reduce the danger of nuclear war, and also the opportunity to expand economic trade, of vital importance to their plans for continued economic development of their country. Both national survival and economic interests remained the principal forces in the following decades sustaining "peaceful coexistence:"

These new policies pointed to the necessity for agreements to improve the security of both sides and to restrain the armaments race. Although Soviet and U.S. leaders were fearful of making concessions, they both understood as well the danger presented by military confrontation. The partitioned lands of Central Europe constituted the principal areas of potential conflict. In 1955, both sides agreed to withdraw from Austria, made by international treaty a neutral state. More than a decade passed until they found the basis for a German treaty, which formally recognized the partition of the country and of Berlin (see Chapter 12).

As important as territorial agreements were efforts to control the armaments race. Again the principal obstacle came from the reluctance of either side to accept any limits

if not of immediate advantage and of no harm to their power of "deterrence." Both Soviet and U.S. nuclear strategy was predicated on the assumption that these weapons were needed to deter the other side from beginning, or threatening to begin, nuclear war. A decade of fitful negotiations passed until Soviet and U.S. leaders agreed on this fundamental premise of their relations, namely, that each side sought a balance of destructive power (labeled appropriately by one American leader Mutually Assured Destruction—MAD). The only feasible arms agreements were those which did not impede that defensive capacity. The first of these was the nuclear test-ban treaty (on above-ground explosions) in 1963, followed by the nuclear nonproliferation treaty in 1968. These modest first steps were followed by far more substantial treaties in the 1970s (see Chapter 12). Although divided still by interests of state and by differing political cultures, the superpowers had to reach some agreements on nuclear weapons. Their own survival was at stake.

The Decline of the Soviet Empire in Eastern Europe

Gradually Communist rule in the satellite states of Eastern rule became less harsh. Under pressure from the peoples of these lands, their Communist leaders ended police terror, made efforts to improve living conditions, and permitted the national identity of their population to find once again public voice. The degree of opposition to Stalinist-type leaders became evident a few months after Stalin's death. In Communist East Germany, political oppression and miserable pay pushed workers to begin a spontaneous protest movement of strikes and demonstrations. Only Soviet troops and tanks could repress the uprising; the rocks thrown by East

Stones against Tanks: Soviet Forces Repress the Uprising by East Berlin Workers, June 1953. *(German Information Center)*

Berlin workers at the Soviet tanks were no match for the might of the occupying Red Army units. In that "worker's state," the Soviet Union stood behind the Communist regime.

Still, the Soviet leaders had to improve political and economic conditions in the region. East Europeans discovered that powerless subjects could by such acts of hopeless protest as well as by everyday passive resistance obstruct political dictatorship and impede state-imposed economic goals. The Berlin workers' revolt was the most visible sign of the decay of Communist rule. The Soviet leaders agreed that they had to improve social conditions there and accepted also the necessity to end Stalin's ruthless domination of the Communist regimes. He had been responsible for the quarrel with the Yugoslav Communists, breaking all ties and declaring a Communist "anathema" on the rebels. Khrushchev ended this schism, hoping to bring Yugoslavia (along with China) into his "socialist camp." He had to pay a price, however, apologizing for Stalin's campaign against the Yugoslav Communist leadership and admitting publicly in early 1956 that there existed "many roads" to socialism, in other words, that the Stalinist system was not the only "progressive" model for Communist countries.

The new Soviet policies encouraged East European non-Communists and Communists alike to believe that freedom from Stalinist rule and Russian domination was possible. In Poland these hopes led in 1956 to political confrontation with Moscow, and in Hungary to a popular revolution, brutally repressed by the Red Army. As in East Germany three years before, the resistance found its strength partly in resentment, especially among workers, at the economic exploitation and hardship imposed by Stalinist leaders, and partly in nationalist solidarity and hostility toward the Russians. In mid-1956, worker strikes and demonstrations forced the Polish Communist party to remove from office its Stalinist collaborators, judged traitors to Poland. The real conflict in that country erupted when Moscow attempted to prevent the Polish party from appointing a new leader, previously a prisoner of the Stalinists. The Polish people rallied around the party, and the Soviet leaders reluctantly approved this modest form of "self-rule" for Communist Poland.

When later that year the Hungarians sought real independence, Moscow proved that it would not tolerate an end to Communist dictatorship and to the Soviet military alliance. Taking encouragement from Polish events, in late October Hungarians, led at the start by students and workers, organized a mass uprising against all forms of Stalinism in their country. In Budapest, one of their first acts was to destroy a giant, sixty-foot statue of Stalin in the middle of the city. With the support of the Hungarian army and many leaders of the Hungarian Communist party, the uprising produced for a few days an independent government and free public life. New Communist leaders, under Imre Nagy, quickly introduced a series of reforms to restore civil and political liberties, and declared their intention to make Hungary a free, neutral state. Their dream clashed, however, with Soviet insistence on military control in Central Europe and on the preservation of Communist dictatorship, regardless of the wishes of the population. The "socialist camp" would not tolerate desertion, and the Soviet leaders, with the backing of the Chinese Communists, were prepared to use force against the rebellious Hungarians. In bloody fighting in November 1956, Soviet troops repressed the Hungarian uprising and imposed on the country Communist leaders loyal to the Soviet Union. Hungary lost its attempt at independence.

In the two decades that followed, the Soviet leaders continued to rely on force when they feared losing political control of bordering countries, and at the same time made limited concessions to ease the danger of revolt or war. Twice in Eastern Europe, Communist rule was threatened. In Czechoslovakia in 1968, the Communist party appeared unable to stem a popular movement—within the labor unions, within parliament, even among its own members—for internal freedom. Although Czech fidelity to the Soviet military alliance was never in doubt, the Soviet leaders feared a democratic state in Czechoslovakia and therefore decided to invade the country with their military forces and to impose Czech Communist leaders of their own choosing.

Shortly afterward, the Soviet leader, Leonid Brezhnev, stated publicly what Red Army troops had already demonstrated. The Brezhnev Doctrine asserted the right of the Soviet Union to intervene in the affairs of any allied state in the "socialist camp" to enforce Communist rule. A decade later it was applied once again when Soviet troops invaded Afghanistan to maintain in power a new Communist regime unable to repress a revolt by the country's Muslim population. Nearly 100,000 Soviet troops remained in the country, fighting Afghan rebels in a war they could not end.

The weakness of these Communist satellite governments was made most apparent in Poland. There opposition to the Communist party came not only from intellectuals and workers, but also from the powerful Catholic church. In 1980 underground resistance came into the open when Polish workers throughout the country supported a general strike to protest their lack of freedom as well as difficult living conditions. This massive but peaceful revolt culminated in the formation of a nationwide free labor movement, called Solidarity, with which the government was forced to negotiate in 1980. The Polish Communist party was powerless to repress Solidarity, whose leader, Lech Walesa, enjoyed greater influence with the people than it did. For a year Communist rule collapsed in that country, but that period of relative freedom was ended by military rule. Polish generals, aware of impending Soviet military intervention, preferred to step in themselves, declaring martial law, outlawing Solidarity, arresting many of its supporters, and turning Poland into a semimilitary dictatorship. The Soviet sphere of influence remained intact but only at the price of periodic intervention to contain and repress political opposition to its satellite leaders.

Popular unrest did not end Russian diplomatic domination, but it did force the Communist governments to reform in a variety of ways their cumbersome centralized economic system, permitting greater individual initiatives and allowing greater freedom in the private lives of their citizens. This trend became most apparent in Hungary in the years after the 1956 revolution was crushed. The Soviet-imposed leader, Janos Kadar, using what limited autonomy he could obtain, slowly modified the socialist economic system to permit private farming to replace collective farms, to allow private commerce, and to make state-run industry compete for profits (ideas the Chinese Communists borrowed when they introduced "market socialism" in the late 1970s). The reformed Hungarian socialist system created what observers called "goulash communism," by the early 1970s raising the standard of living of the people there to a level higher than that of most other East European countries (including the Soviet Union). Intellectuals in the satellite countries, proud of their peoples' resistance to Stalinist dictatorship, began in the 1970s to speak of their lands as Central Europe, divided by what they imagined to be an invisible but real barrier from the political oppression of the Soviet Union.

Nonetheless, the single most important border in Europe separated the Communist from the non-Communist countries. That line ran through the middle of Germany. To the east, 15 million Germans in the German Democratic Republic were under Communist rule. Although no serious unrest broke out there after the revolt of 1953, many East Germans (between 150,000 and 250,000 yearly) chose in the late 1950s to flee to West Germany by traveling to West Berlin, still open then to citizens from both sides. The Soviet government several times threatened to force the Western powers out of West Berlin, for it was intent on bringing the entire city under Communist rule and thus ending the flight of East Germans to the West. Each time, the United States refused any concessions.

To avoid an international crisis and the threat of war, Khrushchev decided in 1961 to turn the invisible line around West Berlin into an impenetrable physical barrier. That year, the Communists constructed a wall through the middle of the city, isolating West Berlin and preventing further flights. The U.S. government preferred not to challenge the Communist action, for fear of provoking a military confrontation with the Soviet Union. Nuclear deterrence prevented forceful measures to end the partition of Berlin. Europe remained divided between Communist and Western military alliances, the legacy of Stalinism and the Cold War. The wall became to many Europeans a symbol of the failure of postwar peacemaking.

Political Stability in Western Europe

The recovery of Western Europe from the destruction of the Second World War was remarkably rapid, constructive, and long lasting (see Chapter 7). The democratic reforms put in place in the late 1940s established the framework for political life in Italy and West Germany, where fascism became for most people a distant, painful memory.

The Divided City: Berlin Wall, approx. 1980. *(German Information Center)*

Only the French, confronted with a bitter political crisis over the colonial war in Algeria, altered their postwar constitutional regime. The North Atlantic Treaty Organization (NATO) joined most European states in a defense alliance with the United States, committed to the "first use" of nuclear weapons to protect its allies in the event of Soviet attack. The policies of partial nationalization of industry and of state planning continued to guide economic development in Great Britain, France, and Italy. Their welfare revolutions, making economic security for the citizens a political right, became a permanent feature of public life. These "mixed economies" prospered and became closely linked by trade, stimulated by the creation of a "common market" among six of the coun-

tries. The antagonism dividing the old nation-states, though it did not vanish, occupied an increasingly unimportant place in the lives of the people and their political leaders.

Parliamentary government opened the way to changes in political leadership in these countries but did not alter basic foreign and domestic policies. In Great Britain the Conservative party governed during most of the 1950s and part of the 1960s, leaving in place Labor's social reforms in the knowledge that abandonment of welfare would lead to their immediate defeat by an irate British electorate. The Conservative cabinet developed Britain's own nuclear weapons in the 1950s but still relied heavily on U.S. military collaboration. When Eisenhower opposed the war on Egypt in 1956, the British leaders accepted the humiliating withdrawal and loss of the Suez Canal. They completed the process, begun by the Labor party, of dismantling the empire. Great Britain had become once again an island state, and its leadership had to adjust to its new position as a second-rate power.

Democratic elections brought a new party to power in West Germany following the retirement of Chancellor Adenauer. A controversial, authoritarian leader, he had guided his country to full independence, the revival of parliamentary politics, and the remarkable "economic miracle" of the 1950s. Memories of nazism and defeat in war became increasingly faint. Adenauer's government recognized Germany's guilt in the Holocaust, making yearly reparations payments to Israel. Most Germans preferred to forget that part of their country's past, turning instead (as did the Japanese) to enjoy the prosperity their hard work had brought. Forced to abandon dreams of being a great power, they relied on the U.S. alliance and nuclear armaments for protection.

This passive acceptance of Cold War conditions did not satisfy the new leadership of the Social Democratic party, principal rival to Adenauer's party. In the late 1950s its leader, Willy Brandt, obtained from his party a formal renunciation of Marxism, for him a vestige of a bygone past and a political liability. He judged that success for the Social Democrats had to come through political moderation and social reform. His new platform of compromise with the "bourgeoisie" was rejected in the 1960s only by some young radicals (including Brandt's own son). Visions of revolutionary struggle against "imperialism" and "capitalism" formed the ideological foundation of the German student youth revolt in those years, but German voters preferred reform. Brandt's most important and contested objective was West

German recognition of the partition of the German nation, for him a gesture of diplomatic realism and peace but to conservatives, including Adenauer, an intolerable concession to Communist aggression.

The rise to power of the Social Democrats occurred gradually, and had its most dramatic effect on relations with the Soviet Union. Brandt's electoral strategy succeeded, first increasing Social Democratic legislative representation sufficiently in 1966 to join their rivals in a coalition government, then in 1969 after new elections forming its own cabinet. Brandt became West German chancellor with a program of welfare policies and of improved relations with the Communist countries. His "eastern policy" (*Ostpolitik*), reversing Adenauer's adamant opposition to Soviet hegemony in the east, included establishment of relations with East Germany and acceptance of the postwar frontiers of Poland. Through a number of separate agreements, a kind of informal peace treaty emerged confirming the permanence of the division of the German nation into two states. The former Allies were by then prepared to accept the partition of Germany and Berlin, for all saw no alternative for peaceful relations between East and West. In 1972 the division of Berlin was formally recognized in a Four Power treaty.

These treaties constituted a very important step toward the stabilization of East-West relations in Europe, ending the most dangerous Cold War conflict. The partition of Germany was a permanent feature of postwar Europe, as was Communist rule in East Germany. Although the danger of war had diminished significantly, the military alliances (NATO and the Warsaw Pact) remained armed and prepared for conflict. Neither side was ready to risk reducing its preparedness for fear of ceding the advantage in the balance of power to the other. When the Soviet Union introduced hundreds of new intermediate-range nuclear missiles in Europe in the late 1970s and early 1980s, the United States did the same. The arms race itself had become the principal force upsetting the international security and stability of Europe.

Political turmoil in France in the late 1950s transformed the constitutional structure of the country. It brought a new nationalist conservative leadership to power, yet even there the postwar policies of social reforms and economic collaboration in European affairs were preserved. In 1958 a military revolt ended the brief life of the French Fourth Republic, founded in 1946. The origins of the revolt lay in the Algerian uprising by Arab nationalists. Blaming politicians for their inability to repress the revolt, the French military and a majority of French voters supported in 1958 the return to power of General Charles de Gaulle, who promised to restore French national unity and to resolve the Algerian war. His ideas on political rule emphasized strong government and the national strength of France. A new constitution created the Fifth Republic, endowing France with a powerful president (stronger even than the U.S. presidency). Until 1969 France's leader was Charles de Gaulle.

To enhance French national power and international prestige was de Gaulle's great ambition. He sought to expand France's role in European and world affairs. Decolonization to him appeared a historical necessity. He laid out the basic policies for the replacement of France's African empire by the French Community and conceded independence to Algeria despite bitter opposition among his generals and from the Europeans in Algeria. His formula to make France a great power mixed modern technology and the belief that in the Third World France could play a role as influential as the superpowers. He encouraged the development of the French nuclear industry, both for peaceful use and for armaments, and of the aeronautic industry, which constructed the first (and only) supersonic passenger plane, the Concorde. In the early 1960s France became the fourth state in the world to possess nuclear weapons and, at the same time, launched a program for nuclear power plants to provide ultimately most of the country's electric power.

The new French nationalism did not alter France's Western ties, however. Although de Gaulle refused to let French naval and infantry forces be commanded by NATO officers, France remained allied with the NATO states. De Gaulle even accepted the participation of his country in the new Common Market, which began operations the year he came to power. French security and economic interests, like those of the other European states, depended on collaboration with other Western countries. De Gaulle was correct in thinking that the division of the globe into Soviet and U.S. "blocs" was ending—the Soviet-Chinese conflict and the Cuban defiance of the United States made that trend obvious. He had to recognize as well that France was itself integrated in new political and economic units. Nationalism in Western Europe could no longer guide a state's policies. The nineteenth-century era of absolute independence of the nation-states of Europe was gone forever.

Europe and the Common Market

The most important indication of the new relations among these states was the economic integration of Western Europe, which had begun in 1952 with the formation of the European Coal and Steel Community (ECSC) and included soon after a free trade community among these same countries. The ECSC created "supranational" institutions (i.e., superior to national governments in a particular respect) with the authority to set for the six member states (Germany, France, Italy, and the Benelux countries) trade and production levels in coal and steel. The principal architect of this radical new idea in European economic relations, Jean Monnet, anticipated that real economic integration had to include free trade in all industrial, commercial, and agricultural products. In the mid-1950s the six states agreed to his plan for a European Economic Community (EEC), to begin in 1958 the dismantling of tariffs on trade among themselves and the formation of one unified economic market. It represented the most significant step yet undertaken toward his dream of a politically united Europe.

Although all trade barriers never actually disappeared, the restraints on commerce did decline dramatically and far more quickly than the treaty had specified. By the mid-1960s Western Europe had begun a new era of economic collaboration. The Common Market operated on the basis of market competition, whether conducted by private or state-owned enterprises, by small farmers or agribusiness. All the states of Western Europe agreed both on the desirability of economic growth and on the ultimate goal of political integration—though no one could say when a "United States of Europe" might appear. With that common agreement, they ceded part of their sovereign powers to supranational Common Market institutions.

The EEC proved an economic success. It was supported by the U.S. government, which in 1963 signed with the EEC the most significant agreement lowering tariffs in its history. Freer trade between Europe and America benefited business on both continents and reinforced the economic and financial ties among the Western democratic nations. Living conditions improved so rapidly in Western Europe that in some

countries they were equal to or higher than the standard of living of Americans. The obvious ability of the EEC to stimulate economic growth overcome finally the hostility of the British government to integration. Great Britain entered the Common Market, along with Denmark and Ireland, in 1971. After two wars and in the midst of the Cold War, the Western European nations had evolved toward economic interdependence and political cooperation, developing extensive social welfare programs while retaining the political liberties of free countries.

Between Europe and the outside world there existed new bonds to replace the old empires. Only the Portuguese empire in Africa still remained, to disappear in the 1970s when Mozambique and Angola received independence. The trend, first apparent at the end of the First World War, of growing American influence and ties to Europe accelerated through the 1950s and 1960s.

The United States and the First World in the 1960s

In those years, the United States itself was slowly changing. The election in 1960 of John F. Kennedy to the U.S. presidency began a period of rapid social and political reforms, carried on by Lyndon Johnson after Kennedy's assassination in 1963. This Great Society, the name Johnson gave his 1964 platform, included new laws to protect the civil and political rights of all citizens, seeking to end the century-long segregation and oppression of blacks. It also encompassed sweeping welfare policies, in spirit and in intent resembling those social welfare measures introduced in Europe at the end of the Second World War.

While these reforms were going into effect, an economic boom in the United States was expanding rapidly the role of U.S. interests in the new global economy. The U.S. government promoted and encouraged increased trade and financial investments abroad, believing that free enterprise constituted a vital element in developing industries and improving the living conditions in Third World countries. U.S. foreign aid in larger amounts than ever went abroad, a substantial part for the first time to Latin America in the "Alliance for Progress" program. One important reason for aid was the U.S. government's concern to discourage socialist revolutions, for radical leaders such as Fidel Castro in Cuba proclaimed that only popular insurrection and socialism could end American imperialist exploitation.

The global economy was dominated by the Western, "developed" countries, among whom trade and investments expanded at a rapid rate. This trend received the backing of the U.S. government, which ever since the end of the war had placed particular importance on stimulating the free movement of goods and moneys, of vital importance in those years to the continued growth of the U.S. economy. Through the 1960s economic trade and investment between the Western European countries and the United States increased rapidly. The new prosperity of Europe attracted major U.S. companies, such as General Motors and International Business Machines (IBM). Termed "multinational" because of their vast financial resources invested throughout the world, these firms set up new factories and created new European markets for their goods. The total U.S. funds in Europe jumped between 1950 and the mid-1970s from $2 to $60 billion, making Western Europe the single largest area of U.S. investment in the world. U.S. banks set up branches in Europe and soon in other parts of the developing world, laying the foundations for a new global financial market dominated by U.S. capitalist interests.

In those years the dollar was the international currency of the global enconomy. U.S. dollars were flowing across the Atlantic to pay for an increasing amount of goods imported, particularly from Germany. Although inflation in the United States began in the late 1960s to reduce the value of the dollar, the U.S. government attempted to carry out the policy begun in 1944 of guaranteeing a stable, fixed value for its currency, which continued to buy one ounce of gold for $30 until 1971. By then, however, the price was too cheap. The dollar no longer was the sole desirable currency for international investors, who saved and speculated in the currencies of the two new industrial powers, Germany and Japan. In 1971 the U.S. government abandoned the gold standard, allowing the value of the dollar to sink (it soon fell to $300 for an ounce of gold).

The global economy was evolving in those years toward greater competition among countries, on the one hand, and increased technological innovation in those lands with the necessary wealth and skills. The electronics and computer industries became the centers of development, and their managers set up production in developed and developing countries, wherever costs would be lowest and profits highest. Although the dollar remained the major international currency, American producers were forced increasingly to compete for markets with other countries in a world where the United States was no longer the center of productivity and enterprise. Financial power and technological innovation spread to Europe and East Asia, while the enormous appetite in the West for petroleum poured dollars into the oil-producing countries. These fundamental new conditions of global interdependence made unthinkable a return to the economic isolationism of depression years.

The Catholic Reawakening

The defense of social justice and concern for the vast numbers of impoverished in the rest of the world roused new voices in the 1960s. They came partly from protest movements which found inspiration in the Marxist denunciation of class exploitation and promise of social equality. They came partly from religious movements, including Muslim organizations like the Muslim Brotherhood. Among the world's religions, the voice of the Catholic church became particularly forceful when its leaders were called by a new pope to a great international conference to renew the message of Catholicism in the world. The largest and most widespread faith in the world, it numbered over .5 billion members in over 130 countries, with the greatest concentration in Latin America. There its new social doctrine had the most forceful impact and caused the greatest political conflict.

The "reawakening" of the Catholic church was launched by Pope John XXIII, elected in 1958, and was implemented by the Second Vatican Council, which met between 1962 and 1965. Among the many reforms and policies approved there, those with particular significance for global problems of economic inequality addressed the so-called "pastoral" mission of Catholics to care for their fellow man. The council looked to the needs of "the whole of humanity," calling on the clergy and the faithful alike to take an active role in social and economic reform to help the poor and oppressed. It welcomed state welfare policies and suggested that the faithful could organize outside the church to assist in this enormous task. The Catholic church did not back political revolution, but the consequences of its call "to all people of goodwill" to work toward peace and social justice had a profound political impact, particularly in Latin America.

THE UNITED STATES, LATIN AMERICA, AND THE CUBAN REVOLUTION

Latin America in the 1950s

The one area of the world where the United States continued to enjoy uncontested international influence until the 1960s was Latin America. In the Cold War years, the U.S. government used its dominant influence there to win support for its Cold War policies (see Chapter 7). U.S. foreign aid was primarily military in the 1950s, even though the arms and training received by Latin American armed forces encouraged the political ambitions of military leaders, who intervened often in affairs of state to overthrow civilian governments and to protect the interests of the small social elite of these areas. The problems of internal rule and social reform took second place in the U.S. assessment of Latin American needs. The U.S. government was content that the Latin American rulers, whether conservative dictators or populist nationalists, adhere to its Cold War policies.

In a tradition that had emerged a century before, politics in most Latin American states was the privilege of an oligarchy, that is, a small segment of the population, who used power to preserve and enhance their wealth and social domination. The principal obstacle to nation building in these lands was the great gulf separating the wealthy oligarchy and the impoverished lower classes. The Catholic church, whose leaders were themselves largely from these upper classes, ministered to the spiritual needs of the faithful. It condemned "Godless" radicals who sought an end to poverty by class war and, by its own social indifference, became the collaborator of the oligarchy. Occasionally populist mass movements challenged these regimes, but only in Mexico did revolution lead in the

1920s and 1930s to social reforms intended to redistribute land and property to aid the urban and rural laboring population.

Conditions in Latin America resembled somewhat those of the Third World countries in Africa and Asia. This area had won independence from European empires a century before. The dependence of Latin America on North American economic interests, with close ties to the oligarchies there, fits well the pattern of "neocolonial" lands. The influence of Iberic culture and of Catholicism tied the area closely to Europe, but the impoverishment of the masses of the population in many areas was as grim as that in Asia. The underlying problems of economic development were similar to those elsewhere in the Third World. For this reason, a political and social revolution in Cuba became a model for rapid reform in other

Contemporary Latin America

developing lands. It also was the origin of one of the most serious international crises in recent times.

Latin American Plans for Development

The most notable political trend after the Second World War was the emergence of Latin American governments which for the first time took an active role in promoting economic development. The war itself had expanded the demand for the primary goods (food and minerals) on which Latin American economies had depended for a century, and also opened new markets for manufactured products. This new direction to economic development offered an escape from the dependency on unpredictable international demand for raw materials and encouraged the production of domestic substitutes for expensive industrial imports. It appeared to be a "strategy" that would permit countries to enter the ranks of developed economies and to raise the living conditions of the population. It became the objective of political movements uniting industrialists and the working population, both groups hoping for quick results.

The results were generally disappointing, however. Economic growth increased only slowly and was barely adequate to keep up with the rapid population growth. The reasons for these meager benefits lay both in the inadequacy of Latin resources and in the conservative leadership implementing development plans. After wartime demand declined, Latin American industries did not expand, and states increased tariff barriers to protect their producers. These countries remained primarily agrarian economies, short of investment capital and lacking the skills necessary for industrial expansion.

With U.S. backing, Latin American governments adopted two techniques to support economic development. On the one hand,

they encouraged international business investments, primarily from North America. U.S. corporations, protected by their state and by Latin American rulers, purchased mines, plantations, and important industrial enterprises throughout the continent. Their investments did not grow as rapidly as hoped in the 1950s, when Europe constituted a far more rewarding market. On the other hand, without adopting the socialist policies of some Asian countries, Latin American states introduced new forms of state subsidies to private economic activity. Conservative in their social policies, they were prepared to experiment to a limited extent in new economic measures.

Their leaders turned, like many other Third World regimes, to outside financial assistance. They relied heavily on Western banks for large loans to stimulate industrial growth and also to raise the standard of living of the population. These policies proved difficult to sustain, for inflation usually resulted from excessive state spending and foreign debts required repayments difficult for the states to make. Populist political forces defended the social and economic needs of the people, accusing their rivals of collaborating with foreign business interests (a common practice) and demanding state welfare policies for the poor (for which funds usually were insufficient). Leaders who resisted ran the risk of provoking mass protests. Those who supported the populist program bought popularity at the expense of financial stability.

Political and civil liberties in the Latin American countries represented a democratic ideal frequently ignored in the bitter political quarrels which divided parties and pitted the government against its military. The 1950s was a time when powerful leaders supported by populist coalitions dominated Latin American politics, but their period in power was often cut short by army insurrections followed by a return to military dictatorship.

Populism in Argentina and Brazil

The Argentine leader Juan Perón built up a mass political movement with the backing of labor unions, to whom he granted special favors and whose workers enjoyed a relatively high standard of living. Argentina was rich in raw materials and agriculture, and Perón used his political might to redistribute wealth to the laboring population. The financial price of his policies was high, and when the state attempted to curtail spending, labor unrest grew. Dangerous political enemies appeared when Perón attacked the Catholic church. The country's social elite, losing wealth and fearing Perón's populist backing, encouraged ambitious generals prepared to intervene in the political crisis. In 1955 the Argentine military leaders overthrew his regime. With brief interruptions, they remained in power until the 1980s. They proved oppressive and incompetent rulers, little concerned to find the means to turn the natural abundance their country possessed into material prosperity for the people.

The most ambitious plans for development came from the largest and most populous country of all Latin America, Brazil. They were the work primarily of Getulia Vargas, a dynamic and charismatic political leader who mobilized a broad coalition of the middle and working classes to support a nationalist program of economic growth and state building. He launched policies for the expansion of Brazil's industrial economy, using the powers and revenues of the state to sponsor or found important enterprises such as oil exploitation, armaments manufacturing, and automobile production.

After his death, his heirs for another decade carried on and broadened his ambitious vision of a "new Brazil," until the military intervened in Brazilian politics. The enormous interior regions, still undeveloped, were the target of the greatest colonization drive since the North American occupation of the Great Plains. Over eleven thousand miles of new roads were built, penetrating deep into jungle areas where Indians had once lived in absolute isolation, bringing settlers to cut the trees of the great rain forests and to introduce modern farming. The economic and ecological impact of this project was comparable both in its vision of economic development and in its devastating ecological effects only to Egypt's Aswan Dam. To symbolize the importance of this policy, the Brazilian government spent vast sums on the construction in the middle of the wilderness of a new capital, Brazilia. Intended to be "the capital that will unite the whole nation," it was inaugurated in 1960.

The cost of these mammoth development projects was, however, far beyond the means of the Brazilian government, which had contracted enormous foreign debts. As in Argentina, power-hungry generals were the only ones to benefit from the social unrest and political conflict caused by the resulting financial crisis. With the backing of the conservative Brazilian elite, they ended democratic government in 1964, beginning a twenty-year military dictatorship. The prevalence of the military in Latin American political life in the 1960s and 1970s constituted a depressing return to an old form of rule, bolstered in these years by the anti-Communist policies and military aid programs of the United States.

The United States and Central America in the 1950s

In Central America, the U.S. government found among military dictators its most faithful allies. It treated the region as a sphere of influence whose small states had to adhere closely to its policies of opposition to communism and support for business interests. The failure of a reformist government in Guatemala to do so revived the U.S. policy of intervention, in the spirit of the "gunboat diplomacy" of the first two decades of the century. This new Guatemalan regime, a coalition of reform liberals, socialists, and Communists elected in 1948 and led by Jacobo Arbenz, differed from the other populist democratic movements in Latin America in those years in its overriding objective of social reform. This was to be achieved principally by a land reform, which included the expropriation of one-half the extensive land holdings of United Fruit Company, principal landowner and American-owned enterprise. The Arbenz regime pursued as well its own development strategy to make Guatemala a "modern capitalist state," a visionary dream for so poor a country. By 1953, its program was well under way and had aroused opposition both from within Guatemala and from the United States.

Its program was opposed by the country's conservative elite, including the landowners, who feared the loss of their large estates, the church, which opposed radical reform, and the military, as well as by the U.S. government. By accepting Communist political support, Arbenz challenged the anti-Communist policies of the new Eisenhower administration. Fearing a military *coup* supported by the United States, Arbenz took another daring step away from U.S. domination by agreeing to purchase arms from Communist states. His attempt to assert the independence of his small country, prefiguring later events in Cuba and Nicaragua, led him without any plan toward nonalignment and aid agreements with the Soviet Union. To the U.S. secretary of state, John Foster Dulles, the Guatemalan leader's rejection of

U.S. Cold War policies was sufficient to damn him as a potential Soviet ally.

To end Guatemala's undesirable drift out of the U.S. sphere of influence, the U.S. government revived, in a new form, the old policy of intervention in Central American politics. It authorized the Central Intelligence Agency to train and equip a small group of Guatemalan exiles opposed to the reformist regime. The U.S. ambassador encouraged the Guatemalan army leaders not to defend their government. In mid-1954, the small armed band of exiles (two hundred in all) invaded Guatemala. Their uprising met little resistance, for the generals refused to call out the army, and Arbenz had not armed his supporters. He fled, and a new U.S.-backed military regime banned the Communist party, broke relations with the Communist countries, and restored to United Fruit the nationalized property. Making anti-communism its principal goal, the U.S. government took its Latin American allies where it could find them. Frequently they were conservative military dictators.

One of these was the head of Nicaragua, General Somoza. He had seized power in his country in the early 1930s, capturing and executing his principal rival, the nationalist leader Augusto Sandino. Somoza's rule ensured in the next decades great wealth to his family, security to the landowners, and adherence to U.S. Cold War policies. Rulers such as Somoza remained client politicians in their relations with the U.S. government and business interests.

Cuban Dictatorship in the 1950s

Cuban politics in the 1950s duplicated this pattern of rule. The dominant figure was Fulgencio Batista, dictator in the 1930s and then president in the war years under a democratic constitution he himself had prepared (see Chapter 6). Keenly aware of U.S. political and economic interests in Cuba, he heeded the U.S. wartime call for democracy, withdrawing from politics in 1944 to permit political parties to compete for power. The turbulent era of democratic government lasted only eight years. Batista, sensing the U.S. readiness in the early 1950s to recognize Latin American dictators on the condition that they backed Cold War policies, seized power in 1952 with the support of the Cuban army. He immediately banned the Cuban Communists, who managed still to keep a secret, underground organization, and ended diplomatic relations with the Soviet Union.

Batista's judgment of U.S. priorities was correct. Like Somoza of Nicaragua, he received generous U.S. military assistance to arm and train his small army. His state remained closely in step with U.S. policies and cooperated with U.S. business interests. Many middle-class Cubans benefited substantially from these economic conditions, and the Cuban standard of living was among the highest of any Latin American country. Cuban nationalists condemned the dominant role of the United States in the Cuban economy as "neocolonialism" and accused Batista of subservience to the Yankees. Sugar, the country's major crop sold principally in the United States, epitomized Cuba's continued economic and political dependence on the United States. This situation was radically transformed after 1959, when Batista's rule suddenly ended.

The man ultimately responsible for the fall of the Cuban dictator was a remarkable revolutionary leader, Fidel Castro. Son of a self-made sugar plantation owner, Castro grew up in comfortable conditions, sheltered from the effects of the depression as a child and given the benefits of education largely reserved for well-to-do Cuban youth.

Trained as a lawyer, he entered Cuban politics in the late 1940s as a member of the Orthodox party, whose populist, nationalist program of independence from the United States and of social reform reflected his own rather vague political ideals. In those years, a period in his life Castro later called his "bourgeois thralldom," he was no different from many other aspiring young Cuban politicians. National legislative elections were scheduled to be held in 1952, and he prepared to campaign for office. Batista's military coup blocked the hopes of the Orthodox party to win power. Among its most bitterly disappointed candidates for office was Fidel Castro, whose political career was permanently transformed.

The Batista dictatorship provoked only sporadic opposition in the first years. The Orthodox party had no plan of resistance. Among its members, however, were a few activists prepared to take up arms against Batista. Their political ideals remained freedom and social justice, but their means to achieve that end shifted from elections to insurrection. One of the Orthodox members to turn to violence was Castro.

In late 1952 and early 1953, Castro brought together a group of 150 followers, mostly young factory and farm workers, united in support of what they loosely termed the Revolution. They pledged themselves to the restoration of the 1940 constitution, to "complete and definitive social justice based on economic and industrial advancement," and to liberation from "any links to foreign nations"—that is, to the United States. The emphasis on social reform and anti-imperialism constituted the core of Castro's political ideology, a romantic mixture of revolutionary fervor, defiance of Yankee domination, and concern for the needs of Cuba's poor. It later became the heart of his revolution.

Castro's first effort at mobilizing a revolution in Cuba was almost his last. His insurrectionary plan in 1953 was to seize the Moncada army barracks in Santiago, to take control of the entire city and to trigger somehow a national uprising. The plan was doomed to failure. The attack, launched on July 26, 1953, led to the death or capture of the entire group. Castro, placed on trial, received a fifteen-year prison sentence. He was only twenty-six years old. In later years, that hopeless uprising came to symbolize the heroic spirit of Castro's revolutionary movement. At the time, it represented a minor incident in Batista's reign.

Cuba's new period of military dictatorship lasted only seven years, from 1952 to 1959. Cuba's economy expanded in those years, for its sugar sold well in the United States and tourism boomed. One American gambler looked at Cuba and exclaimed: "The future looks fabulous!" In an action he must have bitterly regretted later, Batista decreed in 1955 a general amnesty for political prisoners, including Fidel Castro. Economic prosperity was not sufficient to ensure Batista's rule. He proved an incompetent and unpopular ruler. For one thing, his repression of political opposition served only to provoke more resistance. A second reason for his brief rule was his exaggerated confidence in his military forces and in U.S. backing. His army was used for internal repression of political enemies, but it failed even at that task. Before the decade ended, Batista was a political refugee and Castro ruled Cuba.

Castro's Revolution

Why did this unexpected political revolution occur? To Batista's ineffective rule and the growing hostility among Cubans toward his dictatorship should be added a third reason. Fidel Castro proved in the years after his release from prison an effective guerrilla commander and an outstanding nationalist leader, around whom the other anti-Batista forces gathered to create a united revolutionary opposition. Upon his release from jail, he organized his own small group which he named the July 26th Movement (so-called because of the date of his 1953 uprising). He soon fled to Mexico to organize a new armed insurrection. In other Third World countries, revolutionary guerrilla forces had attempted, and a few had succeeded, in seizing power from authoritarian regimes backed by the United States. Nowhere in Latin America did a comparable movement exist, and the example of Guatemala suggested that the United States might prove a serious enemy.

In late 1956 Castro and eighty comrades returned to Cuba on an old boat, the *Granma*, to launch a new uprising against Batista. Castro's plans miscarried, leaving the few survivors of his rebel band to flee to the mountains. Within a year, though, he built up his guerrilla force into an organized band of three hundred fighters supported by an underground political movement in most Cuban cities. He had alongside him his brother Raul, once a Young Communist, who had become his loyal aide and most effective political organizer. With him also was a young Argentine doctor named Ernesto "Che" Guevara, a roaming revolutionary who had watched at close hand the destruction of the Arbenz regime in Guatemala. Fighting a regime armed by the United States, observing the opposition of the United States to social reform, Castro concluded that U.S. domination of Cuba was the great threat to his revolution.

Although Castro's guerrilla forces remained small, they constituted a dedicated group of revolutionaries capable of turning back the half-hearted attacks by Batista's troops and, most important, of winning the support of the rural population. Their program of social revolution promised an end to the hardship of the small farmers. Guerrilla bands appeared in other sections of Cuba by 1958, always few in number but able to organize effective armed attacks on Batista's increasingly demoralized army. The rural guerrilla movement created by Castro provided him with the instrument to seize power. Those who fought with him there became the leaders of revolutionary Cuba later.

The success of the revolution depended on winning the backing of large numbers of Cubans. Castro's July 26th Movement by itself was too small, numbering at most twenty thousand members. However, a much larger urban opposition force, the Cuban Revolutionary Directorate uniting political enemies of Batista, had also appeared by 1958. The only other organized resistance force was the Communist party, with trained underground cadres and a strong following among Cuban workers. In early 1958, the Directorate and the July 26th Movement joined forces, signing a Unity Manifesto. It stated their common enemy to be the "criminal dictatorship of Fulgencio Batista," their joint goal the reestablishment of "full constitutional and democratic rights." The means to this end was "armed insurrection."

Did Castro really intend at that point to collaborate with other liberal forces in a constitutional democracy after the revolution? Probably not, for he had fundamentally revised his political objectives since 1952. His definition of democracy stressed rule for the people, not by the people. He was persuaded that he understood better than other Cuban political leaders the needs of Cubans. For the time being, he needed outside support. He was prepared to collaborate with other groups, whatever their political ideology, including the Communist party. His political daring, his charismatic appeal, and his effectiveness in mobilizing the guerrilla movement gave him the standing of a national leader. Castro's cooperation with the other anti-Batista forces was a temporary affair, his promises of democratic rule an act of expediency.

Castro showed the same skill in dealing with the United States as in his relations with his political allies in Cuba. He bitterly opposed American imperialism, which for him meant all forms of U.S. economic and political domination in Cuba. His foremost political goal consisted in freeing his country from its ties with the "giant of the north." Yet he realized that he needed the neutrality of the United States if his uprising were to succeed. As a result, he welcomed U.S. reporters at his guerrilla headquarters and won their admiration by his courage, his opposition to dictatorship, and his apparent support for democracy. He fit easily the image of freedom fighter in the American press.

Suspicious of Castro's independence and anti-imperialism, the Eisenhower administration attempted to encourage Cubans to find another solution to the growing political crisis. In 1958 it decided to end its military aid program to Batista's regime, clearly a losing cause, in the hopes that a new government would emerge uniting a broad coalition of Cuban parties. By not intervening directly, however, its action bestowed on Castro the role of legitimate political successor. The U.S. policy of nonintervention in the Cuban conflict left to Cubans the choice of political leadership and the right of revolution. The consequences proved not at all what Eisenhower had expected.

In 1958 Batista's power slipped rapidly away. Castro had proven an extraordinarily effective opposition leader. That fall small groups of his Rebel Army operated in all areas of the country and were supported openly by many Cubans, who looked to Castro to end Batista's dictatorship. In the cities an urban guerrilla force, the Civic Resistance, fought police and army units. That

December guerrillas under the command of Che Guevara moved out of the countryside to attack the capital, Havana. Batista's army melted away, and his generals fled for their lives. Batista found no one to fight for his regime. On January 1, 1959, he abandoned power and left the country. On his heels came Guevara's Rebel Army and the Revolutionary Directorate, both eager to take control of Havana. Castro arrived a week later, having traveled across the length of Cuba, greeted by hundreds of thousands of Cubans as the national hero of a democratic revolution. Castro, at age thirty-two, was leader of his country.

Socialist Cuba

A political revolution began in Cuba, unlike any which had occurred previously in Latin America. An armed insurrection led by a small rural guerrilla army totaling at most two thousand fighters had ended the rule of a military dictator. Its political organization, the July 26th Movement, numbered only twenty thousand and lacked both a coherent political program and internal discipline. In a country of seven million, Castro's forces were very small. Allied with them was the Revolutionary Directorate, a collection of liberal and socialist politicians and students. It was even more disorganized than the July 26th Movement. He received support also from the Communist party, with about fifteen thousand members and a centralized leadership modeled on the Soviet Communists. It shared Castro's opposition to American imperialism and possessed the experience with mass organizations that the July 26th Movement lacked. There existed great diversity among the victors of the insurrection. Real unity came from Castro's own leadership; the regime's ruling cadres came from the Rebel Army. This was the case in

1959, and it remained so in the years that followed.

Consolidation of power constituted Castro's first objective. His second was rapid reforms to raise the standard of living of the lower classes of Cuba. His third was independence from the United States. In all these he proved at least partially successful. As a consequence, Cuba became within four years a socialist society based on the Soviet model controlled by a one-party state supported by and dependent on the Soviet Union. The political events leading to Communist Cuba were dramatic and contributed to the most serious international crisis in the postwar period. Despite these exceptional features to Cuban revolutionary history, it is important to point out the similarities with other Third World revolutions and with other Latin American political movements. Castro exemplified, in an extreme form, the nationalist hostility toward American political and economic domination. He organized a party whose program and following—but not methods—resembled other populist nationalist movements intent on fighting social injustice and economic inequalities. He, like other nationalist revolutionary leaders, was prepared to turn for help to the Communist Second World. That decision led in the Cuban case to a grave superpower conflict. The events between 1959 and 1962 leading up to that crisis are directly tied to the early history of the Cuban revolution.

During all those years Castro remained the central figure in Cuban politics. He proved capable of maintaining control of the new state and of winning the loyalty of most Cubans, emerging by 1962 as their undisputed national leader. During the first year of power he organized his new revolutionary regime. In the early months he remained simply commander-in-chief of the Rebel Army. Its uniform provided the symbol of the revolution. Castro himself kept his combat clothes and his beard from the guerrilla years. This choice provided one indication that the new revolutionary regime would not become another democratic state.

Castro arrived in Havana in early January 1959, warning that he would not allow the new leadership to behave "like the many revolutionaries of the past [who] roamed around fighting each other." The Civil Resistance groups had to give up their arms. The Revolutionary Directorate was incorporated into the July 26th Movement. Liberal political leaders appeared for a short time in the new revolutionary government. They found, however, that real power lay in Castro's hands. He chose to delay holding new elections and launched the first social reforms. Within two months he assumed the formal powers of prime minister. Gradually all the important government positions passed to his colleagues in the July 26th Movement. When the head of the State Bank objected to violations of property rights by the new regime, he was replaced by Guevara. In July 1959, the Cuban president resigned in protest at the active part taken by Communists in the social reforms. By then the old liberal parties had disappeared, banned as enemies of the revolution. Free elections were never held. In 1961 Castro formally dissolved the constitution of 1940, claiming it was "already too outdated and old for us." In fact Castro refused to permit democratic liberties to weaken his revolutionary powers.

By then the guerrilla leaders had formed a centralized, one-party dictatorship. Castro had little taste for political edicts and systematic administration, preferring to rely on his personal authority somewhat in the traditional manner of a Latin *caudillo* (literally "chief," the term is used to designate any strong leader). His brother Raul and Che Guevara took particular responsibility for the creation of a new state. Both had worked closely before with Communists and applied to Cuba the principles of "vanguard" leadership and of revolution from above practiced by Communist regimes.

Through them a Soviet-type centralized dictatorship began to emerge in Cuba, with the assistance of the Communist party. Leadership of labor unions, once controlled by Batista's supporters, was transferred to Communists. The growing influence of the Communist party angered Cuban liberals and brought protests even from members of the July 26th Movement. They saw in Communist political influence a threat to them and, they believed, to Cuban independence. In late 1959 Hubert Matos, a provincial military governor and former guerrilla commander, resigned to protest Communist activity. Castro personally arrested him and accused him of becoming a "traitor" to the revolution. In fact Matos's only crime was to refuse to follow unquestioningly Castro's revolutionary leadership. He was sentenced to twenty years in prison. Other political opponents received the same treatment, prosecuted by a new security police acting in the name of the "revolution." The state took over control of Cuba's press. Castro called his rule "direct government by the people." Power actually belonged to the former guerrilla leaders.

Although the revolutionary reforms resembled Soviet socialism, the Cuban Communists were not responsible for this trend. Castro was as unwilling to share power with the Communists as with any other political movement. He and his supporters used the party because they needed experienced personnel trained in revolutionary rule. He declared in 1959 that "our revolution is neither capitalist nor Communist." The statement was partly propaganda to quiet American critics, accusing him of a "Communist revolution." It reiterated also his refusal to take orders from anyone. The question of "liberties" played no part in his rejection at that time of the label of "Communist." The real issue was power. The Cuban Communists agreed to be Castro's collaborators in the hopes of increasing their own political influence. Instead, they found themselves Castro's subordinates.

In 1961 Castro publicly attacked the head of the Communist party for "grave errors" and demanded of the "old Communists" an attitude of "modesty." That year he replaced the July 26th Movement with a new political party called the Integrated Revolutionary Organizations (ORI) and ordered the Communists to join it. Later that year he came to regard the term "Communist" more favorably than before, but for his own political reasons. The United States had become his outright enemy and he was desperate for allies.

Cuba Between the Superpowers

The conflict between Cuba and the United States began shortly after the revolution. It originated in the social reforms instituted in 1959. The revolutionary leaders set out to expropriate wealthy property owners, foreign and Cuban, and to redistribute land and wealth to the Cuban lower classes. They ordered housing rents lowered by 50 percent and electric power rates cut as much. In May they seized landed estates of over a thousand acres, including all large sugar plantations. Part of the land went to farmers, while the largest plantations became collective farms (cooperatives) organized by the Communists in the Agrarian Reform Institute. Irate former owners (including United Fruit Company) charged that Castro was a Communist. Nationalization of foreign businesses continued through the rest of the year despite objections from

the U.S. government. Castro was already prepared to defy the Yankees, though he undoubtedly realized the growing threat of U.S. intervention.

Cuba could not escape its dependence on exports, essential to the Cuban revolutionaries to finance their social reforms. They hoped to increase their country's foreign income from the sale of sugar, presenting the U.S. government with the extraordinary request that it double its purchases of the commodity and agree to a 20 percent increase in the price. Their demand represented a public claim on the wealth of the imperialists. At the same time, they proclaimed a new foreign policy of nonalignment, refusing to join in U.S. Cold War policies and attacking capitalist domination. They were beginning to take Cuba out of the U.S. sphere of influence. Relying on the traditional techniques of U.S. Caribbean control, the Eisenhower administration refused to renegotiate the sugar agreement and demanded that U.S. capitalists receive proper compensation from Cuba for property losses.

The U.S. refusal was predictable, though one still can wonder if the two governments might have cooperated on the new terms set by the Cubans. Instead, U.S. leaders warned the Cubans to "calm down" and threatened to cut back sugar purchases. In early 1960 they began secret plans for possible military aid to Cuban anti-Castro exiles. The Guatemalan crisis of 1954 had begun in the same manner.

Rather than retreat, the Cuban revolutionaries moved even further with their new foreign and economic policies. Castro was psychologically prepared for battle, knowing that the odds were against him. Cuba turned for the first time to Communist countries for help. In February 1960 the Soviet Union agreed to buy Cuban sugar on a regular basis and to provide Cuba with a major loan to permit Cuban purchase of Soviet machinery and petroleum. The Soviet leaders viewed the move as part of their new Third World policy of aid to "bourgeois nationalist" leaders opposed to Western alliances. Castro considered the treaty a victory for Cuban economic nationalism. The Soviet petroleum had to be refined in Cuba, and Castro ordered the U.S.-owned refineries to cooperate. After consulting with Washington, the oil companies refused to handle "Red oil." In June 1960, Castro seized their property.

This decision proved the breaking point in U.S.-Cuban relations. The U.S. government halted all purchases of Cuban sugar; later that year, it declared a complete embargo on trade with Cuba. It had in effect begun economic war. Castro responded by seizing all remaining U.S. property in Cuba, to which he added all Cuban-owned industries, banks, and transportation. By the end of 1960, all large trade and banking, most of industry, transportation, and one-third of agricultural land belonged to the Cuban state. The Cuban revolutionaries launched their country on the socialist path of economic development in defiance of the United States. Other revolutionary regimes, such as Nasser's Egypt, had moved in the same direction. The Cubans, more radical than the Egyptians and challenging the United States on its very doorstep, turned to the Soviet model. International pressures and domestic revolutionary ideals were bringing Cuba and the Soviet Union closer together.

The Cuban economic goals could not be reached without outside help. The Cuban leaders were prepared to begin a Soviet-type "revolution from above" based on command planning, state-financed industrialization, and collective farming. They lacked the skilled personnel and the resources for the task. Even after imitating the Soviet policy of enforcing low prices on farm produce, they still could not find within Cuba sufficient means

for their revolutionary plans. Too poor to pay for its own projects, the Cuban government had to borrow heavily from the Soviet Union. Need for Soviet aid and the U.S. trade embargo made Cuba dependent on Soviet support. With no specific idea of the consequences, Castro had pursued his economic conflict with the United States to its logical conclusion. He had made his country reliant on the Soviet Union and had brought the Cold War to the Caribbean.

Determined to end this new socialist pro-Soviet regime so close to U.S. shores, the U.S. government turned again to interventionist policies. John Kennedy, in his 1960 electoral campaign, had accused President Eisenhower of permitting the Soviet leaders to make Cuba "Communism's first Caribbean base." He promised new, vigorous leadership and warned that "any potential aggressor contemplating an attack on any part of the free world with any kind of weapons must know that our response will be suitable, selective, swift and effective." Containment of Communist regimes allied with the Soviet Union (or China) remained the overriding U.S. strategy, which the new administration planned to implement with what it called the "flexible response." Included in the response was secret aid to anti-Castro rebels.

When CIA officials brought Kennedy their proposals, he agreed to back a large-scale invasion by the rebels. He and his advisers assumed that Castro must be unpopular since the Cuban state was a dictatorship and believed that an invasion by anti-Castro Cubans would trigger an immediate uprising. They underestimated the popular backing for Castro's revolution. The invasion by fourteen hundred Cubans took place in April 1961. It failed even to get beyond the landing beaches of the Bay of Pigs. The police immediately arrested Castro's enemies in Cuba, and effective army and militia resistance defeated the invaders. Victory brought the Cuban revolutionaries the glory of patriots defying the "Yankee imperialists." Like Nasser after the Suez crisis of 1956, Castro became for Cubans and anti-imperialists elsewhere a hero in the struggle against the American giant.

The future of his regime remained uncertain. It confronted the likelihood of further attack from the United States. Castro had come to view his revolutionary struggle as part of the global battle of socialism and national liberation against imperialism. He had seized power in 1959 with no clear vision of history besides that of the Cuban fight for liberty. Force of circumstances placed before him an image of Cuban revolutionary combat which resembled the Marxist-Leninist theory of the struggle against imperialism. His actions in nationalizing the Cuban economy and working for social welfare were sanctioned as well in Marxist-Leninist socialist theory.

These two factors by themselves suggest how he might have become persuaded that his revolution belonged within the world Communist movement. Another important reason, however, was his desperate need for allies against the United States. The Soviet Union alone possessed the military might sufficient to deter another U.S.-backed invasion. In December 1961, he announced that "I am a Marxist-Leninist and shall remain a Marxist-Leninist until the day I die," an affirmation of faith which contained a direct appeal to the Soviet Union for protection.

The Cuban Missile Crisis

The Soviet leaders proposed to him only part of what he sought. He hoped for a Soviet military alliance, but neither the Soviet Union nor the Warsaw Pact extended the offer then or later. Instead, in the spring of 1962 Khrushchev proposed to place intermediate-range ballistic missiles in Cuba, installed and controlled by Russians. Castro agreed, believing that his country was obtaining military protection in the fight against world imperialism. He was wrong, for the Soviet leaders had other aims in mind.

Khrushchev was attempting a major gamble to alter the nuclear balance of power and was using Soviet missiles for that purpose. His own general in charge of the Soviet missile force resigned that spring, probably in protest over his reckless action. Of what use would Soviet missiles be in Cuba? The military and propaganda value to the Soviets would be enormous. It is also possible that Khrushchev hoped to use the new military balance for a form of "nuclear blackmail." His principal diplomatic objective in those years was to force the Western evacuation from West Berlin. He may have considered that, to obtain Soviet withdrawal of its Cuban missiles, the United States would finally abandon the city to the East Germans.

Whatever his long-term objectives, Khrushchev was gambling for high stakes and taking terrible risks. The greatest danger of military conflict in the U.S.-Soviet global rivalry would come if one side provoked an "accidental war" like that which had begun in August 1914. At that time, a regional power move by Germany and Austria-Hungary in the Balkans had escalated into military confrontation throughout Europe when diplomats ceased negotiating and trusted military leaders to protect their interests. Khrushchev risked creating just such a situation by installing Soviet missiles in Cuba. Both sides might be losers as a result. In that dangerous game of power politics, Castro was really only an observer.

To prevent a sudden shift in the military balance of power and a humiliating diplomatic defeat, the U.S. government came very close to war on Cuba. The missiles began to appear on Cuban soil in early fall 1962. In mid-October photographs from U.S. spy planes revealed the rapid construction of several missile sites. In Washington some political and military leaders called for immediate invasion of Cuba, a reckless action which, if Soviet military forces intervened to protect their missiles and personnel, could quickly lead to nuclear war. Kennedy preferred the approach suggested by "flexible response," starting with a naval blockade of Cuba and proceeding with invasion only if the Soviet Union did not negotiate. The United States possessed the naval forces for such a step, which began October 22. It received the backing of U.S. allies both in Europe and in Latin America. Kennedy sent messages to the Soviet government calling for peaceful negotiation for the withdrawal of the missiles and warning of further action if a settlement was not quickly reached. After five days of growing tension, Khrushchev agreed to pull out the missiles. He obtained in exchange the U.S. promise not to invade Cuba. War was averted.

Both sides had compromised. The Soviet Union appeared the loser, having had to remove its nuclear weapons under threat of war. Still, the agreement by the United States not to support another anti-Castro invasion represented a major concession as well. It amounted to a defeat of the Cold War policy of keeping Communist parties and the Soviet Union far from Latin America. U.S. economic and diplomatic domination of the entire Caribbean area had ended. The most important aspect of the crisis was the fact that both sides were deterred from war by the nuclear might of the other, preferring to accept a negotiated settlement. The system of deterrence, though crude, had worked to avert nuclear war.

Castro did not share in the satisfaction at the settlement. His government received only a U.S. promise of nonintervention. It did not obtain military protection from the Soviet Union, and, worst of all, he had had

no voice in the resolution of the crisis. Soviet missiles vanished from Cuba without his approval. From a front-line position in the world struggle against imperialism, his island was reduced to a side-show.

DICTATORS AND REFORM IN LATIN AMERICA

Pressures for Reform

The two decades that followed the missile crisis were years of political conflict and pressure on Latin American governments to take heed of the basic needs and aspirations of their peoples. Three important factors help explain the new situation. First, the Cuban revolution and Castro's stature as revolutionary leader crystallized social opposition to Latin American oligarchies. Castro first laid down his guidelines for Third World revolution in early 1962 in his Second Declaration of Havana. He placed Cuba in the forefront of the "upward march of history." The liberation of the "dependent and colonial peoples" since World War II marked "the final crisis of imperialism." He was convinced that "the Cuban Revolution shows that revolution is possible, that the people can do it." He spelled out the nature of that revolution in later speeches, arguing that "guerrilla war" was the "only solution." He held up the Cuban revolution as the model for revolutionary insurrection in all Latin countries.

The second factor was the decision of the U.S. government in those years, pushed by fears of socialist revolution, to promote social reform in Latin America. Kennedy's Alliance for Progress called on the governments in the region to propose development plans which would receive U.S. economic and financial assistance, totaling $20 billion over a ten-year period. U.S. advisers strongly encouraged the Latin American leaders to impose heavy taxes on the wealthy to help make their own fiscal contribution and to institute land reform to provide farms for the rural poor and landless workers. At the same time, the U.S. government increased its military aid, directed specifically at repressing guerrilla movements like that Castro had led to power. The United States remained adamantly opposed to Communist influence elsewhere in Latin America.

The third force behind social reform came from the Catholic church. To implement the decisions taken at the Second Vatican Council, the bishops of all Latin America met in 1968. In the presence of the pope, the delegates laid down the principles of social action by Catholic priests and laity. The goals were those fixed at the Vatican conference—the need for peace based on human justice, human liberation by social action, and major social reforms. The impact of these decisions was profound, though they are not easily measured. Within a few years, nearly a million Brazilian Catholics, mainly from the poor laboring classes, had joined local religious groups (called *cebs*) to undertake reform measures. In the years of repressive military dictatorship in the 1970s, they represented the only mass political movement in the country. The effect among Catholic clergy was equally profound. While upper-class bishops resisted the reform movement, other bishops and priests began to speak out openly against injustice, at times at the risk of their own lives. While supporters of Castro called for Marxist revolution, the Catholic church proposed its own ideology of social reform.

Latin America Between Dictators and Democracy

The political results of these conflicting pressures varied widely. On the one hand, military dictatorships became the dominant form of Latin American rule in the 1960s and 1970s. Even Chile, once a model of democratic compromise, was caught in a bitter political contest which ended in oppressive military rule. A reform movement, led by the socialist Salvador Allende and backed by socialists and Communists, was voted into office in 1970 with the support of workers and peasants. It undertook a sweeping program of socialist reform, which brought out strong opposition from the middle classes and created by 1973 virtual civil war. The outcome resembled in some respects Brazil in 1964. The Chilean army, with secret encouragement from U.S. agents, seized power in a violent revolt. Bloody repression by the military rulers followed. All social reforms ended. Although later even the Catholic church attacked the dictatorship, it remained firmly in power.

Yet Chile appeared within a few years to be the exception, not the rule, among Latin American countries. On the contrary, the trend turned toward democratic reform governments, and even in one case a revolutionary regime resembling Castro's Cuba. Although military dictators ruled in Argentina and Brazil until the 1980s, they proved increasingly unpopular and incapable of governing their countries. They had accepted enormous loans from international banks in the 1970s, and were incapable of repaying the debt when global economic recession began in 1981. They were unable to control wild inflation within their own economies, which had been growing and then entered in turn a period of recession and increasing hardship for the laboring population. Opposition to their rule grew so great that in both cases the military leaders withdrew from power without popular revolution. Argentina returned to democratic rule in 1984, and Brazil in 1985. In both cases the new governments were based on broad coalitions with middle- and working-class support and were headed by political leaders intent on resuming social reform under democratic rule.

In Central America, the conflict between conservatives and reformers was more acute. Military dictatorship allied with and protecting a small social elite had long dominated politics. Following the 1968 conference of Latin American bishops, Catholic clergy there took the lead in denouncing military rule and economic injustice. When conditions worsened, they even spoke out in favor of insurrection, the only means left to seek freedom and justice. Military repression of Catholic opposition became so brutal in El Salvador that in 1980 officers even assassinated the archbishop. In those years radical guerrilla forces were operating in the rural areas. U.S. diplomatic pressure forced the military there to allow in 1981 democratic reformist leaders to take control of the government, weakened by enemies from both sides.

In the 1970s one Central American country followed the Cuban path of revolution. Castro's hopes for popular socialist revolution in Latin America had been disappointed in the 1960s. Throughout Latin America a few Communist parties attempted to follow the Cuban example, but their uprisings were crushed by military forces. In 1966 Che Guevara, one of Castro's closest colleagues, left Cuba to organize a rural insurrection in Bolivia, only to be betrayed the next year by peasants, arrested, and shot. Brazilian revolutionaries in the late 1960s had also failed to find strong popular support. In Nicaragua a decade later, however, opposition to the Somoza family's dictatorship, which had lasted almost forty years, grew to such proportions it did constitute a real revolutionary movement. It was organized around a coalition of resistance groups, radical and liberal, calling themselves the Sandinistas (Sandino was Somoza's first political enemy to be shot).

Peasants, middle classes, and the bishops of the Catholic church supported their revolt to overthrow the dictator. In 1979, the Sandinista movement seized power, the only popular revolution in Latin America since Castro's forces had taken Cuba.

The revolutionary forces quickly encountered serious obstacles. Divided among themselves, their regime fell under the leadership of radicals whose policies were closely modeled on those of the Cuban revolution in its first years. Their liberal and Catholic supporters became increasingly critical. While some Catholic priests remained active in the regime, the archbishop soon began attacking the authoritarian policies of the Sandinistas. These internal conflicts were overshadowed, however, by the opposition of the U.S. government. The Sandinistas provided aid to insurrections elsewhere in Central America, including El Salvador. They welcomed support from Cuba and the Soviet Union, and initially from the United States as well. But the new Reagan leadership viewed their socialist revolution in the same light Kennedy had judged the Castro regime, namely, a threat to the political stability of the region and to the security of the United States. It began in 1981 to organize and support Nicaraguan guerrillas fighting the Sandinistas, reviving policies of intervention to eliminate a revolutionary regime from an area it considered a U.S. sphere of influence.

The Soviet Union and Cuban Socialism

Castro's regime had liberated itself completely from that sphere as a result of the Cuban missile crisis. The Cuban revolutionaries' freedom of action remained restricted, however, both by the influence of the Soviet Union and by the limited resources of their own country. Their principal concern in the 1960s was the search for a successful path of socialist development. They had begun in

1960 by imitating the Soviet model, emphasizing industry and neglecting Cuban agriculture. After 1962, they set out in a new direction. One reason for the change was the disastrous results of the "crash" industrialization drive. By 1962 the Cuban government had to impose food rationing and had scant manufactured goods from its new factories to compensate for the sacrifices imposed on the population. Industrial production actually fell between 1960 and 1963 by 25 percent. The country remained economically underdeveloped and dependent on its sugar exports to pay for loans and imports of needed machinery. The Soviet Union was the source of this aid and demanded as firmly as any Western bank repayment on the loans. Sugar remained at the foundation of Cuban economic wealth.

In reaction to these failures and to disillusionment with Soviet leadership, the Cuban revolutionaries set out to discover a new path to socialism. In 1965 their movement appropriated the title of Communist party. Castro told a great crowd of followers that year that "all shades and all types of origin distinguishing one revolutionary from another must forever disappear." The only real Cuban Communists from that point on were Castroites. The positions of leader of the party, its first secretary, and president of the Cuban Republic were all held by Castro himself.

The Cuban vision of the future became for several years, as one observer explained ironically, "socialism in one island." Castro's plans for a socialist Cuba sought economic development through increased agricultural instead of industrial production. He told his followers in 1965 that Cuba had no need of socialist models from other countries and would not go around "mechanically copying formulas." He had thrown out the Soviet socialist example. Calling his country a "giant greenhouse," he proposed that the people construct their socialist society and even "communism to a certain degree" by extracting the wealth from the land. His goal for Cuba was the production by 1970 of ten million tons of sugar, twice as much as in the mid-1960s and more than Cuba had ever produced. Cubans had to provide the extra effort for the good of Cuban socialism. All those who did not share this dream had no place in the new Cuba. Permitting temporarily mass emigration, Castro argued that Cuba lost "absolutely nothing" with the departure of "parasites" and "speculators." Another 250,000 Cubans migrated, as many as had left between 1959 and 1962.

The goal of achieving a sugar harvest of 10 million tons acquired a symbolic value, proof that Cuba had no need of outside help or foreign socialist models. It represented in its own way the same dream of economic and social miracles as Mao's Great Leap Forward of the late 1950s. Food rationing was extended in 1968 to include sugar itself. The harvest of 1970 reached 8.5 million tons, but the cost was crushing. Production of other food products and industrial goods fell drastically. The situation was so critical that, without the help of Soviet aid, it might have led to economic collapse. Castro himself admitted that serious "difficulties" existed and took personal responsibility for the failure. Revolutionary Cuba did not have the resources to become an independent socialist state.

Its only recourse was dependence on Soviet economic aid and political supervision. Under pressure from Moscow, Castro had to moderate his foreign policy and to approve Soviet power politics. When Soviet troops invaded Czechoslovakia in 1968, Castro called the action a "bitter necessity" required to preserve the unity of the "socialist camp." In later years he praised the "glorious services rendered to the human race" by the Soviet Union. In exchange, his army received Soviet military aid. It served him as an arm, with

Soviet approval, for the support of African Marxist regimes, first intervening in the Angolan civil war in 1975, then in Ethiopia in 1978. In both cases its intervention proved decisive in maintaining the revolutionary leaders in power, reassuring Castro that his state still participated in the "upward march of history."

Did the Cuban people benefit by his revolution? Their living conditions did finally begin to improve in the 1970s. The Soviet socialist system reappeared in Cuba. A special Soviet-Cuban economic committee supervised the use of the imports from the Communist countries, giving Soviet authorities direct control over their economic aid. Slow economic development did not eliminate shortages, but did under Cuban socialism avoid the extremes of wealth and poverty of other countries. Economic growth throughout Latin America beginning in the 1950s had enlarged the middle classes, but only in Cuba was abject poverty no longer in existence. Women in Cuba enjoyed greater opportunities and rights than in most other Latin American countries. A sign of the profound changes in Cuban social relations was the fall in the birth rate, lowest of all societies in Latin America and an indication of the low priority Cubans gave to large families.

Despite these social and economic improvements, the Cuban state remained a repressive party dictatorship. While in the early 1980s other Latin American countries rid themselves of military dictators to return to constitutional democracy, Castro permitted no liberalization. Political dissenters received long prison terms; Hubert Matos, imprisoned in 1960, served his full twenty-year sentence, leaving immediately after for the United States. Although most Cubans remained loyal to their Communist leaders, discontent was sufficiently widespread that, when Castro briefly permitted emigration to the United States in 1979, over 100,000

Cubans left. Cuba resembled in many respects the Eastern European Communist states, its leadership free to pursue their own policies within the limits set by the rigid model of Soviet socialism and by Soviet international interests.

SUMMARY

The world in the 1970s was evolving away from the simple East-West division of the postwar years. The United States, economically and militarily at the height of its influence in the early 1960s, had a decade later to adjust to new economic rivals in Europe and Asia, to a far more powerful Soviet Union, and to independent nation-states, often nonaligned, throughout the Third World. That period witnessed major changes in international political and economic relations. The visit by the U.S. president to Peking in 1972 represented the major diplomatic event in East Asia, not the departure of U.S. fighting forces from Vietnam. Concern over U.S.-Chinese ties provided one strong incentive to the Russian Communist leaders to agree that year to new treaties with the West (including the Berlin treaty and the nuclear arms limitations treaty), opening a new period in U.S.-Soviet relations termed *détente*. Although competition between the two superpowers continued, they were able for a few years to improve their relations so substantially that it is fair to say that the period of the Cold War had come to an end.

The age of colonial wars and national revolutions had ended as well. The map of the world revealed everywhere the emergence of new nation-states. The borders remained those drawn by the Western imperial rulers, replaced by nationalist leaders whose political ideology, even when Marxist-Leninist, stressed the unity of the nation within those frontiers. When threatened by foreign domination, they could rely on their people for support, even great sacrifice. Although the Cuban Communists had ended democracy, their opposition to the United States plus their social reforms expanded and deepened their backing among the Cuban population. Only after the anti-imperialist struggle faded did the repressive nature of the state and the shortcomings of state socialism become apparent. The Communist leaders there as elsewhere refused to concede any power to a political opposition, claiming their revolution "irreversible."

Their plans for internal social reform encountered the same economic obstacles of meager resources and poverty as other Third World countries, leaving them dependent too on outside aid. In the early twentieth century the most visible division among peoples was that separating the Western empires. Toward the end of the century, it became the line between rich and poor societies, between "North" and "South." Political ideologies, religions, and military alliances added their own boundaries to this complex pattern. No single vision of the future made clear how social justice and a better life might be attained. Increasingly interdependent economically, the nation-states of the world remained deeply divided.

RECOMMENDED READING

U.S. Power Politics in the Postwar Years

*STEPHEN AMBROSE, *The Rise to Globalism: American Foreign Policy 1938–1980* (fourth ed., 1985)

RAYMOND ARON, *The Imperial Republic: The U.S. in World Affairs, 1945–1973* (1974)

STEPHEN KINZER AND STEPHEN SCHLESINGER, *Bitter Fruit: The Untold Story of the American Coup in Guatemala* (1983)

Postwar Latin America

CARMELO MESA-LAGO (ed.), *Revolutionary Change in Cuba* (1971)

*THOMAS SKIDMORE AND PETER SMITH, *Modern Latin America* (1984)

TAD SZULZ, *Fidel: A Critical Portrait* (1986)

HUGH THOMAS, *Cuba or the Pursuit of Freedom* (1971)

Postwar European History

GHITA IONESCU, *The Breakup of the Soviet Empire in Eastern Europe* (1975)

ANTHONY SAMPSON. *The Anatomy of Europe* (1968)

MICHEL TATU, *Power in the Kremlin: From Khrushchev to Kosygin* (1970)

DEREK UNWIN, *Western Europe since 1945* (third ed., 1981)

Memoirs and Novels

*ROBERT KENNEDY, *The Thirteen Days* (1968)

*HEDRICK SMITH, *The Russians* (1976)

chapter 12

A NEW AGE?
THE WORLD IN THE
LATE TWENTIETH CENTURY

International wars and political revolutions have been the most prominent features of the history of the world in the twentieth century. The prospect of renewed violence and war leading to a nuclear holocaust gives pause to any thoughtful observer of our times. Can the conditions that have nurtured civilized life endure? The gloomy forecast of the "decline of the West," made in the 1920s by Oswald Spengler, was only the first of many predictions of doomsday, whose potential scale became far more appalling with the appearance of nuclear armaments. The threat of a third world war, the grim subject for military strategists and for simulated war games in Moscow and Washington, is as real as the missile silos clustered in remote regions of the Soviet Union and the United States and as the submarines armed with ballistic missiles constantly on patrol off the coasts of the two countries. Yet the Soviet Union and the United States did devise in the 1970s new policies to reduce the danger of war and to restrain the armaments race. The direction in which superpower relations have evolved in these new post–Cold War conditions is a subject that deserves special attention in this concluding chapter.

The turmoil of this century has another, less fearful, aspect as well. The end of the orderly world of pre-1914 opened a period of extraordinary change and creative endeavor which some observers believe includes promising trends in constructive social relations and individual fulfillment. We no longer share the naive faith of pre-1914 Westerners in "mechanical miracles" or in inevitable progress. Still, technology has come to occupy a central role in global development, and popular aspirations for more fulfilling social and economic conditions have become more widespread than ever before.

The period since the Second World War, the "second twentieth century," reveals some indications of what some observers consider the beginning of a new age. Recent world's fairs have moved from the ostentatious displays of national power and grandeur of the 1900 Paris Exposition. They have tended to emphasize innovation in transportation and communication, optimistic symbols of a world of opportunity opened up by technological creativity.

In the background, new patterns of social relations which have begun to appear in the major societies are of great importance but difficult to characterize accurately. One perspective offering insight into important global trends is provided by the concept of "feminist revolution." Although the term itself arouses political controversy and opposition in many countries, the subject provides a valuable and revealing measure of social change. Addressing the crucial issue of the relative autonomy and control of women over their lives, it raises fundamental questions regarding family and kinship, marriage and employment, children and education. All these dimensions to the feminist revolution help us to evaluate and to understand the degree to which the late twentieth century marks the beginning of a new era in world history.

TECHNOLOGY AND THE GLOBAL ECONOMY

Economic and social change in the postwar years was accelerated by the speed with which scientific discoveries were transformed into tools for human activity. Although the bulk of the innovations were made in Western countries, they spread quickly to other regions of the world as a result partly of international cooperation, partly of private investment and trade. Public health agencies began to apply to their struggle against infectious diseases a vast new array of medicines. Penicillin, first introduced on a large scale shortly after the war, was only the first antibiotic effective in this campaign. Medical research turned to the development of artificial drugs, a move facilitated by the emergence since the 1960s of the field of genetic engineering. Through the manipulation of genetic material to create new species of life, researchers vastly enlarged the possible bacterial base for antibiotic drugs.

The effect of the generalized distribution of the basic vaccines and drugs was visible in the declining death rate throughout the world. This trend in turn contributed to a rise in the 1980s of the average life expectancy to between fifty and sixty years in many Third World countries. This level was still far below that of Western societies, but it represented a substantial increase from the life expectancy of thirty to forty years prevailing in the early century.

The Green Revolution and Economic Growth

By providing protection from devastating infectious disease, modern medicine made more secure the lives of many millions of people throughout the world. By contributing to rapid population growth, it also placed great demands on Third World economies to sustain and to improve living conditions, and on agriculture in particular to raise food production at a rapid rate. Warnings of a "population time bomb" pointed to the accelerating expansion of world population, which doubled in only forty years after the Second World War—from 2.5 billion in

1950 to 5 billion in 1987. Without a substantial improvement in agricultural productivity, many countries confronted a return to the brutal natural limits put on population growth by famine and disease. In this area, too, technological innovation provided a new breakthrough. The discovery and introduction of new crops, achieved largely with the assistance of international and state research agencies, increased agricultural yields so rapidly that their appearance was termed the Green Revolution. In India, for example, high yielding varieties of wheat introduced in the mid-1960s doubled the harvest within six years.

A second condition for expanded food production was state encouragement to farmers, either by subsidies to cooperative farming or, more frequently, by support for private farming. Communist China provided a dramatic illustration of the improvements that farmers achieved when given the proper incentives. China's most recent famine had occurred in the early 1960s as a result in large measure of Mao's experiments in communal farming. In the late 1970s, the post-Mao leaders abandoned the collective farm policy, permitting farmers to sell their own crops and retain the profits from their labor (see Chapter 8). This reform, plus the spread of better varieties of grain and rice, increased by one-fourth the yearly food production per person between 1975 and 1985, making possible the export of grain even though the population by then exceeded 1 billion. In sub-Saharan Africa, however,

North-South Divisions: Relative Sufficiency of Food Intake, 1970. (*From The State of Food and Agriculture, 1974, Rome, Food and Agriculture Organization of the United Nations, 1975, Table 3-C*)

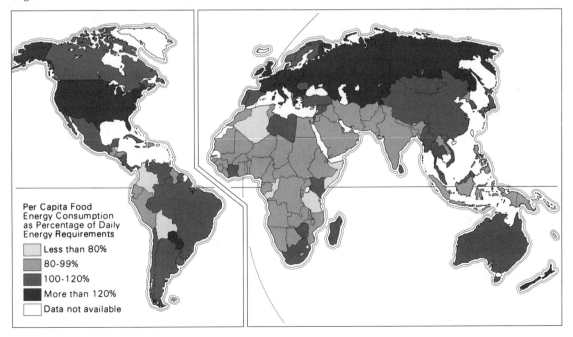

Per Capita Food Energy Consumption as Percentage of Daily Energy Requirements

- Less than 80%
- 80-99%
- 100-120%
- More than 120%
- Data not available

drought and government interference in farming led to massive prolonged famine in the early 1980s.

The disparity between the developed and the developing countries, between the "North" and the "South," changed in character in the decades after the war. The ability of agricultural production to keep up with or to increase more rapidly than the population was essential to improved living conditions among the masses of the population. Rapid improvements in agriculture in the 1970s proved a key factor as well in the ability of many Third World countries (with the major exception of most sub-Saharan African lands) to begin sustained economic growth, that is, to set in motion the long-run processes by which more goods and services are produced every year, even with population rise. In China, economic expansion between the mid-1970s and mid-1980s more than doubled the average per capita income. These benefits were spread unevenly among the population. The middle classes were growing in numbers, and many were living in quite comfortable conditions. Among the rural population, successful farmers growing the new crops could earn a high income, while many families of petty farmers and laborers could no longer survive on their meager resources and had to migrate to the cities. By the 1980s the extent of internal inequalities within many Third World societies was as great as, or greater than, the extent of those between developing lands and the West.

Large urban centers in the Third World became areas in which were concentrated the pressures of population growth and the struggle for an improved life. Cities such as Calcutta, Cairo, and Mexico City grew in large part because they offered a refuge to rural migrants, many of whom did succeed in creating for themselves better living conditions than they would have had in their villages. But there too were vast slums where the unsuccessful lived in terrible impoverishment. The numbers in the world living in "absolute poverty," defined as a standard of living so miserable it cannot ensure survival, probably grew much less rapidly than the total population as a result of economic expansion. The margin of improvement was often slim, at times nonexistent. In some areas of South Asia, population growth was so great that in the mid-1980s food supplies per inhabitant were no larger than twenty years before. Trends in the 1970s and 1980s elsewhere in Asia and in Latin America indicated that the possibility did exist to break out of this vicious circle. The long-term solution had to include a decline in birth rate (to be discussed in the next section), but in the short term it had to include growth in sectors other than agriculture where technology offered new opportunities for development.

Energy

Economic growth and the hope of improved living conditions for the population came increasingly to depend on the availability of energy. New forms of transportation and industrial production, lighting and communication required ready access to energy sources. The global demand for energy expanded after the Second World War at an extremely high rate until the late 1970s, when it was four times greater than in 1950. The highest level of consumption was in the developed areas, but it was rising rapidly as well in developing areas of Latin America and in the newly industrialized countries of Asia. That period experienced a fundamental shift in the energy sources. Coal, principal fuel for the Industrial Revolution, was rapidly displaced by oil. By the 1960s the West derived over half its total energy from petroleum, fueling power plants and automobiles, airplanes and industries.

Since most countries lacked sufficient oil reserves for their growing needs, they looked to alternative energy sources, among which nuclear energy appeared the most promising. The policy of "atoms for peace" held out the possibility of technological miracles, among which the most spectacular was atomic energy. Nuclear power plants began to appear in large numbers in the 1960s; by the mid-1980s over three hundred plants were in operation around the world, and another two hundred were under construction. Their power output represented the energy equivalent of the total yearly production from the world's major oil country, Saudi Arabia. France, with the most active nuclear program, obtained by the 1980s over two-thirds of its total electricity from nuclear plants.

By then, however, many other countries had cut back or stopped nuclear power development, for the new technology hid risks of grave accidents and its cost had become appreciably greater than that of either petroleum or coal. Heightened concern over safety led to complex design changes and delays in plant construction which raised expenses. In the Soviet Union, where safety had not been a major issue, the rapid expansion of nuclear power was suddenly slowed in 1986, when at the nuclear plant in the Ukrainian city of Chernobyl an explosion produced radiation rendering hundreds of square miles of land around the plant uninhabitable. The accident, the worst in the history of nuclear power, did not however lead the Soviet government to alter its plans to open forty more nuclear generating plants in the following years. Other countries such as Japan and France continued to invest heavily in this energy source. Governments everywhere confronted complex issues of public concern over nuclear accidents, the cost of energy production, the need to avoid an energy shortage, and the increasing awareness of atmospheric pollution caused by hydrocarbons created by the use of coal and petroleum for energy.

The rising consumption of energy raised the crucial issue of the availability of natural resources. Two solutions to make better use of energy opened up through technological developments. The sudden rise of oil prices in the 1970s increased costs to a point where efficiency in energy use became a national priority in the industrial countries. The United States, having for a century expended its coal and petroleum at a prolific pace, began a major program of energy savings in industrial and home use and in transportation. In the decade between 1973 and 1983, it reduced energy consumption (measured in relation to gross national product) by one-fourth and curtailed its use of petroleum by one-fifth. This trend, repeated throughout the developed areas, constituted in the opinion of one observer a Conservation Revolution as important to future world development as the Green Revolution in food production.[1]

The possibilities for effective use of available energy in developing countries depended in part on making appropriate use of simple, inexpensive technology. The goal of adapting machinery to the social and economic conditions of particular regions became the principal cause of the economist E. G. Schumacher. His book *Small Is Beautiful*, published in 1973, challenged the idea that expensive, complex technology (such as the giant Aswan Dam) was inherently superior. He proposed the introduction of "intermediate" technology, that is, of machinery which used little energy, demanded no complex skills, and promoted production suited to the needs and capacity of developing areas.

---

[1] William Chandler, "Increasing Energy Efficiency," in *State of the World: 1985* (New York, 1986), p. 117.

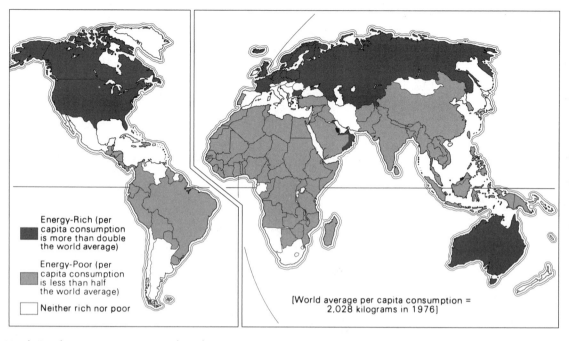

North-South Divisions: Energy-Rich and Energy-Poor Nations, 1970s.
(*From* World Energy Supplies: 1971–1975, *United Nations, Series J, No. 30, 1977, Table 2*)

No spectacular achievements marked the spread of this approach to development, adopted by many governments and by international agencies. It appeared in a variety of forms, from tools for rice cultivation in the Philippines to simple wheel-making equipment employed by blacksmiths in India. Its emphasis on using available labor and resources revealed its very limits, however, for complex technology and intensive use of energy were also necessary and desirable for these same countries. Third World societies needed to combine both the simple tools of "intermediate technology" and the sophisticated machinery of modern technology to achieve their goals of nation building and economic development.

Telecommunications

The most advanced equipment applied to global economic relations, in developed as well as developing countries, was that of the electronic and telecommunications industries. We still have some difficulty grasping the notion that processing and communicating information can be an important part of a country's economy, for our image of development is still fixed on factory smokestacks and production lines turning out heavy machinery. Information had long been essential as a tool of manufacturing and commerce, and of government policymaking. In the decades after the Second World War, that tool became an industry in itself, one of the most revealing indicators of a country's ability to expand its economic productivity and wealth. These activities proved indispensable for global economic operations and facilitated, for good or for ill, the enhanced power of governments to penetrate the lives of their citizens.

Electronics and telecommunications did not exist as distinct industries until the 1950s. They began to expand at a rapid rate in direct response to new discoveries. Technological innovations in this area combined the sophistication of rocketry and earth satellites, the extraordinary power of the computer to analyze information, telecommunications equipment for instantaneous transmission around the world, and the simple television set. The scientific and technological work that went into these inventions was complex and expensive, concentrated principally in the United States and Japan where research was well funded from private and public institutions. Much of the new equipment went to private companies, who brought it to other countries in their trading and investment operations. In many respects, these new sectors have come to epitomize the modern "postindustrial age."

The role of television had the greatest direct impact on popular culture in developed and developing lands. It provided the channel of communication to enlarge people's awareness of social and political conditions through images as well as the spoken word. Invented before the war, it did not spread widely among Western countries until the 1950s. Almost immediately it began to appear in the newly independent nations of the Third World. Privately owned and operated in the United States, it came in most countries under state control. Two factors explain this trend. The choice and interpretation of information to be made publicly available

has always been a source of power. When used to promote a political cause such as nationalism and reinforced by visual images, messages communicated by television proved the most potent tool of propaganda ever invented. In addition, the cost of television production in most countries required state financing. Both economic and political reasons explain why private ownership of television programming became the exception and why television, the most complex form of communication, quickly came to play a central role in plans for nation building in the Third World countries. A means everywhere of education and entertainment, television represented potentially a revolutionary means to overcome the barriers of misunderstanding and prejudice dividing peoples. At the same time, it constituted a potent force for national unification and political indoctrination.

New inventions created the capacity to link peoples of all countries in a network of television transmission to form what one observer termed a "global village." Communications satellites, relaying signals from one continent to another or between distant regions of one country, first went into service in 1965. Ten years later, they were in place over the Atlantic, Pacific, and Indian oceans. In addition, large countries such as the United States, the Soviet Union, India, and Indonesia operated their own domestic satellites. Although India had in 1980 fewer than 5 television sets for every 1,000 people (in the United States the proportion was 650 per 1,000), the government concluded that a national television network constituted a vital part of its program to make its citizens aware of themselves as members of one Indian nation. In the early 1980s, it launched its own communications satellite, which created one integrated national television network. African states set up their own national networks. In Zaire, a vast and diverse land of many tribes and cultures, the first image that television viewers saw every day was that of President Mobutu. Television and nation building went hand in hand in those lands.

Transnational programming, however, was restricted largely to entertainment. Sports competition proved immensely popular; the 1984 Olympics attracted an estimated one-half billion viewers. The principal source of foreign programs was the U.S. television industry, whose sale abroad of drama and comedy series (such as *Dynasty* and *Dallas*) provided global audiences their most vivid images of "life" in America. Images of a larger world did not represent a high priority to governments or a particular attraction to viewers.

The new tools of international communication served principally business and political needs. The use made of the satellites was overwhelmingly for telecommunications, linking far-flung branches of multinational corporations with the central offices, foreign personnel with their governments, and military units with command centers. The superpowers applied their technological advance to create the most elaborate networks. Russian and American spy satellites equipped with elaborate sensory devices were stationed permanently in space, providing instantaneously information on military activities of the other state and becoming the principal technique for verification of nuclear arms limitation agreements. The U.S. government made use of the extraordinary precision of satellite photography for firsthand information on crops throughout the world. Private industry found this technique valuable also; mining companies were able to conduct from space global geological surveys for deposits of valuable minerals. Access to this information remained tightly controlled, either by corporations or by states. The new communications

technology, beyond the means of most Third World countries, revealed as clearly as the disparity in wealth the gap separating the developed and developing countries.

The Global Economy

The link between new information processing technology and communications served also to enhance the efficiency and power of large states and multinational corporations. The invention and development of computer technology transformed the mode of operation of every field in which vast quantities of information constituted the foundation for decision making, from scientific research to economic surveys, from industrial production techniques to missile launching centers. The computer, essentially a tool for the storing and analysis of data, moved out of research laboratories into the public domain in the 1960s and 1970s. In those years, transistors and then integrated circuits (silicon chips) were introduced to operate all analytical and memory commands within such a small space that machines no bigger than a piece of furniture could replace room-size computers.

One area where the computer quickly acquired a central role was international business and financial operations. It could process the information needed for corporations whose operations extended throughout the world. Linked through telecommunications equipment and satellites with other continents, it provided instant information on all phases of business, from production to sales. The international oil corporations were able to keep track at all times of the movement of their petroleum, from wells in Alaska or Nigeria to the supertankers traveling to refineries, and finally to the point of sale. The world's largest banks began in the 1970s to conduct their international financial transfers through telecommunications with no more difficulty than a bank customer obtained funds through an automated teller. The "free flow of information" became an essential aspect of global business operations.

The principal features of the international economic system of the postwar years differed from the earlier period principally in three respects—first, the global dimensions of production by private corporations; second, the global financial ties created by international bank loans; and, third, the effort by the governments of the developed countries to supervise international trade and financial affairs. The Western world remained the area of most intensive activity, though the expansion in the 1960s of the newly industrialized countries of East Asia shifted trade and production toward the "Pacific rim" as well.

Major corporations placed their factories on all continents of the globe, moving to locations where labor was cheap and governments willing to grant special financial benefits. Since these conditions existed primarily in developing countries, industrial plants owned by U.S. companies such as General Motors and International Business Machines began to appear in places as distant as Taiwan and as near as Mexico. So extensive was this dispersal of production that it came to constitute a "global factory" as important in the world economy as international trade. U.S.-owned corporations occupied the principal place among multinational enterprises. Alongside them appeared as well European and Japanese businesses and the companies created by the wealthy oil-producing states of the Middle East.

Economic growth expanded the total funds available for investment, but this wealth was in the hands of a relatively small number of Western financial enterprises. In the 1950s U.S. investments in Europe began to increase the amount of dollars in those countries (see Chapter 9). These Eurodollars were the international currency of the postwar economic boom; later, other economies with funds for foreign investment, such as Germany and Japan, and then the Middle Eastern oil countries, added their own funds to this enormous financial pool, the monetary dimension of the international economy.

The existence of these funds in private hands—investors or banks, both searching for new sources of income—provided the incentive in the 1970s for extensive loans to developing and diversifying countries. The poorest countries, without the means to repay private loans, had to depend on foreign aid. Those lands with abundant natural resources such as Mexico could rely on banks to extend billions of dollars in credits as long as oil prices remained high and interest rates relatively low. By the late 1970s these private foreign loans had climbed so rapidly—over five times in just a decade—that they were greater than all official loans (nearly $100 billion).

The increased dependence of the Third World borrowers on the Western economies became painfully apparent when Western financial and political leaders (principally in the United States) decided to fight rising inflation by suddenly raising interest rates. The resulting international recession of the early 1980s curtailed foreign trade and prevented most of these debtor countries from repaying their loans, some not even the interest on the loans. Mexico was the first state temporarily to cease payments, and many other countries soon did the same. International agencies and banks had to accept the loss of their loans, demanding only the repayment of interest and withholding new credits. Reckless lending spurred by the search for profit and the misuse of funds by governments slowed new international lending and forced the people of these countries to curtail severely their standard of living. The expansion of the global economy was leading to dangerous conditions of economic instability as well as increased prosperity.

These complex international economic operations were beyond the control of any separate government. Yet the well-being of countries throughout the world (with only the Communist countries somewhat sheltered) depended in large measure on global economic growth, for which the key force was the economies of the developed countries. The need for economic coordination led the leaders of seven industrialized states (the major Western powers and Japan) to begin regular meetings in the 1970s specifically to deal with industrial, trade, and financial problems. Though they were able at times to agree on issues such as interest rates, some questions judged of vital interest by one government were closed to discussion. The U.S. government under President Reagan spent yearly hundreds of billions more than it received in taxes and refused demands from the other leaders that it reduce its deficit to stop massive international borrowing. In these discussions the priority on which all concurred was the need to facilitate production and trade. On the other hand, they could not agree on a common policy of economic assistance to developing countries, for some called for international aid, others for reliance on private enterprise.

The international economic system, increasingly interdependent, remained primarily in the hands of private corporations. The postwar experience of economic development revealed that state socialism as practiced in the Soviet Union did not assure adequate economic growth. Communist China turned to the use of private incentives and market decisions of profitability, and even encouraged private foreign investment. Competition among enterprises and choices for consumers, whether organized by states or through private enterprise, appeared preferable to an increasing number of Third World countries to the inefficiency and corruption of state bureaucratic systems. But these policies did not constitute a development plan, only the admission that the state was not all wise and all powerful in economic affiars. No economic theory held the key to ending the poverty of peoples in great areas of the world or to guaranteeing that expectations for a better life could be satisfied year after year.

SOCIAL CHANGE AND THE FEMINIST REVOLUTION

The transformation of political and economic conditions after the Second World War entailed basic changes in human relations, the result partly of global forces, partly of the efforts of organized reform groups. The direction taken by these changes and the extent to which they represent significant new trends are subjects still of discussion and debate. It is clear that social relations have substantially altered among classes, between youth and their elders, and between the sexes. The last will be the focus of our discussion.

The issue of relations between men and women touches on essential features of the human condition as it has evolved over the millennia. It provides us with a valuable perspective on questions of birth rates, of employment, and of family structure, subjects to be discussed briefly here. The term "feminist revolution" (and "feminism") refers specifically to the movement to ensure women greater control over their lives through equality of rights. Whether this movement is in fact desirable remains a subject of bitter controversy in many countries of the world. Its importance, however, was recognized when the United Nations approved the first

International Women's Year in 1975 (since repeated in 1980 and 1985) and declared the years 1975–85 to be the Decade for Women. Participation in the conferences organized in connection with these events was worldwide, one indication that the feminist issue has become another global concern. Our focus here is not on the ideological dimensions to the movement, but rather on changes in the concrete conditions which directly involved. the social relations between men and women.

Women in the Work Force

Until recent years, the place of women in most societies was separate and unequal within a patriarchal system. We can draw a portrait of their life cycle which, though oversimplified, helps better to appreciate changes in the postwar period. In most traditional societies, women's condition throughout their lives left them in an inferior position in society. As infants, they were less desired than boys, and could, under conditions of extreme hardship, become the victims of infant neglect when parents had to curtail family size. As children, their education was very restricted or nonexistent, for they had to help with domestic work until marriage, which came at an early age.

Women's principal role subsequently was childbearing and care of the household under the authority of their husband. In this patriarchal system, he controlled family property and was responsible to ensure the proper protection, even seclusion, of the women within his kin group. Only poverty created a kind of equality of labor, forcing women in peasant families to work in the fields alongside their husbands. If women reached old age, they often acquired some authority and prestige, endowed with the power to discipline the younger women and children. Although relations varied widely from one society to another, some aspects of

this pattern existed in all complex civilizations.

Global economic and political trends described in earlier chapters placed the relations between men and women and the pattern just outlined in a new context. The movement of the population from rural areas into cities, partly in search of better work, partly to escape rural poverty, has characterized all regions of the world to a greater or lesser extent. By the late twentieth century one-half of Europe's population lived in urban areas. In the Third World, the move occurred more slowly, the proportion of townspeople there rising from about 5 percent at the end of the First World War to almost 25 percent in 1980. At a time of rapid population growth, this trend came about through a massive shift to towns of hundreds of millions of people.

Families adjusting to this new environment entered new economic relations, for most shifted from agricultural work to wage labor. They experienced the clash of cultural values brought by contact with different ways of life. In the same period, political revolutions and state building brought new laws on women's rights and family relations which attacked many traditional practices. Western societies had undergone these changes earlier and were, in the midtwentieth century, the center of the feminist movement. Theories and images of feminism became equated in non-Western countries with a Western version of women's emancipation. Thus the reaction against Western imperialism was often associated with a rejection of Western cultural models, including feminism. In these conditions of economic, cultural, and political turmoil, new opportunities and old constraints were thrust upon women and the family throughout the world. We should not wonder, therefore, that the issue ignited heated discussion and that the response of diverse societies, each with their own cultural and social traditions, varied widely. Our problem here is to seek to assess the overall consequences of these opposing forces.

One of the most revealing indicators is the change we can observe in family size, directly connected to the birth rate in various countries. The trend which first appeared in the West saw a decline first in death rates, followed by birth rates as parents came to expect that most of their children would survive until adulthood and judged desirable a smaller family. This "demographic transition" (to low death and low birth rates) represented the crucial factor in reducing population growth. It opened up new perspectives for women no longer tied to childbearing through much of their adult lives. The growing concern about the global population explosion led to concerted campaigns in many countries to encourage the use of birth control methods. Their effectiveness, however, depended on voluntary cooperation everywhere save China, where the "one-child family" became law in 1980.

The trend in family size has been downward, though the pace of decline has varied enormously. In many European countries, families in the 1970s were averaging two children, while in most Muslim and African countries and in India the number varied between six and seven. Throughout Latin America, birth rates began a sudden decline in the 1960s, which two decades later had fallen one-third to one-half. Overall, the figures suggest that the demographic transition was taking place, though at a much faster rate in Latin America and in East Asia than in the Middle East, South Asia, and Africa. Can we interpret these findings to indicate some change in relations between husbands and wives? Two points appear most clearly. First, the reduction in family size resulted from the conscious choice of parents to limit births, not, as had occurred in previous centuries, from famine and disease. Second, although this decision involved complex personal, economic, and cultural issues, the determining condition appeared most often to be the entry of women into the work force.

Driven by economic need, by rising expectations of better living conditions, and by the desire of women for their own income, husbands were increasingly prepared to allow their wives the freedom of outside work. In certain countries, the state consciously encouraged and supported female employment. This policy was most extensive and effective in the Communist countries. By the 1970s over four-fifths of adult women in the Soviet Union had paid jobs. Soviet men's wages did not provide sufficient income for the standard of living desired by most families, and an increasing number of women sought and had access to skilled or professional jobs. The rising female work rate was directly related to the fall in the size of Soviet families, limited in many Russian urban areas to one child. A similar trend was apparent in many other European countries.

Another important factor was "consumerism," that is, the desire for a higher living standard. In Brazil, it appeared the dominant motivation in bringing large numbers of women into the labor force (probably over one-third of adult women by 1980) and in lowering family size (down from an average of six to four children between the 1960s and 1980s). The actual improvement in living standards over those years may not have been appreciable, for economic conditions worsened there as in other Latin countries in the recession of the early 1980s. The case of Brazil, as in other areas at a similar level of development, suggests how important new economic pressures and expectations were in lowering family size and in bringing more and more women into the work force.

The possibility for wage labor was very limited for most women in the Third World, where their education remained inferior to men. Opportunities for schooling were spreading among youth, but even in China, with a major literacy program, girls were three times as likely as boys to be illiterate (18 versus 5 percent). Among Indians a similar disparity existed and at a level four times higher. The lack of education meant that most female employment had to be in unskilled jobs.

This working population, unorganized and prepared to accept work at low pay, proved advantageous both to small businesses and to multinational corporations. The latter's total work force in developing countries grew in the 1970s to between three and four million, of whom the largest proportion were women employed in the new electronics industry, garment manufacture, and assembly work. Dependent on a distant employer and earning low pay, this unskilled female labor force constituted a new proletariat. Only a small group of educated women had in most countries the possibility to enter high-paying, skilled jobs. Lack of sufficient education and male prejudice represented substantial obstacles to their economic advancement. Still, female wage earning and activity away from the home constituted a major shift away from the patriarchal family pattern. The trend toward outside labor undermined the traditional roles of women and their relations with men, a threat in some societies more important than economic need in deciding the question of female work.

Women and the Family

The subject of women's rights within the family appeared in public debates in most new nations soon after independence. Political leaders often judged social improvements a necessary companion to national freedom and looked to Western reform movements

Literacy for Women: Adult Reading Class in Yemen Arab Republic, 1983. *(U.N. Photo 153539/John Isaac)*

for inspiration. More important to reforms than feminism were the Western socialist parties, which had made equality between the sexes an integral part of their struggle for social justice since the nineteenth century. Western states had gradually introduced laws enforcing equal rights of women in the family, a process greatly speeded by post-1945 reform governments. In the Soviet Union, laws very soon after the revolution had granted full legal equality to women in the family.

New laws took effect much more slowly in non-Western states. The Chinese Communists confronted a deeply rooted patriarchal system, which included child marriage and exclusive male right of divorce. Shortly after taking power they introduced sweeping reforms intended, as in the Soviet case, to eliminate patriarchal privileges and to integrate women into their revolutionary society. Their radical methods were not followed in India, where parliamentary debate went on for years before laws established women's rights in marriage and property holding for the Hindu population (see Chapter 9). Fearing communal conflict, the Indian government made little effort to enforce equality on Muslim families, where, as in most other Muslim lands, patriarchal powers included exclusive male divorce and unequal inheritance rights. Among Muslim countries, Turkey was the only large state where Islamic law was replaced by Western family law. The complexity and tenacity of the patriarchal system in most Asian, Middle Eastern, and African countries presented reforming leaders with virtually insoluble problems. No matter how many laws were passed, customary practices of male domination yielded only slowly to pressures for greater equality for women within the family.

This process was linked directly to the new social conditions outlined above and to the cultural values of the various societies. The process of adaptation to urban life, which broke rural ties and opened up new occupational opportunities, left wives in the early stages more closely bound than before to the household. The obligation to care for the children fell directly into their hands, while husbands often took advantage of higher incomes to enforce on their wives patriarchal customs associated with the upper classes. This reverse trend was apparent in Africa, the Middle East, and South Asian countries where seclusion (called in Hindi *purdah*) had been practiced for centuries among the wealthy. The pressures of legal rights and desire for more income pushing toward equality, on the one hand, and customary male authority and cultural values stressing patriarchy on the other, created conditions for acute conflict and personal tragedy.

The consequences became readily apparent in India, where the state's campaign for family equality was reinforced by a feminist movement promoting observance of the new standards. The laws on child marriage did have the effect of raising the average age of marriage for women to seventeen in 1970, itself a substantial change (Gandhi's wife had been twelve when they married), and contributed to the falling birth rate. Still, the social demand on all young women to marry remained overwhelming. Laws against the dowry proved ineffective. The custom, originally a luxury afforded only by wealthy families, became a source of bitter conflict, resulting even in death, when the family desire for more consumer goods conflicted with a husband's insistence that the wife remain in seclusion.

Social pressures among the new urban middle class in India led at times to exorbitant demands for dowries on brides' families, at the time of marriage and even for years afterward. When the parents refused further payment, the consequences for the wife could be tragic. Rarely punished or publicly acknowledged until the late 1970s, dowry murders of wives by husbands' families numbered by official count at least three thousand cases in one year, and the real number was probably far higher. In a country where legal reforms had in theory laid the foundations for equality between the sexes, these murders were a cruel reminder of the limits to state reforms. The clash between the powerful customs enforcing patriarchal rights and the new social conditions of urbanization and consumerism created its own victims among women.

Conditions changed even more slowly in those Muslim countries where Islamic law remained in effect. There family size declined and female seclusion ended only among relatively few upper-class families, where wives had access to education and to well-paying jobs. Elsewhere, the pattern remained that of large families (these societies had among the highest birth rates in the world), low participation by women in the labor force, and segregation and subordination of women in the family. In countries such as Pakistan, fewer than one-tenth of adult women found paid employment. Custom continued to dictate female veiling in public, a symbol of the extent to which men's sense of honor rested on control of the women in their family. Marriage came for women at an early age, and families averaged still in 1980 five to six children.

Why did these countries show the least change? The hold of Islamic religious law remained very strong, for, in most Muslim lands, states made little effort to counter the patriarchal practices sanctioned by the Koran. Yet the influence of religion is only part of the answer. Even in Soviet Central Asia, where secular law fixed family relations, where the practice of the Muslim faith was repressed, and where many women had outside work, the pattern of male authority and large families was repeated. These practices were embedded in centuries-old social custom, which set the basic rules for family life and protected the security and stability of society. The price was the subordination of women.

Based on their own experience, Westerners have a tendency to assume that family relations adjust relatively easily and quickly to new social and economic conditions. The experience of the postwar decades in non-Western lands reveals that where traditions were sanctioned by many generations of practice, even revolutionary regimes could not enforce family equality. After thirty years of revolutionary Communism, a study of women in Communist China in the early 1980s concluded that "socialism and patriarchy exist in stable harmony," for "a woman's life is still determined by her relationship to a man."[2] Declining family size and the increased participation of women in the workplace represented important new features in women's lives in China. Yet standing in the way of women's social and economic emancipation were patriarchal practices, diminished but still powerful there as in many other societies.

In many lands, the struggle against Western domination reinforced the tendency toward social conservatism within families in non-Western societies. The image of Western society projected to other nations included by the 1960s the emancipated woman, liberated sexually as well as politically and economically. Although it represented a simplified picture of a very complex situation, it was profoundly shocking to peoples whose background emphasized stability and who confronted very unsettling political and economic changes. We might best understand the vehement rejection of the feminist ideals in many other parts of the world in

[2]Margery Wolf, *Revolution Postponed: Women in Contemporary China* (Stanford, Calif., 1985), p. 261.

part as a refusal to permit Western cultural values to undermine national traditions as well as a reflection of the importance of male dominance in world cultures. Muslim peoples of the Soviet Union had to bow to the laws of the Russian state and ideals of Communism in their public activities, but they protected their own culture within the family by maintaining important patriarchal customs.

One of the most sweeping attacks on Western influence accompanied by the reinforcement of customary social practices, including the seclusion of women, occurred in Iran following the revolution of 1979. After years of relatively liberal social policies under the shah, the Islamic Republic reimposed all the rigorous restrictions on public activities of women and reestablished the Koranic laws governing the family. To its religious leaders, the Western societies represented demonic forces threatening the essence of Muslim life. Although they welcomed Western technology and modern industry, they categorically rejected the transformation of social relations. To succeed, their Muslim revolution had in their opinion to end all manifestations of Western culture in Iranian life, including the relative freedom enjoyed by women. One fervent supporter of the revolution, asked to explain what the establishment of the Islamic Republic meant to him, responded: "Getting women back into the veil, getting them off television."[3] His insistence on the subordinate role of women represented far more than the protection of the family; it constituted an important aspect for many Iranians of their defense of Muslim traditions and of Iranian nationalism against Western imperialism.

Although the movement for the rigorous enforcement of old customs appeared to gather force in the 1970s and early 1980s in

certain Muslim countries, in the larger historical perspective it appeared exceptional. The overall global pattern was toward a fundamental transformation of social relations, including a reduction in the authority of men in the family and an increase of women's control over their lives. These changes were most apparent in the reduction of family size and female participation in the labor force. Cultural and social traditions, on the other hand, remained extremely powerful restraints on women's equality. They ensured that in the 1980s only modest adjustments could occur in the social relations of the sexes. A global feminist revolution remained still a distant perspective.

GLOBAL CONFLICT AND THE SUPERPOWERS

While rapid political, economic, and social changes in the postwar decades opened perspectives of a new era in world history, a major conflict between the superpowers threatened to destroy all that humanity had achieved. Their relations did change in the 1970s, in some areas augmenting and in others diminishing the risk of confrontation. The world remained their imaginary battlefield, made ever more dangerous by new developments in military technology.

Why did their antagonism endure? To place the responsibility entirely on one side distorts the character of international relations among great powers. An underlying condition contributing to Soviet-U.S. competition was the very nature of international relations in recent centuries. As in 1900, power politics remained in the closing decades of the twentieth century the principal means to adjust the balance of power among states and to ensure their security. A second reason, peculiar to the circumstances after the Second World War, emerged out of the

---

[3] V. S. Naipaul, *Among the Believers: An Islamic Journey* (New York, 1981), p. 28.

turmoil of ideological conflict and revolution throughout the world. In those conditions, the Soviet Union and the United States were rivals in establishing not only diplomatic alliances but also the basic guidelines for state building for the new states. By linking Communist rule with diplomatic domination in Eastern Europe, the Soviet leaders in the postwar decades kept in place the Iron Curtain and ensured the division of Europe into two blocs. The third factor was a direct consequence of the Cold War, namely, the deadly arms race, in which fear of weakness or vulnerability fueled on each side the effort to build ever more effective weapons of war. Nuclear arms, the core of each state's defense system, had expanded to such a point by the late 1960s that the stockpiles possessed the capacity (measured in megatons—millions of tons of TNT explosives) to inflict damage far beyond the demands of simple military victory.

The Arms Race on Parade: November 7th Celebration in Red Square, Moscow, approx. 1965. *(Patty Ratliff Collection/Hoover Institution Archives)*

Détente

By then, both the Soviet and U.S. governments were prepared to place some restraints on their competition. The term détente came into use to designate the possibility of relaxation of tensions between the superpowers. Each side saw that improvement of relations was desirable. Their reasons were not identical, and in that divergence lay the grounds for future disagreement and hostility. In the Soviet Union, leadership was in the hands of the Politburo, where disagreement continued on the improvement of U.S. relations. The general secretary, Leonid Brezhnev, played an active role in support of détente, but powerful voices insisted on the expansion of military forces to protect Soviet interests.

Brezhnev had three principal objectives in backing détente. One was the Soviet need for Western imports of technology and capital to help improve the economy. A second was the desirability of reducing international tension in the West at a time of growing danger of Soviet war with China. Finally, Soviet leaders recognized that nuclear war would be so catastrophic, and the continuing armaments race so expensive, that agreement with the United States was essential to establish limits on new arms. By the late 1960s they possessed nuclear weaponry roughly equivalent to that of the United States. They were prepared to negotiate as equals and expected to have a voice alongside the United States in "all major international problems." In their eyes, armaments agreements with the United States were part of a larger goal of obtaining a greater voice in world affairs than ever before. Competition and cooperation were to them part of the same process of rivalry between capitalist and socialist systems.

In the United States, the new Nixon administration began in 1969 the most exten-sive revision in Soviet policy since the beginning of the Cold War. These changes were due partly to the recognition that serious limits had appeared to American global influence, caused by economic and political problems in the United States—inflation, the Vietnam war—and by new trends in world relations. New centers of political and economic power had appeared, including Western Europe, Japan, and China. In addition, the United States was prepared to recognize the essential political interests of Communist states and to negotiate with them on this basis. Nixon's security adviser (later secretary of state) Henry Kissinger made this clear when in 1969 he argued that "we have no permanent enemies. We will judge other countries, including Communist countries, on the basis of their actions and not on the basis of their domestic ideology."

Readiness to deal with Communist states within one global diplomatic system led to Nixon's visit to Peking in 1972. This opening ultimately brought diplomatic recognition of China, trade agreements, and even some military collaboration. But the same new orientation toward Communist lands also implied a readiness to negotiate directly with the Soviet Union. The U.S. government in those years no longer sought superiority over the Soviet Union in all areas of strategic armaments. The key concept was the maintenance of "sufficient" might to deter attack and to protect those areas of the world, especially Western Europe and Japan, of vital importance to U.S. security. Fundamentally, the impetus to improved relations lay in the awareness within the U.S. government, as in Moscow, of the disastrous consequences of a third world war, made more likely by unrestricted armaments competition.

The readiness of both sides to make concessions in exchange for agreement on basic issues led to a series of treaties and understandings, most of which went into effect in the early 1970s. One was the treaty recognizing the partition of Berlin and permanent Western protection of West Berlin, incorporated in the German Federal Republic (discussed in Chapter 11). A second, which was signed when Nixon visited Moscow in mid-1972, dealt with the complex problems of nuclear arms limitation. Negotiations on the subject, the Strategic Arms Limitation Talks (SALT), had been under way for several years. The final agreement was primarily concerned with antiballistic missiles (ABM), that is, nuclear-armed rockets whose objective was to destroy attacking missiles.

The purpose of these weapons was defensive, to prevent a successful enemy attack (an idea revived in the early 1980s in President Reagan's Strategic Defense Initiative, or "Star Wars"). The side possessing an effective ABM system would, however, acquire overwhelming military superiority, since its invulnerability would give it the potential ability to destroy the enemy without fear of damage. Consequently, to avoid possible domination, each side had to match the defensive ability of the other, a situation which in the early 1970s was pointing to a new armaments race. The only realistic alternative was an agreement banning ABM systems, leaving both the Soviet Union and the United States vulnerable to destruction and assuring that deterrence would dissuade either side from considering or threatening war. In the absence of nuclear disarmament, a distant utopia, the concept of mutually assured destruction remained the least dangerous nuclear strategy which superpower diplomacy could devise to reduce tensions. Restraints on development of new offensive missiles were also incorporated in the agreement, but they were not comprehensive and were only temporary. These restrictions and limits on defensive and offensive missiles constituted the core of the arms treaty (SALT I), signed in 1972.

A permanent agreement on offensive weapons proved far more difficult to achieve. Neither side was prepared to accept any real limitations without the assurance that the other was doing the same. But what was the equivalence between nuclear warheads (capable of carrying several bombs each with separate targets) and missiles, between submarines armed with nuclear-armed rockets and intermediate-range missiles? A treaty signed in 1979 (SALT II) finally set an array of limits, principally on the number of intercontinental ballistic missiles (ICBM) and submarine-launched missiles. It was unable to resolve the thorny questions of modernization of weapons and of intermediate-range missiles. These shortcomings in the treaty, not actual violations, rendered it ineffective in slowing research and deployment of new nuclear weapons.

It appeared more and more that scientific and technological innovations in weaponry, not the strategic interests of the two powers, were pushing the arms race ahead. The Soviet Union developed an improved intermediate-range missile, and installed hundreds in the late 1970s, most targeted on the NATO countries of Western Europe. The United States responded by deploying in the 1980s its new, highly accurate missiles in Europe and by reaffirming its policy to defend NATO allies if necessary by initiating nuclear war in that theater in the event of Soviet attack (the "first-use" policy). By the mid-1980s the number of nuclear warheads at the disposal of the United States was so great that major Soviet cities each were the target of over twenty warheads. The policy of deterrence required a small fraction of this number. The terrible logic of the arms race and of military planning stood in the way of what sanity itself dictated.

Other agreements proved only partially satisfactory in bringing the two superpowers the objectives they sought from détente. No trade agreements gave the Soviet leaders the benefits they hoped from exports to the United States, but private loans from Western banks did assist in the import of Western technology and of large amounts of grain, bought principally from the United States. In 1975 the Soviet government signed the Helsinki Agreements which included the commitment to promote human rights. Nonetheless, until Gorbachev came to power in 1985 it resisted easing its repression of political dissent and imposed similar policies on its European satellites. These shortcomings diminished the attraction to both sides of further concessions.

At the core of their disagreements lay very different expectations and views on global relations. Although ready to acknowledge the desirability of slow reform, the United States was committed to the preservation of basic elements of the new pattern of global relations, including the economic system protecting international capitalist trade and finance, and the independence of nationalist, non-Communist states around the world. Soviet leaders continued to view world relations, on the contrary, as a "struggle between the two systems," capitalism and socialism, and to protect and encourage those "progressive" states and political movements opposed to Western imperialism.

Power Politics in the Third World

Several conflicts in the Middle East, Africa, and Asia in the 1970s made these divergences apparent and worsened relations between the superpowers. Problems emerged in African countries when radical movements were able to use Soviet assistance to take power. When in 1975 Portugal freed its colony of Angola, it could not obtain agreement on the leadership of the new state among competing political movements, divided as much along tribal as political lines. A prolonged civil war began, in which the United States and the Soviet Union supported opposing sides. Soviet aid was more effective since it included the intervention of ten thousand Cuban soldiers, whose presence assured the victory of the Marxist party. Cuban direct military assistance, financed by the Soviet Union, proved equally effective after 1978 in Ethiopia, where a revolutionary group of officers was attempting to repress tribal revolts and introduce socialist reforms. Soviet supplies and Cuban troops kept this regime in power, though in conditions of political disorder and economic collapse. When a severe drought struck the region in the early 1980s, the Marxist officers welcomed international and Western aid while still persevering in a revolution they formally proclaimed to be "communist." As in Cuba two decades before, communism arrived there by official proclamation along with vital Soviet support.

In both Angola and Ethiopia, an activist Soviet policy backed a "progressive" revolutionary regime, which otherwise would have fallen from power. In Afghanistan, Soviet military intervention in 1979 (discussed in Chapter 11) ensured that the feeble Communist leaders, allied with the Soviet Union, were not defeated by Muslim rebels. In so doing the Soviet leaders were moving their forces deep into South Asia, occupying a land which for a century had remained neutral. Although probably defensive in intent, the effect of the Soviet action disrupted the balance of power in South Asia. The U.S. government, unwilling and unable to intervene directly, protested vehemently this dangerous military initiative and began providing military aid to the Muslim rebels. Opinion in the United States swung once again toward the view of the Soviet Union as a revolutionary expansionist power, with whom real relaxation of tensions was neither possible nor desirable. Heightened fears of Soviet intentions, combined with the actual cases of Cuban and Soviet military intervention, made U.S. leaders think back again to the forceful policies of containment of the 1950s.

The Middle East was the area where endemic instability and war made most visible the deep disagreement between Soviet and U.S. leaders regarding revolution and political order. The United States sought with limited success to keep peace among the regimes in power, for it was bound to the protection of Israel and, along with the other Western states, had a direct interest in preserving access to the oil fields of the conservative states in the Arabian peninsula. The Soviet government, on the contrary, backed those radical regimes and movements most fervently committed to war and to revolutionary upheaval. Although it exercised at times a moderating influence on these leaders, it nonetheless sympathized with their socialist, anti-imperialist ideals and was prepared to provide economic and military aid in return for greater influence in Middle Eastern affairs.

Once again the United States and Soviet Union had very little common grounds for collaboration, and were on opposing sides on many issues. As in the past, relations with Israel proved the greatest source of dispute. The Soviet leaders had demanded that no peace treaty be signed unless all the Arab countries participated, possible only if Israel abandoned all the territory seized in 1967 and recognized the Palestinian claim to an independent state. When the Egyptian leader, Anwar Sadat, indicated in 1977 that he was prepared to sign a separate peace treaty with Israel, the U.S. government welcomed and supported eagerly the negotiations leading to the 1979 treaty. It permitted no voice in the affair to the Soviet Union. In other words, the two powers defined peace in terms so different that no cooperation between them on Middle Eastern politics was possible.

The Soviet government, for its part, lent its diplomatic backing and provided economic and military aid to militant, anti-Western nationalist regimes in Syria and Libya, and to the radical Arab movements both states supported. The attainment of a Palestine state and opposition to the West constituted the two common goals of all these groups, which in the late 1960s incorporated terrorism in their plans of political action. Although the Soviets did not themselves initiate terrorist acts, they were ready to furnish aid and training to those who did, thus becoming accomplices in the ugliest form of international conflict of the postwar years.

Terrorism, that is, acts of violence to advance a political cause, had been used by small groups of fanatics since the middle of the nineteenth century. Most often employed when all legal means of action were either fruitless or impossible, it sought to communicate a set of political demands and, at times, through assassination or intimidation, to force concessions. It constituted a serious danger to governments and had once contributed to the outbreak of a major war— the immediate origins of the First World War lay in the terrorist murder of the Austrian archduke (see Chapter 1). Terrorism threatened the public at large as well. "Propaganda by the deed," in whatever form it took, represented in the words of one observer "the most primitive form of language." Occasional indiscriminate violence turned innocent bystanders into tragic victims, unwitting instruments for the terrorists' cause.

When Palestinians and other radicals resorted in the late 1960s to terrorism in their struggle against Israel, they received financial and material assistance from Arab states and from the Soviet Union. Soviet arms and training camps in Soviet satellite countries helped them acquire the weapons and skills for their new battles. The Soviet government looked sympathetically on their revolutionary ideals; how and when their revolution actually occurred was their affair.

Terrorism, growing in violence and scope through the 1970s, amounted to "war by other means" both on Israel and on what radicals referred to as the "multinational imperialist state," including all Western democratic countries. Small groups of Western radicals had in the late 1960s first made use of terrorism. Disillusioned in their hopes of popular revolution, they turned to direct action, assassinating political leaders, kidnapping wealthy individuals for ransom, and bombing public installations. In Italy, the so-called Red Brigades were responsible for two hundred assassinations, culminating in the death in 1978 of a former Italian prime minister. This outpouring of violence had its origins partly in frustrated idealism, partly in the ideological fixation of a few fanatics on the supposed absolute evil of Western imperialism and on the vision of a total revolution of which they believed themselves the leaders.

Their operations soon joined those of the Palestinian terrorist organizations. The crushing defeat of the Arab states in the 1967 war led young Palestinian radicals to adopt the terrorist methods of the Westerners and to initiate their own private war directed as much against moderate Arabs as against Israel and the West. Any Arab leader who proposed negotiation with Israel, either to improve conditions for Arabs in Israeli-occupied lands or to seek a Middle Eastern settlement without an independent Palestine, was a possible target of assassins. Condemned as traitors by the terrorists, their lives were forfeit to the Palestinian dream of an independent nation-state.

The campaign against Israel and the Western states grew in scope and intensity, including bombings, killings, and random acts of violence in every Western European country. Arab terrorist attacks on Israel itself, however, failed to disrupt public life. Israeli police controls combined with the policy of punishing the families of terrorists effectively curtailed the operations of the groups within Israel. Outside the country the terrorists found targets in airports and airplanes, in embassies and public gatherings, even the 1972 Olympic games where they murdered several Israeli athletes. The hijacking of commercial airplanes proved the most effective action in spreading fear and attracting publicity for the Palestinian organizations. The technique was employed first in 1968, when three planes were seized within a few days, flown to Jordan, and then destroyed in full view of Western television cameras. When the United States moved troops into Lebanon in 1982 in an effort to maintain peace there after the Israeli invasion, terrorists attacked the U.S. embassy and later the Marine camp, causing hundreds of dead and wounded. In the rising wave of violence, the proclaimed goal of free Palestine appeared to dwindle in importance, leaving in its place the determination to destroy Western and Arab enemies.

Operating in a lawless world of violence and sudden death, these terrorist organizations became instruments of intimidation, which by the late 1970s were manipulated by a few Arab states for their own political ends. Secret reports indicated that Syria, Libya, and Iran originated most important terrorist operations. In 1986 the U.S. government turned to the Israeli method of direct retaliation to punish the state of Libya for its presumed complicity in terrorist attacks of U.S. military personnel. U.S. bombers attacked Libyan military installations and the residence of the Libyan leader, Qaddafi, in what in earlier times would have constituted an act of war. The roots of the violence lay, however, in the continuing Arab-Israeli confrontation. The Middle Eastern troubles in turn kept the United States and the Soviet Union on opposing sides, worsening their relations and presenting the continual danger of the escalation of local war into a superpower conflict.

The End of Détente

Relaxation of tensions ceased being a priority in superpower relations in the early 1980s. There is no easy explanation why the promising initiatives of the 1970s gave way to an accelerated arms race and to power politics in place of negotiation. For one thing, Soviet readiness to intervene directly or indirectly in political conflicts in Third World countries fed a new wave of anti-Communism in the United States. This view, as misleading and oversimplified as before, was particularly popular after 1981 in the Reagan administration. Its opposition to the Sandinista leadership of Nicaragua expanded until the United States was virtually at war with that tiny country. It intervened indirectly with military aid to Nicaraguan guerrillas in the hope of overthrowing the Sandinistas, an objective as unlikely to succeed there as in Cuba in 1961 at the time of the Bay of Pigs invasion.

A second immediate factor undermining détente was the acceleration of the arms race. The appearance of new Soviet armaments led the U.S. government to undertake a major expansion of its military might, including a much larger navy. The most expensive armaments program was the elaborate (and very problematic) space defense system dubbed Star Wars, an enormously complex scheme whose objective resembled the antiballistic defense systems banned in the SALT I treaty. In place of "sufficient" armaments for deterrence, the U.S. government again sought military superiority. Instead of restricting, as it had in the 1950s, its aid to Third World countries primarily to economic aid, the Soviet Union expanded its assistance to include military arms, advisers, and in a few cases Cuban troops. The two governments shared responsibility for the worsening of tensions which by the mid-1980s created an atmosphere reminiscent of the Cold War in the 1950s.

What was left of détente? The objective of arms control remained a subject of negotiations. When the new Soviet leader, Mikhail Gorbachev, came to power in 1985, meetings between Soviet and U.S. heads of state began again. In a world in which peace depended above all on the decisions of a handful of people in Moscow and Washington, these efforts provided some assurance that reason prevailed. Yet it was clear as well that global competition between the two powers would not vanish. While new nation-states struggled with their problems of development and internal instability, and while innovations in social and economic affairs offered the hope of new, better conditions for the five billion inhabitants of the globe, power politics remained a powerful influence in global and regional conflicts. Even India, under Nehru dedicated to internationalism and conciliation, joined the ranks of nuclear powers to reinforce its defenses against Pakistan, which in turn acquired its own nuclear bomb. Israel became the eighth nuclear state. In every case intended for defense, these weapons threatened atomic destruction even in regional wars.

SUMMARY

This chapter opened by raising the question whether the world had entered a new historical era in the late twentieth century. The previous decades had been a period of great violence caused by wars and revolutions. Did the mid-century mark the beginning of new constructive trends in the history of humanity? The evidence we have examined does not offer an easy answer. It can be read to suggest either an optimistic or a pessimistic view. In the latter perspective, one might argue that nationalism has become a pervasive force dividing peoples. The spread of nuclear armaments has increased the likelihood that conflicts among nation-states might lead to nuclear war. The superpowers found a new arena for military competition in space, unsettling once again the strategic balance between the two states. Another major source of global antagonism has been the increased interdependence of the global economy. Economic recession in developed countries has quickly spread to the developing lands, where widespread poverty and social discontent threaten democratic government and the protection of human rights.

The events of recent decades offer, however, a positive interpretation as well. The terrible suffering of the Second World War was followed by political turmoil in many lands as Western empires fell and revolutions brought new leaders to power. That chaotic time was followed by decades of profound political and social change. Nation building slowly brought greater stability into the lives of the peoples of the Third World. Economic growth of greater scope and speed than ever in the history of humanity reduced the scale of human poverty while offering a considerably higher standard of living to a growing proportion of the population of most countries. International conflicts between the superpowers were contained within diplomatic bounds. Though arms limitations agreements did not end the arms race, the negotiations between the Soviet Union and the United States did constitute the assurance that the Cold War would not return

and that their global competition would remain political and diplomatic.

We are perhaps incited toward the pessimistic view partly by the great hopes which accompanied the end of the two world wars. Both Woodrow Wilson and Franklin Roosevelt spoke for many people in looking forward to universal peace and prosperity. Their promises did not come true, casualties of the complexity of human relations and the violence of social and ideological conflicts which accompanied the wars and revolutions of this century. We have more somber, but also perhaps more realistic expectations of possible improvements in the human condition in our rapidly changing world. Realism by itself is not justification for pessimism. World history of the twentieth century is a story of great rebuilding as well as destruction, of creative vision as well as despair. It provides substantial reasons to conclude that the world has passed beyond the era of wars and revolutions into another era calling for renewed building and a new vision truly global in scope.

RECOMMENDED READING

Technology and the Global Economy

LESTER BROWN, *The Interdependence of Nations* (1972) and *World Without Borders* (1972)

*LESTER BROWN ET AL., *The State of the World: 1985* (1985)

AKIE HOOGVELT, *The Third World in Global Development* (1982)

JAMES MARTIN, *The Wired Society* (1978)

*ANTHONY SAMPSON, *The Money Lenders: The People and Politics of the World Banking Crisis* (1983)

Social Change and the Feminist Revolution

MARGOT DULEY AND MARY EDWARDS, *The Cross Cultural Study of Women* (1986)

NIKKIE KEDDIE AND LOIS BECK (EDS.), *Women in the Muslim World* (1978)

JONATHAN LIEBERSON, "Too Many People?" *The New York Review of Books,* Vol. 33 (June 26, 1986), pp. 36–42.

DEBBIE TAYLOR (ED.), *Women: A World Report* (1985)

Global Conflict and the Superpowers

SEWERYN BIALER, *The Soviet Paradox: External Expansion, Internal Decline* (1986)

JOHN GADDIS, "The Rise, Fall, and Future of Détente," *Foreign Affairs,* Vol. 62 (Winter 1982–83), pp. 354–77.

WALTER LAQUER, *Terrorism* (1977)

JAMES NATHAN AND JAMES OLIVER, *United States Foreign Policy and World Order* (third ed., 1985)

CLAIRE STERLING, *The Terror Network: The Secret War of International Terrorism* (1981)

INDEX

Excellent sections and Ch. 9 on India & Pakistan.